BASIC MARKETING
MANAGEMENT

£3.
4/48.

BASIC MARKETING MANAGEMENT

Second Edition

Douglas J. Darymple
Indiana University

Leonard J. Parsons
Georgia Institute of Technology

JOHN WILEY & SONS

New York • Chichester • Weinheim • Brisbane • Singapore • Toronto

ACQUISITIONS EDITOR	Brent Gordon
MARKETING MANAGER	Jessica Garcia
SENIOR PRODUCTION EDITOR	Patricia McFadden
SENIOR DESIGNER	Karin Gerdes Kincheloe
PHOTO EDITOR	Lisa Gee
ILLUSTRATION EDITOR	Anna Melhorn
PRODUCTION MANAGEMENT	Hermitage Publishing Services

This book was set in 10/12 Times Roman by Hermitage Publishing Services
and printed and bound by Hamilton Printing. The cover was printed by Phoenix Color, Inc.

This book is printed on acid-free paper. ⊗

ISBN 0-471-35392-2

Printed in the United States of America

10 9 8 7 6 5 4 3 2 1

PREFACE

This book is designed to help the reader learn marketing management concepts and apply them to solve business problems. Marketing is the driving force that helps firms succeed in the new era of the information explosion, instant Internet communications, and global competition. Every manager must appreciate the key role that marketing plays in the creation and distribution of goods and services to business and consumer buyers. The importance of marketing to business prosperity means that marketing has become an important pathway to move to the top of the executive career ladder.

Marketing works closely with other functional areas. Business problem-solving and planning today is multidisciplinary. Students must understand the linkages among the functional areas.[1] Taking a flexible multidisciplinary approach in thinking and problem solving prepares one for not only that first position in marketing but also for the ultimate move to general management.

Approach and Objectives

The 2nd edition of *Basic Marketing Management* focuses on the activities of managers who make the everyday decisions that guide the marketing of goods and services. To operate successfully in a business environment, students need to understand what marketing executives do and how marketing builds sales and profits. This book provides in depth coverage of all elements of the marketing mix and shows how they are used in the business world. Our approach to marketing management is comprehensive, up-to-date, and practical. We use many real-world examples and present them in an easy-to-read style. Stories in boxes highlight recent applications of marketing management (Marketing in Action boxes) and unique marketing strategies (Marketing Strategy boxes).

We believe that the new edition offers instructors flexibility to employ different methods of instruction. Some instructors may want to supplement this book with specialized readings or to add cases. We encourage instructors to have students subscribe to *The Wall*

---

[1] Rhett H. Walker, Dallas Hanson, Lindsay Nelson, and Cathy Fisher, "A Case for a More Integrative Multidisciplinary Marketing Education," *European Journal of Marketing,* Vol. 32, No. 9/10, 1998, pp. 803–812.

Street Journal, read general business publications such as *Business Week* and *Fortune*, and get exposure to specialized marketing publications such as *Admap* and *Promo* magazines.

We have suppressed some of the citations that appeared in the previous edition. Our objective is to simplify the appearance of the book, not to claim the ideas of our colleagues as our own. Much of the theoretical material embedded in the book first appeared in academic publications such as the *Journal of Marketing* and the *Journal of Marketing Research*. At the end of each chapter we include Suggested Readings and References. Suggested Readings are usually articles that help flesh out and illustrate the material in the book. References are often books containing details about the material contained in a chapter since each chapter topic could be given as a course by itself!

Changes in This Edition

The most important content change in the new edition is our expanded coverage of electronic commerce and the Internet. We now have extensive discussions of the impact of the Internet on marketing activities in the distribution, direct marketing, advertising, and promotion chapters. To highlight our increased focus on interfunctional coordination, we added "Applying to" and "Integrating with" icons in the margins to point out relevant text discussions. We have also updated eighty-five percent of the boxed inserts to provide newer and more interesting examples. To increase awareness of the societal environment, we have included a business ethics or social responsibility question at the end of each of the chapters. One question at the end of most chapters encourages the use of SPSS statistical software for student analysis.

We have chosen to reduce the length of the new edition to make it easier for students to use. Our goal was to shorten the book by eliminating secondary material without hurting coverage of important topics. For example, the forecasting material was integrated with the product development chapter so the book now has 16 chapters. We would note that although all the chapters have been shortened, they have been thoroughly revised with new material, updated tables, figures, and references.

Supplements

Successful marketing management courses require a well-written text and an effective set of supplementary teaching materials. We have assembled an outstanding package of these aids to support *Basic Marketing Management*.

- Instructors Resource Guide. Includes suggested course syllabi, chapter outlines, lecture notes, and answers to chapter end questions.
- SPSS Student Version for Windows 9.0. This software is available to package with the text to help students analyze the data. The SPSS CD includes the data for SPSS end-of-chapter questions.
- PowerPoint Files and NBR Videos. A topic outline and key figures from the text are now available in PowerPoint files that can be downloaded from the book's Web site for use in class. The Web site is www.wiley.com/college. At this point, users can access the site in two primary ways:
  1. Search for Book Site by Author Name:

     |A|B|C|D|E|F|G|H|I|J|K|L|M|N|O|P|Q|R|S|T|U|V|W|X|Y|Z|

     Selecting "D" will provide you a listing of Web sites of lead authors with last names beginning with D.

2. By selecting:
   Business
   Marketing
   Marketing Management

The Web site will be open access except for the Instructor's resources. Secured Instructor Resources (PowerPoint files, *Instructor's Manual*, and the like) can be accessed only by using a password. Instructors can register for the password online. They will simply need to follow the registration instructions.

NBR stands for Nightly Business Report (PBS). The Wiley Nightly Business Report Business Video Series contains segments from the highly respected Nightly Business Report, which have been selected for their applicability to marketing management principles and for their reinforcement of key concepts in the text. Each of the segments is approximately three to five minutes long and can be used to introduce topics to the students, enhance lecture material, and provide real-world context for related concepts. The videotape is available to adopters of the text. Please see your Wiley representative for details.

Acknowledgements

This book could not have been published without the spirited comments and suggestions from a host of colleagues and reviewers. Although we don't have room to mention everyone, we would like to express our appreciation to the following professors who provided valuable tips for the seventh edition: Craig Andrews, Marquette University; Connie Rae Bateman, University of North Dakota; Terry Bristol, University of Arkansas, Little Rock; Kevin R. Coulson, Northeastern Illinois University; Susan Dann, Queensland University of Technology, Australia; Craig Kelley, California State University, Sacramento; Eldon Little, Indiana University Southeast; Charles L. Martin, Wichita State University; Richard M. Reese, Clemson University; Dennis Rosen, University of Kansas; and Nader H. Shooshtari, University of Montana.

We would like to thank the people from John Wiley & Sons for their guidance and support: our editor, Brent Gordon, and his (then) editorial assistant, Jennifer LiMarzi; our senior production editor, Patricia McFadden; our photo editors, Marge Graham and Lisa Gee; and our assistant editor for supplements, Cynthia Rhoads. The quality of the educational package was enhanced by Larry Meyer of Hermitage Publishing Services (editing and production), by Diane Hambley, University of South Dakota, and Tracy Clark, Multimedia Lab, DuPree College of Management, Georgia Institute of Technology (PowerPoint presentation), and by Stan Maddock, Maddock Illustration (jpeg files of figures). In addition, we would like to belatedly thank Stephen Walsh, State University of New York, Oneonta, who prepared several hundred unsolicited multiple-choice questions for the previous edition after its *Instructor's Manual* was published.

We are especially indebted to Linda Sharp for typing countless drafts and revisions. Last, but certainly not least, we thank our wives, Nancy and Julie, for their help and encouragement.

Douglas J. Dalrymple
Leonard J. Parsons

ABOUT THE AUTHORS

Douglas J. Dalrymple is Professor of Marketing in the School of Business at Indiana University. He received his DBA degree in marketing from Michigan State University and his MS and BS degrees from Cornell University. Professor Dalrymple has taught at the University of California, Los Angeles, the Georgia Institute of Technology, the University of San Diego, and the University of North Carolina, Greensboro. His research emphasizes forecasting and sales force issues. Publications in which his articles have appeared included *Journal of Personal Selling & Sales Management, Decision Sciences, Industrial Marketing Management, International Journal of Forecasting, Journal of Business Research, Business Horizons, California Management Review,* and *Applied Economics.* Professor Dalrymple is the author or coauthor of 24 marketing books including *Basic Marketing Management* (2nd ed.), *Sales Management: Concepts and Cases* (6th ed.), *Cases in Marketing Management,* a computerized *Sales Management Simulation* (4th ed.) and two retailing texts. His books and articles have been translated into Spanish, Chinese, Japanese, and Hebrew.

Leonard J. Parsons is professor of marketing at Georgia Institute of Technology's Dupree College of Management. He received his S.B. degree in chemical engineering from the Massachusetts Institute of Technology and his M.S.I.A. and Ph.D. degrees in industrial administration with a specialization in marketing from Purdue University's Krannert School. He has taught at Indiana University and the Claremont Graduate School, and has been a visiting scholar at M.I.T., a Fulbright-Hays Senior Scholar at Katholieke Universiteit Leuven (Belgium), a visiting professor at INSEAD (France), the Norwegian School of Marketing (Oslo), and U.C.L.A., an Advertising Educational Foundation Visiting Professor at Anheuser-Busch, and an Intercollegiate Center for Management Science Visiting Professor at the Center for Research on the Economic Efficiency of Retailing of the Facultés Universitaires Catholiques de Mons (Belgium) and at the European Institute for Advanced Studies in Management (Brussels). He has been a member of the European Marketing Academy's Executive Council, a member of the Graduate Management Admission Council's Research and Test (GMAT) Development Committee, chair of the American Statistical Association's Section on Statistics in Marketing, and a member of the

Advisory Board of the American Marketing Association's Marketing Research Special Interest Group. He has served as marketing departmental editor of *Management Science* and associate editor of *Decision Sciences,* and has been on the editorial boards of the *Journal of Marketing Research,* the *Journal of Marketing,* and the *Journal of Business Research.* He has coedited special issues of the *International Journal of Forecasting* and the *International Journal of Research in Marketing.* He has coauthored or coedited five books, and *Market Response Models: Econometric and Time Series Analysis,* two programmed learning texts, seven chapters in books, and articles in journals such as the *Journal of Marketing Research, Management Science, Operations Research, and Applied Economics.* He has received several awards from the American Marketing Association, including the first place award in its National Research Design Competition, and a grant from the American Association of Advertising Agencies. He is a member of Beta Gamma Sigma and Phi Kappa Phi and is listed in *Who's Who in America.* He is an expert on market response models, and his main interest is in marketing productivity.

CONTENTS

1

THE ROLE OF MARKETING IN ORGANIZATIONS AND SOCIETY

> Marketing today is not a function; it is a way of doing business.
>
> REGIS MCKENNA

*T*he field of marketing in the new millennium is full of challenges and risks. Domestic firms in every country find that they can no longer ignore foreign competition and foreign markets. Organizations that let their costs and prices get out of line with the rest of the world see their market shares plummet. Companies also learn that they cannot ignore emerging technologies and new forms of organizational structure.

Some firms seize market opportunities and grow while others fade away. Why? We believe that one reason is vision. Another reason some organizations grow is that they choose chief executive officers with marketing backgrounds. Research has shown that more top executives come out of marketing than any other field. A marketing emphasis can make the difference between organizational success and disaster. We believe it is essential that you acquire strong marketing skills so that you can operate in today's competitive environment. This book has been specifically designed to show you how to develop and implement marketing strategies and tactics for organizations of the new millennium.

WHAT IS MARKETING?

Marketing is one of the most powerful tools employed by organizations in their never-ending struggle for survival and growth. One definition of marketing is

> the process of planning and executing the conception, pricing, promotion, and distribution of ideas, goods, and services to create exchanges that satisfy individuals, organizations, and society.[1]

This definition points out that the objective of marketing is to satisfy customers' needs. Thus, the first challenge is to find a set of customers and identify their needs so that appropriate goods and services can be developed. Once an organization has a product, marketing personnel design pricing, promotion, and distribution plans to make these items leap into the hands of the customer. Executives are responsible for meeting organizational goals while ensuring that the customer and the public are not harmed by marketing activities. When we speak of exchanges, we do not restrict ourselves to the onetime, arm's-length transaction between a buyer and a seller.

In a single-event transaction, all that counts is the sale.[2] Price is the most important factor. More often, instead of only one transaction, there are repeated transactions between parties. This is true for some industrial components and most consumables: frequently purchased consumer goods and business supplies. Advertising and sales promotions are used to gain and retain customers. Concepts such as brand loyalty now have meaning. Nonetheless, there may be little direct contact between the marketer and the customer in many consumer markets. When we examine business-to-business markets, we often see long-term agreements among parties. Frequently, a buyer has a list of qualified vendors. The buyer encourages competition among these vendors, perhaps by using a competitive bidding process, to get the best price. The buyer monitors product quality by inspection on delivery. Thus, although this is a long-term relationship, its basis is adversarial. However, the picture we have painted of the marketplace so far, which could be called *transactional marketing,* is changing.

Relationship marketing emphasizes the interdependence between buyer and seller. Even for frequently purchased consumer products, you need to move beyond a repeat transaction mentality to relationship marketing. This has been made possible by the technical ability to create large databases, which identify customers and their needs. You can reach specific customers through direct selling or direct marketing. This approach to relationship marketing is known as *database marketing.* It could also be considered a form of transactional marketing but one that allows you to get somewhat closer to your customer. When using advanced information technology based on individually addressable and interactive media, database marketing is known as *interactive marketing.*

> **INTEGRATING**
> *. . . with*
> *Information*
> *Techonology*
> *Management*

Facing new pressures, once contending parties, especially in business-to-business markets, are realizing the value of cooperation. Quality, delivery, and technical support as well as price, enter into negotiations. Quality is built into the production process. Product design becomes a collaborative process. Individuals in the seller organization interact with their counterpart in the buyer organization in a process known as "customer partnering." Thus, social exchange (i.e., personal interactions) to create value for both parties is paramount. This approach to relationship marketing is known as *interaction marketing,* and should not be confused with interactive marketing.

In today's world, it's important to develop long-term, mutually supportive relationships with your customers—whether they are channel members or end users. This approach can be extended to embrace suppliers and, at times, competitors as well. In some cases, the relationship takes the form of a partnership or a strategic alliance. For example, the Coca-Cola Company and Nestlé S.A. have a joint venture, Coca-Cola Nestlé Refreshments Company. Among other things, this joint venture sells a canned beverage, Nestea Iced Tea. The product is produced and distributed by Coca-Cola bottlers in various countries. This approach to relationship marketing, which is known as *network marketing,* takes into account the totality of the relationships in a market or industry, and it is a more holistic view of interaction marketing. Interaction marketing emphasizes the focal relationship of the firm in the network as indicated in Figure 1-1.

> **APPLYING**
> *. . . to*
> *Consumer*
> *Beverages*
> *Marketing*

A perceptual map showing transactional marketing and the three types of relationship marketing is shown in Figure 1-2. Certain types of marketing practice are more common in some sectors than others (as indicated in Figure 1-2). While one type of marketing may be predominant in a firm, others are also practiced. A comparison of the characteristics of the four types is given in Table 1-1.

In sum, a contemporary view of the purpose of marketing is

> to identify and establish, maintain, and enhance relationships with customers and other stakeholders, at a profit, so that the objectives of the partners involved are met; and this is achieved by mutual exchange and fulfillment of promises.[3]

Nonetheless, for most organizations, transactional marketing remains relevant and is practiced concurrently with various types of relationship marketing. Some of the interplay that

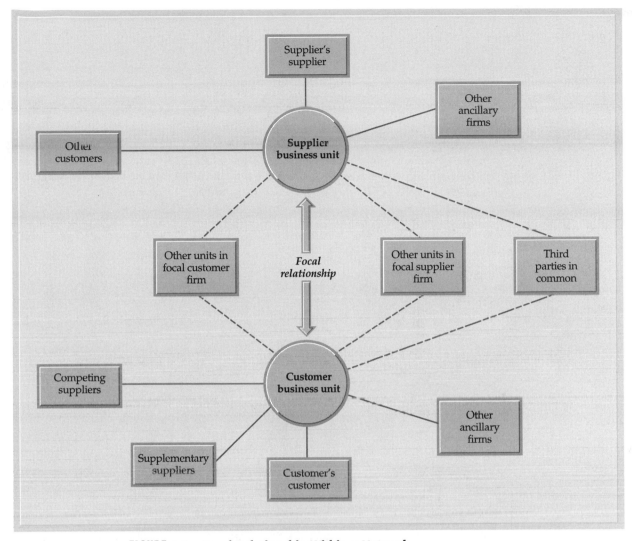

FIGURE 1-1   Focal Relationship Within a Network
(From James C. Anderson, Håkan Håkansson, and Jan Johanson, "Dyadic Business Relationships Within a Business Network Context," *Journal of Marketing,* Vol. 58, No. 4 [October 1994], p. 3)

takes place is hinted at in the Ocean Spray example given in the Marketing in Action box 1-1.

The role marketing plays in an organization varies by organizational level (Table 1-2). At the corporate level, *marketing as culture* is emphasized; at the strategic business unit level, *marketing as strategy;* and at the operating level, *marketing as tactics.* This chapter emphasizes marketing as culture: the basic set of values and beliefs about the central importance of the customer that guide the organization, as articulated by the marketing concept.

WHO IS THE MARKETING MANAGER?

A marketing manager is anyone responsible for making significant marketing decisions. Except in the case of very small firms, no single person is accountable for all the decisions described in this book. The responsibility for marketing is diffused throughout the organiza-

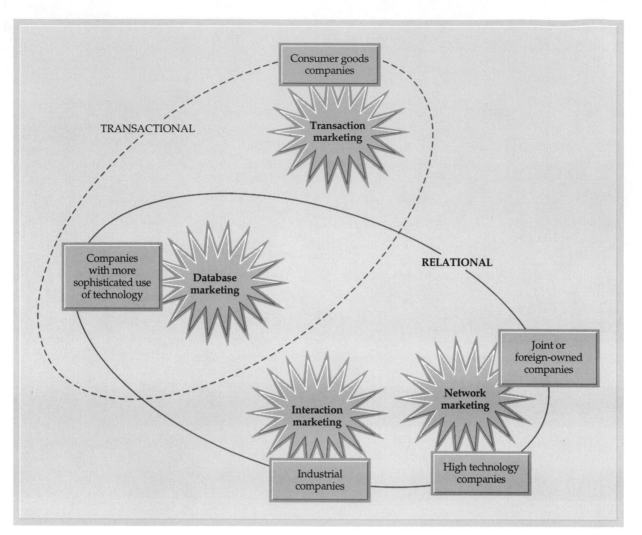

FIGURE 1-2   A Perceptual Map of the Four Types of Marketing (with exemplars).
(Constructed from information in Roderick J. Brodie, Nicole E. Coviello, Richard W. Brookes, and Victoria Little,
"Toward a Paradigm Shift in Marketing? An Examination of Current Marketing Practices," *Journal of Marketing
Management,* Vol. 13, No. 5 [July 1997], pp. 383–406.)

INTEGRATING
*. . . with
Engineering
and Finance*

tion. Senior managers are continually making pricing and strategic marketing decisions. But
engineers are also involved in marketing because they have to design products that meet
customers' needs, wants, and quality standards, as are corporate treasurers who oversee the
credit terms and credit availability that directly affect buying decisions.

Several managers in an organization specialize in marketing decision making. These
include *brand and product managers,* who make the day-to-day decisions for individual
items and prepare the annual marketing plan. The brand manager is charged with managing
and further developing the brand equity. *Category managers* coordinate the marketing
strategies of related products and brands. The evolution of the brand manager system at
Procter & Gamble is described in Marketing in Action box 1-2. There are also line sales
managers who guide the implementation of the marketing plan by the field sales force. In
addition to these line managers, there are a variety of staff managers. Advertising and promotion managers control the preparation of print ads, TV commercials, direct-mail

TABLE 1-1   Types of Marketing

	Transactional Perspective	Relational Perspective		
	Transactional Marketing	Database Marketing	Interaction Marketing	Network Marketing
Managerial intent[a]	Customer attraction (to satisfy a customer at a profit)	Customer retention (to satisfy the customer, increase profit, and attain other objectives such as increased loyalty or decreased customer risk)	Interaction (to establish, develop, and facilitate a cooperative relationship for mutual benefit)	Coordination (interaction between sellers, buyers, and other parties across multiple firms for mutual benefit, resource exchange, market access)
Decision focus[a]	Product or brand	Product/brand and customers in targeted market	Relationships between individuals	Connected relationships among firms (in a network)
Relational exchange focus[b]	Economic transaction	Information and economic transaction	Interactive relationships between a buyer and a seller	Connected relationships among firms
Parties involved[b]	A firm and buyers in the general market	A firm and buyers in a specific target market	Individual sellers and buyers (a dyad)	Sellers, buyers, and other firms)
Communication pattern[b]	Firm "to" market	Firm "to" individual	Individuals "with" individuals (across organizations)	Firms "with" firms (involving individuals)
Type of contact[b]	Arm's-length, impersonal	Personalized, yet distant	Face-to-face, interpersonal (close, based on commitment, trust, and cooperation)	Impersonal – interpersonal (ranging from distant to close)
Duration[b]	Discrete (yet perhaps over time)	Discrete and over time	Continuous (ongoing and mutually adaptive, may be short or long-term)	Continuous (stable yet dynamic, may be short-or long-term)
Formality[b]	Formal	Formal (yet personalized via technology)	Formal and informal (i.e., at both the business and social level)	Formal and informal (i.e., at both the business and social level)
Balance of power[b]	Active seller–passive buyers	Active seller–less passive buyers	Seller and buyer mutually active and adaptive (interdependent and reciprocal)	All firms active and adaptive
Managerial investment[a]	Internal marketing assets (focusing on product/service, price, distribution, promotion capabilities)	Internal marketing assets (emphasizing communication, information, and technology capabilities)	External market assets (focusing on establishing a relationship with another individual)	External market assets (focusing on developing the firms position in a network of firms)

(continued)

TABLE 1-1   Continued

	Transactional Perspective	Relational Perspective		
	Transactional Marketing	Database Marketing	Interaction Marketing	Network Marketing
Managerial level[a]	Functional marketers	Specialist marketers (e.g., customer service manager, loyalty manager)	Managers from across functional areas	General manager
Time frame[a]	Short-term	Longer-term	Short or long-term	Short or long-term

[a] Managerial dimension
[b] Relational exchange dimension

Source: Nicole E. Coviello, Roderick J. Brodie, and Hugh J. Munro, "Understanding Contemporary Marketing," *Journal of Marketing Management,* Vol. 13, No. 6 (August 1997), pp. 501–522.

APPLYING
. . . to
Consumer
Beverages
Marketing

MARKETING IN ACTION *1-1*

Ocean Spray, the Number One Cranberry Brand

Ocean Spray, a farmer's cooperative, markets cranberry juice. Traditionally, Ocean Spray considered its product an all-family beverage. It viewed Mom buying a big bottle for the whole family to drink at home. More recently, it realized it should view each family member as buying a different product outside the home. For example, a 13-year-old might get off a school bus and hit a convenience store on the way home. Ocean Spray expected bigger growth from away-from-home and international than in-home. Consequently, it formed three strategic marketing groups to tackle away-from-home, in-home, and international campaigns. It also set up a brand development group to serve as a resource.

Ocean Spray was eager to break into the broader beverage category to establish the same status as Coke and Pepsi in consumers' minds. To this end, Ocean Spray and Pepsi began a joint venture in 1992. However, the relationship was downgraded to that of distribution agreement in 1995, leaving each company free to develop its own new products and marketing. Ocean Spray didn't give Pepsi as much control over the brand as Pepsi wanted. Pepsi then decided to buy its own juice company so that it could be in control without having to please a farmer's coop. In 1998, Pepsi proposed buying Tropicana. This deal could eventually edge Ocean Spray off Pepsi trucks. Ocean Spray could lose as much as half of its single-serve sales, the portion now handled by Pepsi-owned bottlers. This would kill its momentum in single-serve products—its main vehicle to reach younger consumers. Pepsi maintained that it would honor the current distribution contract. Nonetheless, Ocean Spray filed suit against its distribution partner to block the purchase of Tropicana. The relationship has been contentious but it expanded Ocean Spray's single-serve sales from 1.5 million cases to 22 million cases in five years.

In the meantime, Ocean Spray took its eye off the juice aisle and lost ground with grocers and consumers. Ocean Spray growth historically relied on new products but few had been forthcoming. The trade asked Ocean Spray, "Where are you? We need you spending money and bringing us new products." Grocers wanted help in growing the shelf-stable juice business. While Ocean Spray was not paying attention, newcomer Northland Cranberries made inroads with its 100 percent cranberry juice. Ocean Spray responded by bringing out Wellfleet Farms, an upscale line of 100 percent fruit blends with flavors such as Georgia Peach. In addition, although predominately broker sold, Ocean Spray began to rely more on its own sales staff as grocer consolidations expanded accounts beyond the territory of individual brokers. The company centralized customer sales reps at headquarters from seven scattered plants.

— *Marketing is an interpersonal process based on ongoing contact, mutual goals, trust, and commitment.*

Source: Betsy Spethmann, "Second Wave," *Promo,* October 1998, pp. 38–40, 170–172.

TABLE 1-2   Marketing's Role in the Organization

Organizational Level	Role of Marketing	Name
Corporate	To promote a customer orientation by being a strong advocate for the customer's point of view, as called for by the marketing concept. To assess market attractiveness by analyzing customers' needs and requirements, as well as competitive offerings in the markets potentially available to the firm, to assess potential competitive effectiveness. To develop the firm's overall value proposition in terms reflecting customers' needs and to articulate it to the marketplace and throughout the firm.	Corporate marketing
Strategic business unit	To determine how to compete (market segmentation, targeting, and product positioning) in your chosen business through a more detailed and careful analysis of competitors and of the firm's resources and skills for competing in specific market segments. To decide when and how to partner.	Strategic marketing
Operating	To formulate and implement marketing programs based on the marketing mix—products, pricing, distribution, and marketing communications. To manage customer and reseller relationships.	Marketing management

Source: Developed from Frederick E. Webster, Jr., "The Changing Role of Marketing in the Corporation," *Journal of Marketing,* Vol. 56, No. 4 (October 1992), pp. 1–17.

MARKETING IN ACTION *1-2*

**APPLYING
. . . to
Consumer
Goods
Marketing**

Procter & Gamble Redefines the Brand Manager

The Procter & Gamble Co. is generally credited with developing the brand management system. Brand managers had near absolute power and responsibility to run their brands. Being a P&G brand manager was one of the greatest jobs in the world. Over time, however, the brand managers' clout has eroded. This can be seen in the evolution of P&G's brand management:

1931	brand management system approved
1979	customer business teams instituted
1987	category management implemented
1990	everyday low pricing started
1993–95	marketing staff cut through restructuring
1995	global success models sought
1997	media buying and planning consolidated

The managers of P&G brands within the same category once competed fiercely against each other, even to the extent of refusing to share data. The implementation of category management to stop this fratricide naturally took away some the brand manager's power. The introduction of value pricing meant that slower moving brands and stock-keeping units as well as promotional budgets were trimmed. Restructuring cut the marketing staff by 30 percent by eliminating brand assistant and assistant brand manager positions for some smaller brands. Needless variations in products and packaging internationally were weeded out. Global strategic teams, made up of brand and category managers worldwide, were made responsible for identifying "global success models" in product development and ad copy. Once a model is in place, brand managers have little authority to change it. Seeking to improve cost effectiveness in media spending worldwide, ad planning and buying was centralized in an ad agency, shifting media responsibility away from brand managers. Thus, while brand managers still have responsibility for positioning of brands based on consumer needs and for developing broad media strategy, they have lost their grip on such areas as new product development, advertising copy, media planning, and promotions. The brand managers have become more tactical and get more involved in account-by-account, store-by-store marketing.

— *The brand manager today is no longer the final decision-maker but must be brand champion and multi-functional team captain.*

Source: Jack Neff, "P&G Redefines the Brand Manager," *Advertising Age,* October 13, 1997, pp. 1, 18, 20.

brochures, and contests that help to boost the sales of goods and services. Larger firms also have managers of product development and marketing information.

WHAT DOES A MARKETING MANAGER DO?

A marketing manager is, first and foremost, someone who has control or direction of an organization or organizational unit, that is, a manager. There are fundamental aspects of a manager's job that apply across functional areas. Managers have been shown to play 10 roles: figurehead, leader, liaison, monitor, disseminator, spokesperson, entrepreneur, disturbance handler, resource allocator, and negotiator. These roles can be classified as interpersonal, informational, or decisional. Table 1-3 describes these roles and gives examples of how they might apply specifically to a marketing manager. For example, a national account manager for a health and beauty aids company often negotiates sales and promotional terms with the central purchasing offices of large national supermarket chains. As you can see, many of these roles require not only knowledge of marketing concepts and practices, but the exercise of interpersonal skills as well.

The full range of marketing activities in the firm is described in Figure 1-3. Note that the marketing manager is in the center of interactions with a host of people both inside and outside the organization. Marketing talks to customers, research and development, production, finance, suppliers, ad agencies, and marketing research firms. The net result of these interactions is products delivered to satisfied buyers plus profits to fuel innovations for tomorrow. Your most important role is to understand customers.

Customer Contact

Marketing people continually interact with customers. Customers must be your first and most enduring concern. Close attention to their needs is essential for success. Some of the

TABLE 1-3   The Marketing Manager's Job

Role	Description	Example
Interpersonal		
Figurehead	Performs some duties of a ceremonial nature.	Takes important customer to lunch.
Leader	Assumes responsibility for work of subordinates.	Motivates the sales force.
Liaison	Makes contacts outside the vertical chain of command.	Meets with an account executive from a direct marketing firm.
Informational		
Monitor	Scans the environment for information.	Hears from a supplier about a competitor's new product.
Disseminator	Shares information with others, especially subordinates.	Provides feedback from meetings with prospective clients at their locations.
Spokesperson	Sends some information to people outside the organizational unit.	Makes a speech to lobby for favorable legislative treatment.
Decisional		
Entrepreneur	Seeks to improve the unit, adapting it to changing conditions in the environment.	Assigns a new idea to the product development team.
Disturbance handler	Responds to high-pressure disturbances.	Address a consumer boycott initiated by a special interest group.
Resource allocator	Decides who will get what in the organizational unit.	Determines the allocation of promotion budget across brands.
Negotiator	Bargains with others.	Negotiates sales terms with a channel member.

Source: Developed from Henry Mintzberg, *Mintzberg on Management,* New York: The Free Press, 1989, pp. 7–24.

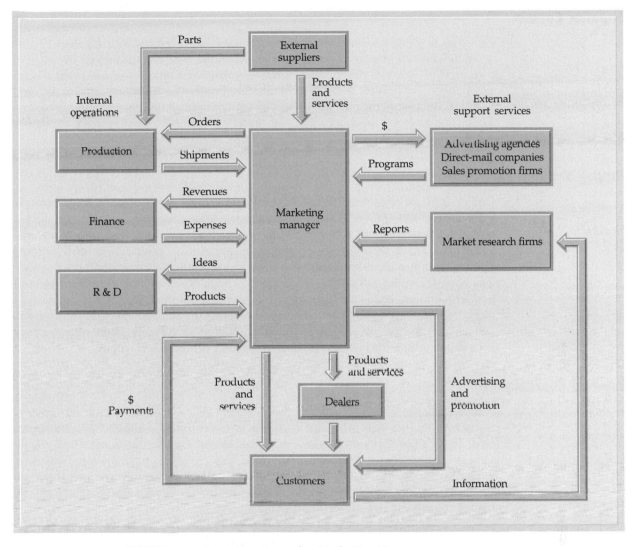

FIGURE 1-3 Operating Areas for Marketing Managers

ways that marketing managers relate to customers are shown in Figure 1-3. The diagram shows marketing managers interacting with two types of customers: dealers who resell your products to others and final users. Both types have unique needs that demand specialized marketing programs. Because these customers are typically located some distance from the office, you have to go into the field to talk with them. You also have to set up distribution systems to make goods and services available when and where they are needed.

The marketing manager has responsibility for directing persuasive communications to dealers and ultimate customers and arranging for payment for purchases. In the case of fast-moving consumer goods companies that face the growing power of the retail trade, *customer business teams*, made up of sales, finance, logistics, and perhaps brand management staff, often work with major retail accounts to develop promotion strategy. In this situation, promotions are funded through a single business development fund for each retail account. In addition, marketing managers have responsibility for collecting information on customer satisfaction, customer loyalty, and future needs. Managing customer relations is a tremendous responsibility and can represent the difference between achieving the goals of the organization and failure.

Supplier Contact

An expanding role for marketing managers is more direct contact with suppliers (Figure 1-3). In the past, the emphasis was on vertical integration, whereby the firm produced all of its own parts. Companies thought that in-house production would lower costs, but it actually raised them. Today some of the most successful firms rely on suppliers for parts and production so that they can focus on core activities such as product design, marketing, and service. These new *strategic alliances* mean that marketing managers must spend more time with suppliers to make sure product quality is maintained and delivery dates are met.

Buying External Services

One of the least understood facts about marketing is that much of the work is assigned to external suppliers (Figure 1-3). In the past, many firms had their own in-house marketing research, advertising, and promotion staffs. Today most companies hire outside advertising agencies to create their advertising and a separate firm to handle direct-mail campaigns. Contests and display materials are developed by special organizations, and market research data are gathered by still another organization. The reliance on outside suppliers means that in your job as marketing manager, you become a buyer of these services. It also means that marketing managers spend a lot of time coordinating the activities of these separate groups and making sure that the work is done on time. Victory in the marketplace often depends on your ability to hire the right service suppliers and to evaluate their output.

Internal Coordination

A third challenge to marketing managers stems from their role as coordinator with other areas of the firm (Figure 1-3). Although marketing is responsible for maintaining good customer relations, as a manager you often have no formal control over the production of the goods and services customers buy. Thus marketing has to work closely with the production department to make sure that orders are filled on time, at an affordable price, and meet customers' specifications. Sometimes this means that production and marketing personnel have to find ways to modify the product to meet the needs of the market. Less successful firms are often those in which production and marketing are unable to work together to get this job done.

Another key interaction for marketing managers involves their ability to work with the research and development department (Figure 1-3). Marketing often comes up with good ideas for new products, but R&D is responsible for turning them into salable products. Thus your success as a marketer may depend on the relationship you develop with the R&D staff. Marketing managers also have to interact with the financial managers of the firm (Figure 1-3). Marketing activities are often expensive, and marketing managers have to meet with financial managers to prepare budget requests. If funds are tight, marketing managers have to find ways to reorganize their activities to make them more efficient. Some of the areas that require financial support are advertising, product development, maintenance of dealer inventories, and credit lines to finance customers' purchases.

If you take a position in marketing, some of the work-related tasks you will encounter are illustrated in Marketing in Action box 1-3. Marketing is much more than a list of things to do; it is a natural sequence of events that leads to greater sales and profits.

THE MARKETING MANAGEMENT PROCESS

Marketing managers plan and implement a sequence of activities that help the firm achieve its goals. The precise actions taken vary with the product or service to be promoted, but a

MARKETING IN ACTION *1-3*

Marketing Activities of One Manager

The Australian biscuit (cracker/cookie) company Arnott's is the giant in its marketplace, with a dominant 60 percent share in its home country. It has manufacturing plants all over Australia. Arnott's New Zealand also does a big biscuit business. Here, Arnott's turnover is some $85 million a year, though they rank second in this market to Griffins. In 1996, its South Auckland, New Zealand, plant was in need of a major upgrade to bring it up to the year 2000. Because of that extra expense and Arnott's new state of the art factory recently completed in Sydney, the company decided to close the New Zealand plant and supply all of its product from Australia.

When Arnott's decided to close its manufacturing base in New Zealand and concentrate entirely on a sales and marketing force, it needed a savvy, new-wave manager to drive the operation. Enter Janine Smith as general manager for Arnott's New Zealand. After years of manufacturing, her big challenge was to refocus Arnott's on marketing. There was great complexity in gradually closing down 150 different product lines and at the same time gradually reducing staff numbers. Smith had to manage that closure before she could begin a new culture, which brought some special management challenges. "The company had always had strong marketing but because of the sheer weight of numbers involved in manufacturing, you can't help but be dominated by that arm of the business," said Smith. "With the manufacturing gone, we can now concentrate solely on the service and marketing arm."

"The first important lesson was having to manage through other people rather than manage direct," said Smith. "In the past, if we ran short of one line we simply cranked up production. But with supply coming from Australia that doesn't work. Now we're constantly in communication with each other so situations like that don't get out of hand. We have lots of partnerships with people, and we have to understand that we are managing through other people."

But the transformation wasn't without its glitches. Arnott's in Australia received extortion threats during 1997 and was forced to pull 40 percent of its stock off the shelves. This directly impacted on the New Zealand operation, as Arnott's struggled to supply its home market, let alone New Zealand. Some lines went out of supply until Australia could make the product and that lost some market share points. Yet overall the company has retained its 32 percent share of the market, something Smith can point to as a credit to her management skills.

Forecasting demand has become an integral part of the new culture. Smith's team has to make sure they don't have any repeats of undersupplying their customers, mostly the supermarkets. A lot of time and energy now goes into accurately judging supply and demand.

Another deliberate strategy was to recruit an almost entirely new team. Seventy percent of the 30 management staff under Smith's control have been in the job less than a year. Many of the former management staff were repatriated to Australia or left of their own volition, something that suited Smith. "We are building a whole new company culture and when you're doing that it's easier to start from scratch," she said. "To generate a 'can-do' culture you need consistency, and if you have someone who's been there, done that, bored with their job, that can affect the whole culture. A lot of the people here are in their particular role for the first time, and there's a terrific energy about that, a willingness to take risks and go the extra mile. Of course that's the upside, the downside is that we did lose knowledge—a little too fast in the short term."

With so many new recruits Smith uses more than just instinct when hiring. Potential recruits are tested with an occupational personality questionnaire—the Saville and Holdsworth OPQ. This details areas of potential strength and weakness of people in areas such as strategy, problem solving and customer service. Though Smith agreed that such tests are not always 100 percent accurate, she said they identify focus, energy and drive. It also identifies team styles that the company uses to develop teams more effectively.

Smith's own style is energetic and one suspects she would score highly on the "can-do" scale of her own questionnaire. She doesn't spend time agonizing over problems, preferring to move on to the solution. "The way I look at life, these are the cards we've been dealt and now we have to rise to the occasion and make it work. I believe you only go after what you can change; if you can't change it then you forget worrying about it."

(continues)

MARKETING IN ACTION 1-3   (continued)

INTEGRATING
... with
Cross-
Functional
Terms

Smith is also fluent in modern management styles. "Cross-functional teams" is part of her everyday vocabulary. "I like to encourage people to look at the bigger picture. We'll get teams from various disciplines together to solve a problem, and we get a wealth of perspectives. People understand their own job best, and if you ask them to think about it they have the greatest opportunity to see ways of doing it better."

And while they're doing that, Smith provides the overview. With the experience of 20 years of management, she likes to think outside the square. "As a manager, more and more, you have to become a very good listener. You have to objectively listen and work out the consistency and logic of a particular argument." Smith said that's also a skill that requires asking the right questions. Often, she says, junior managers will be trying to make decisions on imperfect information. When you ask the right questions you can open minds to a new direction or solution. Management, she says, is about more thinking and less doing—the ability to see the big picture and understand the wider implications of decisions.

Hierarchical management is not her style and as she strolls around the office, greeting staff and popping her nose round doors, it's obvious she's no stranger to the impromptu meeting. She believes in talking directly to her staff as well as a regular monthly meeting with everyone in which they discuss what went wrong and celebrate their wins. Smith also likes to get out with the salespeople—some 100 of them—so on a monthly basis she gets in the car with the territory managers and goes out with them, calling on customers. The new management team had to accept working without a lot of processes to begin with. Initially there were few structures in place and so, again, it demanded people with faith in their own ability.

INTEGRATING
... with
Suppliers

Part of Smith's philosophy of managing through people also means building partnerships with suppliers. "Some people treat their suppliers as dependent on them, but I believe suppliers are part of our business. When you involve them you get them thinking about your business from your point of view, and their contribution can be all the greater." Smith invites suppliers to corporate functions because she believes she's in partnership with them as much as her clients. It's a move that has apparently taken some of the suppliers by surprise, but enriched their relations with Arnott's.

In the long term, Smith said her company is looking to make significant inroads into the "share of mouth." Throughout the restructuring the company held its category share, and Smith says that's a positive in the face of the upheavals of any restructuring. Closer contact with the parent company has its advantages. In the past six months Arnott's has introduced new lines without having to go through complex research and development because it's already been done in Australia.

What has not changed throughout the transition is a focus on brands. The "Farmbake" brand is now, as before, the biggest biscuit brand in New Zealand and Smith doesn't intend to let that slip. Growth in the future will come from nurturing other key brands, and to that end Smith is fostering a culture of "loving the brand." Underscoring the lot is service to the customer, which mostly means the big supermarkets.

Looking back on the change in the culture, Smith says most of it went exactly right, the result of planning and the commitment of people to make it work. It's also a reflection of the ability of the general manager.

— *Senior management is responsible for creating the enabling conditions that ensure future decisions generate value for both customers and shareholders.*

Source: Wendy Colville, "Taking the Biscuit," *Management-Auckland,* October 1998, pp. 22–26.

general idea can be obtained from the flowchart shown in Figure 1-4. This diagram provides a basic framework for the book. First, managers need to adopt a marketing philosophy. This chapter explains why organizations should be customer driven and in tune with the goals of society. Although you are charged with promoting the sale of goods and services, you must also learn to balance these objectives against the long-term needs of society for a safe and healthy environment. In addition, you need to know which marketing activities are ethical and which violate current business standards.

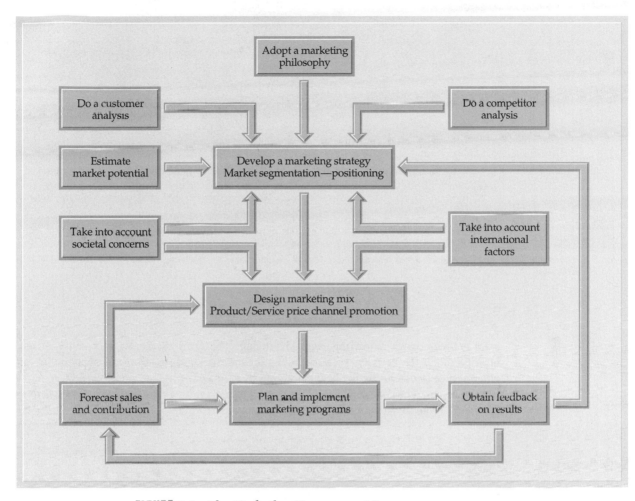

FIGURE 1-4   The Marketing Management Process

Second in the management process is a concern with marketing strategy (Chapter 2): our emphasis is on achieving a sustainable competitive advantage for the organization. A problem-solving approach is used throughout the book and the cases at the end of the chapters provide opportunities to apply what you have learned.

Customer Focus

Before sound marketing strategies can be created (Figure 1-4), you have to know who your potential and/or existing customers are and why they behave as they do (Chapter 3). In developing marketing strategies, the manager must select appropriate market segments to be targets of the marketing effort (Chapter 4). You also have to understand your competitors and where they are going (Chapter 5). A critical decision here is how your organization's offerings should be positioned against those of your competitors. Perhaps the most creative and challenging step in marketing is designing the right mix of marketing activities to tap the target segments. The *marketing mix* is the specific collection of actions and associated instruments employed by an organization to stimulate acceptance of its ideas, products, or services (Table 1-4). The basic functions included in the mix are product development and policymaking, pricing, channel selection and control, and marketing communications—per-

TABLE 1-4   Marketing Mix

Element	Description	Examples
Product	Instruments that mainly aim at the satisfaction of the prospective exchange party's needs	Product characteristics, options, assortments, brand name, packaging, quantity, factory guarantee
Price	Instruments that mainly fix the size and method of payment for goods or services	List price, usual terms of payment, usual quantity discounts, terms of credit
Distribution	Instruments that determine the intensity and manner in which goods or services will be made available	Different types of distribution channels, density of distribution system, trade relation mix, merchandising advice
Marketing communications		
Personal selling	Face-to-face, personal communication efforts	Amount and type of selling, compensation plans
Direct marketing	Other one-to-one communication efforts	Number of direct-mail pieces and telephone calls
Advertising	Mass communication efforts	Theme advertising in various media, permanent exhibits

Source: Based on Walter van Waterschoot and Christophe Van den Bulte, "The 4P Classification of the Marketing Mix Revisited," *Journal of Marketing,* Vol. 56, No. 4 (October 1992), pp. 83–93.

sonal selling, direct marketing, and advertising. The term *marketing mix* can be used to describe either the activity, such as pricing, or the marketing instrument, such as list price. When trying to determine the best marketing mix for your product, you face a large number of alternatives. The only way to reduce these alternatives to a manageable number is to take a strategic focus. That is one reason why we emphasize strategy in a marketing management book.

New Products

Product development activities focus on the conversion of customers' wants into real products or services (Chapter 6). Since existing products and services lose their attractiveness over time, product development is essential to the survival of all organizations. Marketing managers are responsible for designing the systems needed to find, screen, and evaluate new ideas. Product policy (Chapter 7) emphasizes the management of a product over its life cycle. This involves reformulating old products and getting rid of some of them. Since more money is being spent in highly industrialized countries of the world on services than on manufactured goods, the special marketing needs of intangible merchandise are discussed (Chapter 8).

A critical dimension of your job as marketing manager is making decisions on what prices to charge for goods and services to generate desired levels of sales (Chapter 9). Marketing also has the task of organizing brokers, wholesalers, and retailers into channels of distribution so that merchandise and services will be available where customers need and want them (Chapter 10). Personal selling (Chapter 11) is required for many products, and marketing managers have the job of hiring, training, and deploying the right number of salespeople to meet the needs of potential buyers. Direct marketing (Chapter 12) has become increasingly important with the creation of large databases. Direct marketing includes telephone marketing, direct mail, and the Internet. Advertising (Chapter 13) focuses on nonpersonal communication through measured media. This means that you have to choose among newspapers, radio, television, billboards, direct mail, and magazines. Sales promotions and public relations (Chapter 14) support the basic marketing mix. You must determine budgets for point-of-purchase displays, contests, and other promotional activities.

Building the Plan

After an appropriate marketing mix has been selected, it is your job as marketing manager to prepare and implement a detailed marketing plan. Vital to developing marketing strategies and tactics today is the international dimension (Chapter 15). The production and marketing of many goods are now on a global basis, which leads firms to consider the impact of such things as cultural differences and currency exchange rates on pricing and distribution plans. Responsibility for implementing marketing programs (Chapter 16) rests with brand managers, who continually monitor the results of marketing activities and recommend program improvements.

Although we have shown marketing management as a sequence of steps that follow the chapters of this book, you should realize that brand managers often work on several of these activities at the same time. Also, feedback in terms of results and customer reactions provides continuous inputs for strategy revisions and updated sales forecasts (Figure 1-4). Marketing management is a highly interactive process, and your success as a marketing professional will depend on your ability to coordinate and work through others.

The marketing management process begins with the adoption of the marketing philosophy. We will now focus on what makes a firm marketing driven.

THE MARKETING CONCEPT

Organizations must adapt to changing economic environments and meet competitive threats to prevent loss of market share, stagnation, and perhaps even bankruptcy. Some companies take an operations orientation. They are primarily concerned with cost cutting and production. Others are technology driven. They want to do something new and exciting. Both may founder because they ignore their customers or their competition.

The belief that organizational goals can be reached by satisfying customers has grown so much in importance among managers that it has become known as the *marketing concept.* The marketing concept is a business philosophy that maintains that the key to achieving organizational goals is to determine the needs of target markets and deliver the desired merchandise more efficiently than do competitors. This idea of focusing a whole organization on attending to customer needs has gained widespread acceptance among managers. Three important dimensions of the marketing concept that you must understand are these:

1. A customer orientation
2. An integrated company effort
3. Goal-directed behavior

Although these three factors interact to help improve marketing activities, they will be discussed separately.

A Customer Orientation

The basic idea of the marketing concept is to give customers what they want. This means that organizations must decide who their target customers are and then determine their wants and needs. The net result should be the creation of goods and services that satisfy customers' expectations.

The advantages of a customer orientation seem so obvious that it is hard to understand why the concept has not been more widely adopted. However, some organizations still take a very narrow view of their mission, a problem that has been called *marketing myopia.* Banks, for example, once thought of themselves as protectors of their customers' money. They hid behind bars, and their hours were from 10:00 A.M. to 3:00 P.M. a few days a week.

Following the marketing concept, banks have added branch locations that are open on Saturdays, have extended weekday hours, and feature drive-up windows. They have also installed 24-hour teller machines that dispense cash and perform other services to serve customers better. Now you can even do your banking over the Internet.

An Integrated Company Effort

A second dimension of the marketing concept suggests that marketing activities should be closely coordinated with each other and with the other functional areas of the organization. Under the marketing concept, sales, finance, production, and personnel all work together to satisfy customers' needs. With the production orientation, production emphasizes rigid schedules so that costs could be kept low through long production runs. If the sales department said that a customer needed 21-day delivery of 100,000 cases of perfumed, two-color facial tissues in boutique boxes, the likely answer was that it couldn't be done because it would raise costs. Under the marketing concept, the major task of the production department is to learn how to rearrange schedules to meet customers' needs at an acceptable cost. One result has been the emergence of flexible manufacturing systems.

In the past, marketing has emphasized sales goals, production has attempted to minimize costs, and R&D has been concerned with unique ways to apply technology. Although these objectives may be useful performance standards for individual departments, they are incompatible with the marketing concept, and it is unlikely that the goals of the firm will be achieved when they are pursued separately. The objective should be to operate each part of the firm in order to reach overall targets. The marketing concept has been a useful mechanism in helping to unify the independent functional areas to increase customer satisfaction and improve profits.

Goal-Directed Behavior

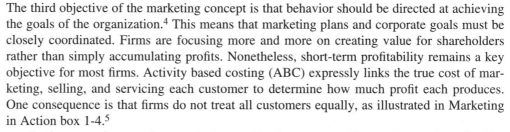

The third objective of the marketing concept is that behavior should be directed at achieving the goals of the organization.[4] This means that marketing plans and corporate goals must be closely coordinated. Firms are focusing more and more on creating value for shareholders rather than simply accumulating profits. Nonetheless, short-term profitability remains a key objective for most firms. Activity based costing (ABC) expressly links the true cost of marketing, selling, and servicing each customer to determine how much profit each produces. One consequence is that firms do not treat all customers equally, as illustrated in Marketing in Action box 1-4.[5]

In the case of nonprofit organizations, objectives are usually stated more broadly. For example, one goal of the U.S. Army is to get recruits and reenlistments, municipal bus lines try to make their services as convenient as possible to maximize the number of passengers, and the goal of Big Brother – Big Sister programs is to get volunteers to contribute their time.

Organizations often have multiple goals. While community orchestras seek to enhance their audiences' appreciation of music, they also must sell enough seats to meet their operating expenses. This means that they need to offer young people's concerts to make sure that future generations will support the orchestra. Also community orchestras must balance their programs with a mix of new selections to educate customers and enough traditional favorites to maintain financial support.

Implementing the Marketing Concept

One of the most successful advocates of the marketing concept is the highly profitable Wal-Mart retail chain. At Wal-Mart, customers come first and are welcomed at the door

MARKETING IN ACTION *1-4*

The Non-Egalitarian Approach to Customers

APPLYING
*. . . to
Financial
Services
Marketing*

Fielding phone calls at First Union Corp.'s huge customer-service center in Charlotte, North Carolina, Amy Hathcock is surrounded by reminders to deliver the personal touch. Televisions hang from the ceiling so she can glance at the Weather Channel to see if her latest caller just came in from the rain; a bumper sticker in her cubicle encourages, "Practice random kindness and senseless acts of beauty." But when it comes to answering yes or no to a customer who wants a lower credit card interest rate or to escape the bank's bounced-check fee, there is nothing random about it. The service all depends on the color of a tiny square—green, yellow or red—that pops up on Ms. Hathcock's computer screen next to the customer's name. For customers who get a red pop-up, Ms. Hathcock rarely budges—these are the ones whose accounts lose money for the bank. Green means the customers generate hefty profits for First Union and should be granted waivers. Yellow is for in-between customers; there's a chance to negotiate. The bank's computer system, called "Einstein," takes just 15 seconds to pull up the ranking on a customer, using a formula based on minimum balances, account activity, branch visits and other variables.

INTEGRATING
*. . . with
Information
Technology
Management*

"Everyone isn't all the same anymore," says Steven G. Boehm, general manager of First Union's customer-information center where agents will handle about 45 million customer calls this year. After years of casting a wide net to lure as many consumers as possible, banks and many other industries are becoming increasingly selective, limiting their hunt to "profitable" customers and doing away with "loss-leaders." Wielding ever-more-powerful computer systems, they are aggressively mining their vast databases to weed out losers, or at least to charge them more, and to target the best customers for pampering.

For banks, a typical "bad" customer makes frequent branch visits, keeps less than $1,000 in the bank and calls often to check on account balances. The most profitable customers, who keep several thousand dollars in their accounts, use a teller less than once a month and hardly ever use the call center. And while favored customers generate more than $1,000 in profits apiece each year, the worst customers often cost the bank money—a minimum of $500 a year.

What's more, the top 20 percent of typical bank customers produce as much as 150 percent of overall profit, while the bottom 20 percent of customers drain about 50 percent from the bank's bottom line, according to Market Line Associates, an Atlanta bank-consulting firm.

First Union, the sixth-largest bank in the United States, estimates its Einstein system will add at least $100 million in annual revenue, or less than one percent of its 1997 total revenue of about $12 billion. About half of that increase is expected to come from extra fees and other revenue from unprofitable customers, and from holding on to preferred customers who might otherwise leave the bank if not for the extra pampering.

First Union acknowledges that it is still figuring out how to track profits generated by its new strategy. "It's not so much that it can't be done, but we need to refine the mechanism," says Sandy Deem, a First Union spokeswoman. Part of the problem is that most banks haven't married their disparate computer systems. While one database may track how many times a customer visits ATMs, how much the bank spends on marketing to get that person there might be in another system, with a third system estimating how much interest income an account generates.

The profit obsession, of course, has many risks. For one, future profits are hard to predict. A high-school student on his way to an engineering degree, a master's degree in management of technology, and a plum job in a high technology industry might be worth courting. So might an unprofitable customer who suddenly inherits a lot of money and wants to purchase certificates of deposit or other financial products

— *A policy of bending over backwards for your most profitable customers pays off, but at the risk of straining relations with nonpreferred customers.*

Source: Rick Brooks, "Alienating Customers Isn't Always a Bad Idea, Many Firms Discover," *Wall Street Journal*, January 7, 1999, pp. A1,A12.

by people greeters; once inside, hourly employees (called associates) approach customers and ask how they can help, and checkout lines are kept short. The whole operation is designed to be responsive to customers' needs. In addition, most senior managers spend four days a week on the road making sure that the 1300 stores are clean and operating smoothly. Wal-Mart helps to integrate company activities by sharing cost, freight, and profit margin data with department heads and hourly associates. Also, when a store's profit goal is exceeded, the hourly associates share in the additional profit. To help control losses from damage and theft, Wal-Mart has instituted a shrinkage bonus when employees keep store losses below company goals. Group harmony is fostered by encouraging troubled employees to talk about their problems with management. Wal-Mart has shown that when employees work together to meet customers' needs, they are better able to meet company sales and profit goals.

Marketing-driven firms must always keep in mind the interests of all the players with whom they interact: customers, channel members, competitors, regulators, and society as a whole. The ultimate success of a firm rests on obtaining sustainable competitive advantages based on long-run customer and channel franchises.

MARKETING AND SOCIETY

Some people question whether the marketing concept is an appropriate organizational theme in an era of environmental deterioration, poverty, and neglected social services. Is society better off when firms sell goods to satisfy individual wants and needs or should marketing managers adopt a longer-run goal of maximizing human welfare? Perhaps we should use a broader definition of the marketing concept:

> The societal marketing concept holds that the organization's task is to determine the needs, wants, and interests of target markets and to deliver the desired satisfactions more effectively and efficiently than competitors in a way that preserves or enhances the consumer's and the society's well-being.[6]

This definition asks marketers to balance customers' wants, company profits, and the public interest. Instead of just maximizing profits, marketing managers are beginning to consider the interests of society when they make decisions. The relative positions of marketing and several environmental variables are highlighted in Figure 1-5. We show marketing plans surrounded by the marketing mix variables under your control. However, most of the factors in the outer ring cannot be changed by individual organizations. You are generally at the mercy of economic conditions and international trade agreements. You also have little control over changes in consumer tastes and the actions of competitors. Two areas that are influenced by marketing activities are responsible marketing conduct, such as environmental responsibility, and business ethics.

Responsible Marketing Conduct

In our rush to create products that sell, we sometimes select packaging that is bulky and does not degrade over time. Marketing is often blamed for the mountains of trash that are filling up landfills, polluting our rivers, and desecrating the landscape. The "green" movement believes that the answer is for business to produce more environmentally safe products. However, sales of products that help the environment have been slow. One problem is that recycled paper and other green items often cost more. Although people say they will pay 7 to 20 percent more for green merchandise, this sentiment has not held up at the cash register. Also, some people do not like the performance or texture of recycled paper and other household products. Some tissue, for instance, isn't as soft.

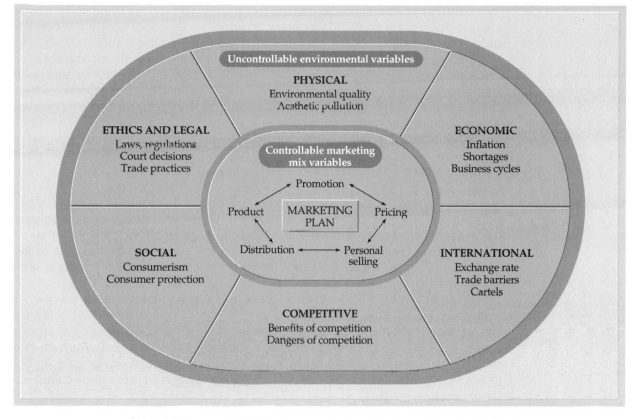

FIGURE 1-5   Societal & Environmental Factors Impacting Marketing Programs

The dilemma for marketers is to find ways to help the environment, satisfy customers, and make a profit. A popular solution is to make packages smaller. This is not as easy as it appears because smaller packages are harder to see in the store and offer less space for promotional messages. Procter & Gamble (P&G) has had some success in Europe with refills for cleaners and detergents that come in throwaway pouches. These have not worked in the United States and the trend is to a reduction in package sizes. For example, P&G has devised a concentrated Ultra Tide powdered detergent that provides savings for both the manufacturer and the retailer. Consumers get a smaller box to carry around, but the cost per wash is somewhat higher. Other successful green programs include the replacement of Styrofoam hamburger containers with cardboard boxes by McDonalds. Also, P&G has eliminated the cartons from Secret and Sure deodorants, keeping 80 million cartons from going to the landfill. These examples show that creative managers can find ways to balance customer wants, environmental needs and profitability. This approach is known as *green marketing*.

Environmentalism is only one aspect of responsible marketing conduct. Yes, you should design your products for recyclability where possible. Also, products should be reusable without discarding, but they also must be built with integrity and quality for safety, accessibility by the disabled, longevity, and more. A second problem area is knowing what marketing tactics are ethically acceptable.

Business Ethics

Business ethics is a set of standards governing the conduct of members of the business community. These standards evolve from interactions among businesspeople and reflect how firms expect to be treated by others. In recent years, the drive for short-term profits has been a major threat to American business ethics. When the next quarter's bottom line outweighs all other considerations, ethical shortcuts lead to insider trading and payoffs.

You should understand that companies are not unethical; people are unethical. This implies that if you hire the right employees—people with principles—you are ahead of the game. However, even the right people can go wrong if they are not given proper guidance in moral decision making. A common problem is that standard company solutions simply do not work. Often there are no applicable laws or court decisions to guide you in specific situations, and actions must be taken in the "twilight zone" between the clearly right and the clearly wrong.

SUMMARY

Our book is concerned with showing you how managers develop marketing plans and manipulate marketing variables to meet long-run customer needs in the presence of business rivals. We believe marketing managers are the driving entrepreneurial force that allows organizations to compete successfully in the race for customer acceptance.

This chapter has introduced you to the role of the marketing manager in business and non-profit organizations. The basic functions of marketing have been described as planning, pricing, promoting, and distributing goods and services to customers. We suggest that organizations must have a marketing focus if they expect to succeed. One such philosophy, called the marketing concept, helps organizations achieve their goals by emphasizing customer satisfaction through close coordination of marketing with the other operating areas of the institution.

Marketing activities must also be coordinated with a number of environmental factors that are largely outside the control of individual organizations. This means that organizations need to spend more time educating their employees about which marketing activities are ethical and making sure that products are safe before they are introduced.

Marketing is a creative and ever-changing occupation with few rules. The position of marketing manager is stimulating because you associate with a wide variety of people in a continuously changing environment. Moreover, marketing management is an excellent training ground for advanced assignments within any organization. Because marketing managers have to work with so many areas of the firm, they are often tapped for positions as general managers. Research has shown that marketing jobs offer the fastest route to the top. Today organizations are turning away from the financial executives, engineers, and lawyers once favored for CEOs and are looking to marketing managers to provide leadership for the future. We believe that marketing is the path to your own marketability.

NOTES

1. Adapted from the official definition of marketing prepared by the American Marketing Association.
2. This section draws heavily on Frederick E. Webster, Jr., "The Changing Role of Marketing in the Corporation," *Journal of Marketing,* Vol. 56, No. 4 (October 1992), pp. 1-17 and Roderick J. Brodie, Nicole E. Coviello, Richard W. Brookes, and Victoria Little, "Toward a Paradigm Shift in Marketing? An Examination of Current Marketing Practices," *Journal of Marketing Management,* Vol. 13, No. 5 (July 1997), pp. 383–406.
3. C. Gronroos, "The Rebirth of Marketing: Six Propositions about Relationship Marketing," Swedish School of Economics and Business Administration, working paper 307, Helsinki, 1995.
4. Selection of goals determines success criteria. See Tom Ambler and Flora Kokkinaki, "Measures of Marketing Success," *Journal of Marketing Management,* Vol. 13, No. 7 (October 1997), pp. 665–678.

5. Bob Donath, "Fire Your Big Customers? Maybe You Should," *Marketing News,* June 21, 1999, p. 9.
6. Philip Kotler, *Marketing Management,* 9th ed., Prentice-Hall, 1997, p. 27.

SUGGESTED READING

Berthon, Pierre, James M. Hulbert, and Leyland F. Pitt. "Brand Management Prognostications," *Sloan Management Review,* Vol. 40, No. 2 (Winter 1999), pp. 63–65.

de Mortanges, Charles P., Jan-Willem Rietbroek, and Cort M. Johns. "Marketing Pharmaceuticals in Japan: Background and the Experience of U.S. Firms," *European Journal of Marketing,* Vol. 31, No. 8 (1997), pp. 36–51.

Han, Jin K., Namwoon Kim, and Rajendra K. Srivastava. "Market Orientation and Organizational Performance: Is Innovation a Missing Link?" *Journal of Marketing,* Vol. 62, No. 4 (October 1998), pp. 30–31.

Homburg, Christian, John P. Workman Jr., and Harley Krohmer, "Marketing's Influence within the Firm," *Journal of Marketing,* Vol. 63, No. 2 (April 1999), pp. 1–17.

van Waterschoot, Walter, and Christophe Van den Bulte. "The 4P Classification of the Marketing Mix Revisited," *Journal of Marketing,* Vol. 56 (October 1992), pp. 83–93.

Webster, Jr., Frederick E. "The Changing Role of Marketing in the Corporation," *Journal of Marketing,* Vol. 56, No. 4 (October 1992), pp. 1–17.

REFERENCES

Hankinson, Graham and Philippa Cowling. "Branding in Practice: The Profile and Role of Brand Managers in the U.K." *Journal of Marketing Management,* Vol. 4 (May 1997), pp. 239–264.

Partridge, Mike and Lew Perren. "An Integrated Framework for Activity-Based Decision Making," *Management Decision,* Vol. 36, No. 9 (1998), pp. 580–588.

Srivastava, Rajendra K., Tasadduq A. Shervani, and Liam Fahey. "Market-Based Assets and Shareholder Value: A Framework for Analysis," *Journal of Marketing,* Vol. 62, No. 1 (January 1998), pp. 2–18.

Turner, Gregory B. and Barbara Spencer. "Understanding the Marketing Concept as Organizational Culture," *European Journal of Marketing,* Vol. 31, No. 2 (1997), pp. 110–121.

Wethey, David. "Is It Really Marketing versus Finance?" *Admap,* Vol. 34, No. 1 (January 1999), pp. 46–48.

QUESTIONS

1. Why has the emphasis in marketing moved from exchanges to relationships?
2. Alitalia Airlines and Starwood Hotels & Resorts Worldwide teamed up with a cross promotion backed by a $1 million ad campaign. For three months (January through March), a print ad featuring the stained glass dome above the posh lobby of Madrid's Palace Hotel ran in a dozen upscale publications including *Architectural Digest, Bon Appetit, W,* and *Town & Country* with the headline, "No Wonder the Rich Get Richer." Body text explained that travelers who flew Alitalia Magnifica class to Europe, Africa, and the Middle East and stayed three nights in any participating hotel in Starwood's Luxury Collection would receive a fourth night free. The deal included breakfast, hotel taxes, and tips. Magnifica is the Italian carrier's new brand for its in-flight service and vacation packages. Amenities include chauffeur service from the airport, leather seats with lots of legroom, and gourmet Italian food and wine. The Luxury Collection is Starwood's roster of more than 50 tony hotels such as the St. Regis in New York. What is the purpose of this tie-in for each company?
3. Give another marketing example of each of the 10 roles a manager plays.
4. Is media selection a good use of a brand manager's time?
5. The marketing concept defines a specific organizational culture—a shared set of beliefs and values centered on the importance of the customer in the organization's strategy

and operations. How can managers create, preserve, or change organizational values and behaviors to implement the marketing concept?

6. Social critics have charged that "Marketers are the primary source of false consciousness. This is because they refocus people's thoughts away from reinforcing personal bonds toward acquiring material possessions, from community sharing resources to selfishly hoarding them, and from feeling empathy with other persons to wanting to feel superior to them." How would you respond?

7. Prepaid cellular phone service plans have caught on with drug dealers and other criminals. With no contract and no bills, there is no paper trail—a feature that also makes the service attractive to tax evaders. What is the responsibility of marketers when making products that may facilitate illegal activities?

8. Not long ago, Nestlé Company, of White Plains, New York, became the target of a U.S. consumer boycott sponsored by a group called the Infant Formula Action Coalition (INFACT). INFACT was concerned about the sales techniques used to sell powdered infant formula in third world countries. INFACT claimed that Nestlé's baby product division used uniformed "milk nurses" to promote the product together with free samples and magazine and radio ads. INFACT believed that the general lack of pure water in third world countries made the powdered infant formula more dangerous than mother's milk. Because the infant formula is not sold in the United States, should Nestlé Company of White Plains be concerned about INFACT? If so, how should Nestlé respond to the boycott?

9. Pager Networks Inc., a paging service provider, for several years essentially gave away its pagers in a race to build market share. In the process, it attracted heavy users who receive a flurry of messages but often pay only a rock-bottom monthly fee. How should PageNet address this situation?

10. Nabisco, in a cost-cutting mode, killed its slow-selling Crown Pilot cracker. The cracker was sold only in New England, where it was mostly munched with New England clam chowder. Consumers protested with more than 3,500 angry calls and letters. What should Nabisco do?

2 MARKETING STRATEGY

> Results are gained by exploiting opportunities not by solving problems.
>
> PETER DRUCKER

Marketing strategy is concerned with finding sustainable ways for organizations to compete in a continuously changing world. This chapter is concerned with helping you select marketing strategies to exploit the opportunities of tomorrow. Organizations that fail to plan for the future will find themselves fading into the sunset.

WHAT IS MARKETING STRATEGY?

A strategy is a plan of action designed to achieve the long-run goals of the organization. Marketing strategies evolve from more general business objectives. Marketing strategies usually include the following dimensions:

1. The product or service market in which you expect to compete.
2. The level of investment needed to grow, maintain, or milk the business.
3. The product line, positioning, pricing, and distribution strategies needed to compete in the selected market.
4. The assets or capabilities to provide a sustainable competitive advantage (SCA).

Successful marketing strategies are based on *assets* that are strong relative to those of competitors. These assets include brand equity, the scale, scope, and efficiency of operations, financial condition, location, and government support. For example, Nestlé, a Swiss company that is the world's largest food company, has performed well in the marketplace with strong brand names including the Perrier and L'Oréal lines. Some companies believe that, as the world opens up to business, the operating model for today's exemplary companies no longer needs to include ownership of significant manufacturing assets. For example, Sara Lee Corp., whose stable of famous brands includes Legg's hosiery, Sara Lee frozen desserts, Wonderbras, Coach briefcases, and Kiwi shoe polish to name a few, has moved to contract out its production.

Strategies also spring from *capabilities* to do a good job. Capabilities are complex bundles of skills and accumulated knowledge, exercised through organizational processes, that enable firms to coordinate activities and make use of their assets.[1] The capabilities of market-driven organizations are classified in Figure 2-1. Marketing strategies take assets and capabilities and forge them into sustainable competitive advantages. For example, see Marketing Strategies box 2-1.

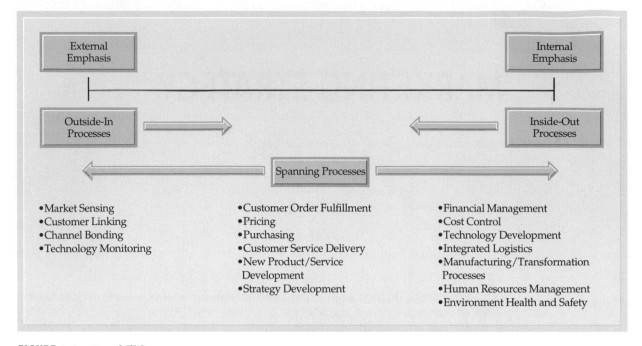

FIGURE 2-1   Capabilities
(From George S. Day, "The Capabilities of Market-Driven Organizations," *Journal of Marketing,* Vol. 58, No. 4 [October 1994], p.41)

Searching for SCAs

Organizations are continuously looking for ways to achieve SCAs. Some of the most important SCAs in a survey of businesses are shown in Table 2-1. Note that a wide variety of SCAs are mentioned, and the top few do not dominate the list. The average business reports 4.6 SCAs, suggesting that it is probably foolish to base your marketing strategy on a single SCA. Table 2-1 reveals some interesting differences in SCAs across industries. High-tech firms, for example, favor technical superiority, quality, and customer service. This often applies to less high-tech industrial firms as well, as illustrated in Marketing Strategies box 2-2. Service companies build their success around quality, good management, name recognition, and customer service. Firms in the "other" category are most interested in SCAs based on quality, name recognition, and low-cost production. On the other hand, technical superiority and low-cost production are not key SCAs for service companies.

Although two of the most important SCAs have been thought to be differentiation and low costs, these SCAs are ranked fifth and twelfth in Table 2-1. Differentiation strategies enhance profits by developing products with unique design, performance, quality, or service characteristics. The objective is to make your product different from that of your competition. Once customers perceive your product as unique, they are less sensitive to price and you can charge more for the product or service.

Low-cost strategies seek to build volume by achieving SCA in the areas of production or marketing. Low costs can be captured through economies of scale, access to raw materials, automated equipment, or outsourcing. (With regard to outsourcing, see Solectron's strategy for growth in Marketing Strategies box 2-3 near the end of this chapter.) Firms with low costs can charge low prices to build market share, or they can use the margins to increase profits. Low costs elsewhere may also allow firms to spend more on advertising and promotion.

Two organizations with low-cost SCAs are Goodyear in tires and Whirlpool in appliances. Goodyear has reduced costs through volume and vertical integration and Whirlpool

MARKETING STRATEGIES *2-1*

Building on Innovation and Customer Loyalty

Although United Knitting has only been in operation less than two decades, the firm has made its mark as a leader in some major niche markets—specializing in performance fabrics. The firm started out producing gussets for hosiery. [A gusset is a small, triangular piece of material inserted in a clothing item to improve the fit or for reinforcement.] Even though United has gone on to new markets and

(continues)

Keeps you warm while you shiver with fear.

When your playground is an icy perch 100 feet off the deck, the last thing you should fear is the cold.

Thermologic fabric provides safe refuge for your goosebumps by using a special

THERMO

knit to trap air and still transfer moisture. So if you're still shivering, it won't be from the cold.

LOGIC

Jagged Edge
Mountain Gear

Courtesy United Knitting

MARKETING STRATEGIES 2-1   (continued)

more exotic products, those gusset operations continue today as one of the company's niche markets, accounting for 10 to 15 percent of production. "We have some of the most loyal customers in the hosiery industry." From gussets United expanded into liners, primarily swimwear in 100% nylon. Early on, the main customer was Jantzen. A highlight was development of the CoolMax lining, which currently has a widespread distribution. United continues to build products around DuPont's CoolMax fiber.

The last decade or so has solidified the foundation of United: performance fabrics. "We have built this company on performance. Our ability to provide stretch and recovery—and to repeat those characteristics in literally thousands of rolls of fabric, has established our niche in this marketplace."

Key to United's business approach is developing friendships with customers. "We want to talk to them." Typical of management's commitment to working with the customer was the relationship United built in development of the popular JogBra. Convinced of the growing market demand for a bra for female runners, two women began searching the industry for a fabric with stretch and recovery properties that would enable a runner to jog comfortably with the appropriate support. Given United's developmental talents, this challenge was right down its alley. After some experimentation and several sample runs, the plant shipped the women a 10-yd piece of fabric. This was rapidly followed by ongoing modifications, accompanied by increasing production volume. Today, JogBra is a staple in women's sportswear. Champion (a division of Sara Lee) owns the product, but United is still JogBra's principal fabric supplier.

Other products have mushroomed. United worked with DuPont, Glen Raven, and Danskin to develop a fabric using Supplex nylon. Beginning in body aerobics wear, it has grown to the point its applications now include sportswear, fashion and children's wear. Along with this growth in applications has come increasing sophistication in marketing techniques. "Performance hangtags are important. The objective is convincing consumers they are looking at a garment that's made of fabric that performs with the objective of having products that think."

INTEGRATING
. . . with
Production

A tour of United's manufacturing operations underscores management's drive for quality and efficiency. For example, most knitting machines operate in clean rooms to offset fly contamination. Commitment to preventive machinery maintenance is evident. Fabric testing is also crucial to operations. Included in the full-service laboratory is a sophisticated system for testing fabric stretch and recovery. These characteristics are critical in United's performance products. United performs 100% inspection of finished fabrics. An Error Source Analysis program quickly provides summary and analysis of any problems.

Recent mergers have greatly expanded United's technical expertise, production capabilities, and markets. The mergers allowed United to tell a common color story that correlates across all fabrics. Finally, the mergers provided United with greater purchasing leverage, from raw materials and dyestuffs to machinery. "Although United is growing in many markets, we don't lose focus on the necessity of giving the customer products that perform, while providing value, quality, speedy delivery and service."

— *Developing and supplying innovative and inspired products ensures customer loyalty.*

Source: Walter N. Rozelle, "United Builds on Innovation and Customer Loyalty," *Textile World,* August 1998, pp. 29–31.

through the use of automated equipment. At the same time, Michelin and Maytag have had success in the same industries with differentiation strategies. Michelin is well known for the safety of its steel belted radial tires and Maytag for the durability of its appliances. For these firms, differentiation has led to a sustainable price premium.

Other successful marketing strategies include focusing on special classes of customers and preemptive strikes. With focus strategies, a clothes retailer might focus on the needs of hard-to-fit buyers or a limited line of sportswear. A preemptive move stakes out new territory, and it is often difficult for competitors to make an appropriate response. Coca-Cola built a

TABLE 2-1   Most Important Sustainable Competitive Advantages

		Type of Firm		
Rank	SCA	High-Tech	Service	Other
1	Reputation for quality	2	1	1
2	Customer service/product support	3	4	5
3	Name recognition/high profile	16	3	2.5
4	Retain good management and engineering staff	6	2	17
5	Low-cost production	5	14.5	2.5
6	Financial resources	12	5.5	6
7	Customer orientation/feedback/market research	7	5.5	11
8	Product-line breadth	12	20	7.5
9	Technical superiority	1	6.2	11
10	Installed base of satisfied customers	4	9.5	18.5
11	Segmentation/focus	17	9.5	4
12	Product characteristics/differentiation	9	14.5	9
13	Continuing product innovation	9	12.5	14
14	Market share	9	12.5	11
15	Size/location of distribution	14.5	17.5	7.5
16	Low price/high value offering	18	11	14
17	Knowledge of business	20	7	18.5
18	Pioneer/early entrant in industry	12	17.5	14
19	Efficient, flexible production/operations adaptable to customer	19	16	18.5
20	Effective sales force	14.5	19	18.5
	Average number of SCAs	4.63	4.77	4.19

Source: David A. Aaker, "Managing Assets and Skills: The Key to a Sustainable Competitive Advantage," *California Management Review* (Winter 1989), p. 94.

MARKETING STRATEGIES 2-2

A Niche for a Quality Supplier

APPLYING
. . . to
Industrial
Marketing

Over the past few years, Greer Steel Co., Dover, Ohio, has invested over $21 million to improve quality, shore up its niche in cold-rolled strip, and drum up new business. A subsidiary of privately-held Greer Industries, Greer Steel views itself as "a mill that happens to own a service center." Its Dover cold-rolling mill operation is the primary focus of its efforts. The mill produces carbon and alloy cold-rolled strip steel, flat wire, and flat bar for applications ranging from home appliances to automotive and hardware. It is "really a specialized service center dealing in products that most service centers don't handle. There are a few that do. But, by virtue of flat wire, narrow slit product (under 1 in.), round edging, and things of this nature, we're somewhat unique. We think it's a growth situation, and we're certainly tuning it up in anticipation."

Because Greer views its Dover facility as a mill, it approaches the mill's market much differently than it does Ferndale's service center market. "In some arenas, many service centers are handling business that rightfully should be produced or distributed by a mill. Many are fortunate to secure a position with tonnages that are not historically service center tonnages; they're way too big to be considered service center business. There are instances where that business has reverted back to mill-direct distribution, and that means growth for Dover. The customer is only going to pay so much for your product. By going to the service center, the product gets marked up, so they're paying healthy premiums for services on larger orders which are available in Dover via JIT and stocking programs.

INTEGRATING
. . . with
Production/
Operations
Management

We perform JIT where it is necessary and feasible. It costs a lot of money, and has to be carefully managed. At Dover, we put in a lot of stocking programs this past year with our major accounts to ensure on-time delivery. We'll continue in that posture, and add more and more accounts." However, at Dover, JIT is usually limited to customers that buy in larger lot sizes and can forecast usage on a quarterly basis. "We don't necessarily want to stock 1,000 lb. of an item here. It becomes totally unmanageable—and it's really a service center function at that level."

(continues)

MARKETING STRATEGIES *2-2*   (continued)

With Ferndale organized to handle smaller orders, JIT is more of a factor in its operations. "More of its business depends on the ability to satisfy those JIT customers. We carry more inventory up there than we'd like to, but we have to do it. It's not quite as feasible for a mill as it is for a service center. With the pressure on suppliers to hold and ship material in a very timely manner, we feel that on a long-term basis, Ferndale will continue to grow, and that the need for the JIT services they provide will grow. JIT, of course, is nothing new. But, we are feeling it more and more every year in performing and aligning ourselves to satisfy customers. We are going to do whatever is economically feasible to service our customers."

Although Greer's Dover cold-rolling mill handles orders that are usually larger than service-center-sized shipments, its niche is in shipping loads smaller than those typically handled at an integrated mill or larger processor. "There is a trend now where larger processors are partnering up with mills to perform finishing and distribution. In most cases, those are very large tonnage items. We try to work at our Dover mill on a minimum of 6,000-lb. orders; we'll take a 500-lb. order at our service center. Larger processors and producing mills will typically handle orders over 20,000 lb. Many of our competitors are not oriented toward specialty products, which we are. So, there is a niche there, we feel. And that market is quite substantial. Most of these outfits are bigger than we are."

Greer sells to many large manufacturers, including Black & Decker, Harley Davidson, Toastmaster, Caterpillar, as well as divisions and suppliers of General Motors, Ford, and Chrysler. But it also has a number of small customers: job shops, and spring, fastener and bearing manufacturers. "With the precision product we have and because most of these companies buy in medium quantities, we have a lot of customers. We're not selling '10,000 tons' to one company. We're covering a large cross section."

INTEGRATING
... with
Suppliers

Naturally, suppliers are also important to Greer. The company has about seven suppliers with a concentration on three. "But we're constantly qualifying new sources looking for better product, better gauge control, chemistry, and competitive pricing. This is an ongoing thing that really doesn't stop. We're buying low carbon steel, high carbon steel, alloy, and a little stainless."

Greer's suppliers include integrated mills and minimills; representatives from a new minimill startup were recently at Greer's facility seeking qualification. "We've worked very hard in developing our supply line. We have a very strict qualification procedure for materials. We have a General Motors-approved lab. So, we really react like a fully-integrated mill—except we don't make steel."

Overall, Greer Industries is content with the niche its steel subsidiary fills. But market pressures are forcing the unit to expand its niche in cold-rolled strip. Greer deals heavily in the highly competitive appliance and automotive sectors. For instance, automotive has become particularly tough in recent years; manufacturers have continually reduced their supplier bases, while boosting quality and delivery requirements. "Anytime you are dealing direct with automotive, the cost pressure is very intense," the president adds. "We are very cognizant of that. Staying on the cutting edge of technology is the only way we or any company can remain competitive in that environment. So, we have to spend money to do that. We are, and that will allow us to continue to compete."

One of Greer's major expenditures was the upgrading of its cold reduction/reversing mills in Dover. Greer needed to improve on its gauge control and surface conditioning for its customers' sake; defects have costly effects on overall material yields. "A big factor is the continuity of their processing operations (presses and roll formers); they don't want to experience downtime trying to work material that varies in gauge. They want to set up and go. We need to provide a product that will allow them to do that, coil after coil, day after day, without requiring them to tweak their equipment to make it work. It is a cost savings for the customer with more productivity and a better product."

Packaging is an extremely important function at Greer. "We're on the jewelry end of the steel business, if you will. So, we're dealing with very sophisticated surfaces that can be easily ruined. Our packaging reflects the nature of the product. We're very careful about the way we handle material: pack it, ship it, etc."

But Greer has been making more than just physical changes in Dover and Ferndale. The company has made quality and labor changes as well. For instance, in 1994, Greer established its Employee

(continues)

MARKETING STRATEGIES 2-2 (continued)

Involvement Team (EIT) program, which empowers workers and management to address production, quality, and service problems jointly, as a team. "We have union folks and management people attacking problems by department to get to the root cause and make suggestions on how to correct them. EIT is now part of Greer's corporate culture. Team play and working together to make things happen."

INTEGRATING
. . . with Quality Improvement

Quality improvement has been another priority of the new president. Greer established its Greer Quality Plus (GQ+) total quality management program in 1994, which was viewed by the company as the first step toward ISO and QS certification. In November, Greer's Dover plant was recommended for ISO 9002 certification, and it did it without the use of an outside consultant. Instead, Greer used its EITs to make it happen.

"To get any benefit out of it, the people have to do it," states Greer's manager of quality assurances. "There is no right, no wrong; it's what works best for your company. We were fortunate in that we had actually started putting together quality procedures a number of years ago, so we had the baseline items done. We utilized our EITs, and had them start by looking at the work instructions in their particular areas. We had all the resources here, and used our teams." Greer's employees, therefore, have a better understanding of ISO procedures and documentation because they were the ones who actually developed the system; "They're not just memorizing stuff."

Consistency is the number one benefit of ISO. For example, before ISO, inside salespeople were not asking the same questions of customers, using the same forms, et cetera. Now, salespeople are performing their jobs similarly, and that should be the most immediate benefit for customers. Down the line, he says, deliveries and quality should improve further. He notes that for Greer, ISO is an extension of GQ+, which had emphasized accuracy, good service, and quality. ISO, he notes, has more to do with record keeping.

Ferndale will eventually be ISO-certified as well. After that, Greer will target QS 9000, the automotive quality standard. "Quite honestly, we have a long way to go before we achieve QS 9000, it would take a year of concerted effort. It's a monumental leap over and above ISO." QS requires, for instance, more sector-specific requirements, documented strategic planning, a functioning preventive maintenance program, and proven effective use of statistical process controls.

INTEGRATING
. . . with Information Technology Management

Greer is also experimenting with electronic commerce and performs bar coding. Its systems are in compliance with the Automotive Industry Action Group, which sets standards and specifications for the automotive sector. "We currently service about six accounts on an EDI basis. We feel that that will intensify. There is no question about it: the more sophisticated we are in this arena, the better we are going to be able to service our customers who are demanding these kinds of services and communication."

— *Bigness is not necessarily the goal for a niche player; it can be being a high-quality producer and performer.*

Source: Kevin Nolan, "Greer Steel's CR Strip Growth Shows No Sign of Waning," *Metal Center News* (January 1997), pp. 74–83.

dominant position in the Japanese beverage market by signing up all the best distributors. Pepsi and other firms were preempted and had to make do with weaker sales organizations.

Advantages of Strategic Marketing

A strategic approach to marketing has a number of advantages. First, a strategic emphasis helps organizations orient themselves toward key external factors such as consumers and competition. Instead of just projecting past trends, the goal is to build market-driven strategies that reflect customer concerns. Strategic plans also tend to anticipate changes in the environment rather than just react to competitive thrusts.

Another reason strategic marketing is important is that it forces you to take a long-term view of the world. Many people believe that the problems of U.S. automobile and steel companies are due to their obsession with short-term quarterly profits. The Japanese, on the other hand, have had great success in the U.S. electronics and auto markets using a long-run focus. The ability of the Japanese to penetrate U.S. markets also shows that marketing strategy must have an international dimension. Today firms with global marketing strategies are better able to meet customer needs and the growth of international competition.

Strategy-Building Process

The basic dimensions of strategy development are described in Figure 2-2. The first step is to establish a comprehensive mission for the organization. Then a detailed assessment of each strategic business unit must be performed. This usually includes both external and internal analyses of current strengths and weaknesses. Next, appropriate marketing strategies are identified for each business unit. The remainder of Figure 2-2 shows how basic strategies are converted into detailed marketing plans for implementation.

We strongly believe that you first decide what you want to do, your strategy; then you decide how to do it, your tactics. The elements of the marketing mix are highly interrelated, and the best mixes are achieved when you take a strategic approach. For example, a new product might be positioned as a soap with lotionlike properties or as a lotion with soaplike properties. The appropriate price and advertising appeal depend on this positioning. One price level might cause consumers to perceive the product as a soap, while another price level might cause them to perceive it as a lotion. Of course, market strategy itself must be based on a sustainable advantage on one or more elements of the marketing mix.

WHAT IS OUR MISSION?

A well-defined organization provides a sense of direction to employees and helps guide them toward the fulfillment of the firm's potential. Managers should ask, "What is our business?" and "What should it be?" The idea is to extract a purpose from a consideration of the firm's history, resources, distinctive abilities, and environmental constraints. A mission statement should specify the business domains in which the organization plans to operate.[2] These are usually spelled out in product terms, such as "we are a copy machine company," or more broadly as "we are an office productivity company." The firm should try to find a purpose that fits its present needs and is neither too narrow nor too broad.

Effective mission statements should cover the following areas:

1. Product line definition
2. Market scope
3. Growth directions
4. Level of technology

Marketing strategies often involve decisions on which products to add, which to drop, which to keep, and which to modify. Thus it is logical to construct mission statements around product dimensions. For example, Famous Amos is in the cookie business rather than in the more general bakery business. Individual products can lose favor, and some firms prefer to define their mission in terms of customer needs. AT&T can be viewed as being in the communications business rather than in the telephone business. Xerox, best known for its copiers, advertises itself as being in the document business.

Organization missions must also be defined in terms of the market for their products or services. This can be expressed in geographical terms or as customer groupings. For example, Coors beer is not pasteurized, so the company has been limited to markets within refrigerated

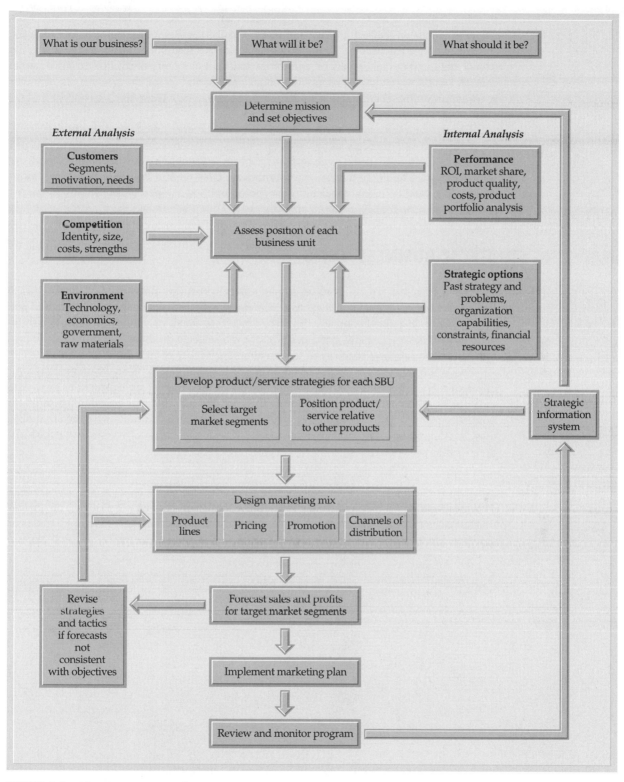

FIGURE 2-2   **The Strategy Development Process**

trucking distance of its breweries. Pontiac dealerships, on the other hand, are located everywhere but focus on the performance and sports-minded segment of the automobile market.

Technology has become so important to business success that mission statements need to indicate the types and levels of technology that will be emphasized. For example, American steel mills were slow to adopt continuous casting and to see the advantages of melting scrap in minimills. Their inability to recognize and seize new technology has depressed their profits and growth potential.

Finally, mission statements should give management direction on areas for growth. Some firms expand by penetrating existing markets, others by expanding product lines, or by building up present markets, by diversifying, or by growing with new technology or distribution methods. The mission statement tells management what it should not be doing, as well as what it should be doing. Once an organization has a mission, the next step is to focus on the activities of individual business units.

ANALYZING STRATEGIC BUSINESS UNITS

Marketing strategies are designed for use by strategic business units (SBUs) (Figure 2-2). An SBU is any organizational unit that has a business strategy and a manager with sales and profit responsibility. In a small company the SBU would include all operations. SBUs can also be a division of a larger company, product lines, or even selected products. General Electric popularized the SBU concept as a way to foster entrepreneurial spirit in a diversified firm.

Marketing planners operate on the principle that individual business units should play different roles in achieving organizational objectives. Some units are expected to grow faster than others, some units will be more profitable, and not all units will generate the same cash flow. The concept that the organization is a collection of business units with different objectives is a central belief of modern management. These collections of business units are often described as *portfolios.*

Product Life Cycles

The life-cycle concept helps managers keep track of their product portfolios. This proposition suggests that products are born, grow to maturity, and then decline much like plants and animals (Figure 2-3). During the introductory period, sales grow rapidly but high expenses

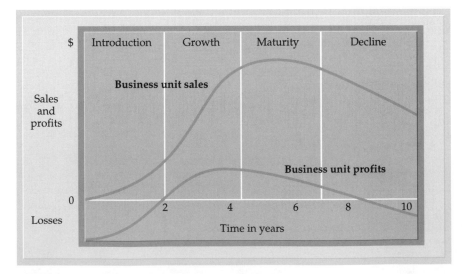

FIGURE 2-3   Impact of Product Life Cycle on Strategy

keep profits negative. Near the end of the growth stage, the rate of expansion of sales begins to slow down and profits reach a peak. During the maturity phase, sales reach their peak and profits are slowly eroded by increased competition. If something is not done to revive declining products, they eventually have to be dropped from the product line.

The life-cycle concept helps managers think about their product line as a portfolio of investments. Ideally, the firm wants to have some business units in each phase of the life cycle. If most of the items are in the mature and declining phases, the company will have trouble reaching its growth objectives. Similarly, if all the products are bunched in the introductory and declining phases, the firm is likely to experience serious cash flow problems. The best plan is to have enough business in the growth and maturity stages spinning off cash to finance the introduction of new products and the reformation of products in decline. The advantage of the product life-cycle analysis is that it makes executives realize that products do not last forever and must eventually be replaced. On the other hand, it is sometimes difficult to know when a product is leaving one stage and entering the next.

Portfolio Matrix

SBUs can be evaluated by positioning them on a diagram that compares relative market shares with market growth rates. Figure 2-4 shows a portfolio matrix developed by the Boston Consulting Group. Each circle in Figure 2-4 represents a business unit in a firm's product portfolio. The size of the circles shows the dollar sales being generated by each unit. The horizontal position of the circles shows their market share in relation to their competitors. A logarithmic scale is used for relative market share that goes from $1/10$ to 10 times the size of the next largest competitor. Thus, business units located to the right of the value 1.0 are smaller than the competition and those to the left are larger.

Portfolio matrices are often divided into four separate quadrants for analysis purposes. The positions of the lines separating the sectors are arbitrary. In Figure 2-4, high growth rates would include all businesses expanding faster than the overall economy. SBUs in each

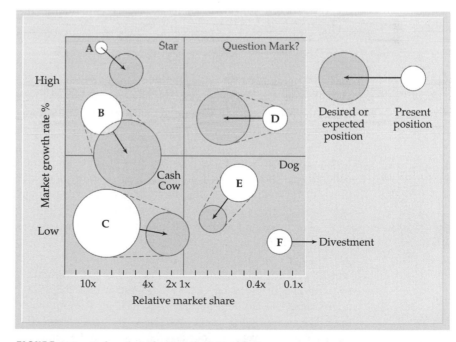

FIGURE 2-4 Balancing the Product Portfolio

corner of the portfolio matrix have sharply different financial requirements and marketing needs.

Stars   Products that fall into the *star* category have strong market positions and high rates of market growth. The primary objective with stars is to maintain their market positions and to increase their sales volumes. Stars are the keys to the future because they provide growth, technological leadership, and enhanced respect in the business community. Although stars increase revenues to the firm, they tend to use more money than they generate from earnings and depreciation. To maintain their high rates of growth, stars require extra cash for expanded plant and equipment, inventories, accounts receivable, field salespeople, and advertising programs. Thus, stars are both a blessing and a curse because of the strain they put on the firm to constantly expand working capital.

Another problem with stars is that their high growth rates attract competition. The entry of other firms can help expand a market, but eventually the market will become saturated, and growth rates will decline.

Cash Cows   Business units described as *cash cows* are low-growth, high-relative-market-share operations (Product C, Figure 2-4). These products are likely to be in the mature stage of their life cycles and do not require extensive funds for production facilities or inventory buildup. Cash cows also have established market positions and do not need large advertising expenditures to maintain their market shares. As a result, their high earnings and depreciation allowances generate cash surpluses that can be used to invest in other growing products, to support research and development, or to buy into new lines of trade. Cash cows thus provide the basic fuel on which portfolio management of business units depends.

Question Marks   Products with low relative market shares in fast-growing markets are called *question marks*. These products have the potential to become stars of the future or to fade into oblivion. Because question marks have such small market shares, they usually absorb more cash than they generate. Thus, in the short run, question marks just eat money, and when their market growth slows, they become dogs.

The preferred approach with question marks is to increase their relative market shares and move them into the star category (Product D, Figure 2-4). However, this often takes a pile of cash, sophisticated marketing plans, and a good measure of luck. If the prospects for improving the market position of a business are not attractive, the firm must consider phasing the business out. Large multinational companies are often concerned not only with weaker brands but also with otherwise successful brands that don't have the potential for global reach. One popular approach is simply to sell the business to a competitor. Another technique is to withdraw all promotional support and try to make a few dollars as the product withers away.

Dogs   Businesses that fall into the low-growth, low-relative market share quadrant are called *dogs*. These products are often in the decline phase of their life cycles and show little prospect for gaining market position or generating much cash flow. Even worse, dogs can become *cash traps* and absorb more money than they generate as firms try to revive a lost cause. The usual approach with dogs is to sell them when the opportunity occurs or to deemphasize marketing activities (Products E and F, Figure 2-4).

APPLYING
. . . to
Consumer
Beverages
Marketing

Quaker Oats, for example, sold its Snapple juice and iced-tea business for a fraction of what it paid for this business only three years before. While adding Snapple to its Gatorade sports drink lineup made Quaker the number three beverage company in the United States after Coca-Cola Co. and PepsiCo Inc., Quaker's timing could not have been more inopportune. The fast-growing market for "New Age" uncarbonated drinks such as water, lemonade, and tea began to plateau. Coke and Pepsi got into the game under the Lipton and Nestea brand names. Snapple fell to third place with only an 18 percent share compared with leader Lipton's 33 percent share. The impact on relative share was even more devastating. Quaker thought it was buying a star and found itself being bitten by a dog.

The most common criticism of the portfolio matrix approach is that it does not have enough dimensions to assess a product portfolio accurately. Despite these limitations, the terms *dog, star,* and *cash cow* have become a standard part of the vocabulary of business planning.

Multifactor Methods

Other approaches to strategic planning include those by Arthur D. Little, Shell Chemical, PIMS (Profit Impact of Marketing Strategy), and future scenario profiles. Arthur D. Little has a 24-sector grid. It uses a four-stage product life-cycle concept and stresses that risks increase as products age and market positions weaken. Shell compares prospects for business sector profitability with company competitive capabilities. PIMS uses historical evidence collected across industries on factors contributing to performance. This information permits assessment of the current performance and future strategy options of a business unit. Future scenario profiles focus on projections of what the future may hold given different strategies that might be adopted by a business unit. In addition, some firms have developed their own in-house approaches.

General Electric, for example, has developed a nine-cell matrix based on industry attractiveness and company strength in each business. Units with the best scores are candidates for further investment, and those with the lowest scores are harvested or sold off. Business units in the middle fall into a hold or cash cow category and are used to finance growth. Business units chosen for additional investments have included microwave ovens and industrial plastics. On the other hand, lamps and large appliances followed a hold strategy, and small appliances were sold off.

One survey of industrial firms found that heavy equipment manufacturers preferred the Arthur D. Little and PIMS approaches, light equipment manufacturers preferred the Boston Consulting Group and market attractiveness approaches, and component parts manufacturers preferred the Arthur D. Little approach. Arthur D. Little's 24-sector grid has the most satisfied users.

SELECTING MARKETING STRATEGIES

Once a portfolio of business units has been evaluated, you are ready to assign strategic roles for the future management of each business. This requires creative thinking on your part. You also can consider what businesses like yours usually do by examining what are known as *generic marketing strategies*. The objective is to come up with strategies that lead to sustainable competitive advantages.

Creative Strategic Thinking

Managers must be able to step back from the existing situation and view the product and the market from another angle. This is easier said than done. Some approaches that have been suggested to encourage strategic thinking include the following:

1. Challenge the present strategy.
2. Look for strategic windows.
3. Play on the vulnerabilities of competitors.
4. Change the rules of the game.
5. Enhance customer value.

We elaborate on these approaches in later chapters, especially Chapter 5, which stresses looking for strategic windows and playing on competitors' vulnerabilities. Throughout the book enhancing customer value is emphasized.

Generic Marketing Strategies

The nature of marketing strategies may be seen in what companies actually do.[3] Empirical research based on marketing factors—marketing objectives, strategic focus, market targeting, and quality and price positioning—has shown that many businesses follow one of five strategies.

1. Companies have aggressive growth or market dominance goals. The targeting approach aims at the whole market. The *scope* of the target market in this case is said to be broad. Positioning involves marketing high-quality products at prices similar to those of competitors. This may be considered a differentiation strategy.
2. Companies seek steady sales growth through either market share gain or market expansion. Selected segments are targeted through higher-quality products at higher prices than those of competitors. This may be considered a focused differentiation strategy. *Focus* means narrow market scope.
3. Companies pursue steady sales growth through an emphasis on market share by concentrating on selected segments of the market. Their positioning is average quality at average prices. This may be considered a stuck-in-the-middle strategy, as no real advantage through quality differentiation or low costs is created.
4. Companies strive for steady growth, with a focus on total market expansion or on winning market share by targeting selected segments or individuals. The positioning is higher quality at the same prices. This resembles a variant of a focused differentiation strategy that emphasizes value. It provides a powerful incentive for the expansion of the market as a whole.
5. Companies have defensive objectives, with a focus on cost reduction and productivity improvement. Very selective targeting of individuals is coupled with a positioning of similar quality at similar prices.

While not all firms exactly match one of these profiles, they are usually similar to one of them. As you would expect, differences in deployment of the five strategies correspond to different stages of market maturity (Table 2-2).

Some believe that "All successful strategies are differentiation." The implication is that all strategies are based on some form of differentiation. Where one firm will differentiate on the basis of costs, another will use products, or size of market, or distribution, or some other dimension. If you think of differentiation as the common denominator, then it is easier to see how marketing strategies blend together to achieve the goals of the firm.

STRATEGY EXECUTION

Having a good strategy is a necessary but not sufficient condition for success. You must ably implement your strategy. For example, the 100-year-old bandage maker Johnson & Johnson (J&J) has pursued a strategy of constantly pushing into new areas to cater to evolving customer needs. J&J views itself as a healthcare company. Its major consumer products are Tylenol painkillers, Band-Aids, baby products, and Nutrogena skin products. Its major professional products are coronary stents—tiny metal scaffoldings that prop open arteries, minimally-invasive surgery products, and wound closure products. Its major pharmaceutical products include Risperdal for schizophrenia, Levaquin for infections, and

TABLE 2-2   Generic Marketing Strategies

	Aggressors	Premium Position Segments	Stuck-in-the-Middlers	High-Value Segmenters	Defenders
Strategic objective	Aggressive sales growth/ domination	Steady sales growth	Steady sales growth	Steady sales growth	Defend/pre-vent/decline
Strategic focus	Win share/ expand market	Win share/expand market	Win share	Win share/expand market	Cost reduction/ productivity improvement
Market targeting	Whole market	Selected segments	Selected segments	Selected segments	Individual customers
Competitive positioning	Higher quality/same price	Higher quality/higher price	Same quality/same price	Higher quality/same price	Same or higher quality/same price
Market type	New, growing; fluid competition; rapid change in customer needs	Mature and stable	Mature and stable	New, growing	Mature and stable
Corporate attitudes	Pro-active NPD;* marketing important; take on any competition	Pro-active NPD; marketing important; take on any competition	Imitate/lead in NPD; take on/avoid competition	Pro-active NPD; take on/avoid competition	Follower in NPD; marketing of limited importance; take on/avoid competition
Performance	Best across financial and marketing based criteria	Good across most criteria	Mediocre	Mediocre, esp. on profit criterion	Worst performance overall

* NPD = new product development.

Source: Graham J. Hooley, James E. Lynch, and David Jobber, "Generic Marketing Strategies," *International Journal of Research in Marketing,* Vol. 9, No. 1 (March 1992), p. 87.

APPLYING
. . . to
Industrial
Marketing

MARKETING STRATEGIES 2-3

Solectron's Strategy Execution

Solectron Corp. is a "stealth manufacturer" of computers, printers, cellular phones, and other high-tech gear. Its American-based factories produce products stamped with famous names such as IBM, Hewlett-Packard, and Mitsubishi Electric. This allows Solectron's customers to become "virtual firms" that do little besides design and market products. Solectron is a leader in the global contract manufacturing business—a business that is growing almost twice as fast as the electronics industry it serves.

Solectron lands orders because it is considered among the world's most efficient manufacturers. It keeps assembly lines running 24-hours a day, spreading the costs of its buildings and machines across more products. Every line looks exactly the same everywhere in the world. Thus, Solectron can shift jobs or add capacity quickly. Moreover, as a massive purchaser of electronic components, it gets low prices and precisely scheduled deliveries that minimize inventory.

Somewhat surprisingly, Solectron's biggest plant is not in Asia but in California's Silicon Valley. This proximity to its customers is prized because it facilitates quick product development. Speed is crucial because high-tech products have short life spans—and the first to market often reaps the

(continues)

MARKETING STRATEGIES 2-3 (continued)

Bob Day/Courtesy Solectron Corp.

largest rewards. As Solectron expands it risks the nimbleness behind its success. Thus, in order to manage its growth, it sometimes turns away a prospective customer.

Solectron relies on high volume and low overhead. Its profit margins are thin. It tracks every efficiency and every expense carefully. It has little room for error. Thus, it must emphasize quality. It asks 150 customers each week to grade it on quality, responsiveness, communication, service, and technical support. These grades are posted inside factories and help determine bonuses for both workers and managers. Solectron is a two-time winner of the Malcolm Baldrige National Quality Award for manufacturing.

— *One strategy is to be the low cost producer; nonetheless, quality is a must.*

Source: Scott Thurm, "Some Firms Prosper by Facilitating the Rise of the 'Virtual' Firm," *The Wall Street Journal,* August 18, 1998, pp. A1, A6.

Procrit for anemia. In the late 1990s, Johnson & Johnson encountered numerous woes. Six experimental drugs fell through late in development. Rivals of the company's coronary stent grabbed 90 percent of its market. Plans for a cholesterol-lowering margarine suffered a regulatory setback. And the company lost a critical battle over rights to a future version of a top-selling anemia drug. J&J suffered setbacks in executing its strategy. In contrast to J&J, an example of a successful implementation of strategy is given in Marketing Strategies box 2-3.

SUMMARY

Marketing strategy is concerned with forging assets and capabilities into sustainable competitive advantages. Strategies are created for portfolios of business units using multifactor evaluation matrices. Remember that your job is to manage product portfolios so that cash cows generate funds for rising stars and dogs are harvested or sold off. We will pursue our discussion of marketing strategy in more detail after we have covered customer and competitive analysis and the crucial concepts of market segmentation, product differentiation, and product positioning.

NOTES

1. Definition from George S. Day, "The Capabilities of Market-Driven Organizations," *Journal of Marketing,* Vol. 58, No. 4 (October 1994), p. 38.
2. The mission statement is sometimes called a *business statement.*
3. This section is taken from Graham J. Hooley, James E. Lynch, and David Jobber, "Generic Marketing Strategies," *International Journal of Research in Marketing,* Vol. 9, No. 1 (March 1992), pp. 75–89. The authors relate their research to that of two other well-known works: R. E. Miles and C. C. Snow, *Organization Strategy, Structure, and Process* (New York: McGraw-Hill, 1978) and Michael E. Porter, *Competitive Strategy* (New York: The Free Press, 1980).

SUGGESTED READING

Cruvens, David, Gordon Greeley, Nigel F. Piercy, and Stanley F. Slater. "Mapping the Path to Market Leadership," *Marketing Management,* Vol. 7, No. 3 (Fall 1998), pp. 29–39.

Day, George S. "The Capabilities of Market-Driven Organizations," *Journal of Marketing,* Vol. 58, No. 4 (October 1994), pp. 37–52.

Hooley, Graham J., James E. Lynch, and David Jobber. "Generic Marketing Strategies," *International Journal of Research in Marketing,* Vol. 9, No. 1 (March 1992), pp. 75–89.

Menon, Anil, Sundar G. Bharadwaj, Phani Tej Adidam, and Steven W. Edison, "Antecedents and Consequences of Marketing Strategy Making," *Journal of Marketing,* Vol. 63, No. 2 (April 1999), pp. 18–40.

Williams, Jeffrey R. "How Sustainable Is Your Competitive Advantage?" *California Management Review,* Vol. 34, No. 3 (1992), pp. 29–51.

REFERENCES

Aaker, David A. *Strategic Market Management,* 5th ed. New York: Wiley, 1998.

Day, George S. *Market Driven Strategy: Processes for Creating Value.* New York: The Free Press, 1990.

Douglas, Susan. *Global Marketing Strategy.* New York: McGraw-Hill, 1995.

Jagpal, Sharan. *Marketing Strategy and Uncertainty.* New York: Oxford University Press, 1999.

Jain, Subhash C. *Marketing Planning & Strategy,* 5th ed. Cincinnati: South-Western, 1996.

Schnaars, Steven P. *Marketing Strategy,* 2d rev. ed. New York: The Free Press, 1997.

QUESTIONS

1. KeyCorp is one of the top 15 largest banks in the United States with assets of about $65 billion. KeyCorp is the market share leader in northern metropolitan areas such as Cleveland and Seattle. For a number of years it followed a "snowbelt strategy" of acquiring small, cheap branches in the northern half of the country. Many of the acquired banks are in small towns. Is this strategy consistent with KeyCorp doing targeted selling by market

segmentation? With it being a supermarket of financial services? Would you shift Key-Corp's strategy away from the snowbelt strategy? If so, how?

2. Procter & Gamble is the world's largest consumer products company. P&G sells more than 300 brands to 5 billion consumers in 140 countries. Nonetheless, P&G recently reorganized, shifting product management from four geographical regions to seven essentially self-contained global business units, ranging from baby care to food products. Each unit is completely responsible for generating profits from its products and controls product development, manufacturing, and marketing. Why did P&G restructure its operations?

3. More and more firms have the policy that "marketing will never be constrained by manufacturing." What is the role of manufacturing as a weapon in the ever-present battle for market share? Give an example.

4. Hudson Bay is Canada's largest retailer. Hudson Bay owns The Bay general department store chain and the Zellers discount chain. Hudson Bay has been slow to respond to new competitors, and has been hobbled by dated information systems and poor customer service. One result was that Wal-Mart Stores surpassed Zellers to become Canada's biggest discount chain. Hudson Bay has responded by acquiring K-Mart Canada, Canada's third-largest discount retailer. What did Hudson Bay gain with this purchase?

5. International Business Machines abandoned giant, "bipolar" machines to move to a new technology, CMOS (complementary metal oxide semiconductor). The move resulted in mainframes that are much smaller and consume a lot less power, which allows them to be cooled by air instead of chilled water. This means they cost customers less money to run. They are also cheaper for IBM to make, resulting in higher profit margins. There has been one big drawback—they are slower than the old-style machines that they replaced. Customers who needed high-end machines switched to competitors. In particular, Hitachi Data's Skyline series, which combines the older bipolar technology with some new CMOS technology, became a big hit. IBM's world-wide mainframe share fell from 81 percent in 1995 to about 67 percent in 1998. IBM's new mainframe, System 390 G5 (for fifth generation) for the first time matches the processing speed of the bipolar machines it abandoned. Nonetheless, there is still a performance gap between IBM and Hitachi: 125 MIPS (millions of instructions per second) to 150 MIPS. Assess IBM's strategic decision.

6. Zippo Manufacturing makes lighters. Zippo became a legend by wisely taking up World War II correspondent Ernie Pyle's suggestion that it send lighters to GIs free of charge. The move won Zippo good feelings from an entire generation. Now, however, anti-smoking groups have made lighting up a social no-no. A historic settlement between states and tobacco companies has ended a barrage of marketing that has inadvertently assisted the company. How should Zippo address its evolving marketplace?

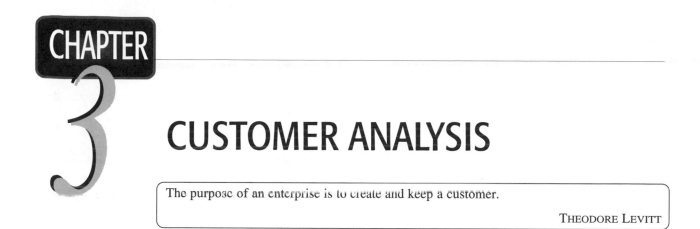

CUSTOMER ANALYSIS

> The purpose of an enterprise is to create and keep a customer.
>
> THEODORE LEVITT

*T*he most important ingredient in the success of any organization is a satisfied customer. Indeed, some believe that an "obsession with customers" can lead to a sustainable competitive advantage. This means more than getting close to the customer.

WHY ARE CUSTOMERS IMPORTANT?

Customers are essential because this is where the life of an organization begins. Until customers place orders, nothing really happens. Once customers think enough about your goods or services to buy them, you are in business. Also, when customers stop placing orders your organization starts to die. Customers thus have a great deal to do with the success or failure of an enterprise. We believe that customers are the engine, the critical driving force that powers a market economy.

When executives were asked what were the most important issues managers will face, customer wants was second only to product quality. The implication is that marketing managers can never know too much about customers and their needs. This chapter is concerned with answering seven questions you must ask yourself about your customers, their motivations, and your relationship to your customers.

1. Who are my customers?
2. Where are my customers?
3. When do customers buy?
4. What do my customers want?
5. How do customers buy?
6. How do you learn about customers?
7. How does a firm become customer oriented?

Once you understand customers and develop a customer focus, you are ready to design products and marketing programs to fill their requirements.

WHO ARE MY CUSTOMERS?

The issue of who customers are seems at first to be an easy question. After all, we can look at our current invoices and identify everyone to whom we ship. These firms can be classified by size and industry to give a detailed picture of who buys. Consider the case of McElwee Paper Company.

McElwee Paper Company is a prototypical independent corrugated packaging manufacturer. It faces an ongoing challenge of remaining competitive and profitable in a price-sensitive business dominated by commodity-oriented purchasers. It has developed a sensitive acuity to the needs of its customers. It has been successful by thinking of itself as not just a corrugated box company but as a "packaged solution provider"—even if that solution involves a material other than corrugated. This is not to say that McElwee Paper yielded market to plastic, flexible packaging, and other forms of alternative packaging without a fight. It has stressed one major area of market impact—the environment—where corrugated has the upper hand. McElwee Paper has developed bulk containers or bins, improved coating for increased water resistance, used stronger adhesives for joining and forming, and improved graphics with multicolor flexographic printing. This has allowed it to elevate the status of its corrugated product from that of a basic shipping container to an effective merchandising tool that can be used in point-of-purchase displays and in club stores, warehouse-style stores, and large discount stores. McElwee Paper's goal is to serve its customers' needs efficiently and profitably. To help achieve this goal, McElwee Paper tracks its end-use markets. Nondurable goods consume about 80 percent of its shipments. Of this group, food and beverages make up the largest end-use market with a share of nearly 40 percent, followed by paper and printing at more than 20 percent. A detailed breakdown is given in Table 3-1.

Although customer shipping point data may be useful, they can give a distorted view of who your customers really are. The problem is that deliveries may go to fabricators or channel intermediaries that resell your products to others. This raises the difficult question of whether your most important customer is the OEM, the distributor, the retailer, or the ultimate user. The results also suggest it may be useful to distinguish between business and consumer buyers.

Consumer Customers

Consumer buyers include everyone who purchases goods for their own or family members' consumption. Firms that sell low-priced products such as paper towels often focus their attention on the final buyer. After all, paper towels are branded products that are presold with a heavy use of magazine and television advertising. This suggests that paper towel manufacturers must understand consumer preferences for features such as wet strength, durability, color, number of plys, and price. Firms that accurately measure these preferences are in a better position to create products and ads that will draw customers to grocery stores.

An alternative argument is that towel *brand loyalty,* or the degree customers repurchase, is really low. Can you, for example, name five brands of paper towels? The answer is no and neither can the authors or most anyone. The truth is that all brands of paper towels are similar and buyers do not have strong emotional attachments to items in this product class. Most consumers of fast-moving consumer products have *split loyalties* to several

TABLE 3-1   Corrugation Customer Identification at the McElwee Paper Company

	Proportion of Shipments to				
Year	Food and Beverages	Paper and Printing	Chemical	Rubber	Other
Current	39.1%	22.5%	5.0%	5.3%	28.1%
Last	40.6	21.4	5.0	5.2	27.8
Previous	39.6	22.5	5.1	5.1	27.7

brands; that is, they are multi-brand buyers. Consumers buy from brands in their idiosyncratic repertoires of one or more individual brands.[1] Under these conditions, the marketing activities of grocery stores may be more important than the preferences of the final buyer. Retail stores determine shelf locations, number of shelf facings, final selling prices, the existence of end aisle displays, and whether a brand of towels is "featured" in the weekly store ad. Thus manufacturers that cater to the grocery store buyer with special deals, discounts, display racks, signs, banners, cooperative advertising support, and contests may be able to sell more paper towels than firms that advertise only to the final user.

APPLYING
. . . to Consumer Semi-durable Marketing

Okay, this may work for low-priced paper towels, but does the same concept hold true for higher-priced consumer durables? With durables the costs of development and manufacturing are so high that companies surely focus on the final users and their preferences. The answer is yes. When manufacturers ask customers to spend $1,000 or more they usually make an effort to tailor the product to their needs. However, customer contact can be expensive and there may be a cheaper way. For example, a Japanese camera manufacturer wanted to expand its position in the U.S. high-priced camera market. Instead of asking users what features they wanted in new cameras, the firm sent a vice president to America to visit a number of retail camera stores. The executive observed customers buying cameras and then held in-depth conversations with store managers about what features were desirable. He then returned to Japan and developed a new line of cameras that were very successful in the U.S. market. Why did a focus on retail store employees work so well? The answer is that people do not buy $500 cameras off the shelf; retail salespeople sell them cameras in this price range. Thus a key factor was the manufacturer's ability to include features that the clerks could use to sell the cameras to the final buyer. Much of consumer marketing is *transaction marketing*.

Business Customers

The issue of customer identity is even more complicated with products sold to businesses. Remember that business goods and services are used to create merchandise that is then sold to final users. This means that the demand for business products is *derived* from the demand for the final product. Thus the identity of components and services is often lost when selling to business buyers. As a result, the importance of brands is reduced and the role of specifications, timely delivery, and price is increased. Under these conditions, identifying the "right customer" is extremely difficult.

A common approach with goods sold to businesses is to treat the purchasing agent as the "customer." After all, purchasing agents often select qualified suppliers and negotiate contract terms. However, purchasing agents usually rely on engineers and company scientists for technical expertise. This means that the most "important" customer may actually be some obscure technician who uses the product in the plant or laboratory. Other key business customers are plant managers and the controller. Production managers typically have some input on the type of equipment installed in their plants. Also, controllers pay for supplies and equipment, and they have to approve orders before they can be sent out to vendors. Obviously, business marketing involves satisfying a large number of different customers. Here you often encounter *interaction marketing*.

Another complication with business markets is that buying committees frequently make purchasing decisions. Because membership on these committees may be secret and meetings are usually off-limits to outsiders, the identity and the buying criteria of key business customers may not be readily available.

APPLYING
. . . to Business-to-Business Marketing

Firms selling engines for commercial airplanes provide an example of business customer identification problems. The most logical customer for engine manufacturers is the airframe builder such as Boeing or McDonald-Douglas. Engines are a key component and have to be matched carefully with the airframe to give the desired lift, range, and capacity.

However, engine manufacturers have begun to sell directly to the airlines using features such as durability and low fuel consumption. If this were not complicated enough, a third customer, the leasing firm, has entered the picture. Airplanes have become so expensive that they are commonly sold to a finance company and are then leased to the operating airline. This means the engine supplier has to satisfy the sometimes conflicting demands of three customers: the airframe manufacturer, the financing company, and the airlines. The engine supplier may work together with the airframe manufacturer and financing company to meet the requirements of the airlines. This is an example of *network marketing*.

Nonprofit Customers

Another important class of customer is the not-for-profit sector. This includes community orchestras, the United Fund, public radio and TV stations, credit unions, hospitals, and schools. Each of these organizations is managed by a local board of directors. As a result, purchase orders for supplies and equipment often go to firms that maintain offices in the community. In addition, it is not uncommon for nonprofit groups to place orders with companies associated with friends, relatives, or members of particular political parties. Marketers who expect to sell to nonprofit organizations need a great deal of information on how customers make purchase decisions.

Choosing the Right Customer

Our discussion has shown that consumer, business, and not-for-profit suppliers are often expected to serve multiple customer constituencies. This can complicate product design and the creation of marketing programs. Firms that try to be all things to all customers may fail because they lack the resources to get the job done. Some organizations focus on specific groups of customers and succeed by becoming specialists. Most firms need to cater to the ultimate users as well as dealers and other channel intermediaries. Polaroid sells to retailers (its customers) and markets to instant camera and film users (its consumers). Certainly an ability to set priorities helps put the issue of customer identification in proper focus. Perhaps the best solution to the dilemma of customer emphasis is to take guidance from the strategic plan. A good strategic plan should identify who the company expects to work with not only now but in the future. The relative importance of intermediate and final buyers may change over time. See Marketing in Action box 3-1.

WHERE ARE MY CUSTOMERS?

Knowing where customers are located can be very useful to marketing managers. Existing customers are sometimes traced through invoice data. Service Merchandise catalog stores, for example, make it a point to ask for the address of each customer who makes a store purchase. These addresses are stored in the computer and used to select newspaper and radio media to cover their customer base. They are also used to send catalogs and sales notices directly to customers' homes.

Another way to locate customers is through the use of *warranty cards*. These cards are enclosed with merchandise and customers are asked to fill them out and return them to the manufacturer. Warranty cards are primarily used to notify customers in case of recalls and safety updates, but they can also be used for marketing purposes. Some firms use these names for telephone solicitations for extended warranties and for mailing direct mail offers. Unfortunately, only about 20 percent of warranty cards are returned and large numbers of customers are still unidentified. One solution is to use postage paid warranty cards so customers are more likely to return them.

MARKETING IN ACTION *3-1*

APPLYING
. . . to
Consumer
Toy
Marketing
and
Retailing

The Impact of Changing Buying Patterns

For much of the past 15 years, the toy industry's "Big Three" players—the retailing chain Toys "Я" Us and the manufacturers Mattel (Barbie) and Hasbro (G.I. Joe)—grew together. Toys "Я" Us pioneered the category-killer retailing philosophy of building big stores with huge selections and great prices that wiped out traditional smaller toy stores. Even two superstore imitators, Child World and Lionel, could not compete with Toys "Я" Us and went out of business. Toys "Я" Us swooped down to pick up these chains' best locations. The two big manufacturers acquired smaller ones, cut new toy development, boosted spending on movie- and TV licensed products and relied on Toys "Я" Us to move the goods while spurning smaller stores.

But over the past three years, a number of trends have started to chip away at these strategies. First, lots of time-strapped parents no longer make Toys "Я" Us a destination for routine toy buying, opting instead to use the increasingly well-stocked toy aisles at Wal-Mart stores and other discounters. A recent national online survey by Digital Research showed a pronounced migration away from toy superstores. Over 40% of the households responding shopped at toy superstores less often than they did four years ago. Second, many upper income parents are turning to specialty-toy retailers for more service or for toys that are marketed for education and enrichment value rather than for instant appeal. The president of one chain of stores promoting higher-end, specialty merchandise has said, "Today, with both parents working, there is a desire to give children the best they can give them. You could define it as guilt." Third, buying surveys, such as by the NPD Group, show that children are outgrowing toys earlier, moving on to computers and electronic games. Toy spending in the U.S. now peaks with three-year-olds! Toy spending steadily drops after that for each age category, with 12-year-olds receiving about half as much. Parents who work longer hours have less time, and so do the kids. Between computer tutoring, after-school activities, organized sports programs, and homework at lower grade levels, children have less time to do what they want. They are even watching less television than five years ago. Toys are playing a smaller role in the time budget of kids.

Age compression is taking place. A survey of households with children under 12 showed that while 46 percent of seven- and eight-year-olds listed playing with toys as a favorite pastime, only 24 percent of 9- and 10-year-olds did, and a mere five percent of 11- and 12-year-olds did. The older groups list reading, going to the park, playing video games, and listening to music higher on their preference lists. Where once girls were interested in Barbie until they were nine years old, they now leave Barbie at five or six. A lot of toys consequently face a compressed product life cycle.

Toys "Я" Us remains the nation's largest toy retailer and most sought after outlet during the holiday season. Nonetheless, it has had to cope with stalled growth rates, falling market share, and earnings that peaked in 1995. Toys "Я" Us is planning to alter its operations to deal with market changes.

(continues)

Courtesy Toys "Я" Us

MARKETING IN ACTION *3-1* **(continued)**

It believes that there are a number of categories in which it would be possible to extend the age groups to older children. It plans merchandising initiatives to respond to customers' desires for convenience and more educational products. To deal with customers' time pressures, Toys "Я" Us has started selling toys over the Internet rather than only through stores. It is coping with the age compression problem by expanding its demographics by emphasizing baby needs at one end of the spectrum and looking seriously into electronics at the other end. It acquired the largest baby products retailer and renamed it—surprise—Babies "Я" Us.

— *Changing buying patterns impact the relative importance of intermediate and final buyers.*

Source: Joseph Pereira, "Toy-Buying Patterns Are Changing and That Is Shaking the Industry," *The Wall Street Journal,* June 16, 1998, pp. A1, A8.

A locational breakdown of the McElwee Paper Company is shown in Table 3-2. A conservative reaction would be to focus the efforts of your salespeople, distributors, and advertising on the growing South Central market. This approach seeks to make money by concentrating on areas where the firm currently does well. A more aggressive reaction would be to ask why your organization is showing slippage in some areas. Is there something wrong with your product or is it just a marketing problem? Perhaps customers expect local production facilities to assure quick delivery. Perhaps the firm is using the wrong mix of pricing, distribution, and promotional activities.

A further complication for marketing managers is a customer who operates from multiple locations. For example, a plant manager in Oklahoma may want to buy your product but the order may require approval from a parent organization located in New York City. This means selling efforts have to be coordinated and conducted in two widely separate environments. An even more difficult situation occurs when the Oklahoma plant wants to buy your corrugated product and the Florida plant wants another brand. Under these conditions, the New York parent is likely to demand standardization on one product and suppliers will have to sell at three or more locations if they expect to land the order. These examples suggest sellers need to know where customers are located and they must be prepared to conduct extensive marketing activities at a variety of sites.

WHEN DO CUSTOMERS BUY?

At first glance the question of when customers buy does not seem to be a serious problem. If these are the periods when customers want to order, then the marketing concept suggests the marketing manager should adapt production and distribution systems to meet these customer demands.

TABLE 3-2   Location of McElwee Paper's American Customers

	Proportion of Shipment to					
Year	Northeast	Southeast	East Central	North Central	South Central	West
Current	15.8%	19.3%	14.1%	12.0%	21.7%	17.1%
Last	15.4	19.6	14.2	12.2	21.6	17.0
Previous	15.8	19.6	14.0	12.1	21.2	17.3

Adapting to Customer Buying Patterns

Demand variation exists for many products. When enough customers want to rent videos at 10 P.M. or on Sundays, alert stores adjust their hours to fill this need. In a similar fashion innovative banks have added teller machines so customers can withdraw cash 24 hours a day, and mail order firms have toll-free numbers so customers can order at night and on weekends. Even financial service companies have toll-free numbers so customers can trade securities 24 hours a day. The success of these activities depends on knowing a great deal about when customers want to buy.

Changing Customer Buying Patterns

Perceptive marketers not only know when customers buy, they take advantage of those times when they do *not* buy. For example, airlines, resorts, and telephone companies build capacity to meet peak seasonal demands. This means that they have excess capacity sitting idle during the off-season. Marketing managers can help utilize this capacity by implementing special pricing and promotional programs to attract new customers when demand is low. The trick is to see the opportunity to expand sales even though customers do not seem to be interested.

A classic example of extending the period customers will use a product occurred with that old American favorite the turkey. Turkeys were traditionally served during the Thanksgiving and Christmas holidays and were not eaten the rest of the year. An entire industry was created to grow and process turkeys for sale during a two-month period. Although turkey is low in fat and economical, the birds are packaged in 15–20 pound units and take a great deal of time and effort to cook. This is not a problem during holidays when friends gather to celebrate, but turkey is inconvenient during the week when family members may be working. The key to extending turkey sales beyond the normal holiday season is to make it easier for the customer to prepare. Turkeys are now sold year round in pieces, slices, and as breasts for even the smallest buying unit. This example shows that the time when customers buy products can be extended with careful attention to marketing activities.

WHAT DO MY CUSTOMERS WANT?

Determining customer wants seems simple enough, just monitor current sales to see what they are buying. A somewhat more sophisticated approach would record sales by price range, size, and color so that product offerings could be matched with customer preference. While an analysis of internal sales data is straightforward, what do you do if you are not currently selling the item? This problem can be resolved by buying the sales figures for your competitors from independent research firms (ACNielsen) or send observers into their stores to count the number of purchases being made.

There is, of course, more to determining customer wants than just checking out what sells. The main reason is that many new concepts and products have yet to be invented and are not currently for sale. In these cases market research may help you understand customer tastes (see Marketing in Action box 3-2).

You must be careful not to let your preconceptions about customers cloud your thinking. Experienced managers frequently misjudge what customers really want. For example, the Reflective Products Division of 3M sells reflective materials to a wide variety of city, county, and state governments and to sign and barricade manufacturers. 3M is a major player in this market and they have a good idea what product characteristics, delivery times, prices, and services are important. However, when they asked each group of customers to rank these criteria they were stunned by the results. While all the customers' rankings

APPLYING
... to
Business-to-
Business
Marketing

MARKETING IN ACTION 3-2

Carmakers Use Research to Cater to Weekend Warriors

Early on in the car-as-home-trend, Toyota researchers measured every possible drink size—even camping out to watch people's drinking habits in their cars and trucks. Other carmakers were doing their own research, and the cup-holder war began. General Motors Corp.'s Chevy Venture boasted 17 cup holders, or nearly two cup holders for every passenger.

While another cup holder might be too much of a good thing, a superabundance of pockets is something else. Car companies say market research told them that having a map pouch in the door, a glove compartment, and maybe a hidey-hole in the console just didn't provide enough places to stash the necessities of life. In focus groups and surveys, drivers said they were tired of tennis balls rolling around the gas pedal or skis poking out of the trunk. They wanted a place for everything and everything in its place. Toyota's product manager found that younger and more active customers were easygoing about how storage spaces should look. Netting and mesh were fine.

Hoping to distinguish its new vehicle from the competition, Nissan equipped its new small sport utility vehicle with pockets upon pockets. The new Nissan has a cubbyhole in the rear tailgate that can house dirty soccer cleats, wet snowshoes, or a kid's filthy backpack. Under the carpeting in the rear cargo area, there is a hidden compartment for small objects, like tools or tent stakes. And in the rear cargo space are hooks for various different types of storage nets. For sports equipment and other bulky items, Nissan added an overhead cargo area on the roof of the vehicle.

— *You can use market research to understand consumer preferences.*

Source: Emily R. Sendler, "Car Makers Cram Vehicles with Pockets Pouches," *The Wall Street Journal,* August 11, 1998, p. B1

Courtesy Toyota Motor Corp.

included the same factors, there was *no* agreement on which was most important. This meant that the same appeals could not be used for different reflective customers as had been done in the past. 3M was forced to revise its marketing program to emphasize separate criteria for each customer group. Customer wants in this case were not as generic as the managers believed.

HOW DO CUSTOMERS BUY?

By far the most complex issue in customer analysis is figuring out how customers buy. The problem for marketers is that much of the decision-making process takes place inside the buyers' heads, which makes it difficult to observe exactly how choices are made. Fortunately, extensive research has revealed the basic dimensions of the decision process.

A simplified model of the customer buying process is shown in Figure 3-1. Note that the procedure is sequential and time constrained. Also purchase decisions are influenced by a variety of internal and external factors. The first step is for the buyer to recognize that a problem or need exists. In a common situation, the buyer is reminded by the computer that the inventory of parts or supplies is low and needs to be replenished. Sometimes needs arise from the breakdown of the old product or from a constant demand for repairs. Also, advertising or store displays can make people aware of unfilled wants. Social interaction with friends or associates can often lead to buyer interest in new products. Finally, many consumer needs arise from internally generated desires for food, shelter, and clothing.

The second step in the buying process involves a search for alternative ways of solving the problem or filling the need. The inclusion of a detailed search process in Figure 3-1 means the customer is engaged in extended problem solving. Many routine purchases are much simpler than Figure 3-1 suggests. If you just want a candy bar, for example, you are likely to pick one up from the next available vending machine or candy counter rather than shop around at different stores. In the case of depleted business inventory, search may be limited to rebuying the item from a regular supplier. If an item is broken, can it be repaired? How much will repairs cost compared to the cost of buying a new unit? If a new product is needed, what brands are available? What features are offered by the different models? The information search phase of the process is important because this is where marketing can help the buyer gather necessary data. Marketing helps train the salespeople so they will have the information necessary to answer customer questions. Marketing prepares the tags and brochures that inform buyers about the merchandise. Marketing also designs the point-of-

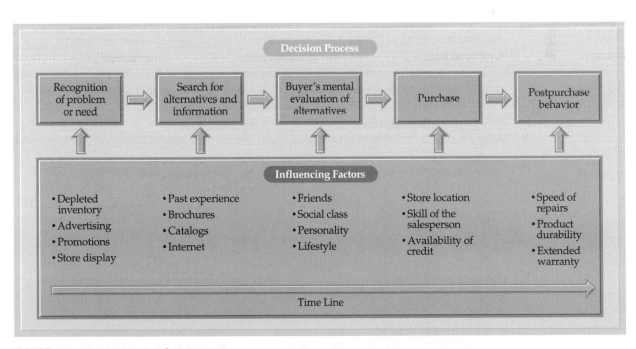

FIGURE 3-1   Customer Buying Process

purchase displays, newspaper ads, TV ads, radio commercials, and Web sites that give customers information on prices, product availability, and desirable product features.

The third step in the buyer's decision process is the evaluation of the alternatives. This part of the process involves little action for the seller; it occurs primarily in the customer's brain. The buyer weighs the advantages and disadvantages of the various alternatives and eventually makes a decision. Because this part of purchase behavior is a mental process, it is hard to observe and, consequently, is more difficult for marketing people to influence.

Once the customer has decided to buy, the next step is to complete the purchase transaction. The job of marketing is to make the product conveniently available so customers do not have to travel great distances or wait in lines for it. Also, marketing can help complete the purchase by simplifying credit arrangements, packaging, and delivery. It is not enough just to interest customers in your product; you must make the product easily available if you expect to sell in any volume.

The final step of the buying process deals with postpurchase behavior. Most products wear out or are used up and have to be replaced. This means that it is important to keep customers satisfied with the purchase so they will buy the item again. Marketing people carefully monitor postpurchase activities of customers so that interest in the product is maintained. The way customers are treated on returns, repairs, and warranty service will influence the decision process for subsequent purchases. A firm that handles postpurchase doubt and anxiety properly is more likely to build a loyal cadre of repeat buyers.

Problem Recognition

The buyer decision process begins with problem recognition. This occurs when a person perceives a difference between what he or she has (poor TV reception) and what he or she would like (a sharp, clear picture). Problem recognition can be awakened by information on past experiences stored in memory, basic motives, or cues from reference groups (Figure 3-2). Motives are enduring predisposition toward specific goals that both start and direct behavior. For example, some people must have the very latest equipment, and others like to avoid uncertainty caused by mechanical breakdowns. Problem recognition also can be activated by an outside stimulus such as advertising.

You should realize that not every difference between actual conditions and the ideal state will lead to purchase. Threshold differences must be exceeded before decision making is started. Buyers will often put up with minor inconveniences for a long time prior to actually becoming aware of their needs and starting to search for a solution. For example, many people will endure a headache for many hours before they go to the drugstore to choose a remedy.

Motivation   Needs tend to be arranged in a hierarchy and consumers usually satisfy their needs on one level before they move to higher levels. Once consumers have satisfied their

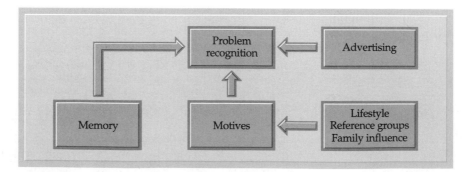

FIGURE 3-2   Factors Influencing Problem Recognition

requirements for food and shelter, they become more concerned with safety and products such as health insurance and radial tires. At the next level, a need for belonging is filled by churches, clubs, and family associations. The fourth level in the hierarchy is concerned with status, and some people satisfy this need by buying paintings or jewels. The highest need level is for self-actualization; this implies doing something to develop the talents of the individual, such as taking art lessons or working toward a new occupation.

Although basic needs influence many purchase decisions, we all buy things for other reasons. Some people have an unusually strong concern for their health, for example, and stock up on vitamins and nutrition books. Others are anxious in small groups and purchase quantities of deodorants and mouthwash. Still others crave excitement and take up skydiving and travel to exotic locales. Marketing managers can also appeal to pride in personal appearance or possessions to sell soap, cosmetics, and house paint. Another powerful motivating factor in buying situations is economy.

Reference Groups   One factor that influences the awakening of customer needs is membership in various social groups. Customers often buy products similar to what their friends and business associates own, so it is important to study membership in social groups.

For consumer goods, buyers are sometimes grouped into social classes based on occupation, source of income, type of housing, and residence location. The important thing to remember is that social class membership often determines when people buy products and what they buy. Research has shown that the middle classes are good markets for insurance and travel and the lower classes are prime customers for appliances and automobiles. The upper class is small in numbers, but it controls a lot of wealth that can be steered into various investment opportunities.

Family Influences   The role and influence of family members in consumer decision making vary depending on the product and family characteristics. For example, the six major stages of the family life cycle are (1) young single people, (2) young married couples with no children, (3) young married couples with dependent children, (4) older married couples with dependent children, (5) older married couples with no dependent children, and (6) older single people. The consumer's arrival at each stage of the life cycle initiates needs for new classes of products. When single persons move into their own apartment, they need to buy basic household equipment. When these persons marry, there is a need for more furnishings, and the arrival of children triggers a host of infant-related purchases. Thus, each stage of the family life cycle opens new vistas of needs that can be met by marketing managers who watch for these opportunities.

Joint decision making by the husband and wife tends to decline over the family life cycle as each of the partners becomes more aware of what the other considers acceptable. Usually, one partner will be responsible for decisions concerning a given product class. For example, the husband may be an expert in insurance whereas the wife may be more knowledgeable about children's clothing. This division of responsibility is based on relative expertise. Joint decision making is more important where large expenditures are involved.

Search for Alternatives

Once buyers become aware of their needs, the next step in the decision process is to gather information on products and alternative solutions to the customer's problem. A diagram explaining the search process is shown in Figure 3-3. The search usually begins when buyers consult their memories for information that might solve their current problem. Previous experiences of the buyer with similar merchandise can be reviewed to see what product solutions worked in the past. Memory can also be consulted for recommendations of friends, articles, and advertisements. If memory does not provide enough, buyers start to consult out-

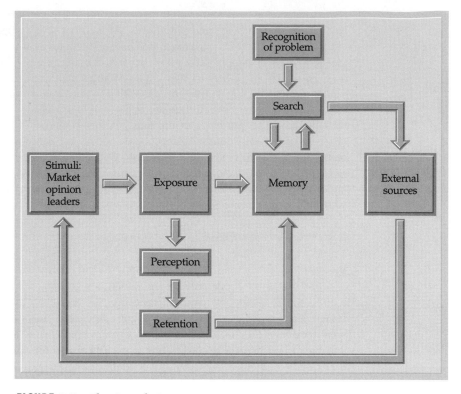

FIGURE 3-3   The Search Process

side sources of information. These include both market-oriented sources such as reading newspaper ads and talking with salespeople and nonmarketing sources such as articles in *Consumer Reports* magazine and conversations with friends.

For outside sources to be effective, buyers have to be exposed to their messages. This means the buyer has to own a radio or TV set, subscribe to magazines and newspapers, read trade journals, see billboards, and be close enough to visit and talk with dealers. After the buyer is exposed to market information, some of the data are sent directly to memory, where it is processed for decision making. However, most of the information goes through a series of filters, where it is often distorted or discarded. This process of interpreting data is called perception.

Perception   In a marketing setting, perception means values attached to communications about products received from salespeople, friends, advertisements, and independent test reports. Variations in the behavior of buyers in the marketplace can be explained partly by individual differences in the way products and services are perceived.

The perceptual process controls both the quantity of information received through attention and the quality or meaning of information as it is affected by bias. Attention is the mechanism governing the receptivity of the buyer to ads and other stimuli to which the buyer is exposed. Bias, on the other hand, is distortion of incoming data caused by previous exposure to the product, other promotional material, or family background. Two aspects of the perceptual process that have important marketing implications are selective attention and perceptual bias.

In the case of selective attention, consumers have frames of reference that they use to simplify the information they are continually receiving from their friends and marketing communications. Although the sorting-out process prevents consumers from being overwhelmed by their experiences, it does mean that they are sensing only part of their environment. For example, people can sit in front of a TV set and read in a room full of children. When they are called to dinner, they often do not hear the summons because they have effectively "tuned out" all sound messages and are receptive only to what they see in magazines or newspapers. In addition, they are likely to notice only some of the ads depending on their preferences for articles or news coverage.

An example of perceptual bias can be described by referring to some research showing that brand names influence taste perception. One brewer asked consumers to explain their preferences for beer and found the answers centered on the physical attributes of the product, such as flavor. Then an experiment was conducted to determine whether the beer drinkers could distinguish among major brands when they were not labeled. The consumers failed this test, and when these same consumers were subsequently asked to rate labeled beers, their ratings differed from those in the unlabeled experiment. These results suggest that brand names influence preference, and the success of a brand of beer may be highly dependent on the effectiveness of its marketing effort. The sense of taste is especially subject to bias and distortion, and product development for items in which flavor is an important attribute must be designed to accommodate this phenomenon.

Perceived Risk   The amount of risk buyers believe is associated with a purchase decision also affects behavior. The degree of risk varies with the costs at stake in a decision and the buyers' degree of certainty that the outcome of the decision will be satisfactory. The costs of a bad decision include monetary loss, time loss, ego loss, social risks, and losses related to the failure to satisfy the aroused need.

Individuals often pursue different risk reduction strategies. Some buy only for cash; others buy the most expensive items as an assurance of quality; still others buy the least expensive to minimize dollar investment. Some risk reduction actions by consumers are inconsistent. Frequently, the amount of deliberation for an expensive product is *less* than for an inexpensive one. Some buyers seem uncomfortable with decisions involving high perceived risk and act hastily. This suggests that perceived risk interacts with the amount of *time* that can be used for decision making.

Opinion Leaders   The search for nonmarket information (Figure 3-3) often involves interpersonal communications with friends, neighbors, relatives, or people at work or school. Individuals who provide others with information for the buying process are called opinion leaders, influentials, or change agents. These nonmarket sources can have a positive effect on purchase, or they can discourage people from buying a product. Research has shown that interpersonal communications are influential in the purchase of durable goods, food items, soaps, motion picture selection, makeup techniques, farming practices, clothing, selection of doctors, retail stores, and new products.

The term *opinion leader* must be used carefully because it is often interpreted as meaning that influence trickles down from members of higher social classes to members of lower social classes. However, influence usually occurs horizontally within strata. Influentials tend to be more gregarious and possess more knowledge in their area of influence. Often this knowledge has been obtained through greater exposure to relevant mass media.

According to the two-step flow of communication, the firm directs its advertising at the influentials in its product category, and these people influence their followers by word-of-mouth communication. The amount of word-of-mouth communication varies according to adopter categories. The purchaser of a product can be classified into one of five groups on the basis of the time of his or her adoption in relation to that of other buyers, as shown in Figure 3-4. The five categories are innovators, early adopters, early majority, late majority, and laggards.

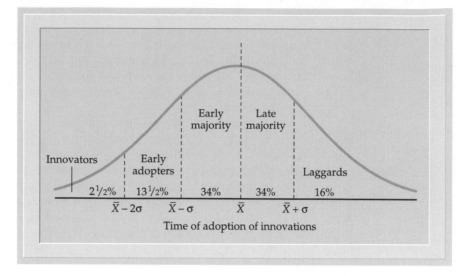

FIGURE 3-4   Adopter Category as a Function of the Relative Time of Adoption

Innovators are important in new product introductions because they affect later adopters and retail availability. However, innovators are usually not influentials. They are too innovative to be credible. They do help create awareness of a new product, however, and perform a product testing function which is observed by the influentials. The most important group of opinion leaders are the 13 percent classified as early adopters (Figure 3-4). These people are highly respected and have the most extensive social networks. The early majority also have some value as opinion leaders. However, the late majority and laggards are slow to adopt and have no value as influentials.

Evaluation of Alternatives

The evaluation phase of the customer decision model is the most complex and the least understood part of the process. A great many factors influence individual decision making, and it is difficult to observe what is going on inside the buyer's head. However, a general outline of the evaluation phase is shown in Figure 3-5. Sometimes evaluation occurs as a buyer is searching for information, as when he or she is flipping through a rack of clothes. In other cases, evaluation takes place after the search process is complete. The first stage involves a comparison of the data with the buyer's evaluative criteria. The buyer asks whether various brands would deliver the benefits sought in the product. The outcome of this process is a set of beliefs about the brands available for purchase. These beliefs are stored in memory and tell the buyer the consequences of different purchases based on the evaluative criteria. As a rule, you should view the buyer's evaluative criteria as a given and learn to adapt your product, price, promotion, and distribution elements to these key buying determinants.

The next step occurs when the buyer's beliefs and evaluations are combined to form attitudes (Figure 3-5). Attitudes are mental states of readiness to purchase that are organized through experiences and influence behavior. In general, prospects will purchase items when attitudes toward the product are favorable. If attitudes are negative, the purchase is likely to be postponed, whereas positive attitudes are associated with a strong intention to act. Measurement of intentions is important because it tells you the probability that a purchase will be made. This discussion has described the basic steps of evaluation, and we will now move on to some of the details of the process.

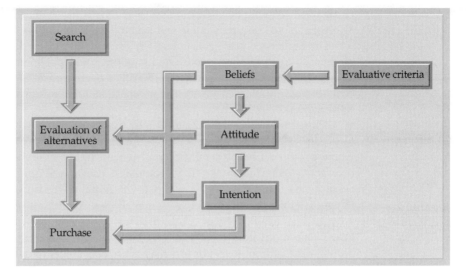

FIGURE 3-5   Alternative Evaluation

Learning   Buyer evaluation of product alternatives is enhanced through learned behavior. Learning can be defined as changes in response tendencies due to the effects of experience. Learning occurs when buyers respond to a stimulus and are rewarded with need satisfaction or are penalized by product failure. For example, a consumer might see an ad for beverages on a hot day and respond by trying different brands such as 7-Up, Slice, or Sprite. If Sprite satisfies the taste, then on future occasions he or she will buy Sprite again. The customer has learned. Theories that explain this adaptive behavior include problem solving, stimulus response, and reinforcement.

Advertising programs are often built on stimulus response theory. For example, a TV commercial of a pleasant outdoor boy–girl situation is shown as a stimulus to the prospect. The idea is to elicit a positive emotional response that can be sent into memory when the brand name "Sprite" is presented in a voice over the commercial.

Marketers also use a learning theory called *operant conditioning,* which says that the probability of a favorable response (read the ad) can be increased by following up with reinforcement or a reward. A print ad might show a person performing an unpleasant household chore (cleaning the oven) with a new spray product. People who read the ad are rewarded with a 50-cents-off store coupon that is placed at the end of the ad copy. Other examples of the use of learning theory in marketing include techniques such as giving out samples of new products and refund offers that are designed to achieve product trial.

Consistency Paradigm   Consistency is another useful concept that helps explain how customers make decisions. Buyers attempt to maintain consistency in their attitudes, behaviors, and the interaction of the two. Exposure to conflicting information produces internal strain. Customers seek to find solutions that minimize this tension. Conflict reduction alternatives include (1) changing behavior to conform to new information, (2) changing attitudes, (3) discrediting the source of the conflict-causing new information, (4) acquiring additional information to reinforce their original position, (5) avoiding the information sources that contribute to the dissonance (selective exposure), (6) distorting the new information, and (7) forgetting the content of the new information (selective recall).

Consistency theory also provides insight for planning new product prices. Often a new product is temporarily offered at a low introductory price. This is done to encourage trial of the product. Although many marginal users will be lost when the price is raised, it is hoped that some of these consumers, who would not have tried the product at the regular price, will be retained. Although this reasoning seems plausible, consistency theory suggests that the effort may be counterproductive and lead to lower rather than higher eventual sales.

The higher the price consumers pay for a new product, the greater will be the pressure on them to justify their purchase by liking the product. The greater liking will, in turn, produce greater repeat purchases. On the other hand, consumers who buy the product on a cents-off promotion can justify the purchase as a bargain and need not alter their attitude toward the product.

Thus, attempts to change attitudes by first changing behavior must involve commitment to product trial. This suggests that sampling a new product would be ineffectual in cases where consumers have established preferences. In one case, housewives resisted cold-water detergents and stated that they would not use a free sample. Some commitment was achieved by using cents-off coupons in the initial advertising and forcing the consumer to pay most of the purchase price.

Fear One motivating force that is risky to use in marketing communications is fear. The problem is that high levels of fear may cause consumers to distort advertising messages and thus may actually reduce the sales of the product. To sell antilock brakes, for example, auto manufacturers could use films of cars in accidents being smashed and burned. However, consumers might be so horrified by the pictures that they would refuse to consider that accidents might occur. Lower levels of fear help sales by creating interest in the product message, a facilitating effect. The inhibiting and facilitating effects of fear appeals may balance each other out. In this case, a moderate level of fear is optimal. One successful use of fear to sell products has been the publication of personal experiences with household fires to help sell smoke alarms. An example of a fear appeal is given in Marketing in Action box 3-3.

Attitude Formation and Change

Attitudes may affect the buyer's decision-making process (Figure 3-5), and you must understand attitude formation and change if you expect to direct marketing activities to influence sales. *Attitude* is a mental state of readiness, organized through experience, exerting a directive influence on the individual's response to objects, and situations with which it is related. This implies that attitude is a hypothetical construct that intervenes between marketing communications and product purchase. Most discussions of attitude recognize three components: cognitive (perceptual), affective (like-dislike), and conative (intentions).

An interesting synthesis of the relationships among the components of attitude and behavior suggests that at least three alternative sequences of cognitive, affective, and conative (behavioral) change may exist. These may be summarized as follows.

1. The Standard Learning Hierarchy
   Sequence of Change: Cognitive   →   Affective   →   Conative
                              (Perceptual)   (Like-Dislike)   (Purchase)
   Conditions: Buyers are highly involved.
                      Alternative products are clearly differentiated.
                      Mass media promotion is heavy.
                      Product is in early stages of its life cycle.
2. The Dissonance-Attribution Hierarchy
   Sequence of Change: Conative   →   Affective   →   Cognative
                              (Purchase)   (Like-Dislike)   (Perceptual)
   Conditions: Buyers are highly involved.
                      Products are similar.
                      Personal selling is more important than mass media promotion.
                      Product is in early maturity stages of life cycle.

MARKETING IN ACTION 3-3

Soothing the Fear of Germs

Soap used to be a social thing, but now it is a selfish thing. This explains why Dial soap, a 50-year-old brand, is struggling and has pulled the plug on its long-running campaign: "Aren't you glad you use Dial?" in an effort to appeal to a younger crowd. Famous as the old slogan was, Dial decided that it wasn't relevant any longer because of what is going on inside of soap users' heads: When we lather up, we aren't simply primping or worrying about offending others in the outside world. Rather we want to scrub the outside world away. "People are looking at germs in a very different way," says the group account director for Dial's advertising agency, which created the new Dial campaign after talking to consumers. "It used to be, 'I'm trying to make myself presentable to you.' Now it's more about 'Hey, I've got to wash you off of me.'"

In focus groups, Dial discovered that many consumers know Dial as the famous "gold bar" but view the soap as a masculine product, a big drawback in a category where women primarily make the purchase decisions. In addition, Dial users tend to be older, a less-appealing demographic target than young families, whose grimy kids and outdoor activities simply require more soap. Hence, Dial decided on an emotional appeal to women 25 to 49 years old with families. "You might feel your very best when you get out of the shower in the morning, and after that, you start to come into contact with a world that has germs. We can restore you to a safe haven, that area of comfort when you are clean and feel very good about yourself."

A new black-and-white spot, which debuted on NBC's "Today" show, begins with a little girl climbing into a bathtub. A voice-over evokes a scene from "The Wizard of Oz" movie, with the voice of the late Judy Garland wondering if there might be "someplace where there isn't any trouble ... far, far away." As she begins to sing "Somewhere Over the Rainbow," a soothing woman's voice tells viewers: "You can get there and feel clean, healthy, restored." The tagline: "Doesn't that feel better?" Although Dial won't discuss the campaign's cost, the budget is nearly three times what the company spent on Dial soap last year, and more than it has spent on any single product campaign in seven years.

The commercial is part of a broader effort to suds up sales of Dial, the first antibacterial soap. While Dial is the No. 2 brand in the bar-soap category, its sales last year fell eight percent despite a growing consumer craze for antibacterial products. Sales of bar soaps were flat last year as many consumers switched to shower gels and liquid soaps, which increased about seven percent, according to Information Resources Inc. But sales of Dial liquid soaps and shower gels also plummeted last year, even as bar-soap competitors cleaned up at the checkout. Sales of market leader Dove, from Unilever, rose 5.5 percent, while Unilever's Lever 2000, the third-ranked soap, increased 6.5 percent. In the No. 4 slot, Colgate-Palmolive's Irish Spring jumped 14 percent.

Dial, like other aging brands, must walk a fine line between updating its image and alienating its core consumers. That is what happened in the late 1970s when Dial, feeling pressure from Procter & Gamble's Coast soap, abandoned the "Aren't you glad you use Dial?" slogan. It switched to "A new Dial morning," promoting Dial as an invigorating soap with a refreshing scent. Market share tumbled, and the company returned to its famous old slogan. But this time, Dial says the slogan change capitalizes on the soap's heritage, but still broadens its appeal. "It's good heritage and that's fine, but this is intended to be a departure. We're making a strong attempt to change the way people feel about Dial."

— *Fear appeals can be effective.*

Source: Tara Parker-Pope, "Dial Soap Aims at Soothing Fear of Germs," *The Wall Street Journal,* January 20, 1998, p. B7.

---

3. The Low-Involvement Hierarchy

Sequence of Change:	Cognitive	→	Conative	→	Affective
	(Perceptual)		(Purchase)		(Like-Dislike)

Conditions: Buyers have low involvement.

Products are similar.

Broadcast media are important.

Product is in late maturity stage of life cycle.

Attitudes may be positive; yet no sales result. You probably have extremely positive attitudes toward Rolls Royce cars and Steinway pianos, but do not own either, and probably never will. It is even worse than this. Scanner data, which provide irrefutable evidence of buyer choice behavior, are showing direct contradictions to attitude measurements. For example, those consumers who have the highest positive attitude toward healthful living and diet are the same people buying the fattening, creamy deserts. Since the link between attitude and behavior is tenuous, attitude research is giving way to behavior research. "If you want to know what your favorite product is, look through your trash can."

Purchase

Once consumers have selected a product alternative, the next step in the behavioral model is to complete the purchase (Figure 3-6). The purchase part of the transaction is influenced by the buyer's intentions and other special conditions that exist in the marketplace. A buyer may intend to purchase a Sony TV, but if this brand is out of stock, he or she may end up with an RCA. Also, the buyer may want the remote control console model but can only afford to buy a portable TV.

A number of other in-store conditions can influence purchase decisions. The buying process is advanced if the product or service is readily available to the buyer. Consumers may prefer your product, but if they have to travel 50 miles to the nearest dealer, they are not likely to buy it. Similarly, dealers who are open at nights and on weekends have advantages over stores with limited hours, where customers wait in line and in which credit or check-cashing services are not offered. For example, emergency medical clinics that do not require appointments and are open evenings and weekends have siphoned off substantial business from regular doctors and hospital emergency rooms.

In-store displays are another special condition that influences buyer choice. When customers encounter a large display of a new soft drink and are given a free sample, they are more likely to switch brands and try the new item. The display provides new information so that the consumer reevaluates established beliefs and the intention to buy is modified.

A special price at the store level is also a strong inducement to get customers to switch brands. Price is particularly effective when the buyer believes that all brands in a product category are about equal in quality. Under these conditions, a price reduction may temporarily shift customer choice, and then it will revert back when the raided brand makes a counter

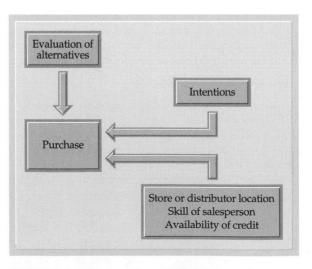

FIGURE 3-6   The Purchase Decision

price adjustment. For example, automobile tires, batteries, and shock absorbers fail on a random basis, and the buyer rarely has time to shop for preferred brands. Thus, the buyer frequently purchases the item that is on sale when he or she comes in for a replacement.

Knowledgeable and helpful personnel at the point of sale are often the key factor that sways a customer toward a particular brand. Salespeople who can explain product features and demonstrate benefits are often able to trade customers up to higher-profit merchandise. One study revealed that three-fourths of those interviewed in five cities said quality of salespeople was a factor in the choice of a shopping center. Clearly, retailers and manufacturers who do the best job of selecting and training salespeople enhance their customer purchase probabilities.

Postpurchase Behavior

Customer postpurchase activity provides several inputs to our model of buyer behavior (Figure 3-7). A major concern is that purchase allows customers to learn more about products or services. Customer expectations are compared with actual product experience; the degree of satisfaction or dissatisfaction assessed; and possible further customer behavior projected. Highly satisfied customers, for example, will alter their beliefs about a product in a favorable direction. These satisfied consumers are likely to be "converted" to repeat buyers and may become advocates of the product in their conversations with others.

Dissatisfaction   Products or services that do not live up to the buyer's expectation for durability or performance result in customer dissatisfaction (Figure 3-7). The most common reaction to product problems is for the customer to return to the dealer and ask for an exchange, refund, or repairs. If the problem is handled properly by the dealer, the buyer's

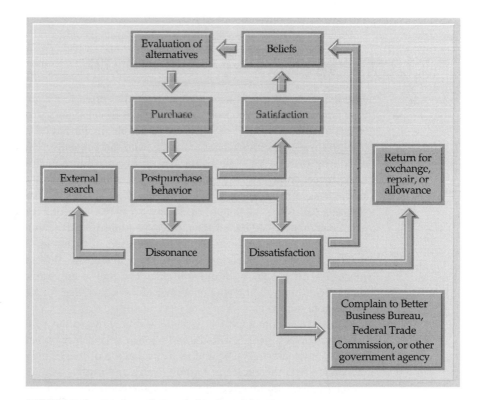

FIGURE 3-7   Postpurchase Behavior

positive attitude toward the product will be restored, and the customer will probably buy again. When customer complaints are rebuffed, a negative attitude structure is formed, and repeat purchase probabilities decline. In the case of low-value goods, dissatisfied customers usually do not return to the dealer for an adjustment and simply show their resentment by not buying again.

When customers' complaints are not handled properly, they may result in appeals to outside agencies. The ensuing publicity can lead to lawsuits, product recalls, loss of goodwill, and reduced market shares. For example, research has shown that customer dissatisfaction is high for services such as employment agencies, auto repairs, nursing homes, moving and storage, and appliance repairs. This suggests that some firms could benefit by improving the quality of their services and providing better methods for handling complaints. Firms that fail to deal with dissatisfied customers may end up having to deal with increased government regulation and decreased revenue.

Cognitive Dissonance   Another important area of postpurchase behavior is cognitive dissonance or postpurchase doubt (Figure 3-7). A purchase decision usually does not eliminate dissonance, for the consumer remains aware of the favorable features of the unchosen brands and must reconcile this knowledge with his or her own decisions. The process of reconciliation often involves a search for new information.

The likelihood that consumers will search for information after a purchase increases with the importance of the decision, with the number of negative attributes of the chosen alternative, and with the number of positive attributes of the unchosen alternatives. The kind of information sought depends on consumers' confidence in their initial decisions. Consumers who are confident that they have made the correct decision are more likely to try to find differing information and refute it. On the other hand, less confident consumers are more likely to seek only information that supports their decision. You should engage in activities designed to give buyers more product information, reduce postpurchase doubt, and turn customers into product advocates.

HOW DOES A FIRM BECOME CUSTOMER ORIENTED?

Many firms say they are customer oriented, but often this is just slogans and window dressing. Some managers profess to be interested in customers just to protect their own departments and chances for promotion. For example, managers of a flow controls company gathered to discuss declining sales, earnings, and market share. The president suggested that the only way to solve their problems was to become more customer driven. Everyone agreed and proceeded to give their version of a customer orientation. First the sales VP said they needed more salespeople to get closer to the customers. Then the manufacturing VP said they needed more automatic machinery so they could deliver better quality. The research and development VP called for more expenditures on research to generate more new products. One division manager asked for separate sales forces for each division and another wanted a special engineering group to tailor designs to customer needs. Although all of the managers displayed a customer orientation, they were primarily interested in using this theme to protect their own functional areas rather than to integrate a customer mentality throughout the firm.

In today's competitive environment, everyone in the firm is involved with marketing. Factory workers, people who answer phones, service people, and clerks in the back room all contribute to customer satisfaction. Thus one job of marketing is to make sure these employees understand their roles in building sales and profits. An Australian public transportation company used the inverted pyramid organization chart in Figure 3-8 to emphasize this new approach. This structure places the customer on top followed by the front-line staff. Man-

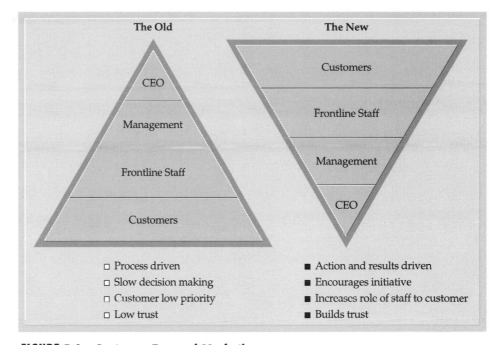

The Old

CEO

Management

Frontline Staff

Customers

The New

Customers

Frontline Staff

Management

CEO

☐ Process driven
☐ Slow decision making
☐ Customer low priority
☐ Low trust

■ Action and results driven
■ Encourages initiative
■ Increases role of staff to customer
■ Builds trust

FIGURE 3-8   Customer Focused Marketing
(From Peter Daw, "Empowering Employees Drives Australian Transportation Customer Service," *Services Marketing Today,* American Marketing Association, July/August, 1992, p. 4.)

agement and the CEO are at the bottom. By empowering front-line staff to make decisions, marketing managers were free to concentrate on strategy development and implementation. This plan also focused everyone in the company on satisfying customers. After the new program was initiated at the transportation company, the number of customer complaint letters dropped by 30 percent.

Customer Checklist

After the president of the controls firm pointed out the need to work together, the managers concluded that they needed more information about present and potential customers. They also prepared a checklist to monitor how well they were doing in their drive to be more customer oriented (Table 3-3). The most common way to gather data for the items on this checklist is through the use of customer surveys. Questionnaires can be prepared, distributed to representative samples of customers, and the results summarized in reports. Useful information can be obtained from surveys, but success often depends on asking the right questions. This means you must know a great deal about customers before you can conduct a survey. Also surveys take time to complete and there is always doubt that the people who return them may not represent all customers.

A faster and more personal way to gather customer information is through some form of direct contact. One of the simplest is to listen in on your toll-free 800 customer call-in number. In some firms cassette recordings of customer calls are routinely distributed to a wide range of executives. If managers are adventuresome, they might even try to answer a few customer calls. An extension of this method is to use the phone to make regular calls on customers. For example, executives at Castle Company find a 5×7 inch sheet of paper with the name and phone number of a customer who has purchased a new piece of equipment on their desk three mornings a week. The executives are expected to call these people to see if

TABLE 3-3 Customer Orientation Checklist

1. *Are we easy to do business with?*
   Easy to contact?
   Fast to provide information?
   Easy to order from?
   Make reasonable promises?
2. *Do we keep our promises?*
   On product performance?
   Delivery?
   Installation?
   Training?
   Service?
3. *Do we meet the standards we set?*
   Specifics?
   General tone?
   Do we even know the standards?
4. *Are we responsive?*
   Do we listen?
   Do we follow up?
   Do we ask "why not," not "why"?
   Do we treat customers as individual companies and
      individual people?
5. *Do we work together?*
   Share blame?
   Share information?
   Make joint decisions?
   Provide satisfaction?

Source: Benson P Shapiro. "What the Hell Is Market Oriented? *Harvard Business Review,* Vol. 88, No. 6 (November–December 1988), p. 125.

they are satisfied with the company's hospital sterilizers. This lets customers know they are important and helps uncover problems before they become serious. You can also call recently lost customers and others who have not purchased for several years. Ask them why they are not buying and what can be done to bring them back as regular customers.

Plant Tours and Customer Visits

Another good way to learn about customers is to invite them in for a tour of your facilities and some informal discussions. The idea for these "How are we doing for you" sessions is to encourage customers to talk about issues that are important to them. One electrical connector company makes it a point to have their customers outnumber company personnel so they will feel free to speak up. Customers are generally delighted to be invited and often provide many new insights on their needs. A variation of this idea is to send executives out to visit customer plants. This approach was used by the controls firm mentioned earlier. They sent out 10 executives in groups of 2 to visit 20 major customers. These visits are more informative if you can talk to operating personnel or actually work for short periods in selected customer operations. Customers can also be contacted at trade shows. Hospitality suites at trade shows are often used to get customers to discuss their problems and needs.

You must realize that it is not enough to conduct one survey or call a few customers to establish a customer orientation for your company. Learning about customers is an ongoing process that reflects the changing business environment. A knowledgeable consultant suggests that senior line managers should spend not less than 30 percent of their time with customers. He also recommends that accountants, manufacturing managers, and MIS people spend 10 percent or more of their time learning about customer needs. There is no one best way to interact with customers, and the most important issue is to make sure that customer contacts are maintained on a regular basis.

SUMMARY

Marketing managers must understand customer needs in order to recognize new product opportunities, to identify meaningful bases for market segmentation, and to improve existing marketing activities. This means you should know who your customers are and where they are located. In addition, you need to know when they buy and why. Managers who understand how customers make purchase decisions are in a better position to design products and more effective marketing programs.

NOTES

1. Neil Barnard and Andrew Ehrenberg, "Advertising: Strongly Persuasive or Nudging," *Journal of Advertising Research,* Vol. 37 (January/February 1997), pp. 21–31.

FURTHER READING

Germain, Richard and M. Bixby Cooper. "How a Customer Mission Statement Affects Company Performance," *Industrial Marketing Management,* Vol. 19, No. 1 (February 1990), pp. 47–54.

REFERENCES

Peter, J. Paul and Jerry C. Olson. *Consumer Behavior and Marketing Strategy,* 5th ed. Boston: Irwin, McGraw-Hill, 1998.

Schiffman, Leon G., and Leslie Lazar Kanuk. *Consumer Behavior.* Englewood Cliffs, NJ: Prentice-Hall, 1997.

Solomon, Michael R. *Consumer Behavior.* Englewood Cliffs, NJ: Prentice-Hall, 1998.

QUESTIONS

1. The 2000 U.S. Census allowed a person to check multiple racial categories for the first time. How will this change marketing practices?

2. Around the world, countries are seeing their populations age. The approximate percentage of people over 65 in the year 2000 were as follows: Italy (17%), Sweden (16.7%), Belgium and Japan (16.4%), Spain (15.9%), France (15.6%), United Kingdom (15.4%), United States (12.4%). These percentages will surge over the next 25 years. How will this trend affect which products and services are marketed and, more important, how they are marketed?

3. The Procter & Gamble Co. developed a new-category brand called Fit, which outperforms water in removing dirt and other residues from produce. The product reportedly caused "a steep learning curve" for consumers. Moreover, produce marketers and retailers were concerned that the brand's advertising would conjure up fears about product safety. What is the right way to sell consumers on a cleanser for fruits and vegetables? Would concentrating on the dangers of produce residues be an effective way to market the product?

4. For years homebuilders have built first, then hoped for the best. Builders fill develop-

ments with a handful of cookie-cutter designs that can be mass produced economically. If a given model doesn't sell, they simply knock down its price. Is there a better approach that builders might take? Explain.

5. The heyday of roller skates, which have a double row of wheels, lasted from the 1960s through the early 1980s. During this period, a big draw at roller rinks was the disco-theme party, with *Saturday Night Fever* soundtracks and costumes to match. At roller rinks near Hollywood, celebrities like David Hasselhoff and Cher could often be spotted. More recently, the growth of in-line skates devastated roller skates, whose sales plunged. In-line skates, with a single row of wheels or rollers on a high-rise boot, move faster and more smoothly than roller skates on bumpy streets and sidewalks. There is a downside. The number of in-line skating accidents more than tripled between 1993 and 1995, prompting the U.S. Consumer Product Safety Commission to issue an advisory that all in-line skaters should wear helmets. The Commission noted that from 1992 to 1996 there were three-dozen deaths related to in-line skating. Meanwhile roller-skate manufacturers have improved their product. Softer plastic wheels cushion the ride. A wider wheel base offers better balance and a steady platform for launching jumps and other tricks. Roller skates also have toe brakes for easier stopping. How might a manufacturer encourage skaters to migrate from in-lines to roller skates?

6. In this chapter we have emphasized that you cannot know enough about your customer. However, some firms may go too far in their zeal to gather data on customers. For example, with so much consumer information now stored on computers, it is possible to find out if customers have been convicted of crimes, if they have gone to jail, if they pay alimony, if they suffer from serious diseases, if they have been treated for alcohol or drug abuse, how often they have filed for bankruptcy, how much they weigh, and how much money they owe on credit cards or previous purchases. Is it ethical for companies to use such personal data, often obtained from questionable sources, to eliminate or target certain prospects on their consideration lists?

7. LSI Logic, a high-tech semiconductor manufacturer, conducted an activity-based costing study of its customers. It found that it was making 90 percent of its profits from 10 percent of its customers. Moreover, it discovered that it was losing money on half its customers. What should LSI Logic do to address this situation?

8. J. P. Morgan & Co. is a master at providing private-banking service to the very rich. Its advertisements historically targeted prospects with $5 million to invest. Recently, however, Morgan has sought to inform investors that it will accept their business if they have $1 million in investable assets and, in some cases, with even less. Why is Morgan doing this? Is Morgan going down-market?

9. A company's main business is selling pharmaceutical products. It acquired a new product line, containing two products—Alpha and Beta, in a recent acquisition. Alpha is sold primarily over-the-counter (OTC) while Beta is sold only by prescription. Before preparing a marketing plan for the new line, the product manager commissioned a user survey to gather some basic consumer information. The resultant data is in file OTCdat.sav. The manager wondered what cross tabulations and other analyses should be run to help design distribution and promotional strategies for the new line.

4

MARKET SEGMENTATION AND PRODUCT DIFFERENTIATION

> Small opportunities are often the beginning of great enterprises.
>
> Demosthenes

*I*n today's competitive environment, many companies are finding it dangerous to treat customers as a single homogeneous group. Mass markets are breaking up into dozens of minimarkets each with its own special needs. This approach to marketing is known as *segmentation* and it often is the key to developing a sustainable competitive advantage based on differentiation or a focus strategy.

Using separate marketing programs to sell to different market segments contrasts with *mass marketing* where the same marketing mix is used for all markets (Figure 4-1). Segmentation and profiling techniques (e.g., see Direct Marketing chapter) may not be worth the trouble in fast-moving consumer goods markets. The belief here is that consumer behavior is becoming more and more homogeneous.

You must decide whether to follow a mass market strategy, to focus on one segment or niche, or to compete in several segments simultaneously with different marketing mixes. Some of the issues involved here are illustrated in the detailed example for consumer appliances given in Marketing Strategies box 4-1.

MASS MARKETING

Dominant brands provide economies of scale and the efficiencies of mass media that reduce unit costs while generating greater revenues. These revenues come from not only heavy brand buyers but from the whole continuum of buyers. Popular brands are not only bought by more people, they are bought more often on average than less popular brands. Thus, brand popularity contributes to a favorable profit picture.[1]

APPLYING
... *to*
Consumer
Grocery
Products
Marketing

Research based on a number of grocery products in different countries has found that, within particular product category subtypes and their variants, competing brands differ little in terms of the demographic and socioeconomic characteristics of their customers.[2] This research has further discovered that even many subtypes and variants with their different physical formulations appealed to much the same kinds of consumers of their category. Thus, you don't try to find a way to appeal to different prospects than your competitors but rather you must market successfully to the same potential customers.

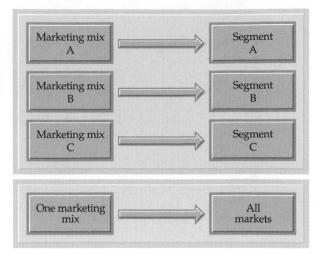

FIGURE 4-1   Segmentation versus Mass Marketing

MARKETING STRATEGIES *4-1*

Globalization of Markets

For many manufacturers, particularly those operating out of Western Europe, the American market offers important lessons that many firms would like to replicate on a regional or global basis. In the U.S. refrigerator market, for example, a fairly standard product design and limited number of standard sizes are marketed using a small number of national brands. High volume output of a range of standard products allows for major cost savings, and efficient, low-cost production is a hallmark of the industry.

In other parts of the world, for example Europe, the market context is more complex. National markets are much smaller and significant regional differences arise because of variance in customer requirements, technical standards, and conditions of product use. In the case of washing machines, for example, national customer preferences differ in respect of two key features: method of loading and spin-speed. Clothes washers sold in northern countries like Denmark must spin-dry clothes much better than in southern Italy, where consumers often line-dry clothes in the warmer weather. Preferences for refrigerators are even more complex: Northern Europeans tend to shop once a week in supermarkets and demand large refrigerators; southern Europeans, many of whom shop at open-air markets every few days, generally prefer small ones. Northerners like their refrigerators on the bottom; southerners want just the opposite. And the English, who are big consumers of frozen foods, complicate things further by insisting on units with 60% freezer space. The impact of these national idiosyncrasies, which mainly result from differences in consumer shopping behavior, are further complicated by variation in the space available for appliances in the home, with resulting pressure for differences in product design and size.

As a consequence of the factors noted above, country segmentation has been a favored approach in the industry. Many U.S. and European manufacturers have thus traditionally focused on their home market, only venturing on a small scale into foreign markets that are not dissimilar to their home base. During the last decade, however, the pressures favoring developing world-scale operations targeted at global markets have increased, and more firms have been putting major efforts into their international business operations. The Swedish firm Electrolux has been a leader in this regard, partly because of its relatively small home market base in Sweden and the need to integrate the operations of the many foreign firms that have been acquired over the past twenty years.

Traditionally, Electrolux has structured its business around individual national markets, and management still recognizes a need to react to variation in the preferences of national customers. However the impact of globalization drivers has also been noted: "Differences are narrowing and market charac-

(continues)

MARKETING STRATEGIES *4-1*   (continued)

INTEGRATING
... *with*
Production/
Operations
Management

teristics converging. By developing the ability to transfer and leverage products, concepts, components and manufacturing techniques from one market to another, Electrolux with more new product launches and shorter development cycles can develop insurmountable advantages over others."

The recent Electrolux approach to segmenting overseas markets thus reflects both country clustering and a search for transnational consumer segments. Electrolux recognizes that some niche markets are valuable. These are typically national-based markets where output of speciality, high-end models can still be viable. Electrolux continues to market a diverse collection of national brands in different ways. At the same time, major effort has concurrently been put into developing two international brands which are used for product lines targeted at a particular regional market customer profile. In Europe, for example, Zanussi and Electrolux are international brands for relatively standard product lines with integrated international positioning and marketing. Life style and behavioral criteria are employed as key segmentation criteria. Products are manufactured in regional production centers with the aim of achieving economies of scale through the output of a product line based on standard components and efficient flexible manufacturing systems.

In summary, Electrolux operates with a mixed mode approach to segmentation. Individual national market segmentation is still undertaken in some cases, normally for premium, speciality products that are viable despite low production runs. Other product lines are targeted at a limited cluster of countries. Finally, larger area country clusters are delineated; and regional transnational customer segments, identified primarily on the basis of life style and behavioral criteria, are targeted with international brands with a key goal being to achieve significant uniformity in respect to prod-

(continued)

Courtesy Electrolux, Sweden

MARKETING STRATEGIES *4-1* **(continued)**

uct features and marketing policy. Electrolux has not sought to identify global demand segments on a world-wide basis. This orientation may change in the future, but segmentation practice in the industry has reflected a view in which major national markets for many household appliances have been perceived to be: "Relatively isolated from others due to differences in customer tastes and preferences, divergent technical standards, and the relatively high cost of transportation for most products of the industry."

Whirlpool holds the leading spot in the U.S. appliance market, with brand names such as Whirlpool, KitchenAid and Roper. It makes washers and dryers for Sears, Roebuck & Co.'s Kenmore brand. Whirlpool is also the No. 1 appliance maker in Latin America, partnering with a Brazilian manufacturer, Brasmotor SA, to make most of its appliances. America's largest maker of home appliances has been thwarted in its ambitious attempts to build a leading presence in Europe and Asia.

Whirlpool wasn't shy about its plans when it first went overseas. Whirlpool's cover-the-globe strategy initially came with some bold promises. After snapping up controlling interests in joint ventures in India and China, it said it would make money, or at least break even, in Asia in two years. With its purchase of Philips Electronics NV's European appliance business, it anticipated making profits in Europe even as rivals were pulling out. In an effort to convince shareholders of the wisdom of the company's Philips purchase, Chairman David Whitwam gave an interview to the *Harvard Business Review* entitled "The Right Way to Go Global." The company even decorated its annual reports to reflect its new, cosmopolitan face. Its 1990 Report featured postage stamps from around the world. The 1993 Annual Report had a gadget attached to the front cover: a tiny, working compass.

Whirlpool has retreated a bit from its global strategy, taking a $350 million charge to exit from two of its four joint ventures in China and to reorganize its European business. Now, with Whirlpool's withdrawals from joint ventures that made refrigerators and air conditioners in China, the company is expected to focus less on manufacturing its own products overseas and more on licensing. That strategy could be especially effective in Asia, where, despite deep discounting, Whirlpool has been unable to unseat General Electric Co.'s appliance business from its leading market position.

Whirlpool didn't count on the difficulty in marketing appliances—largely homogenous in the U.S.—to the fragmented cultures of Europe. Whirlpool was also caught with higher material costs, pinching margins. And the Whirlpool name, which wasn't well known in Europe, took a while to catch on with locals. Distributors were more familiar with brands like Electrolux, Whirlpool's largest European rival. When Whirlpool came on board, "It was like Whirl what?" The company recently redesigned more than half its products in Europe after a string of unprofitable quarters there. Whirlpool insists it remains committed to its foreign operations.

— *Globally integrated strategies may not always be appropriate.*

Source: The Electrolux example is from Peter G. P. Walters, "Global Market Segmentation," *Journal of Marketing Management,* Vol. 13 (1997), pp. 171–173; the Whirlpool example is from Carl Quintanilla, "Despite Setbacks Whirlpool Pursues Overseas Markets," *Wall Street Journal,* December 9, 1997, p. B4.

Mass marketing means broadening brand appeal to many different kinds of households. Mass marketers ask "how many?" not "who?"[3] You want as many category users as possible. Consequently, you want a media message that has wide appeal and a media plan that reaches most category users.

MARKET SEGMENTATION

Segmentation is the strategy of developing different marketing programs for different customer groups or segments. It recognizes heterogeneity in the market. Each customer segment has its own unique demand function based on price, physical product characteristics, and nonphysical attributes reflecting image and performance. You build volume by appealing to group preferences.

First, you need to identify the best ways to segment a market and then pin down the characteristics of each group (this second step is called *profiling*). Next, you must evaluate the attractiveness of the segments and select the most appropriate target markets. Finally, you need to position your product or service relative to competitive offerings within the chosen market segments.

Building Customer Segments

Segmentation sounds like a process of breaking large markets into smaller ones. In the extreme, segmentation involves designing a unique product and marketing program for each buyer. Examples would include designing office buildings and insurance plans to meet the needs of individual corporations. However, segmentation is really a process of aggregation. The idea is to pull together groups of customers who resemble each other on some meaningful dimensions.

Although you can consider each buying unit a segment, there are usually some economies if they are grouped into clusters. Buying units are placed into segments so there is similarity in demand within segments and differences in demand among segments. *The Farm Journal,* for example, groups its 1 million subscribers into 1,134 different segments based on location and type of farm. Content varies across editions and an issue of the magazine might have 150,000 copies for beef farmers, 7,000 copies for beef and dairy farmers, and 36 copies for top producers who raise cotton, hogs, and dairy cows. The idea of mailing out 1,134 different editions of a magazine is mind-boggling and is only possible because the firm has a computerized bindery. A more typical situation would have a company working with 2 to 12 market segments. One of your jobs as marketing manager is to decide the most appropriate number of segments for your organization.

A variety of statistical methods are available to help you with the grouping task. While a discussion of these techniques is beyond the scope of this book, you should have some notion that the choice of technique depends upon the segmentation approach employed and purpose of the analysis. Segmentation approaches can be partitioned on whether they are a priori or post hoc. An a priori approach is one in which the type and number of segments are completely specified by you without regard to the data collected, whereas a post hoc approach is one in which the type and number of segments are revealed to you as the result of your analysis of the data. An a priori approach is used when the complexity of the market can be captured by relatively few variables, you are confident about your understanding of your market, and the main focus is on segment size, and perhaps the relative importance of segmentation variables; otherwise, a post hoc approach is used. The choice of technique also depends on whether you want to identify segments (description) or test the relationship of segmentation variables with purchase behavior (prediction).

Which Characteristics Identify Segments?

The major *bases* for segmentation are geographic, demographic, psychographic, and behavioralistic. These bases, together with their typical breakdowns, are shown in Table 4-1. Some of these buyer characteristics were discussed in Chapter 3.

Geographic Basis   Markets are often segmented on the basis of nations, states, regions, counties, cities, and population density. Product usage tends to vary among buyers on these dimensions. For example, Maxwell House coffee is sold nationally in the United States but is flavored regionally. Campbell's Soup also adapts its products and promotions to local

TABLE 4-1   Alternative Bases for Segmentation

Basis	Typical Breakdown
Geographic	
Country	Canada, England, Mexico, Japan, United States
Region	New England, Metro New York, Mid-Atlantic, East Central, Metro Chicago, West Central, Southeast, Southwest, Pacific
County size	A, B, C, D
SMSA[a] population	Under 50,000; 50,000–99,999; 100,000–249,999; 250,000–499,999; 500,000–999,999; 1,000,000–3,999,999; 4,000,000 or over
Density	Urban, suburban, rural
Demographic	
Age	Under 6; 6–11, 12–17, 18–34, 35–49, 50–64, 65 and over
Sex	Male, female
Family life cycle	Young, single; young, married, no children; young, married, children; older, married, children; older, married, no children; older, single; other
Education	Grade school or less; some high school; graduated high school; some college; graduated college
Occupation	Professional and technical; managers, officials, and proprietors; clerical; sales; artisans; supervisors; operatives; farmers; armed services; retired; students; homemakers; unemployed
Race	Black, oriental, white
Manufacturer's industry	Standard Industrial Classification (SIC) Code
Psychographic	
Social class	Lower; working class; lower-middle; upper-middle; upper
Personality	Gregarious, introverted, compulsive
Lifestyle	Cosmopolitan, yuppies
Behavioralistic	
Decision-making unit	Buying committee, purchasing agent, plant or headquarters
Usage rate	Nonuser, light, medium, heavy
Readiness	Unaware, aware, interested, intending to try, trier, repeat purchaser
Benefits sought	Quality, service, value
Occasion	Regular, special
Brand loyalty	Nonloyal, loyal

[a] SMSA, standard metropolitan statistical area.

conditions. Friday's restaurant chain gives its franchisees the option of offering 30 regional items on their menu—along with 70 national items that they must serve. General Mills sells specialized Super Moist Cake Mix in specific regions. In Pittsburgh, home of the Steelers National Football League team, the mix comes with sprinkles that match the team's colors: gold and black. General Motors, Ford, and Chrysler vary their promotions and rebates by geographic regions. The use of regional marketing plans is made easier by the availability of spot TV, spot radio, local newspapers, and regional editions of magazines. Targeting for some consumer products may be as narrow as an individual neighborhood, or even a single store, thanks to the information provided by checkout scanners.

 Multinational firms often segment markets on the basis of national boundaries. The attractiveness of an international market environment is a function of political stability, market opportunity, economic development and performance, cultural unity, tariff barriers, physiographic barriers, and geocultural distance. In addition, the multinational firm must take into account factors specific to the firm and its industry.

Demographic Basis   Consumer markets can be segmented according to age, sex, stage in the family life cycle, income, education, occupation, and ethnicity of the customer. For instance, eye makeup usage rates tend to be higher for the young, the well-educated, and working women. Shortening usage rates tend to be higher for those who are older and have larger families. Business markets can be segmented according to the total sales, the total assets, or the number of employees of the firm.

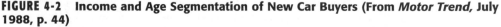

An example showing how income and age can be used to segment new car buyers is provided in Figure 4-2. The advantage of this graphical approach is that it highlights the positions of your products relative to those of your competitors. Notice that General Motors' Chevrolet, Buick, Oldsmobile, and Cadillac divisions all appeal to older drivers. The only division feeding in young customers is Pontiac. To help attract more first-time buyers, General Motors is promoting their Saturn division. Also Figure 4-2 shows that Buick and Oldsmobile appeal to the same market segment. The unpleasant result is that these cars tend to steal market share from each other rather than from competitors. General Motors is currently running some youth-oriented ads for Oldsmobile to try to differentiate these products in the minds of the customer. Another interesting finding is the hole in the middle of Figure 4-2. This suggests there is untapped potential for cars designed for 50-year-old customers with $60,000 annual incomes. When data from Figure 4-2 are combined with information on education and occupation, auto firms have precise profiles on customer segments that can be used for market programming.

Geodemographic Basis   Geodemographic segments are formed when geographic areas, say postal codes or census tracts having similar demographic characteristics, are grouped

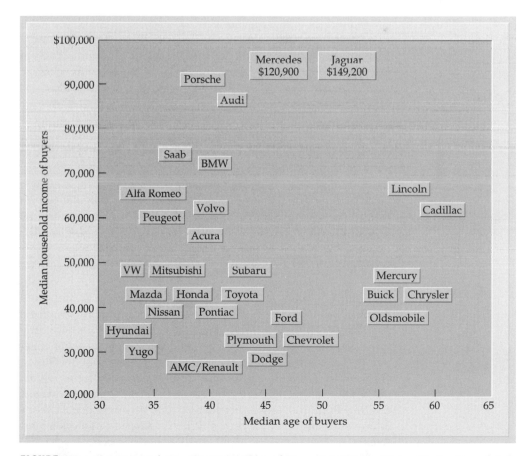

FIGURE 4-2   Income and Age Segmentation of New Car Buyers (From *Motor Trend,* July 1988, p. 44)

together. The geographic areas within a particular geodemographic segment are widely dispersed. Commercial research firms providing geodemographic offerings include Claritas (PRIZM), Donnelley (CLUSTER PLUS), and CACI (ACORN). Geodemographics allow marketers to focus their efforts on specific areas throughout the United States, and they are especially helpful in direct marketing (see Chapter 12). Geodemographics are also used for determining store locations by nationwide chains with multiple outlets.[4]

As marketing has become more targeted, demographics just do not explain enough; although demographics tell you what a customer looks like and what the customer does, they do not explain why the customer behaves as he or she does.

Psychographic Basis   Psychographics provide a useful supplement to demographics. Psychographics focus on general buyer habits, social class, lifestyles, and attitudes as they might relate to a specific product class. Lifestyle is concerned with the *activities, interests, and opinions* concerning leisure time, work, and consumption of the buyer alone or with others, with respect to both general behavior and the specific product class. Researchers find, for example, that buyers of Isuzu Motor's line of Trooper sport utility vehicles tend to be more environmentally conscious and outdoor minded than other consumers. Lifestyle research at Carnation Co. led to the creation of the Contadina line of fresh pastas targeted at two-income couples who like freshly prepared foods but have little time to cook.

Among the best-known psychographic classifications of consumers is SRI International's Values and Life Styles (VALS 2) program. Consumers are classified into eight categories as shown in Table 4-2. How can this information be used? A packager of travel tours, for example, might focus on adventure when talking to the experiencer, but emphasize luxury and service with the achiever.

Lifestyle segmentation has some limitations. Although lifestyle segmentation greatly increases survey costs, lifestyles explain only a small proportion of brand behavior. Many individuals assume multiple roles in life. How then can one lifestyle label be applied to such an individual? Even where lifestyle segments have been identified, the results frequently have not been actionable.

Behavioral Basis   A common way to segment a market is by *volume*. Marketing managers obviously distinguish between users and nonusers of their product or service. However, users consume different amounts. A small proportion of users might account for a large share of sales. Thus, the importance of a buyer is represented by the associated purchase volume. Strategies based on the heavy half are easier to implement if these users have clearly defined demographic profiles. Besides the usage rate, markets can be segmented by the decision-making unit, the end use, buyers' purchasing strategies, the degree of brand loyalty, the response to changes in our own and our competitors' marketing mixes, and the readiness stage. For industrial markets, another possibility is to group customers on the basis of similarities in *their* strategies.[5]

Rather than segment a market on the basis of descriptive factors such as the geographic, demographic, or volume, causal factors related to the reasons for purchase might be more appropriate. These causal factors are the *benefits sought* by the buyer. Once the benefit segments have been constructed, they can be characterized using conventional descriptive factors. As an example, consider the toothpaste market. Four benefit segments can be identified: (1) flavor and product appearance, (2) brightness of teeth, (3) decay prevention, and (4) price. These segments have different demographic strengths, special behavioral characteristics, brands disproportionately favored, and personality and life-cycle characteristics. This information suggests how copy directions and media choices might be tailored to reach different target segments.

The most common way of segmenting a business market is by *end use*. An industrial marketer might want to segment the pollution-control market. Some of the ways this market

TABLE 4-2   The World According to VALS 2

Actualizers
Value personal growth
Wide intellectual interests
Varied leisure activities
Well informed; concerned with social issues
Highly social
Politically active

Achievers
Lives center on career and family
Have formal social relations
Avoid excess change or stimulation
May emphasize work at expense of
    recreation
Politically conservative

Believers
Respect rules and trust authority figures
Enjoy settled, comfortable, predictable
    existence
Socialize within family and established
    groups
Politically conservative
Reasonably well informed

Makers
Enjoy outdoors
Prefer "hands-on" activities
Spend leisure time with family and
    close friends
Avoid joining organizations, except unions
Distrust politicians, foreigners, and big
    business

Fulfilleds
Moderately active in community and politics
Leisure centers on the home
Value education and travel
Health conscious
Politically moderate and tolerant

Experiencers
Like the new, offbeat, and risky
Like exercise, socializing, sports, and the
    outdoors
Concerned about image
Unconforming, but admire wealth, power,
    and fame
Politically apathetic

Strivers
Narrow interests
Easily bored
Somewhat isolated
Look to peer group for motivation and
    approval
Unconcerned about health or nutrition
Politically apathetic

Strugglers
Limited interests and activities
Prime concerns are safety and security
Burdened with health problems
Conservative and traditional
Rely on organized religion

Source: SRI International.

could be segmented are by the type of pollutant (e.g., odors), by the medium being polluted (e.g., water), by the source of the pollution (e.g., municipality), by the entity requiring the control products (e.g., federal), and by the type of control product (e.g., biological organisms). The attributes of a product or service must also be matched with the needs of potential customers. For example, one type of medical equipment can be used in the emergency room of a hospital, and another type in the office of a physician in private practice. Some attributes of the equipment will be more important in one market than in the other. Cost and ease of operation are more important to the individual doctor than to the hospital. The physician must collect from individual patients and use the equipment without help whereas the hospital collects from medical insurance and employs technicians.

A customer might have different reasons for selecting from a product category depending on the motivational circumstance. This gives rise to occasion-based segmentation. For example, the occasion is often a prime factor in wine selection. A wine's status is more important if the wine is served to guests than if it is to be consumed alone. The social occasion may make the buyer willing to spend more, be more sensitive to brand image, and pay more attention to label graphics.

Customer sensitivity to marketing actions is an important aspect of buying behavior. For example, Signode used sensitivity to price and service changes to help it identify buying behavior microsegments (Marketing Strategies box 4-2). Firms can shape the buying behav-

MARKETING STRATEGIES *4-2*

Fine Tuning Signode's Segmentation Strategy

The packaging division of Signode Corporation produces and markets a line of steel strappings used for packaging a diverse range of goods such as brick, steel, cotton, and many manufactured items. Signode has been the market leader for more than 25 years by bundling its strapping with other services. It provides engineering advice on customer packaging needs as well as parts and service for repair of packaging equipment at user firms. All other competitors offer only steel strapping. Despite its success, Signode's market share was being eroded by stiff price competition.

Signode traditionally segmented its customers by size—small, medium, large, and national accounts—and within each of these segments by SIC code. It did not use a buyer-behavior-based segmentation scheme. However, market pressures made customer behavior in terms of tradeoffs between price and service an important additional segmentation criterion. Since Signode could not do an in-depth analysis of the buying behavior of all its customers, it focused on its 174 national accounts whose purchases of Signode's products exceeded $100,000 annually. These national accounts generated nearly 40% of Signode's sales revenues.

(continues)

Courtesy Signode Packaging Systems

To gather information on the customer buying behavior of these key accounts, *key informants* were used because extensive surveys of multiple members of complex decision-making units have been found to be impractical. The key informants were Signode's five national account managers and 20 national account sales representatives. They provided input on 12 variables. Four buying behavior microsegments were then identified by performing cluster analysis on these variables. These segments were called programmed buyers, relationship buyers, transaction buyers, and bargain hunters. Knowledge of segment behavior helped Signode to redirect marketing resources.

— *Segmentation analysis can be used proactively to influence customers' movements to segments.*

Source: V. Kasturi Rangan, Rowland T. Moriarty, and Gordon S. Swartz, "Segmenting Customers in Mature Industrial Markets," *Journal of Marketing,* Vol. 56 (October 1992), pp. 72–82.

iors of potential customers by tactically altering marketing mix variables. Your next task is deciding how to balance the costs of segmentation against the potential benefits.

Evaluating Market Segments

Once you have identified some appropriate market segments, you have to evaluate whether a segmentation policy makes sense. Segmentation has a somewhat negative image as it implies brand managers deliberately abandon part of the market to the competition. However, mass markets do not have to be ignored. Usually the timing of a brand's entry determines whether a firm should segment a market or treat it as a whole. Original entrants should try to dominate the entire market, whereas latecomers might do better going after identifiable submarkets or *niches.* To determine whether segmentation is a good idea, you need a set of evaluation criteria.

Evaluation Criteria A number of factors that have been suggested to help evaluate segmentation strategies are shown in Table 4-3. Segmentation only works when you have groups of customers with common needs or wants. If every buyer wants the product tailored to his or her own specifications, then segmentation will fail. Also you must be able to identify customers in each market segment. This is fairly easy if segments are based on demographic factors such as male/female, age, or income. These characteristics can be observed and measured with some accuracy. Segments based on lifestyles are much more difficult to use, however. For example, you might decide to focus your efforts on marketing to cosmopolitan customers. The problem with this segment is how to measure cosmopolitanism. Worldliness is made up of many traits and is not as easy to scale as age or income.

One of the key requirements for effective segmentation is that group members must respond differentially to marketing initiatives. When prospects are uneducated, illiterate, or speak foreign languages, they are not likely to understand or react to ads and other promo-

TABLE 4-3 Requirements for Effective Segmentation

1. Customers with common wants exist.
2. Segment members are identifiable/measurable.
3. Segment members are accessible.
4. The segment responds to marketing efforts differently than does the market as a whole.
5. Specialized communications media are available.
6. The seller has a competitive edge in target segment.
7. The segment is large enough to make a substantial profit.

tional communications. Encouraging segment members to buy is helped if specialized promotional media are available. This means you must have access to spot TV and regional editions of magazines and newspapers. Other special media that can be useful include ethnic and foreign language radio stations.

Direct mail is also effective with segmentation strategies. Toyota, for example, has used direct mail to build awareness when introducing its Lexus line of luxury automobiles. Since these cars sell for high prices, Toyota needed an economical way to reach a limited number of prospects without the use of mass media. Their approach was to build a mailing list from people who attended auto shows and appeared on executive referral lists and bombard them with multiple mailings about the new model. Toyota included locations of the dealers for the luxury cars so prospects would be encouraged to visit the showrooms to look at them.

Segment Size   Although a project may score well on the first six criteria in Table 4-3, segmentation will not work unless the market is big enough to make the venture profitable. Even if initially profitable, a small *niche* may soon be saturated. The main reason you have to worry about size is that segmentation strategies are more expensive than selling to everyone. Special ads, brochures, and promotions have to be created for individual groups of customers. Also segmentation leads to smaller expenditures in a wide variety of promotional media with a resulting loss in quantity discounts. You have to balance these increased costs against the profits produced by selling to relatively small groups of buyers. This issue is especially true in micromarketing and niche marketing.

Micromarketing   *Store-specific marketing,* often called micromarketing, has become possible for many consumer products because of the detailed marketing information now available. For example, one U.S. market research company, Market Metrics, collects statistics, such as store size, volume, space devoted to various departments, and shopper sociodemographic profiles on 30,000 supermarkets, which it combines with consumption pattern studies. This permits the research company to rank specific stores based on how well they should sell a specific product. Borden, for instance, used micromarketing for its Classico pasta sauce. Classico carries a premium price—40 cents more than Prego and Ragu. The Classico target market is those who earn at least $35,000, live in dual-income households in metropolitan areas, and are interested in gourmet-style pasta sauces. Because a mass market approach would have been inappropriate, a list of the best stores for the Classico consumers was generated. This permitted Borden to spend its money more efficiently. Some additional targeting examples are given in Table 4-4. Micromarketing not only helps big food companies, but it also allows retailers to allocate store shelf space correctly.

Niche Marketing   Niche marketing means serving a small market not served by competing products and of negligible interest to competitors. The real strategic use of segmentation seems to be in identifying underserved customers, then creating a new product category, subtype, or variant for them through product differentiation. You will have a temporary monopoly until the market attracts competitors.

PRODUCT DIFFERENTIATION

Our discussion of segmentation would not be complete without a consideration of product differentiation. Whereas segmentation focuses on groups of customers, differentiation emphasizes product differences to attract buyers. You must keep in mind that, when talking about a brand, what matters is not so much unique, but what is special, consistent, and

TABLE 4-4 Targeting a Product's Best Customers and the Stores Where They Shop

Brand	Heavy User Profile	Lifestyle and Media Profile	Top Three Stores in New York City Area
Peter Pan Peanut Butter	Households with children headed by 18- to 54-year-olds, in suburban and rural areas	Heavy video renters Go to theme parks Below-average TV viewers Above-average radio listeners	*Foodtown Supermarket* 3350 Hempstead Turnpike Levittown, NY *Pathmark Supermarket* 3635 Hempstead Turnpike Levittown, NY *King Kullen Market* 398 Stewart Ave. Bathgate, NY
Stouffers Red Box Frozen Entrees	Households headed by people 55 and older, and upscale suburban households headed by 35- to 54-year-olds	Go to gambling casinos Give parties Involved in public activities Travel frequently Heavy newspaper readers Above-average TV viewers	*Dan's Supreme Supermarket* 69-62 188th St. Flushing, NY *Food Emporium* Madison Ave. & 74th St. NYC *Waldbaum's Supermarket* 196-35 Horace Harding Blvd. Flushing, NY
Coors Light Beer	Head of household, 21–34, middle to upper income, suburban and urban	Belong to a health club Buy rock music Travel by plane Give parties, cookouts Rent videos Heavy TV sports viewers	*Food Emporium* 1498 York Ave., NYC *Food Emporium* First Ave. & 72 St., NYC *Gristedes Supermarket* 350 E. 86th St., NYC

Source: Spectra Marketing Systems, with data from Information Resources Inc., Simmons Market Research Bureau, Claritas Corp., and *Progressive Grocer;* appeared in Michael J. McCarthy, "Marketers Zero in on Their Customers," *The Wall Street Journal,* March 18, 1991, pp. B1, B5.

believed. This is your consistent brand promise (CBP).[6] Both segmentation and differentiation strategies are usually employed at the same time to achieve a sustainable competitive advantage. For example, see Marketing Strategies box 4-3.

Using Differentiation

The coffee market illustrates product differentiation. The first change from ground coffee was the introduction of a powdered instant for busy people. Then a way was found to remove the caffeine from coffee for those who do not want their sleep interrupted or have been told by their doctors to lower coffee consumption. The end result was a proliferation of different types of coffee to appeal to specialized customer segments. A similar explosion of product differences has occurred with Coke. Where once there was a single Coke, we now have Classic Coke, Caffeine Free Coke, Diet Coke, Caffeine Free Diet Coke, Cherry Coke, and Diet Cherry Coke.

Differentiation is more difficult when you are selling standard items like cement or metal strapping to business buyers. Decisions are often made for these commodities on the basis of lowest bid price. The Lonestar Cement people have partially overcome this problem by developing a fast-drying, superstrong cement targeted at four segments: airport construction and restoration, highway and bridge-deck building and repairs, tunnel work, and precast construction. The cement will harden in just four hours instead of the 7 to 14 days required for regular cement to set. Its niche appeal permits Lonestar to charge twice the price of regular cement. Another way to deal with commodities is to broaden the concept of the product

MARKETING STRATEGIES *4-3*

Prepaid Plans Open Cellular-Phone Market

Portugal's main telephone company, Portugal Telecom SA, came up with the idea of prepaid cellular service when they recognized that the existing network of automatic teller machines (ATMs) could be used as "refueling" stations. A user buys an off-the-shelf telephone, along with a card representing a certain value. Dialing a phone number and giving a personal activation number printed on the card activates the phone. When the money runs out, the card can be replenished with a fresh payment: cash at a local store, credit card charge, or ATM deduction (requires digital phone). The plan was a smashing success in Portugal (about 70% of all Portugal Telecom's mobile-phone customers are prepaid), took Europe by storm (about 25% of the European market), and is now catching on in the U.S.

A rival wireless carrier, Telecel Communicacoes Pessoais SA, markets its Vitamina prepaid telephones in brightly colored packages, each shaped in the form of a pill. One version is aimed at corporations. A company can specify exactly how much credit it wants each employee's phone to have and how often the credit can be topped off. Another product, Vitamina K (for kids), is for children ages 8 to 15. The phones look like frogs and have six colorful programmable (by a parent) buttons. The child only needs to know one is for mom, two is for dad, three is for grandma. Yet another variant, Vitamina R (for radicals), is sold to 15 to 24 year olds. Only fashionable Ericsson and Nokia models are featured. These phones provide a running display of the credit available at any one time. If one Vitamina R customer calls another Vitamina R customer, the call is 35% cheaper than a normal call.

— *You should consider marketing different product offerings to different market segments.*

Source: Gautam Naik, "Prepaid Plans Open Cellular-Phone Market," *The Wall Street Journal,* September 16, 1998, pp. B1, B4.

Courtesy Telecel Comunicacoes Pessoais, S.A.

in the eyes of the buyer. A cement company could equip its trucks with radios and advertise itself as the on-time cement company.

Costs of Differentiation

Although product differentiation can help improve sales revenues, it is expensive. Some of the added costs of differentiation include:

- *Product Modifications.*   Adapting products to meet the needs of different segments requires extra payments for R&D, engineering, and special tooling.
- *Shorter Production Runs.*   Product proliferation means producing items in smaller lots. Instead of producing 5,000 units of one item, you have to manufacture 1,000 units of five different products. This raises set-up times and workers have to adapt to different routines.
- *Larger Inventories.*   The more products you offer customers, the larger the inventories needed to meet the demand. This occurs because the safety stock required to meet unexpected variations in demand for several products exceeds the safety stock needed for one product.

The amount of differentiation that you employ should be determined by the impact on profits. For example, not long ago customers could go into the showrooms of American auto manufacturers and order cars built to their exact specifications with regard to color, upholstery fabric, and 25 other options. However, this raised the costs of production and the more standardized Japanese cars were able to grab market share with lower prices. American car manufacturers have found that they can now make higher profits by offering less product differentiation. The use of a differentiation strategy forces managers to choose between additional revenues and the added costs of serving individual segments.

The real danger is that, while incurring higher costs of production, you might not garner enough additional sales to compensate. Even worse, you might alienate your core customers or distributors. Consider what happened to Reebok International Ltd. in the battle with Nike Inc. for the U.S. high-end sneaker market. Athletic shoe companies try to garner the cachet as a maker of performance shoes for serious athletes and thereby kindle sales in the broader consumer market. Runners, like smokers, seldom switch brands once they have settled on something they like. Reebok tried to innovate a running shoe called the Pump, which featured an inflatable bladder that wrapped around the sides. Unfortunately wearers complained of overheated and abnormally sweating feet. Runners and running specialty stores have been skeptical about Reebok ever since.

MASS CUSTOMIZATION

Technology, such as information technology and flexible manufacturing system technology, is making it economically feasible to reach the market of one. For example, Japan's National Industrial Bicycle Company sells made-to-order bicycles. Dealers fax National a set of specifications based on customers' requirements for model, color, components, and personal measurements. Computers digest the specs and print out custom blueprints. The customer's bicycle is created out of cut-to-fit and common parts. Robots do most of the welding and painting while skilled workers complete the assembly—including silk-screening the customer's name on the frame. Within a day, this bicycle is finished, packed, and ready for shipment.[7] Another example is Computer Designed Swimwear, which uses a computer and video camera to measure customers in nine ways. After buyers pick styles and fabric, the computer prints out a pattern that can be turned into a suit within an hour. Mass customization can take many forms. (See Marketing in Action box 4-1.)

MUST SEGMENTATION AND DIFFERENTIATION ALWAYS GO TOGETHER?

Market segmentation and product differentiation often are used together. Unilever's Chesebrough-Pond's division added cleansers and creams to expand its cold-cream franchise. These products largely attract the over-35 market. To extend its franchise to younger women, Pond's launched a new line of skin cleansers, moisturizers, and toners under the Clear Solutions brand name aimed at women 18 to 34 years of age. Mandarina Gatorade, an orange-flavored drink, and General Mills' La Pina flour, good for making tortillas, are sold in only areas with large Hispanic populations.

You should realize, however, that there are situations where segmentation is used without product differentiation and where differentiation is used without segmentation. Apple Computer, for example, sells the same basic machines to educators that they sell to businesses. Separate marketing programs are used to reach these segments and differentiation is a minor issue. Mercedes-Benz has had a great deal of success selling the same cars to different market segments in Germany and in America. In the United States, Mercedes are sold as luxury cars for the rich and famous. In Germany, the Mercedes has a more popular image and is even used as a taxicab. These examples show that advertising and promotion can be used to position products to appeal to particular buyers. Product differentiation without segmentation is shown by P&G's advertising of Charmin toilet paper

APPLYING
. . . to
*Consumer
Products
Marketing*

MARKETING IN ACTION *4-1*

Mass Customization at Duracell

Duracell, a division of Gillette, is the world's leading alkaline battery manufacturer and has the highest U.S. market share. Its U.S. product line includes alkaline major cells, lithium photo batteries, hearing aid batteries, high-powered rechargeable pack batteries (e.g., camcorder and wireless telephone), and specialty batteries. It is a consumer packaged goods company with a component product dependent on the use of devices such as toys, flashlights, pagers and radios. Most of Duracell's batteries are sold at retail outlets. Its distribution includes grocery stores, drug stores, mass merchants, warehouse clubs, hardware stores, home centers, electronics shops, convenience stores, variety stores, and many other trade channels. As the market leader since the eighties, Duracell has close to one hundred percent distribution penetration for its product line.

Duracell's core business is alkaline major cells. These are Duracell's D, C, AA, 9 volt, and AAA batteries you find in stores. The five standard battery sizes are built into thousands of stock keeping units (skus) to ship its customers every month. Consider the more than 20 basic pack sizes such as common AA cell 2 packs, 4 packs, 8 packs, 12 packs and special 20 cell size packs for the warehouse club channel. These pack types go into various types of shipping cartons and trays creating over 80 open stock skus.

Duracell also produces more than 50 standard types of prepackaged displays, mostly to support incremental retail locations. The displays can be shipped using a variety of promotions including standard, seasonal and custom consumer marketing messages/offers. Its sales force works with retailers to optimize their return on these incremental displays using customized promotional offers and different product assortments. This creates thousands of different shipping skus each month.

Marketing and sales has effectively turned five basic batteries into thousands of skus to meet customer requirements. This has boosted Duracell's sales volume. Before this mass customization, its sales were significantly less than the current level.

— *Mass customization applies to intermediaries as well as final users and can include packaging and displays as well as product.*

Source: Rich Gordon, "A Role for the Forecasting Function," *Journal of Business Forecasting Methods & Systems,* Vol. 16, No. 4 (Winter 1997/1998), pp. 3–7.

APPLYING
. . . to
*Consumer
Packaged
Goods
Marketing*

as softer than competing brands. P&G is attempting to persuade customers that there are differences in softness, but they really want to sell Charmin to everyone. The ideal combination of segmentation and/or differentiation strategies varies by products and the competitive environment.

SUMMARY

Individual customers differ widely in their individual brand choices. This does not guarantee that there are identifiable segments with consistently different reactions to similar brands. Consider the case of apparel retailing.[8] Here retailers, especially small ones, define the target market by making an initial retail mix with an intuitive notion of the kind of people to whom it will appeal, seeing who responds, then adjusting the retail mix to better serve the emergent market. In the apparel market, socio-demographic characteristics are poorly related to buying behavior. Other less easily measured variables, such as socio-cultural ones: interests, ways of life, and "mental age"—the age consumers identify with and feel and act like—are more important. Moreover, there is great variability in clothing behavior according to usage situation—"clothing moments." Thus, apparel retailers find that they appeal to every socio-demographic segment, albeit to a greater or lesser degree. The warning here is

APPLYING
. . . to
*Apparel
Marketing*

that you might not always be able to identify your target market in advance but may have to rely on your customers identifying themselves through their purchase behavior. Furthermore, you may not want to limit your market prematurely.

Advances in manufacturing technology and developments in information technologies allow for mass customization. Mass customization makes it feasible for you to reach segments of one. However, for many products, including most frequently purchased consumer packaged goods, individualized products are not justified. There is a continuum between treating the market as a whole and markets of one. You have to decide which level of aggregation yields the most efficiency and profitability.

NOTES

1. Ned Anschuetz, "Building Brand Popularity," *Journal of Advertising Research,* Vol. 37, No. 1 (January/February 1997), pp. 63–66.
2. Hammond, Kathy, A.S.C. Ehrenberg, and G. J. Goodhardt, "Market Segmentation for Competitive Brands," *European Journal of Marketing,* Vol. 30, No. 12 (1996), pp. 39–49.
3. Roger Titford and Roy Clouter, "The Case for Mass Marketing in an Increasingly Segmented World," *Admap,* Vol. 33, No. 10 (November 1998), pp. 37–39.
4. James H. Myers, *Segmentation and Positioning for Strategic Marketing Decisions* (Chicago: American Marketing Association, 1996), pp. 39–45.
5. Sudharshan, D. and Frederick Winter, "Strategic Segmentation of Industrial Markets," *Journal of Business & Industrial Marketing,* Vol. 13, No. 1 (1998), pp. 8–21.
6. Richard Jeans, "Integrating Marketing Communications," *Admap,* Vol. 33, No. 11 (December 1998), pp. 18–20.
7. Hart, Christopher W., "Made to Order," *Marketing Management,* Vol. 5, No. 2 (Summer 1996), pp. 11–16; Ali Kara and Erdener Kaynak, "Markets of a Single Customer: Exploiting Conceptual Developments in Market Segmentation," *European Journal of Marketing,* Vol. 31, No. 11/12 (1997), pp. 882–883.
8. Danneels, Erwin, "Market Segmentation: Normative Model versus Business Reality," *European Journal of Marketing,* Vol. 30, No. 6 (1996), pp. 36–51.

SUGGESTED READING

Hart, Christopher W. "Made to Order," *Marketing Management,* Vol. 5, No. 2 (Summer 1996), pp. 11–16.
Kara, Ali and Erdener Kaynak "Markets of a Single Customer: Exploiting Conceptual Developments in Market Segmentation," *European Journal of Marketing,* Vol. 31, No. 11/12 (1997), pp. 873–895.

REFERENCES

Jenkins, Mark and Malcolm McDonald. "Market Segmentation: Organizational Archtypes and Research Agendas," *European Journal of Marketing,* Vol. 31, No. 1, (1997), pp. 17–32.

McDonald, Malcolm and Ian Dunbar. *Market Segmentation: How to Do it, How to Profit from It,* 2nd ed. London: Macmillan, 1999.

Myers, James H. *Segmentation and Positioning for Strategic Marketing Decisions.* Chicago: American Marketing Association, 1996.

Sarabia, Francisco. "Model for Market Segments Evaluation and Selection," *European Journal of Marketing,* Vol. 30, No. 4, (1996), pp. 58–74.

Walters, Peter G. P. "Global Market Segmentation," *Journal of Marketing Management,* Vol. 13, (1997), pp. 165–177.

Wedel, Michel and Wagner A. Kamakura. *Market Segmentation: Conceptual and Methodological Foundations.* Boston: Kluwer Academic, 1998.

QUESTIONS

1. For years, makers of baldness remedies have made their pitches to men. Most people lose 100 to 150 hairs a day, a small percentage of the 100,000 hairs that grow on the average head. People who suffer genetic baldness problems don't replenish hair at a normal rate. Minoxidil, the generic version of Rogaine, is the only Food and Drug Administration (FDA)-approved baldness remedy. No one knows how minoxidil works on the human head. It began as a blood pressure medication with the unwelcome side effect of excessive hair growth. The drug appears to prolong the growth phase of the hair cycle. The FDA says that the drug spurs meaningful hair growth in only 25 percent of men and 20 percent of women after several months of use. The FDA has approved the drug for sale without a prescription. Most drug companies get a three-year monopoly when a product is converted to over-the-counter use. In an unusual move, the FDA decided that Rogaine failed to meet the criteria for this exclusive status and immediately approved several generic versions of the drug.

   Dermatologists estimate that about 40 million men and 20 million women suffer from hereditary hair loss. Most men eventually come to terms with hair loss. Surveys show only about half the nation's balding men are worried about their plight while nearly every woman with thinning hair is concerned. Moreover, women are more likely to endure the twice-a-day treatment and prolonged use requirements of hair-growth products. Should marketers of minoxidil pursue a risky new market: women? If so, how should Rogaine do so? A generic version?

2. People in the fashion business long held that big women—and teens—didn't want stylish, body-revealing clothes. Let them wear sweat pants and tent dresses! Designers were especially loath to court such customers for fear of losing cachet with trend-setters. Meanwhile the total number of girls ages 10 to 19 in America is rising. They are getting heavier as well as taller as a result of junk-food diets and too little exercise. Feet are growing along with waists and hips. Today's teenagers are more tolerant of body differences than previous generations. Plus-size teenagers crave more body-revealing clothes than heavy adult women tend to wear. Should fashion marketers address this niche within a niche? If so, how?

3. Private-label film accounts for about 5.5 percent of total U.S. film revenue and about 11% of total units sold. Should the Eastman Kodak Co. develop a discounted product, one that wouldn't carry Kodak's name, for the segment of the market that is price sensitive? Kodak could do so with an older-technology film emulsion than used in its branded Kodak film. The new product would have less well defined and less colorful pictures.

4. Some find it useful to classify the bases of segmentation as general (independent of products, services, or circumstances) or product specific (related to the customer and the product, service and/or particular circumstance). Further, these bases can be classified as observable (measured directly) or unobservable (inferred). Construct the corresponding four-cell classification table and put the bases in Table 4-2 into the appropriate cells.

5. In the past, many business owners or managers felt that they either did not need new insurance coverages for their business practices or that their claims would not seriously affect their business on a day-to-day basis. All that has changed as daily news of lawsuits awarding large settlements are reported. How can an individual firm in the insurance industry react quickly to emerging needs for specialized insurance coverage? How should it market these new products?

6. Many U.S. banks have shifted their policy on bounced checks so that the largest check is processed first when multiple checks are received at one time. By processing the largest check first, several small checks may bounce that day and the banks get to charge the

customer more than one $25 bounced check fee. If the small checks had been processed first, the account owner might have had to pay only one bounced check fee. Some banks have projected increases in fee income of $700,000 to $14 million from changing the order of check processing. Since it costs a bank only $.50 to $1.50 to process a bad check, banks make high profits on $25 bad check processing fees. Is it ethical for banks to target customers who bounce checks with a high to low check-processing policy and then say they have no legal requirement to inform customers of this policy?

7. There is a growing segment of up-market consumers who are willing to pay a premium to stand out. The German carmaker, Mercedes-Benz—now Daimler-Chrysler, started its car customization program called Designo in 1995. In 1998, it launched the program in the United States. About 100,000 Mercedes are sold each year in the U.S. market. While customization is needed in Germany, where taxicabs are Mercedes E-class sedans, the need in the United States is not obvious. Adding 10 percent or more to the cost of a car through custom options also runs counter to Mercedes current value theme. Should Mercedes have a customization program in the United States? What is the biggest challenge in implementing the program?

8. A telecommunications company wants to assess the attractiveness of market areas that it has yet to enter. Markets in which subscribers rack up lots of airtime minutes are preferable to those with "deadbeat" subscribers. The company has subscriber billing and demographic information for those markets that it already serves. Some markets—and the counties that comprise them—were selected at random from current service areas. To adjust for the fact that some counties are larger and more populous than others are, all demographic variables were put on a per capita, per household, or similar basis. The data are in file cellulardat.sav. The key performance measure for the telecom is average airtime usage per customer. What are the key demographic variables for predicting it?

COMPETITIVE ANALYSIS AND PRODUCT POSITIONING

> A common problem is the assumption that competitors do things "the same way we do."
>
> ALAN ZAKON

*I*n business environments, domestic and international competitors are constantly attacking existing market positions. Firms that fail to respond to these challenges are destined for the scrap heap. Companies have come to realize that they must focus on global market share, not just domestic share. Toyota's "Global 10" strategy was based on their belief that they need at least 10 percent of the world market to remain strong. Gillette, the American consumer goods company, is the world leader in razor blades and razors. Its Papermate, Waterman, and Parker lines have a 15 percent revenue share of the world pen market—the next-biggest competitor is Societe BIC with 8 percent. Gillette's Oral-B toothbrush is the leading seller in the United States and several international markets and its Braun electric shaver is the top seller in Germany. Gillette sells in 200 countries. A key benefit of big market share is that it gives a company strong bargaining power with suppliers and distributors. Low costs mean that profits can grow faster than revenue.

Competitive analysis flows out of customer analysis. To truly know how you stack up against your competitors, you first need to understand your customers' wants and needs. Then you must identify both current and potential competitors in both your served and unserved markets. Industry analysis is also important. You need to know about the suppliers to your industry as well as channel members who serve as intermediaries between you and your competitors and the end users. These actors impact your competitive position. Once you have identified your competitors, it may be possible to group them by factors, such as degree of specialization or degree of globalization, to make it easier to discern patterns of competitive behavior. Now you should be in a position to do an in-depth analysis of competitors' strategies. You must be careful not to simply focus on what your competitors are doing now. You must consider where your competitors are going.

This chapter focuses on six issues:

1. Who are your competitors?
2. What are your relations with your competitors?
3. Where do you compete?
4. When do you compete?
5. How do you compete?
6. How do you position your product?

In addressing these issues a firm is examining its strengths and weaknesses, its opportunities and threats. This is known as *SWOT* analysis.

WHO ARE YOUR COMPETITORS?

You must know which of the many companies in the marketplace you are really competing with for your served market. You should respond most vigorously to those in direct competition. You also must be aware of those potential competitors who are not now in your market, but who may be in the future.

Current

One way of identifying who your competitors are is through *market structure analysis* using perceptual mapping. Products or brands that are perceived to be close together in perceptual space are more in competition with each other than those far apart.

Perceptual Mapping   Every market has a structure based on the strengths of brand attributes. The positioning of products in a market can be illustrated by a perceptual map such as the one shown in Figure 5-1 for automobiles. Perceptual maps are derived from customer

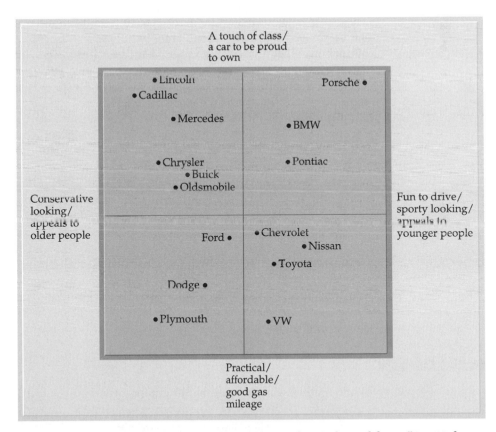

FIGURE 5-1   Perceptual Map of the Automobile Market (Adapted from "Car Makers Use 'Image' Map as Tool to Position Products," *The Wall Street Journal,* March 22, 1984, p. 33. Reprinted with permission of *The Wall Street Journal,* © Dow Jones & Company, Inc. 1984. All rights reserved.)

data measuring similarities among brands. Customers are asked to rate each pair of brands (e.g., Buick-Porsche) on a scale from very similar to very dissimilar. These ratings are fed into a computer program for doing multidimensional scaling. The program determines the relative positions of the brands and prints out a perceptual map.

APPLYING
. . . to
Consumer
Durables
Marketing

The location of the automobiles in Figure 5-1 is a direct measure of similarity across brands. Since Porsche and Plymouth are the farthest apart, customers view them as least similar. Notice that Buick and Oldsmobile are seen as the most similar. This result agrees with the findings of Figure 4-2 that showed these two brands were close in terms of customer age and income. General Motors has a serious problem with Buick and Oldsmobile since you do not want to compete with yourself. Better positioning has been achieved for Cadillac which is near Lincoln and Chevrolet which is near Ford. GM executives are sure to be ecstatic that the high-priced BMW is the closest car to Pontiac. This shows that Pontiac's marketing program has been effective in moving it into a desirable market position.

Map Dimensions　Dimensions for perceptual maps are not named by multidimensional scaling programs. Additional information must be gathered from customers to find the critical dimensions and locate them on the maps. Labeling dimensions of perceptual maps and interpreting these diagrams is rather subjective. This does not lessen the value of perceptual maps, but it does mean you have to evaluate them carefully.

Dimensions for perceptual maps are often obtained by asking customers to describe the benefits (e.g., economy, durability, ease of service) they associate with each of the brands. These ratings are then fitted to the perceptual space as shown in Figure 5-1. In this diagram the vertical axis has been named "a touch of class" at the top and "practical/affordable" at the bottom. The horizontal axis has a "conservative/older dimension" to the left and a "sporty/younger" dimension to the right. You may note that these dimensions are similar to the age and income axes of Figure 4-2. Although Figure 5-1 has two labeled dimensions, some perceptual maps have more and some less.

Perceptual map dimensions are vital in the preparation of marketing plans. Once you understand the dimensions that customers use to evaluate products, you are better able to design products to fill their needs. This applies both to modifications to strengthen the positions of existing products and in the design of new items to fill gaps in perceptual maps. In addition, map dimensions are useful when you want to reposition products through the use of advertising. For example, General Motors has been successful using advertising to give Pontiac a stronger sporty/youth image. In addition, Oldsmobile has run an ad campaign with the slogan "It's not your father's Oldsmobile" in an effort to attract younger buyers.

Ideal Points　Once you have labeled the dimensions of your perceptual map, the next step is to add in some information on personal preferences. Each customer can be represented on your map by a point showing that individual's ideal product. Ideal points are person points. Clusters of ideal points indicate where there are sufficient prospects to justify current and new products.

Potential Entrants

While focusing on your current competitors, you must be alert for the emergence of new competitors. The possibility of newcomers to an industry depends on two things: the barriers to entry that exist and expectations about competitive reactions. The barriers to entry include economies of scale, product differentiation, capital requirements, buyer switching costs, access to distribution channels, other cost disadvantages, and government policy. These factors are often interrelated. The need for economies of scale requires capital for plant construction, whereas overcoming existing brand identification and customer loyalty through product differentiation requires capital for advertising. The costs of a buyer switching to your product from that of your competitor may be formidable. For example, although many new software products are better than those already in use, they fail. The problem is not awareness of the product or the price of the product, but the cost of retraining personnel to use the new software. A new entrant may find the best distributors already under contract and retailers demanding compensation to provide scarce space. Existing firms may also have proprietary product technology, favorable access to raw materials, favorable locations, government subsidies, or other cost advantages. Governments can limit or prevent entry with regulations such as licensing. For example, foreign distillers find it hard to sell vodka to the Russians. One reason is that the Russian government imposed high taxes and import duties to protect the "strategic" vodka industry.

Potential entrants may be deterred if they expect forceful competitive reaction. Conditions under which the likelihood of reaction is high include a past history of vigorous retaliation, established firms with significant resources to fight back, established firms with commitment to the industry, and slow industry growth.

WHAT ARE YOUR RELATIONS WITH YOUR COMPETITORS?

While the primary relationship with your competitors will be a competitive one, your relationship with them may take some other form. The relationship between competitors is a continuum from conflict to collusion, passing through competition, coexistence, and cooperation along the way.[1]

Conflict

APPLYING
. . . to
Consumer
Energy
Marketing

The focus of conflict is your opponent. Confrontation is likely to occur, for example, when you have a market share growth objective in a stagnant market. You can only gain share by wresting it from competitors. More generally conflict may occur when competitors have mutually incompatible objectives. Consider the Georgia natural gas service market. For decades Atlanta Gas Light Co. had a monopoly. Then the state Public Service Commission decided to deregulate the industry, restricting Atlanta Gas Light to the natural gas transportation business only. Nineteen companies jumped in to sell natural gas. Many gave their expected market shares: EnergyOne 20–30 percent, Columbia Energy 10–20 percent, Energy America 15 percent, Shell Energy Services 10–15 percent, Scana Energy 10 percent, United Gas Management 10 percent, and so on. Atlanta Gas Light's new separate gas marketing subsidiary, Georgia Natural Gas Services, simply said that it expected to be one of the leaders.[2] The expected market shares of these gas marketers add up to much more than 100 percent. These market share objectives are mutually inconsistent, and they must lead to a fight. Threats to a company's position may elicit a harsh reaction.

Competition

Competition is object centered. Competitors strive to win the same prize—the customer. The degree of competition will depend mainly on market attractiveness (market size and growth rate, economic climate, possibilities for economies of scale, technological innovation, differentiation, and segmentation) and industry structure (number of competitors, diversity of competitors and their commitment to industry, ease of entry and barriers to exit). The competition among brands in an industry is often called "The Battle of the Brands." An example of the battle of the brands is given in Marketing in Action box 5-1. Much of the remainder of the chapter will focus on these battles.

MARKETING IN ACTION *5-1*

Bathroom Brawl

Kimberly-Clark is a relative newcomer in the $3.5 billion-a-year U.S. toilet paper business. Its original Kleenex toilet-tissue brand struggled after its introduction in 1990. The company merged with Scott Paper, maker of the Scott and Cottonelle brands, in 1995 and created Kleenex Cottonelle, which helped Kimberly-Clark gain a 23% share of the market. But it trails rival Procter & Gamble's Charmin, which has 30%. Among premium tissues, Kleenex Cottonelle still ranks a distant fourth behind Charmin, Fort James's Northern and Georgia-Pacific's Angel Soft.

Overall, bath-tissue sales are flat and premium brands are losing share to economy-priced tissue. Many toilet-paper consumers treat the brands as interchangeable and simply shop for the best deal. Even the industry's most recent innovation—the triple-sized roll from Charmin is about value, rather than improved performance. Marketers of bathroom tissue have used everything from puffy clouds to cuddly babies to advertise their products. Now Kimberly-Clark wants to talk about the real reason that people use toilet paper.

Testing the limits of how much consumers want to hear about what goes on in the bathroom, the maker of Kleenex Cottonelle spent $100 million to promote the brand as the toilet paper that wipes better than regular tissue, thanks to a new "rippled texture." In conjunction with new advertisements, ten million free samples were hung on doorknobs in the Eastern United States, where the product was first introduced.

The rippled texture is the result of a patented technology that dries the tissue during manufacturing without crushing it flat and later embossing it. This method also allows the tissue to hold its rippled shape when wet, allowing it to clean better. Thanks to a $170 million investment in a manufacturing operation, the process uses less fiber while improving the bulk and strength of the tissue. As a result, the company's manufacturing costs per roll are 20% less than those for other premium tissues. With the price to consumers remaining the same, the extra margin will help Kleenex Cottonelle better withstand the price wars plaguing the tissue category and let the company spend more on marketing and advertising to grab market share.

Kimberly-Clark hosted focus groups to talk to consumers about toilet paper, and asked them to compare leading brands with the new Kleenex Cottonelle textured tissue. They discovered that even though tissue advertising doesn't talk about how well a toilet paper wipes, that is what customers are thinking about. Nonetheless, Kimberly-Clark marketing executives quickly discovered there were limits to what they could say.

Talking about the way a toilet paper performs is a major departure for a category that for years has focused on squeezable softness, quilted softness and cottony softness. Are consumers who are used to seeing Mr. Whipple squeeze the Charmin ready to hear even a hint of what he does with the product? Kimberly-Clark is convinced that they are. "It's a very delicate thing, but it has the potential, if it's done right, of taking a major share of the toilet paper market."

Courtesy Kimberly-Clark

The $100 million launch budget was more than double what Kimberly-Clark spent on the brand the previous year. About $20 million to $30 million went toward national television advertising, including 18 weeks of primetime TV. In addition to the door-to-door sampling, another million single rolls were made available in stores for 50 cents each in the Eastern U.S.

— *Meeting consumer needs better than your competitors is important in the "battle of the brands."*

Source: Tar Parker-Pope, "The Tricky Business of Rolling Out a New Toilet Paper," *The Wall Street Journal*, January 12, 1998, pp. B1, B8.

Coexistence

Coexistence is working toward a goal independent of others. Coexistence occurs when competitors define different niches of a market to dominate. For example, this happens in distribution where retail outlets have local monopolies in their core geographic areas.

Cooperation

Cooperation involves working together toward a common goal. A typology of formal forms of cooperation is shown in Figure 5-2. The main types are dyadic, joint activity, and investment in a third party. In the seed business, some major technology developers have acquired distribution networks outright, while others have formed marketing agreements to sell the products of their research. One of the industry's alliances, an illustration of joint activity, is between Novartis and Beck's Superior Hybrids. The companies signed an agreement to bring NK Bt corn hybrids to the eastern corn belt. The partnership benefits Beck's by enabling it to get a Bt product to the market fast, and Novartis gets its Bt technology planted on more acres, which in turn will help it recoup some R&D money. Another illustration of joint activity cooperation is given in Marketing in Action box 5-2. An example of an investment in a third-party alliance is Agri Tech Inc., a joint venture formed by StarSeed Inc. and DeLange Seed Inc. Agri Tech has been licensed to produce and distribute Roundup Ready soybeans. It markets the consolidated soybean line-up of each of its partners.[3] These examples show the business reasons for cooperation: speed to marketplace, new market potential, technology access, and market share protection.

Collusion

Collusion is cooperative behavior designed to injure third parties—customers, suppliers, noncolluding competitors, or the general public. Oftentimes collusive behavior is illegal. Collusion may be explicit involving direct communication among the parties. Such communication may take place at trade association meetings or industry conventions. Sometimes the government is a party to collusion. The intent is to protect existing domestic firms, especially from foreign firms.

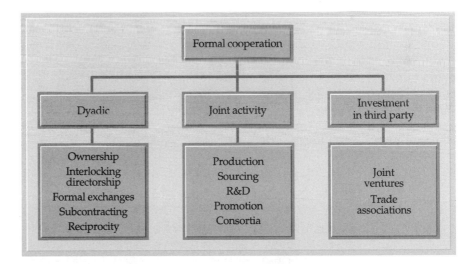

FIGURE 5-2 **Typology of Forms of Formal Intercompetitor Cooperation (*Source: Geoffrey Easton, "Relationships Among Competitors" in The Interface of Marketing and Strategy, in George Day, Barton Weitz, and Robin Wensley, eds. [Greenwich, CT: 1990], p. 73.*)**

MARKETING IN ACTION 5-2

Building Alliances with Competitors

Not so long ago, the American pharmaceutical behemoth Warner-Lambert was regarded with contempt on Wall Street. Its number one prescription drug, the cholesterol medication Lopid, was about to come off patent, imperiling its only bright spot. Regulatory problems and a product recall, which cost it an estimated $1 billion, had brought the company to the edge of disaster. Its product lines were a ho-hum hodgepodge of everything from Listerine to prescription drugs. No new products appeared even close to being market-ready. Things had become so bleak that everybody told the company to sell out while it still could. Or at least get rid of the pharmaceutical division and stick to mouthwash.

Warner-Lambert chose radical surgery, selling two lackluster divisions—Pro toothbrush and Warner Chilcott—and ordering across-the-board cost-cutting to save 10% a year. Warner-Lambert had one promising new product, a cholesterol drug, Lipitor. It threw out the rulebook by striking a deal with rival Pfizer to co-market the new drug. Admitting it couldn't market the product on its own got Lipitor on the shelf two years ahead of schedule. It became the first drug to produce sales of over $1 billion in its first year. Released a few months after Lipitor, Rezulin, a diabetes drug, became a billion dollar drug too. Warner-Lambert's market cap increased an astonishing 750% over four years.

— *You and your competitor may both benefit from working together.*

Source: Stephan Herrara, "Health Care Products: Sow's-Ear-Into-Silk-Purse Tale," *Forbes,* January 11, 1999, pp. 180–181.

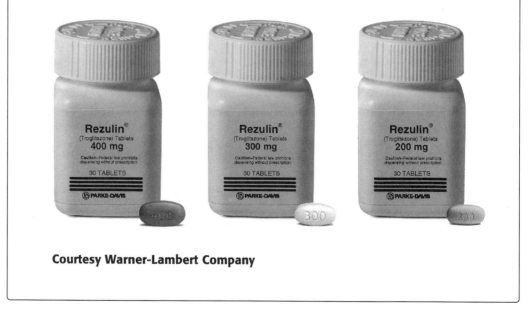

Courtesy Warner-Lambert Company

Collusion is sometimes indirect, which would involve signaling. A firm can make an announcement to test competitor sentiments. Competitive firms then can reply by making announcements communicating their pleasure or displeasure with competitive developments in the industry. If the industry responds negatively, the firm need not follow through with its intended action. Signaling occurs frequently in the airline industry. You must be able to discern between market signals that are truthful indications of a competitor's intentions and those that are bluffs.

HOW DO YOU LEARN ABOUT YOUR COMPETITORS?

The more and better the competitive information available to you, the sounder will be your marketing decisions. For competitive information to be helpful, you must process it in a methodical manner. This involves five steps.[4]

1. Set up an information-gathering system for competitive analysis.
2. Identify your competitors.
3. Gather information through a competitive audit.
4. Evaluate competitive information.
5. Integrate this information into your planning process on a regular basis.

This process forces you to consider competitive actions and reactions in formulating and executing your marketing strategies and tactics.

The *competitive audit* can generate a lot of information about your competitors. You must decide what is worth keeping. Each piece of information has to be evaluated on source reliability and information accuracy. An example of a competitor profile that could come out of a competitive analysis is given in Table 5-1. This profile is for competitors of an Internet service provider.

TABLE 5-1   Competitor Profiling

Company	America Online, Inc./Netscape Communications Corp.	At Home Corp./Excite Inc.
Strengths	• 16 million AOL service members • 31 million viewers of AOL's Web sites, or 54.% of total audience • 17.5 million viewers of Netscape's Web sites, or 30.9% of total audience • Ease of use thanks to AOL's proprietary software which guides users to selected content • Netscape's browser, loaded with features that tie in to Netscape Web site	• 331,000 At Home subscribers • 16.6 million viewers of Excite sites, or 29.2% of total audience • Distribution—thanks to 60 million homes served by At Home's cable partners • Cable operators locked into exclusive deals • On At Home service, users are connected full-time—they don't need to dial up • Extensive personalization features that deliver local news and weather
Weaknesses	• Encroachment upon its core home-user market from high-speed cable services	• Cable partners have been slow to market At Home's services • AOL and competitors are lobbying for access to cable systems, potentially negating At Home's advantages
General information	• Typical users: families looking for an easy way to get online • Acquiring Netscape to reach business customers • The biggest just keeps getting bigger	• Typical users: Power Web users who lust after At Home's high-speed connections; experienced users who prefer Excite to Yahoo • Not the biggest, but at the forefront of redefining portals from Web sites to next-generation telecommunication providers

Source: Thomas E. Weber, "The Emerging Armies of the Web," *The Wall Street Journal,* February 11, 1999, p. B1.

You are now in a position to formulate your marketing strategy by considering three key issues: where to compete, when to compete, and how to compete. We conclude with a discussion of product positioning.

WHERE DO YOU COMPETE?

Choosing market arenas to seek competitive advantage depends on market attractiveness and organization strengths. Your job as marketing manager is to pick the best of a variety of strategic options. Most firms compete somewhere on a continuum from "avoid competition" to "attack market leader." Market leaders go after the core market. Unless the leader experiences marketing inertia or encounters some disruption in the marketplace, you may want to resegment the market and target a niche. You want to establish a niche that is defensible against its imitators. This can be successful, at least in the short run. The danger is that the niche may grow and attract other larger firms.

To the extent that competing companies focus on matching and beating their rivals, their strategies tend to converge along the same basic lines of competition. They share a conventional wisdom about their industry. The companies end up competing on marginal differences. To break free from the competitive pack, you must *create new market space*. A systematic approach to value innovation requires that you "think outside the box" by looking (1) across substitute industries with whom you implicitly compete, (2) across strategic groups within your industry, (3) along the chain of "players" who are directly or indirectly involved in the buying decision, (4) across complementary product and service offerings, (5) beyond the current functional-emotional orientation taken by your industry in making appeals to customers, and (6) ahead to how emerging trends will change value to customers.[5]

WHEN DO YOU COMPETE?

The ability to compete often depends on *strategic windows* of opportunity. Strategic windows are openings in the competitive map that can be exploited at a point in time. Remember that windows that are open one moment can be closed another. To take advantage of strategic windows, you first have to be able to see them, then you have to be ready to make a move before they close. This requires insight and flexibility.

Table 5-2 provides several examples of strategic windows and shows how four firms reacted. The rapid penetration of microwave ovens into American homes opened a large strategic window for cookware. Metal pans could not be used in these ovens and everyone buying a microwave oven was an immediate customer for new pots and pans. Corning was in an excellent position to take advantage of this technology change, because they were experts at making ceramic and glass dishes for conventional ovens. However, they did not read this opportunity correctly and failed to push existing items or develop new ones until competitors had grabbed strong market positions. This lack of attention to market conditions for mature product lines is all too common and may explain why Corning spun off their housewares division to a Mexican firm.

In the case of home-delivered pizza (Table 5-2), Pizza Hut and other national chains had strong national positions in restaurant-served pizza long before Domino's came along. However, Domino's was the first to see the open window of the home-delivered pizza customer and they moved rapidly to capture many of these markets. Domino's strategy put Pizza Hut on the defensive and forced them to play an expensive game of catch-up.

TABLE 5-2   Examples of Strategic Windows

Company	Window Opportunity	Opportunity Seized	Marketing Strategy
Corning Glass Works (microwave cookware)	The microwave oven boom created a major need for "safe" cookware. Corning could immediately meet the needs of this emerging market	No	Delayed aggressively marketing existing products and developing new products until after competitors had gained important market positions
Domino's Pizza (home-delivered pizza)	Recognition of consumers' needs for rapid and reliable home delivery of pizza. No major competitive force was present at the time Domino's entered the market.	Yes	Responsive home delivery of pizza from a network of retail outlets. The company emphasizes quality, speed of delivery, courteous employees, and hot pizza
Lens Crafters (eyewear chain)	Opportunity to develop customer-responsive services in an industry dominated by optometrists.	Yes	Launched a chain of retail shops conveniently located in malls, offering eye exams and one-hour glasses
United Airlines (air travel)	Deregulation, restructuring, and an opportunity for marketing leadership due to dominant position in U.S. market. Held strong market position at the time of deregulation	No	Did not expand services and marketing capabilities to strengthen position and gain advantage. United lost market position to more aggressive competitors.

Source: David W. Cravens, "Gaining Strategic Marketing Advantage," *Business Horizons,* Vol. 31, No. 4 (September–October 1988), p. 53.

Vulnerability of Market Leaders

Market leaders can be vulnerable to external forces beyond their control. These forces include government or environmental challenge, a random catastrophe, a change in industry technology, and a new "personality" in the industry. A government or environmental challenge can distract a market leader and weaken brand loyalty. When concerns mounted about phenolphthalein, the main ingredient in Correctol, Ex-Lax, and Phillips' Gelcaps laxatives, as a potential cancer risk, Correctol reformulated its product. Ex-Lax ran television ads showing two sisters discussing the fact that Correctol officials had "changed their medicine," and suggesting that it didn't work as well. Correctol ran newspaper ads pointing out that a government panel has determined that some laxatives "may cause cancer," and suggesting that Ex-Lax might need to be recalled. It also provided a toll-free number for concerned consumers. Then the U.S. Food and Drug Administration proposed banning phenolphthalein. Ex-Lax's manufacturer immediately announced a voluntary recall and plans to reformulate the product with a different ingredient. Correctol began running ads reminding consumers that Ex-Lax was being withdrawn.[6] A new "personality"—a successful firm in a related, or even different, industry—may be able to transfer its marketing expertise into the market leader's industry.

The technology used in an industry may change because of the expiration of patents or the emergence of new technologies. The expiration of patents is less a problem than would first appear. This is because a firm usually builds substantial brand equity during its period of patent protection. This raises a barrier of high marketing costs that any new entrant must overcome. Perhaps the most common challenge to market leaders is the introduction by competitors of new products for market niches. Two market leaders that handled this confrontation differently are Gillette and Schwinn.

APPLYING
. . . to
Health and
Beauty Aids
Marketing

Gillette invented the safety razor and has long dominated the U.S. wet shaving market. In 1962, a relatively small company, Wilkinson Sword Ltd., introduced the first coated stainless steel blade, cutting sharply into Gillette's market share. Gillette swallowed its pride and brought out its own stainless steel blade. This humbling experience taught Gillette several important lessons: (1) Never take a rival for granted, no matter how small; (2) don't concede market niches to competitors because market niches have a way of growing; (3) don't delay bringing out new products for fear of cannibalizing old ones-if you don't introduce, competitors will. Gillette's obsession with defending its core market has led to the expenditure of hundreds of millions of dollars on new shaving products. These efforts resulted in the innovative twin-blade Track II in 1972, the pivoting head Atra in 1977, the hugely successful Sensor, with independently suspended blades in 1989, and the MACH3 in 1998. The company also rushed out a disposable razor in 1976 to fend off French rival Bic, even though the cheap throwaways cut into sales of higher profit Gillette products. The net result of Gillette's attention to its core shaving business is that it has 64 percent of the U.S, market, 70 of the European market, and 80 percent of the Latin American market.

APPLYING
. . . to
Consumer
Semi-
Durables
Marketing

Schwinn, on the other hand, failed to implement strategies to protect its strong position in the U.S. bicycle market. Schwinn started selling bikes in 1895 and for years was the dominant U.S. brand. Their market share peaked in the 1960s with more than 25 percent of the market. Schwinn's market position was based on a reputation for quality and a powerful distribution system of exclusive dealers. In the 1980s, however, the company made a series of strategic blunders. Customer interest shifted to mountain bikes and exotic frames made of aluminum and carbon fiber. Schwinn refused to spend money to develop new products for these niche markets, and became a follower instead of a product innovator. Unfortunately for Schwinn, the mountain bike niche grew to command 60 percent of the market. Then, in 1981, workers at its main plant in Chicago went on strike. Instead of settling, Schwinn closed the plant and shipped its engineers and equipment to a plant in Taiwan that they did not own. This move cut production costs, but led to quality problems and overdependence on foreign suppliers. Schwinn's delays in developing new products and its shift to overseas production resulted in its sale in bankruptcy court in 1993. The lesson to be learned from Gillette and Schwinn is that firms that fail to protect markets from competitors often regret it.

When there is no strong number-two firm in a market, a competitor seeking to "fill the vacuum" often damages the leader in the process. Ragu held 70 percent of the U.S. spaghetti sauce market to Chef Boy-R-Dee's 11 percent. The lack of a strong number-two brand attracted Hunt's Prima Salsa and Campbell's Prego into the market. Prego emerged as the new number-two brand at the expense of Ragu.

Market leaders may be leery of cutting prices because they will lose the most from a price cut. Even in mature markets, new positioning opportunities arise. A market leader from a small firm with limited resources is very vulnerable. Finally, a strong number two company may not have as much distribution as the leader. The temptation for the number-two firm is to expand its coverage into new markets.

A market leader has only itself to blame if it is lethargic, has a significant strategic weakness, or has alienated a key distribution channel. Lethargy may arise because the leader is "conservative" and fails to make a commitment to "raise the stakes" for competitors, favors financial goals over marketing goals, is in a market that makes up only a small part of the firm's overall business, fears cannibalism, or is preoccupied elsewhere. Family-owned businesses such as Wrigley's gum are often slow to introduce new products, opening themselves up to competitive initiatives. Vlasic was able to attack and become number one in pickles because pickles were a relatively inconsequential market to Heinz and Borden. Coca-Cola was very slow to take advantage of Coke's tremendous market identification because the company did not want to dilute the Coke name. John Deere was able to wrest the farm equipment leadership away from International Harvester because IR was focusing its attention on trucks. A leader may have a significant weakness in its strategy. Hershey's long-standing policy against national media advertising made it vulnerable to a challenge by Mars. Finally, the leader may alienate key distributors which may result in the competition's using the betrayed channel to gain ground or even the channel itself emerging as a competitor. For example, Lee jeans took advantage of the opportunity that arose when Levi Strauss stopped using jeans stores exclusively to add new mass merchandising outlets. These examples suggest that followers must be sensitive to market leaders' problems so they can be exploited to gain share.

HOW DO YOU COMPETE?

In the battle with competitors, organizations must decide on what dimensions to attack or defend. This decision is based, in part, on the size of the firm relative to its competitors. It will also depend on the strategies that are viable in a particular industry.

Offensive Strategies

The guiding principle for attack is to concentrate strength against the competitors' relative weakness. Attack strategies include (1) frontal attack, (2) flanking attack, (3) encirclement attack, (4) bypass attack, and (5) guerrilla warfare. A frontal attack means taking on a competitor head-on. This is one of the most difficult and dangerous of all marketing strategies. To be successful, the firm must have a substantial marketing advantage or deep pockets. For instance, the firm might have a similar product, but be able to sell it at a lower price. A flanking attack is appropriate for segments of the market where customer needs are not being fully met. This may simply mean fighting in geographical regions of a country or the world, where the competition is weak. More likely, it means bringing out new products for emerging segments of the market. Flanking addresses gaps in existing market coverage of the competition. An encirclement attack, known also as an envelopment attack, involves forcing the competitor to spread its resources thin by probing on many fronts at once. Again, superior resources are required. The intent is to break the competitor's will. A bypass attack is one of nonconfrontation. The firm diversifies into unrelated products or diversifies into new markets for existing products. Guerrilla warfare entails small, intermittent attacks on a competitor. One goal might be to slice off small amounts of share while evoking minimal competitive reaction.

Defense Strategies

Defense strategies exist to counter each offensive strategy. The six main defense strategies are (1) position defense, (2) mobile defense, (3) preemptive defense, (4) flank-positioning defense, (5) counteroffensive defense, and (6) strategic withdrawal. The position defense requires that the firm fortify its existing position. The main risk in this strategy is marketing myopia. Redesigning or reformulating your product can keep you one step ahead of the competition. An example is given in Marketing Strategies box 5-1. A mobile defense is a defense in depth. The firm engages in market broadening. Unattacked markets can subsidize the firm's activities in more competitive markets. A preemptive defense is attacking first. This first-strike strategy could use any of the attack strategies previously mentioned. The flank-positioning defense extends the firm's offerings into new segments to protect the positioning of the firm's existing products. The counteroffensive defense involves amassing resources and counterattacking whenever threatened. Sometimes a strategic withdrawal is necessary. With this approach firms consolidate their positions by competing only where they have competitive advantages.

MARKETING STRATEGIES *5-1*

New and Improved

Procter & Gamble Co.'s Downy has a commanding 65% of the $750 million liquid fabric conditioner category. However, Lever recently boosted marketing support for No. 2 brand, Snuggle. And USA Detergents grabbed about a 6% share of the category in the past year with its new Nice & Fluffy value brand.

P&G is protecting its position by rolling out an improved Downy that uses a new technology to protect fabric colors. Procter & Gamble Co. is backing the rollout with an estimated $15 million to $20 million campaign, hoping that color protection technology can do for a fabric softener what it did for laundry detergent. The TV and print campaign is tagged "Come on in to Downy care," and in the advertising P&G claims that "new Downy" can prevent fading.

Downy's color protection differs from the carenzyme technology introduced in recent years in P&G's Tide and Cheer detergent brands to prevent fading and fuzzing of cotton fabrics. Downy's color ingredient is designed to work in the rinse cycle rather than the wash cycle and to prevent hard-water deposits and other impurities from damaging clothes. Though competitors Lever Bros. and Dial Corp. have since added color protection ingredients to their brands, carenzyme helped P&G's Tide and Cheer add several share points earlier in the decade. Combined, the two brands held 45% of the $4.3 billion laundry detergent category.

One observer cautioned that P&G might be stretching color protection too thin. "They may be solving a real consumer problem but is it a fabric softener problem?"

— *You cannot rest on your laurels.*

Source: Jack Neff, "P&G Promotes Downy as 'New' and Improved," *Advertising Age,* September 29, 1997, p. 18.

Defensive Tactics   Most defensive strategies are built around three classes of defensive tactics: raising structural barriers, increasing expected retaliation, and lowering inducement for attack. The emphasis is on deterring a competitor from taking action against you. Market leaders can raise structural barriers by filling product or positioning gaps, blocking channel access, raising buyer switching costs, raising the cost of gaining trial, increasing scale and capital requirements, or encouraging government policies that create barriers. Flanking brands and fighting brands can fill product or positioning gaps. Channel access can be blocked through the use of exclusive dealerships; the proliferation of products, brands, varieties, and sizes; and aggressive trade promotions. Providing special services can raise buyer-switching costs. The cost of gaining trial can be raised by customer sales promotions. Scale economies and capital requirements can be increased by increasing advertising expenditures, introducing new products, extending warranty coverage, and providing below market credit financing.

A market leader must let its competitors know that there will be retaliation for any attacks on it. A firm can signal its intentions through public statements at trade meetings and in the business press. In particular, the firm can resolve to match or beat any competitive move. Disrupting market tests or introductory markets can blunt actual attacks. A market leader can lower the inducement for attack by reducing its own profit targets or by manipulating competitor assumptions about the future of the industry.

A number of promotional tactics can be used to protect the market positions of established brands from new product introductions. The idea is to attack new brands when they are vulnerable to forgo short-run profits to retard or block the entry of competitive items. A classic approach is to introduce additional brands in the same product class to preempt shelf space and to deprive actual or potential competitors of profits or resources needed to compete in a market.

The ability of market leaders to fend off new entrants with defensive tactics is illustrated by events in the orange juice market. Minute Maid, owned by Coca-Cola, and Tropicana, owned by PepsiCo, are the dominant deep-pocket players in this business. Procter & Gamble launched a frontal attack on the two market leaders with its Citrus Hill brand.

P&G advertised heavily, used cents-off coupons, added calcium to its juice, and tried a screw-top spout. Minute Maid and Tropicana fought P&G's every move and prevented it from establishing needed brand loyalty. Citrus Hill never gained more than 8 percent of the orange juice market, and P&G finally abandoned it after an investment of $200 million. Defensive strategies can work for established brands, but when they don't, withdrawal may be necessary.

Withdrawal　　The proper use of withdrawal is one of the more delicate maneuvers you may have to make as a marketing manager. Your objective is to cut your losses so resources can be moved to businesses with better prospects for growth. However, many managers are reluctant to give up on a business for fear the finger-pointing will hurt their careers. An example of a typical scenario occurred at Pet Inc. when the Whitman's Chocolates unit they purchased did not live up to expectations. Pet responded by firing the manager and selling the business. Johnson & Johnson has done a better job of strategic withdrawal. They continuously review their businesses to make sure they are fit and performing up to company standards. J&J takes the attitude that pruning the business tree of unhealthy units is just a natural activity when following a growth strategy. One J&J manager closed down a kidney-dialysis equipment business and a heart surgery equipment business before he became the manager of a successful disposable contact lens business.

HOW DO YOU POSITION YOUR PRODUCT?

You have been introduced to the concepts of segmentation and differentiation, so we now shift our attention to finding out how customers view our products relative to the competition. Product positioning focuses on buyers' perceptions about the location of brands within specific market segments. These positions are based on how well perceived product characteristics match up with the needs of the buyer.

The Majority Fallacy

Marketing managers are often concerned with positioning new products in established markets. Companies that are the first in a market can position themselves to appeal to the majority of customers, but this has less attraction for firms that enter late. Some of the factors influencing this decision can be shown by using the preference distribution shown in Figure 5-3. The distribution shows the proportion of customers that prefers each of three different levels of chocolate flavoring for ice cream. Preferences are displayed both as a histogram and as the smooth distribution that would result if a great many flavors of ice cream had been evaluated by buyers.

This diagram suggests that if three levels of chocolate flavoring were available, 60 percent of the customers would choose medium, 20 percent would select light, and 20 percent would choose heavy. With these preferences known, the first company to enter the market would maximize revenue by selling ice cream with a medium level of chocolate flavoring. However, if three companies divide the medium chocolate-flavored market equally, then the optimum position for succeeding entries is not immediately clear. If a new firm compared customer preferences for a light level of flavoring with the medium level brands already on the market, the medium chocolate ice cream would be preferred by most customers. Unfortunately, the firm might interpret these results to mean that the best way to enter the market would be with a medium chocolate-flavored ice cream. A new medium flavor might be expected to capture one-fourth of the 60 percent in the middle or only about 15 percent of the total market. The potential for a new light flavor, by comparison, is a full 20 percent of the customers. This example shows how the *majority fallacy* can lead an unwary firm into

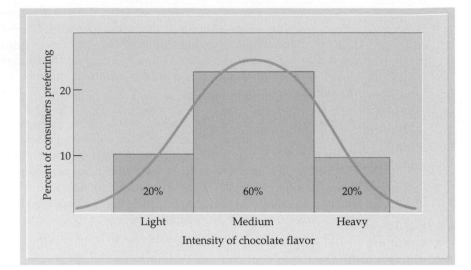

FIGURE 5-3   Customer Preferences for Chocolate Flavoring of Ice Cream

merely duplicating existing characteristics. The "fallacy" is that competition is ignored. Obviously, the "majority" of consumers do not have to prefer a particular product for it to be successful.

APPLYING
. . . to Consumer Food Products Marketing

One product category that illustrates the majority fallacy is spaghetti sauce. A few years ago relatively little product variation existed and most brands imitated the dominant brand Ragu. Ragu occupied a position near the center of a continuum from heavy, rich, spicy sauces on one end to light, thin, and sweet sauces on the other. Hunt tried to exploit differences for spaghetti sauce by introducing its Prima Salsa brand, which was much thicker and zestier than Ragu sauce. Hunt compared its new thick sauce directly with Ragu, using personal testimonials and a heavy schedule of TV and print ads. Prima Salsa's initial success attracted Campbell Soup, which introduced more spaghetti sauce variations under its Prego label. Prego was helped by a *Consumer Reports* article that rated its salt-free flavor as the best sauce available. As a result, Ragu was forced to add a variety of new products of its own. Today Ragu and Prego are continuing to bring out new flavors of spaghetti sauce to appeal to special segments of the market.

Repositioning Strategies

Perceptual maps with dimensions and clusters of customer ideal points are valuable for the management of new and existing products. A frequent problem is deciding whether to reposition a product and in what direction to move. This issue is usually a trade-off between maintaining the benefits of the existing position and possible sales gains associated with new positions. When your current position is weak, it is easier to make a case for repositioning. For example, Miller beer was once sold as the "Champagne of bottled beers" to the high-income, lighter-beer-drinking segment. When Philip Morris bought the brand it had only 3.4 percent of the market and they decided to reposition Miller to appeal to heavier drinking blue-collar buyers. The "Miller Time" campaign featuring working men enjoying a Miller at day's end successfully moved the brand up to 22 percent of the market.

APPLYING
. . . to Consumer Beverages Marketing

Creating Gaps   Repositioning decisions are more difficult when there is something to lose. For example, Chrysler, now Daimler-Chrysler, interpreted the perceptual map shown in Figure 4-5 to suggest that their cars needed a more youthful image. They also concluded that

Plymouth and Dodge needed to move up on the luxury scale. If Chrysler is successful in its efforts to appeal to a more youthful market, then they will give up the conservative older market to Buick and Oldsmobile. Further if Plymouth and Dodge are repositioned as luxury cars, what will Chrysler have to sell to buyers interested in practical low-priced cars? These examples suggest that you have to be sure that repositioning does not create new markets to be exploited by your competition.

In addition, you should realize that a gap in a perceptual map does not necessarily mean that there is an attractive market waiting to be exploited. Customer preferences change over time and a gap may mean that few buyers are currently interested in that combination of product attributes. This suggests that you need to know the number of potential buyers involved before you rush in to fill a "gap" in a perceptual map.

Serving Multiple Segments   Another problem is how to keep one group of customers happy while attracting new segments needed to build future sales. Levi-Strauss's line of casual and dress pants, Dockers and Slates, have sold well, but its blue jeans hit a rough patch. Blue jeans are bought largely by men and Levi's share of men's jeans market dropped from 48 percent to 21 percent in less than a decade. The number of teen boys who cited Levi's as one of their favorite jeans brands dropped from 31 percent to 21 percent in five years. Teens drive fashion trends but that only belatedly seemed to dawn on Levi-Strauss. The company then launched an aggressive series of ads aimed at 15- to 19-year-olds. But Levi's seemed to overcorrect. Its TV commercials were far less mainstream than those of its competitors. Any firm that expects to survive in the long run must find a way to capture a share of the entry-level buyers.

Cannibalism   A common reason for repositioning is a discovery that you have two brands occupying the same location on a perceptual map. This generally leads to an unacceptable level of cannibalism. For example, Procter & Gamble found that customers perceived two of their detergents as being identical. In this particular case, Procter & Gamble dropped one brand rather than attempt repositioning. However, merging Buick and Oldsmobile is not an attractive alternative to General Motors. They have spent millions of dollars establishing name recognition and dealer networks for each of these brands. General Motors is naturally reluctant to throw this money away and they are trying to separate these two cars in the minds of the customer with styling changes and some youth-oriented advertising for Oldsmobile.

SUMMARY

Successful marketing strategies are often based on differentiation, market focus, and lower costs. Firms must identify windows of opportunity and select appropriate attack and defense strategies if they expect to reach organization goals. Measure performance against your corporate mission; this will prevent you from overreacting to competitors.

Strategic marketing involves selecting a target market and positioning one's product relative to competitive products. Various elements of the marketing mix are selected to be consistent with the chosen strategy. This is one of the most fundamental concepts of marketing.

NOTES

1. This section borrows heavily from Geoffrey Easton, "Relationships Among Competitors" in *The Interface of Marketing and Strategy,* in George Day, Barton Weitz, and Robin Wensley, eds. (Greenwich, CT: JAI Press 1990), pp. 57–100.

2. "Who's Who Among Natural Gas Marketers," *The Atlanta Journal-Constitution,* October 4, 1998, p. G2.

3. Michael Kawleski, "Strategic Alliances Can Benefit Many," *Agri Marketing,* Vol. 35, No. 3 (March 1997), p. 14, and Lynn Grooms, "Seed Company Alliances Provide Access Route Genetic Super-highway," *Agri Marketing,* Vol. 35, No. 7 (July/August 1997), pp. 52–55.

4. These steps are from K. Michael Haywood, "Scouting the Competition for Survival and Success," in *Marketing,* A. Dale Timpe, ed. (New York: Facts On File, 1989), pp. 129–141. The many kinds of information you should consider collecting are listed in his Figure 1.

5. W. Chan Kim and Renee Mauborne, "Creating New Market Space, *Harvard Business Review,* Vol. 77, No. 1 (January-February 1999), pp. 83–92.

6. Laurie McGinley, "How Ex-Lax, Trusted for Nearly a Century, Became a Cancer Risk," *Wall Street Journal,* September 26, 1997, pp. A1, A8.

FURTHER READING

Day, George S., and Robin Wensley. "Assessing Advantage: A Framework for Diagnosing Competitive Superiority," *Journal of Marketing,* Vol. 52 (April 1988), pp. 1–20.

Hunt, Shelby D., and Robert M. Morgan. "The Comparative Advantage Theory of Competition," *Journal of Marketing,* Vol. 59, No. 2 (April 1995), pp. 1–15.

REFERENCES

Easton, Geoffrey. "Relationships Among Competitors," in *The Interface of Marketing and Strategy,* George Day, Barton Weitz, and Robin Wensley, eds. Greenwich, CT: JAI Press 1990, pp. 57–100.

Myers, James H. *Segmentation and Positioning for Strategic Marketing Decisions.* Chicago: American Marketing Association, 1996.

Oster, Sharon M. *Competitive Analysis.* New York: Oxford University Press, 1994.

Ramaswamy, Venkatram, Hubert Gatignon, and David Reibstein. "Competitive Marketing Behavior in Industrial Markets," *Journal of Marketing,* Vol. 58, No. 2 (April 1994), pp. 45–55.

Vandenbosch, Mark B. "Confirmatory Compositional Approaches to the Development of Product Spaces," *European Journal of Marketing,* Vol. 30, No. 3, (1996), pp. 23–46.

QUESTIONS

1. The key to dominating the Web is controlling the front door through which users connect to the Internet. The early leaders among the Internet portals were Yahoo! and aol.com. Originally most of the top destinations simply performed search functions but became portal destinations as they added features such as news clips, shopping channels, and travel and financial information. Portals tend to inspire customer loyalty fast because they usually allow their users to tailor site content. The portal strategy is popular because offering a number of features attracts sizable audiences that, in turn, attract large advertising dollars. Portals are potentially a way to make money on the Web. How can General Electric's NBC build Snap.com or Walt Disney build Infoseek into a dominant brand? How can a site without the established awareness of a Yahoo! or without the financial backing of a Disney hope to grab users?

2. W. A. Schmidt is a major manufacturer of custom-built mezzanines and other material handling equipment. A mezzanine creates new floor space in a factory or warehouse by adding a low story of structural steel within an existing higher story. They are engineered for maximum span with minimum obstruction. An example of W. A. Schmidt's material handling equipment is its HF stacking cradle that stores up to four coils of some material on the same floor footprint. The racks adjust to coil diameter when

loaded. The coils are loaded and retrieved from the rack system by overhead cranes with C-hooks. W. A. Schmidt clients include Duracell, Koons Steel, Saks Fifth Avenue, and Volvo. A situation analysis was done to determine what Schmidt's strengths were compared to their competition. The situation analysis revealed that Schmidt is widely recognized as a leader in quality. However, potential customers see Schmidt as a high-priced vendor. Some assume that Schmidt is out of reach. This perception is costing Schmidt the opportunity to even bid on some business. In addition, although Schmidt has a large following of independent, nonexclusive distributors, it wants to boost loyalty among its core distributors. Sketch out a total marketing program to address Schmidt's problems.

3. Software giant SAP AG, maker of the popular R/3 enterprise resource planning (ERP) system, is preparing stand-alone applications that will compete directly with specialty or niche products such as warehousing software. Why is SAP taking on a host of vendors of products ranging from sales force automation applications to advanced planning and optimization systems to business-to-business electronic commerce applications to applications for the management of product data, warehouses, and transportation? How will customers react? How will the niche players react?

4. Comparative advertising is a fact of life in the automobile industry. Nissan Motor Corp. USA ran a commercial that compared its Altima sedan to a Mercedes-Benz. The Altima spot touted Altima's roominess over the Mercedes. It shows the small sedan crashing through a glass display window over a Mercedes, with the words "Mercedes has just been topped." What are the advantages and disadvantages of comparative ads? Assess the Altima commercial.

5. Rob de Zwart, marketing director of Croky Chips, a subsidiary in The Netherlands of United Biscuits, was confronted with a drop in market share of Croky chips from 32 percent in March to 18.5 percent in the fall of the same year. The major cause of this dramatic decrease was the very successful Flippo campaign, launched by competitor Smith Chips in the spring. Flippos are small round plastic discs with Warner Bros. cartoons on them, that are put into the bags with the chips. There are all kinds of different Flippos for example, Regular, Game, Flying, Chester, and Techno Flippos (335 different types in all)—and collecting and exchanging Flippos became a craze among children as well as teenagers and young adults. At the start of the Flippo campaign, Croky did not pay much attention. Flippos were thought to be too "childish" and Croky launched an "infotainment" campaign (trendy texts on chips bags) combined with discounts on CDs. When Croky realized that, against their expectations, the Flippos had actually touched a nerve with teenagers, they had to react. What should Rob de Zwart do?

6. In a survey conducted a month after the 1996 Olympics in Atlanta, consumers were asked to name the official sponsors of the Summer Games. For credit cards, 72 percent named Visa whereas only 54 percent named American Express. Those results were almost identical to a similar survey conducted after the 1994 Winter Olympics, in which 68 percent named Visa and 52 percent named American Express. One might conclude from these surveys that Visa does a better job than American Express in promoting its association with the Olympic Games—except Visa paid $40 million for the exclusive rights to be an official sponsor in the credit card category, while American Express was not an official sponsor of the Olympic Games. How could American Express achieve such a high level of recognition as an official sponsor without being one? Is it fair for companies to associate themselves with the Olympics without being an official sponsor?

7. Airline yield management programs continually change the number and price of seats on future flights so airlines can increase the number of seats sold for each flight and maximize their profits. Some observers suggest that by making their prices instantly available to their competitors, airline yield management programs allow airlines to

engage in a form of price collusion with their competitors. The argument suggests that making prices instantly available to competitors is a form of signaling that discourages price competition and independent price setting. At what point does the exchange of price information among competitors become illegal collusive behavior?

8. The global wholesale vitamin market is dominated by Roche Holdings AG, with about 40 percent of the market, BASF AG, with about 20 percent, and Rhone-Poulenc SA, with about 15 percent. Recently, Swiss vitamin maker Lonza AG plus U.S.-based executives of the Canadian Chinook Group Ltd. and the U.S. firm DuCoa LP pleaded guilty to government charges that they conspired to fix prices in the international sale of vitamins B3, also known as niacin, and B4. Both vitamins are used as nutritional supplements in human and animal products, including livestock feed, baby formula, and daily-vitamin tablets. Lonza agreed to pay a fine of $10.5 million for its role in the price fixing scheme. The U.S. Justice Department is also investigating the pricing activities of the three largest vitamin manufacturers plus at least two Japanese vitamin makers. Why would Lonza Inc. and DuCoa's president, division president, and division vice president and Chinook's vice president of sales and marketing and its U.S. sales manager employ an illegal price-fixing strategy for their vitamins? What are the upsides and downsides of collusion: to the individual? to the firm?

9. Megamergers are creating global oligopolies. What are the advantages and disadvantages of oligopolistic competition from the perspective of business? Consumers? When should government regulators intervene?

10. A national corporation purchased a small Midwestern regional producer of industrial and consumer paper products. The regional producer sold paper towels under the Countess label. As a possible prelude to taking the brand national, 500 Fort Wayne, Indiana, consumers were asked to fill out a questionnaire and to record their purchases for the duration of an 18-week study. The questionnaire, which was completed at the beginning of the study, collected information on: (1) the first brand of paper towels the person could mention, (2) the person's favorite brand, (3) recall of the brand most recently purchased, (4) an evaluation of each brand—with the highest evaluation having an index value of 100, and (5) eleven demographic variables. By the end of the longitudinal panel study, 132 participants had made one or more towel purchases. Persons who claimed to be paper towel users but who did not purchase during this time were dropped from the study. The data are given in file papertoweldat.sav. How does Countess stack up in the marketplace? Is it a strong candidate for being taken national?

6
PRODUCT DEVELOPMENT AND TESTING

> No war, no panic, no bank failure, no strike or fire can so completely and irrevocably destroy a business as a new and better product in the hands of a competitor.
>
> F. RUSSELL BICHOWSKY

INTEGRATING
. . . with
Cross-
Functional
Teams

APPLYING
. . . to
Consumer
Durable
Goods
Marketing

New product development (NPD) is the process of finding ideas for new goods and services and converting them into commercially successful product line additions. In the early 1990s when General Motors was in trouble, they asked a young engineer to design a new car that was bigger on the inside than the Toyota Camry but based on the chassis of the much smaller Chevy Cavalier. The team was given only $1 billion for the project and told the car had to make a healthy profit. The NPD team—including an engineer, an interior designer, and an assistant brand manager—began by dissecting rival cars to set benchmarks for 250 attributes. Then they ran focus groups with customers and hung out in dealerships selling competitive cars. Next they built mockups of the new car's interior and shipped them to focus groups in California. Some Chevy people said that bench seats were preferred over bucket seats by people working out of their cars. However, bench seats flunked with potential buyers and they were dropped. To keep costs down, only two versions of the new car equipped with options they expected customers to order were offered along with one suspension choice and two engines. A name was suggested by the Chevrolet general manager who proposed resurrecting the classic Malibu marque that had been used on 6.5 million cars. The end result of the Malibu NPD project was a car that had the same or more interior space than its competitors, weighed less, got higher gas mileage, was priced hundreds of dollars lower, generated unit profits of $1,000 and was named the *Motor Trend* car of the year in 1997.[1] The Malibu example shows that careful new product development can make companies more successful in the marketplace. The objective of this chapter is to explain each step of the development process from the search for new ideas to the introduction of new products to customers.

WHY DEVELOP NEW PRODUCTS?

The basic reason organizations develop new products is to replace items that have lost favor with customers. Product obsolescence is real and firms need new products to stay alive and prosper. We define new products as goods and services that are basically different from those already marketed by the organization.

New Products Boost Sales and Profits

The introduction of new items helps increase revenues and profits for organizations. A study of the best NPD practices used to introduce more than 11,000 items over a five-year period provides the striking results shown in Figure 6-1. Companies were divided into those with the "best" practices and "the rest." Best companies derived 39 percent of their revenue from new products compared to only 23 percent from the rest. Also best companies had twice the profits from new products as the rest and twice as many of these items were still on the market. The poorer performing firms spent more than 40 percent of their efforts improving old products and tended to ignore cost reductions that could boost profits. Other studies have shown strong positive correlations between research and development (R&D) spending and profits for 24 industries. All of these results demonstrate that NPD is a key factor in the survival and growth of business organizations.

The Product Life Cycle

APPLYING
. . . to
Consumer
Marketing
Business-to-
Business
Marketing

The most important concept supporting NPD activities is the idea that products follow a cycle of birth, growth, and decline. A diagram showing the new product life cycle at Hewlett-Packard Co. is described in Figure 6-2. This chart reveals that new products produce 20 percent of their total revenue the first year they are introduced and 34 percent the second year. In years three through eight, new product sales at Hewlett-Packard drop sharply. Figure 6-2 demonstrates that Hewlett-Packard must continually introduce new items to replace products in decline if they expect to maintain sales and profits. Hewlett-Packard spends about 10 percent of revenues on R&D each year and for the period from 1990–1993 created $13 of new product revenue for each dollar invested in R&D.[2] These results confirm that NPD is a powerful engine for growth at Hewlett-Packard.

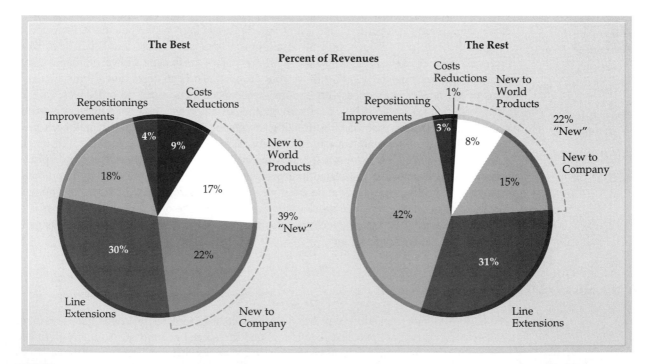

FIGURE 6-1   Innovation Pays Off (From Barton G. Tretheway, "Everything New Is Old Again," *Marketing Management,* **Vol. 7 [Spring 1998], p. 7.)**

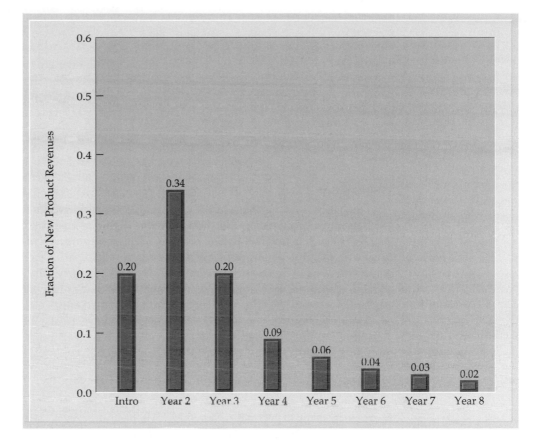

FIGURE 6-2 **The Product Life Cycle at Hewlett-Packard (From Marvin L. Patterson, "From Experience: Linking Product Innovation to Business Growth,"** *Journal of Product Innovation Management,* **Vol. 15 [1998], p. 393.)**

Competitive Obsolescence. Product life cycles, like those shown in Figure 6-2, are becoming shorter in some lines of trade. Competitors have been increasingly quick to copy new items and introduce their own brands at low prices. This can lead to rapid declines in profit margins and market shares for innovators. For example, Johnson & Johnson invented the cardiovascular stent used to open blocked arteries in the heart. A stent is a tiny metal-mesh tube wrapped around a small balloon that is threaded into the heart arteries. At a blockage site, the balloon is inflated to deploy the stent, which is left in place after the balloon is removed. Johnson & Johnson worked for seven years to gain FDA approval and patents for their revolutionary device. Once approved, the new stent racked up sales of $1 billion in 37 months. However, Johnson & Johnson refused to give discounts off the $1,595 price of the stent to catheterization labs purchasing $1 million in stents a year, and they failed to develop longer and more flexible stents requested by doctors. The huge market for stents and the high 80 percent gross margins available, encouraged competitors to develop new designs. Doctors were so upset at Johnson & Johnson's inability to deliver new stents that they lobbied the Food and Drug Administration to expedite approval of competitive designs. When the approval was received, doctors immediately switched to new stents from Guidant Corp and in 45 days Johnson & Johnson's 91 percent market share dropped to only 21 percent. By the end of 1998 Johnson & Johnson estimated stent market share had slipped to only 8 percent.[3] Although Johnson & Johnson has started to bring out new stent designs and offer volume discounts, they will never be able to return to their former position of complete market dominance. This example shows that product life cycles are real and firms that fail to continually innovate can be ruined.

Competition is also shortening product life cycles for calculators, electronic character recognition devices, copiers, and small computers. The model life for fax machines is down to less than four months and for audio components less than six months. Each of these industries has become almost a fashion industry. If the life expectancy of new products continues to decline, firms will need to develop even greater numbers of new items to maintain their market positions.

Chances for Success.   Product development is expensive and you need to understand the chances that new items will succeed. The best product development practices study described in Figure 6-1 found that the most effective firms had 65 percent of new products meet their success criteria compared to only 47 percent in weaker companies.[4] Many new products are lost in the screening stages, and these help account for higher new product failure rates often reported in the trade press. Overall, about one new *idea* in seven is converted into a successful new product. This means that a great deal of money is spent developing products that never reach the marketplace. Research has shown that strength in R&D, engineering, and production helps increase the number of new products. In addition, the average success rate of new products is related to strength in marketing, sales force/distribution, and promotion. These data suggest that most new products succeed and that careful attention to marketing activities can make a difference.

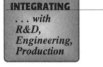

INTEGRATING
. . . *with*
R&D,
Engineering,
Production

SEARCH AND SCREENING

The management of product development has been described as a sequential process that converts ideas into commercially successful product line additions. The procedure is essentially a series of go, no-go decisions in which the best ideas emerge as finished products. Six steps of the product development process are highlighted in Figure 6-3. Product development begins with the search for new product ideas and then moves on to screening, revenue, and cost analysis, followed by development and market testing, and concludes with commercialization. Large numbers of new product ideas are passed into the system at one end, and months or years later, a few successful items reach the market. Ideas that fail to meet development criteria along the way are either dropped or sent back for more testing. The developmental process demands a steady stream of new ideas from which a few choice projects can be selected for more intensive development.

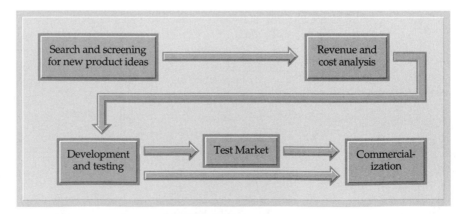

FIGURE 6-3   The Product Development Cycle

Sources of Product Ideas

The most common source of ideas for new products lies within the company itself. A survey revealed that 60 percent of industrial and 46 percent of consumer new product ideas came from the research staff, engineers, salespeople, marketing research personnel, and executives of the firm. Another 26 percent of industrial new product ideas and 30 percent of consumer new product ideas came from users.[5] In addition, consumers are often studied by using depth and focus group interviews to find opportunities for new items in individual product categories. An example showing how a focus group led to new pickle products at Vlasic Foods is described in Marketing in Action box 6-1. Market structure maps such as those discussed in Chapter 4 can reveal gaps that suggest ideas for new products.

Dependence on internally contributed ideas indicates that many firms do not pay enough attention to external sources for new projects. Company-generated ideas seem to gain acceptance easily, and there is a widespread suspicion about products that are "not invented here." An inventor developed a new type of mercury vapor lightbulb that uses much less electricity and lasts considerably longer than incandescent lightbulbs. The inventor took this attractive new product to several lighting companies, but they all turned him away. Apparently, the companies wished to protect their investments in regular lightbulbs and were not interested in gaining access to new technology. Firms that carelessly reject new product ideas that appear promising are likely to suffer in the long run in terms of lost opportunities and reduced market shares.

Good sources of new product ideas also include the U.S. Patent Office, private labs, independent inventors, and university researchers. Some firms have had success by talking to advertising agencies and attending trade shows. For example, U.S. food companies spend less than 1 percent of sales on research and development and they are continually looking outside their own offices for new product ideas. They routinely send teams to the New Products Showcase and Learning Center in Ithaca, New York, to look over an inventory of 60,000 extinct grocery products. Companies pay $750 an hour to search for product ideas that can be revived.[6] American firms also send teams to European trade shows to look at new processes such as one the French have developed to give 30-day shelf life to precooked packaged entrees. Another new idea from Europe vacuums oxygen out of packages to keep baked goods fresher longer. When looking for new products it is best to cast a wide net if you expect to catch any big fish.

Imitation

Rather than create an innovation, a firm may find it expedient to imitate competitive offerings. In the survey mentioned earlier, 27 percent of industrial new product ideas and 38 percent of consumer ideas came from the analysis of competitors. Adapting an existing product created elsewhere is less expensive and time-consuming than creating an innovation.

Even the most innovative firm will not come up with all the new products generated in its industry. Every firm should have a policy to guide its responses to the innovations of competitors. This gives you the advantage of observing the market performance of the innovative new item before launching your own product. Some people believe it is worth spending money on "reverse engineering" to tear apart your competitors' products to gain insights for your copies. Research with automobiles and computers found that reverse engineering of competitors' products tends to reduce the performance benefits to the firm from product development.[7] This suggests that although it is often useful to copy new product ideas from other firms, it may not be productive to spend a lot of time and money on reverse engineering.

APPLYING
. . . to
Consumer
Food
Marketing

INTEGRATING
. . . with
Supplier

MARKETING IN ACTION *6-1*

Vlasic's Hamburger Stackers

Pickle consumption in the United States has been falling 2 percent a year. This has put pressure on the number one pickle packer, Vlasic Foods International, to come up with new products to increase revenues. An idea for a new items surfaced when consumers in focus groups said they hate it when pickles slip out of their hamburgers and sandwiches. A Vlasic product development manager started slicing pickles horizontally into strips and created pickle planks that stayed in sandwiches better than the traditional small round chips. Although Vlasic sold $60 million of these pickle planks the first year, they were not perfect because they contained too much of the soft center seed cavity.

The manager then came up with the idea of creating a new giant pickle chip that would cover the whole surface of the sandwich. These giant chips would need to be cut from bigger pickles than were currently available in America. The manager scoured the world for bigger pickles and found some seeds at a small company in the Netherlands. These seeds produced poorly shaped pickles and it was not until their supplier crossbred them with another variety that Vlasic got a pickle that could be sliced into the desired 3 inch chip. The first year these were planted, hurricanes and insects destroyed all 10 acres of the new plants. Finally in 1998, Vlasic managed to harvest 2,000 bushels of giant pickles despite problems with mildew and the need to hand pick the heavy pickles.

Vlasic introduced the new 3-inch pickles chips as Hamburger Stackers and packed them 12 to a jar. The company is counting on the jumbo pickle chips to deliver at least $20 million in new sales.

— *Firms that push product development come up with new items to expand their markets.*

Source: Vanessa O'Connell, "After Years of Trial and Error, A Pickle Slice That Stays Put," *The Wall Street Journal,* October 6, 1998, p.p. B1, B4.

Courtesy Vlasic Foods International

Acquisition

One of the quickest ways of acquiring new products is to buy other companies that have developed new items. This has the advantages of eliminating all the costs of search, screening, testing, and commercialization, and it involves fewer risks because someone else has

APPLYING
... to
*Consumer
Health and
Beauty Aids
Marketing*

already built up a satisfied group of customers and dealers. Acquisition is common in the drug and consumer products industries. For example, Johnson & Johnson bought the Playtex tampon brand to strengthen its position in the tampon business. Before this acquisition, it was a minor player in the market, with its O.B. tampon holding 9.5 percent of the U.S. market. Despite considerable effort, Johnson & Johnson has been unable to increase the market share of the O.B. brand. Although such tampons are big sellers in Europe, U.S. women prefer tampons with applicators. By purchasing the Playtex brand, Johnson & Johnson grabbed an additional 30 percent of the market and is now second to the market leader, Tambrands.

The main problems with this approach to product development are finding available brands to acquire and paying the sometimes high asking prices. Johnson & Johnson paid $726 million for Playtex tampons, and had to take Playtex nursers, gloves, and Tek toothbrushes as well. Some analysts believe that today it is much easier to buy into a market than to try to create your own brands.

Licensing of New Products

Obtaining new product ideas through licensing offers several advantages for firms that wish to avoid the high cost of product development yet lack enthusiasm for acquiring going concerns. Probably the most important attraction is that there are more firms willing to license their ideas than there are firms willing to sell successful new products. Also, most license agreements involve the payment of royalties on a unit or percentage of sales basis so that initial costs are low and subsequent payments are due only when the product is actually sold. Furthermore, it is unusual for royalties paid on products obtained by licenses to exceed the savings achieved in R&D expenses. Licensing can also reduce lead time compared with the months or years that may be required to develop similar products in the company's own laboratories.

Screening Procedures

Surveys have shown that 76 percent of firms screen new product concepts, an activity that takes about three months (Table 6-1). The objective of screening is to eliminate new product ideas that are inconsistent with the goals or resources of the firm. Screening can be viewed as a filtering process. First, a quick judgment is made on whether the idea is compatible with the company's plans, technical skills, and financial capabilities. This evaluation is made by knowledgeable managers and staff specialists who weed out the obviously unsuitable ideas so that valuable resources will not be wasted reviewing impractical proposals. The second phase of the new product screening process is more detailed and is designed to establish a ranking for the remaining ideas. Rankings are based on an evaluation of factors relevant for product development in a particular firm. A checklist shows the relative importance of the criteria and combines the factor evaluations into a single index number for each product. The main value of a new product index is its ability to separate quickly the best proposals so that priorities can be established for succeeding stages of development. The main problem with such scoring models is that they rely on the subjective ratings of managers; hence, data input may not be very reliable.

A better scoring model would take into account the information available in the success or failure of a large number of past new product launches. One such model is *New-Prod,* a software-based new product screening, evaluation, and diagnostic tool. NewProd was developed from a statistical analysis of 200 projects from 100 companies. Managers were asked to rate their own project on 50 screening criteria. A regression was run relating these dimensions to degree of commercial success. Eight factors linked to product outcomes included product superiority, compatibility, market need, economic advantage,

TABLE 6-1   NPD Activities and Time Spent

Activity	Percent Using	Months Spent
Concept search Includes brainstorming and other creativity-stimulating techniques, preliminary discussions about the product's design, and identifying new product opportunities.	89.9	3.5
Concept screening May include scoring and ranking concepts according to some criteria and eliminating unsuitable concepts.	76.2	3.0
Concept testing Covers preliminary market research to determine market need, niche, and attractiveness.	80.4	3.6
Business analysis An evaluation of the product concept in financial terms as a business proposition.	89.4	2.6
Product development Technical work to convert a concept into a working model.	98.9	14.4
Product use testing, field testing, market testing Offering the product to a preselected group of potential buyers to determine its suitability and/or marketability.	86.8	6.0
Commercialization Launching the new product into full-scale product and sales.	96.3	6.5

Source: Alan L. Page, "Assessing New Product Development Practices and Performance: Establishing Crucial Norms," *Journal of Product Innovation Management,* Vol. 10, No. 4 (September 1993), p. 281.

newness to the firm (negative), technical compatibility, market competitiveness (negative), and size of market. The model is used to predict project ratings from new product screening questions.

NewProd studies in North America, the Netherlands, and Scandinavia have shown correct predictions for 75 to 85 percent of the new product studied.[8] For example, Procter & Gamble used a version of NewProd to assess 60 projects. Of the projects that NewProd predicted to be successes, 80 percent succeeded in test market and 60 percent were rated as financial successes when expanded nationally. On the other hand, of those it predicted to be failures, 25 percent were successful in test market but only 5 percent were financially successful when expanded nationally. NewProd predicts success and failure before development even begins.

REVENUE AND COST ANALYSIS

The business analysis phase of the product development cycle includes a detailed study of the potential profitability of new product ideas. The objective is to eliminate marginal ventures before extensive development and market testing expenses are incurred. An important first step is to measure market potential.

Market Potential

Market potential represents the maximum sales in dollars or units that can be obtained by an industry for a new product with a specified marketing effort. A simple way to estimate potential is as follows:

$$MP = N \times P \times Q \qquad\qquad (6.1)$$

where

    MP = market potential
    N = number of possible buyers
    P = average selling price
    Q = average number purchased by each buyer

APPLYING
. . . to
Consumer
Semi-Durable
Goods
Marketing

For example, digital video disk (DVD) players were first introduced in March of 1997 and by the end of 1998, one million Americans owned a player. Each DVD holds a recording of one movie and sells for about $20. Since each player owner purchases seven disks a year, the total DVD market potential in 1999 would be $140 million (1,000,000 × $20 × 7). Each film studio could then estimate their market share and multiply it times market potential to get their own revenue projection for DVDs. The success of this approach depends on the accuracy of your data and your assumptions. For example, the purchase rate *(Q)* for DVDs will change with disposable income, popularity of films released for DVDs in a season, and the availability of alternative video formats. Also the number of potential buyers *(N)* is often hard to determine. Although there were one million DVD players in homes at the beginning of 1999, more would be sold during the year and the estimate for DVDs would have to be adjusted upward to reflect this expected increase in the number of players.

Chain ratio procedures provide another way to measure market potential. This approach calculates potential by applying a series of ratios to an aggregate measure of demand. A firm could start with population figures and multiply by ratios that discard nonusing segments of the market. For example, a firm estimated demand for a new replacement thermostat by noting there were 32.5 million year-round housing units in populated colder areas of the country. This number was then adjusted by the proportion of units that were owner occupied (62 percent) and the number of homeowners in the relevant age group (78 percent). Next they adjusted for buyers with sufficient income (55 percent) and for units that had central thermostats (67 percent). The final calculation (32.5 × .62 × .78 × .55 × .67) gave a total market potential of 5.7 million units. If the company was able to sell 4 percent of these homeowners their new $40 thermostat, they would generate revenues of $9.1 million (5,700,000 × .04 × $40).

Market potentials for new business products can be estimated using data made available through the U.S. Census of Manufacturers. The government surveys all manufacturers every five years and collects information on the number of firms in Standard Industrial Classifications (SIC), value of shipments, number of production workers, and other data. With the SIC buildup method, market potentials are derived by adding up the number of firms or workers in relevant SIC categories and then converting them to dollar forecasts. If a firm knows how many machines a typical firm uses, market potentials for new items can be derived by multiplying usage rates times the number of firms reported in the Census of Manufacturers. Estimates of potential sales for an individual company would be obtained by multiplying by the firm's current market share and the expected unit price of the item.

Estimating Costs and Profits

INTEGRATING
. . . with
Accounting,
Production

Predicting the costs to build products before they are introduced is a difficult but essential part of the developmental process. Sometimes firms can get an idea on costs from similar products they already make or items sold by competitors. For example, when Johnson & Johnson was developing their coronary stent mentioned earlier, they knew that standard balloon catheters used to open clogged heart arteries in a procedure called an angioplasty were selling for a few hundred dollars each. This meant that they would be able to wrap their metal-mesh stent around a standard balloon catheter for variable costs of about $100. Since they planned to sell their stents for $1,595, they would have $1,495 per unit to cover development costs, new production facilities, advertising and selling expenses, overhead, and profits. Total profits would depend, of course, on the number of units they would be able to sell. J&J knew that 400,000 angioplasties were performed in the United States each year and that 30 percent failed within six months, leading to further treatment. In addition, in five percent of angioplasties, the vessel snaps shut abruptly within minutes or a few days, prompting a life-threatening emergency coronary artery bypass operation costing $40,000 or more. Given that 120,000 angioplasties fail each year, that J&J's stent lasted longer than an angioplasty, was safer, and was less expensive than bypass surgery, J&J might be able to sell 100,000 stents the first year they were introduced. With an anticipated gross margin of $1,495 per unit, J&J could generate a gross profit of $149,500,000 on their new product. Thus J&J's revenue and cost analysis for stents was very encouraging and explains why J&J labored for seven years to show that they worked properly and gain regulatory approval for their sale. As it turned out stents were used in 80 percent of angioplasty procedures, J&J's estimates of sales were low, and stents were much more profitable than they expected.

DEVELOPMENT AND TESTING

Development and testing are concerned with establishing physical characteristics for new goods and services that are acceptable to customers. The objective is to convert ideas into actual products that are safe, provide customer benefits, and can be manufactured economically by the firm. Usually, development includes concept testing, consumer preference tests, laboratory evaluations, use tests, and pilot plant operations.

Concept Testing

The first step in the development process often includes measuring customers' reactions to descriptions of new products. Promising ideas are converted into concept statements, which are printed on cards and shown to small focus groups of customers. Sometimes pictures or preliminary models of the product are included, together with the written descriptions. Participants are asked if they would buy the item and to give reasons for their decisions. Modifications are then made in the product concept, and the revised statement is tested with another group of customers. When the product concept appears well defined in terms of customer acceptance, a real product is developed to go along with the concept. An example of how Ford and General Motors suffered when concept test data were poorly interpreted is described in Marketing in Action box 6-2.

Product Design

The success of new products is often related to how well they are designed. Attractive products catch the attention of customers, and good design makes items easier to use. In addition, products should be designed so that they are easy to manufacture. Gillette's design of its new triple-blade MACH3 razor shows the importance of careful attention to product features. The company wanted to improve on its excellent double-blade razor the Sensor Excel. First, Gillette's designers positioned three blades so that each one was progressively nearer the face. This allowed each blade to shave closer than the one before and reduced skin irritation. The designers also moved the pivot point to increase the cartridge's stability. In addition, the blue lubricating strip was designed to fade over time to indicate wear. Another design change involved coating the blades with a microscopic layer of carbon to make the edge thinner and stronger. As many as 18 percent of Sensor Excel users clip on new razor cartridges upside down. To prevent this problem, Gillette designed the MACH3 with a new single point docking system. These design improvements were expensive and required

MARKETING IN ACTION 6-2

How Many Doors Are Enough?

Chrysler introduced the first minivan equipped with two front doors and one sliding door on the right side to simplify loading. When Ford brought out its new Windstar van in 1995 to compete with Chrysler, it also had three doors as only a third of potential minivan buyers wanted a fourth door. Chrysler saw this one third as a market opportunity and introduced a new van in 1996 with a sliding door on the driver's side. Chrysler's minivan sales boomed and Windstar's sales were badly hurt by the absence of a second sliding door. It took Ford four years and $560 million to add a fourth door to the Windstar. Meanwhile Chrysler sold 90 percent of its minivans with two sliding doors and solidified its hold on the number one position in this market.

Also early in 1998, Chrysler was first to offer four doors on hot selling extended cab pickup trucks. The new Dodge Ram Quad Cab was a runaway hit. Ford was not far behind this time and was the first to offer four doors on its entire line of extended cab pickup trucks in 1998. By the fall of 1998, 70 percent of large pickup trucks were delivered with four doors. General Motors, however, was late to the four-door party. They introduced major revisions to their 11-year-old Silverado and Sierra full-sized pickup trucks in the fall of 1998 with only three doors available for its extended cab trucks. Full-sized pickup trucks account for $14 billion of its annual sales and a huge chunk of GM's North American profits. Since GM loses money on many of the cars it sells, the new Silverado and its cousins needed to be hits for GM to deliver on promises to restless shareholders. GM did not introduce four-door extended cab pickups until the 2000 models were introduced in the fall of 1999. This inability to see the allure of four doors in extended cab trucks was a major blunder in its new product development efforts.

— *Failure to see major changes in consumer preferences can lead to serious NPD problems.*

Source: Donald W. Nauss, "Extra Door Proved Van Marketing Marvel," *Herald Times,* August 9, 1998, p. D1, and Joseph B. White, "GM Set to Launch New Silverado Pickup, Taking Aim at Ford's Top-Selling F-Series," *The Wall Street Journal,* October 8, 1998, p. B12.

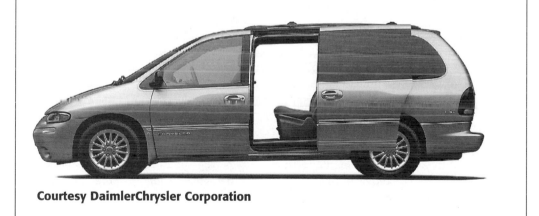

Courtesy DaimlerChrysler Corporation

Gillette to devise new continuous-assembly machinery to build the cartridges at a rate of 600 a minute. The total cost of the design innovations to bring the MACH3 to market was $750 million.[9] This example shows that creative product design is essential if you want to gain competitive advantages in the marketplace.

Preference Tests

Preference tests are employed to compare reactions to different product attributes or quality levels. Consumers usually are given two samples of the product with different characteristics to taste or use, and are then asked which they prefer and why. The idea is to isolate the most desirable characteristics and quality levels so that they can be built into the new product.

A variety of methods has been developed to identify product features that are important to consumers. Perhaps the simplest approach is to interview potential customers and ask them to rate product features on a scale from 1 (unimportant) to 5 (very important). This makes it possible to compare the relative values of product attributes and to construct distributions of customer preferences. Another method submits a full range of sample products to groups of consumers, using a forced-choice, paired-comparison technique. Whatever the method employed, marketing managers need accurate preference data so that they can set product specifications to achieve the best possible market positions.

When Gillette ran consumer preference tests between its old Sensor Excel and prototypes of its new MACH3 razors, men preferred MACH3 by nearly 2 to 1 over Sensor Excel. However, when *Consumer Reports* magazine tested the two products in homes with its own panel of men after the product had been introduced, preferences were decidedly different.[10] Although MACH3 received high marks for closeness of shave, ease of cleaning, lack of drag, and preventing cuts, so did the Sensor Excel. Some *Consumer Reports* panel members found it difficult or impossible to shave under their noses with the MACH3 because of its big head. Others found it tricky to trim sideburns or a beard because it is hard to tell where the blades meet the face. These deficiencies may explain why the Sensor Excel was voted the best overall razor in the *Consumer Reports* preference test. This raises the question of why the Gillette preference test failed to uncover MACH3's inability to shave under the nose and trim sideburns. Was their preference test poorly designed or did they just ignore these problems in their haste to get the new three-blade razor to market? The MACH3 example shows that careful product testing can be critical to new product success.

Use Tests

Once you have a viable product concept and a set of specifications, the next step in the development process is to use test samples of the product to see if they meet the needs of the customer. Usually, this is done through a combination of laboratory and field testing. Lab tests offer the advantage of controlled conditions, and they can often simulate usage of the product and obtain results faster than field trials can. Car doors, for example, can be slammed thousands of times in the lab to see if they are designed to last the lifetime of the automobile. Despite these advantages, laboratory tests are artificial, and most new products are also subjected to lengthy testing by potential customers.

Customer-use tests are designed to determine how a product performs under the realistic conditions encountered in the home or factory. General Electric, for example, tested its electric slicing knife among 800 persons in 26 different cities before introducing it to the marketplace. In another case, a food manufacturer offered 738 women from four cities sample bottles of a new pourable mayonnaise. After 10 days, personal interviews were conducted to gauge customer reactions and to give the women a chance to purchase some of the product at the regular price. Women who bought samples of the new pourable mayonnaise were contacted three additional times to see whether they wanted more of the item. In addition, the respondents were asked to keep a diary to show how they used the product. This research indicated that although consumers liked pourable mayonnaise, they tended to use it as a liquid salad dressing rather than as a mayonnaise. Thus, the use test suggested that some changes were needed in packaging and promotional appeals if the firm expected the item to compete with more traditional mayonnaise products.

Selecting a Name

New products and services are named so that they can be easily identified and promoted to consumer and industrial buyers. The best names tend to be short, distinctive, and easy to pronounce and remember. Also, desirable names often suggest action (i.e., Drano, Sinex, U-Haul).

Suggestions for names are frequently provided by advertising agencies that write promotional material for the product and by computers programmed to make up nonsense words. Sometimes consumers are interviewed to find out what images are associated with prospective brand names and to measure preferences for alternative names. Words that are made up, such as the Exxon name adopted by Standard Oil of New Jersey, are likely to have fewer negative connotations than words that are already in use. Moreover, fanciful words with no preexisting meaning but created for a specific product have the most legal protection. Some examples of the selection of car names are presented in Marketing in Action box 6-3.

A growing problem with naming new products is that it seems that most of the good names have already been trademarked by other firms. For example, a California automobile security firm challenged Chrysler Corporation over the name Viper. Directed Electronics, Inc. owned a trademark for a line of automobile security alarm systems before Dodge claimed it for its muscle car. The two companies reached an out-of-court settlement, agreeing to coexist peacefully.

Names you select do not have to be spelled the same way to cause problems. Toyota coined the word *Lexus* as a play on the word *luxurious* for a new line of high-priced sedans. However, Mead Corporation thought the name had infringed its trademarked Lexis name for computer database systems. Mead won the first round by getting an injunction that prevented Toyota from advertising its new cars. This action hurt Toyota and slowed down the introduction of the vehicle. Toyota appealed and had the initial ruling reversed. These examples show that you have to be careful with names to avoid lawsuits and delays in getting products to market.

Sometimes brand names become so popular they are used by the public to describe a whole class of products (e.g., Scotch Tape). When this occurs, the manufacturer can lose the rights to the name, as happened in the case of *aspirin* and *escalator*. One way to avoid this problem is to insert the word *brand* after the name, as in Scotch Brand Cellophane Tape, to show that the word Scotch is not a generic term.

Packaging

The main concern in designing packages for new products is to protect the merchandise on its journey from the factory to the customer. This is particularly true for industrial goods and appliances whose sales are made from display models. When consumers select products from store shelves, however, packaging becomes an important information and promotional tool. Sales are enhanced by packages that are visible, informative, emotionally appealing, and workable.

An example of how user-friendly packaging can help a new product succeed is provided by Procter & Gamble's Helidac ulcer treatment. Ulcers are caused by bacteria and are treated with a combination of antacids and antibiotics. P&G's treatment program requires patients to take 224 tablets representing three types of drugs over a two-week period. Helidac users have to take four pills every six hours. Missing even a few pills can sharply reduce the cocktail's success rate. P&G needed a package that would remind patients to take their pills at the right time. They came up with a blister pack design that held one day's pills and could be easily slipped into a pocket or purse (Figure 6-4). The blister card was divided into four perforated squares, one for each six-hour period labeled "breakfast," "lunch," "dinner," and "bedtime." The blister cards are packed in a box that is printed with a simple 14-word set of instructions accompanied by three drawings. Compliance instructions become symbols such as a wineglass in a red circle with a line through them in a glossy 20-page booklet that was placed in the box. To remind people to take their pills, P&G gave patients a sheet

MARKETING IN ACTION 6-3

What's in a Name?

What's in a name? is a time-consuming and costly question. Selecting, researching, and legally claiming a name, called a *marque,* for a new automobile can cost as much as $200,000. Here is how some cars got their names:

- *Acura:* A computer-generated name, or neologism, that doesn't mean anything but connotes precision. Created with the understanding that one of Honda's desired hallmarks for the brand was precise engineering.

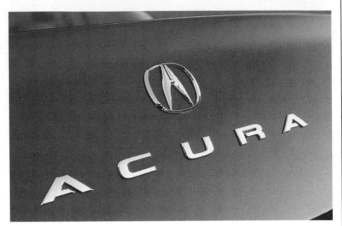

Courtesy American Honda Motor Co., Inc.

- *Altima:* A neologism that hints at ultimate or best. Replaced the Stanza, a name that never caught on with the public in a decade of use.
- *Geo:* A morpheme—the smallest meaningful language unit—that means world in many languages. Used for a lineup of small vehicles sold in Chevrolet dealerships.
- *Mitsubishi:* Means three pebbles in Japanese, but the company portrayed it as three diamonds, which is Mitsubishi's logo.
- *Mondeo:* Means world in Italian. Ford's "world car" designed and engineered in North America and Europe for sale on both continents.
- *Taurus:* The vice president of Ford car product development and one of his top engineers determined that both their wives were born under the Taurus sign of the Zodiac. It was the project code name and eventually became the name of the car.
- *Windstar:* Ford's successor to its Aerostar minivan. The goal was to keep a family relationship with the Aerostar while being different enough to persuade buyers that it was a new vehicle.

Before Villager was picked as the name for Mercury's minivan, the name Columbia was a finalist. Mercury liked the name because of the symbolism of the space shuttle. It was scrapped when consumer research suggested a link with drugs, as in Colombia's cocaine trade.

— *It is very difficult to find a name that is crisp, appropriate, inoffensive, and not owned by someone else.*

Source: Alan L. Adler, "Marque of a Winner," *Atlanta Constitution,* May 7, 1993, pp. S1, S6.

of four stickers decorated with balloons to affix to a visible spot wherever they happened to be when it's time to take their pills. To provide extra motivation, P&G included a set of daily affirmation cards in the box of pills. The cards carry pithy slogans that can be peeled off to mark the passage of each treatment day; day 1 says "let's get started." P&G's creative use of packaging not only helped patients to take their pills correctly, but it also encouraged doctors to prescribe Helidac because the packaging made ulcer cures more likely.[11]

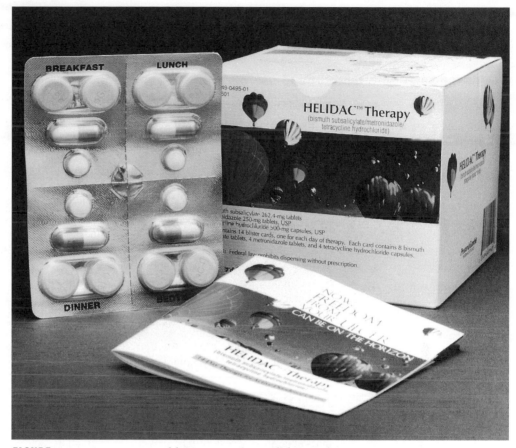

FIGURE 6-4   Procter & Gamble's Innovative Helidac Package.

Good packaging helps move consumer products off store shelves because items with high *visibility* are easier to see. Designs with good informational value tell the consumer at a glance what the package contains. In addition, packages are required by U.S. law to provide information on food additives, flammable materials, net weight, name of the manufacturer or distributor, and other factors. In the United States, the Fair Packaging and Labeling Act also has provisions designed to help standardize package sizes and make comparative shopping easier for the consumer.

Workability in packaging means that the container not only protects the product but is also easy to open and reclose, is readily stored, and has utility for secondary uses once the product is used up. Examples of package designs that have these characteristics include tear-top pudding cups, reclosable pop bottles, and the drinking mugs used to hold margarine. The pump dispenser, aseptic packaging, squeezable and recappable bottles, ultralight plastic, and plastic pouches are consumer packaging approaches that have combined convenience with cost effectiveness. The global marketplace is a good source of innovative designs.

Simulation Tests

Once the basic dimensions of a new product have been established, marketing executives often forecast future sales levels to see whether a project should be continued. The idea is to obtain some customer reactions to the new item without incurring the cost and publicity associated with a full market test. These projections are usually based on concept and product tests, historical data regressions, laboratory test markets, controlled store tests, and sales wave experiments.

Projecting Sales with Concept and Use Tests

With this approach, customers are presented with the idea or physical product, and sales are estimated from purchase intentions. An estimate of first-year trials is obtained by multiplying the percentage of prospective buyers who say that they "definitely will buy" by the percentage incidence of prospective buyers in the population. General Foods, in testing a frozen vegetable line, found that 21 percent of its sample of prepared-vegetable users would definitely buy. The prepared-vegetable segment was thought to represent 50 percent of the total population. The estimate of first-year trials was then calculated as 10.5 ($0.21 \times 0.50 \times 100\%$) percent.[12] This score was compared with data for previous vegetable products. Repeat purchases were estimated using concept fulfillment scores and posttrial attitude scores. This method does a fairly good job of predicting trials for product extensions, but it is not as accurate for repeat purchases of more innovative items.

Computer models have been developed to integrate information from concept tests and other custom marketing research with information from secondary source materials, related product experiences, and informed judgments to make new product forecasts. One such model, called NEWS/Planner, forecasts consumer awareness, trial, repeat purchase, usage, sales, and market share. The model was developed for the clients of a leading advertising agency, BBDO. A more widely available model is Burke's BASES.

Projecting Sales from Historical Data

Market response can also be simulated using *historical data regressions.* Equations are constructed that relate the success of past new products to such factors as category penetration, promotional spending, relative price, and distribution. Once an equation is derived based on past experience, values are estimated for the predictor variables for the new item and plugged into the regression equation. The regression procedure works well in predicting trial but is not as accurate for items that fail to fit existing product categories. Some marketers believe that even a small amount of consumer research data collected for the new brand will lead to more insight and thus better new product decisions than will data collected on other brands.

Laboratory Test Markets

Laboratory test markets expose consumers to commercials for new and existing products and then allow them to make purchases from the product category in a simulated store. The new item is then taken home and used, and a follow-up interview measures satisfaction and repurchase intent. Frequently, repeat purchases are measured by offering consumers a chance to buy the product again after initial home placement. Although the exposure to ads and the store purchases are somewhat artificial, the method has proved to be a quick, inexpensive, and fairly accurate predictor of future sales levels. The method might not work well for highly seasonal products, emerging ill-defined categories, or therapeutic products for infrequent symptoms. Even so, Johnson & Johnson ran a test market simulation of Sundown Sunscreen that proved to be within 5 percent of its equilibrium market share in a concurrent test market.

A computer model called ASSESSOR combines executive judgments on marketing strategy with laboratory data using preference and trial and repeat purchase models of behavior. Although this model has proved to be an accurate predictor of market shares, the method can be used only when new brands seek to enter well-defined product categories. Situations in which innovative products create product categories, or in which products require long periods of usage before benefits are realized, are best evaluated by using extended sales wave tests or regular test markets.

Sales Wave Tests

Product adoption and purchase frequency can also be estimated by using *sales wave* experiments. This approach measures repeat purchase behavior by observing a sample of consumers who receive the new product through a home placement and then are offered a series of opportunities to purchase it at a special price. Forcing the consumer to pay for repeat purchases on several occasions (four to six) simulates the wear-out and adoption process that normally occurs in the marketplace. An advantage of sales wave experiments is that they can be used to forecast performance of category-creating new products. The main problem with these experiments is that they take more time and are more expensive than the other methods that have been discussed. Also, the continual recontact with the customer cannot be duplicated in the marketplace with normal advertising programs.

The market simulation procedures that we have discussed share several advantages that have made them widely used by marketing managers. First, they allow you keep the existence and the special features of new products secret from your competitors. This provides an element of surprise and often allows you to grab and keep a larger share of the market. Second, these simulations take less time to run than traditional test markets, and thus you can get products to the market faster. Third, market simulations are cheaper, and they allow you to develop more new product ideas.

TEST MARKETING

Test marketing is an optional phase of the product development process (Figure 6-2) that involves placing products in selected stores and measuring customer purchase rates in response to promotional activities. It is most often used when new products are radically different and companies do not know how to promote them or whether customers will buy them. The mock fat olestra, one of most controversial food additives ever, provides a good example (Marketing in Action box 6-4). The main drawbacks of test marketing are high costs, delayed introductions, and field tests, which give competitors a chance to steal your ideas. Gillette, for example, did not test market its new MACH3 three-bladed razor because it did not want to reveal the design to its competitors. Also high tooling costs make it impractical to test market appliances, automobiles, and many industrial products. Industrial manufacturers work closely with their customers and rely on feedback from use tests to determine when a new product is ready for national distribution.

Test Procedures

A first step in designing a test market is selecting a representative group of test cities. One rule of thumb is that two or more test areas with a minimum of three percent of all households are needed for national projectability. The objective is to find stable communities in which key demographic statistics are typical of the anticipated buyers of the product. Test cities must also have cooperative merchants and good media coverage to facilitate promotional activities. In addition, test cities should be isolated from each other so that promotional campaigns run in one city do not influence sales in other test areas. The three best-matched markets in terms of demographic profiles, media coverage, and market isolation are reputed to be Erie, Pennsylvania; Fort Wayne, Indiana; and Tucson, Arizona.

MARKETING IN ACTION *6-4*

Assessing Olestra's High Price and Side Effects

Marion, Indiana, is best known as the birthplace of actor James Dean. However, it temporarily has become the world's fake-fat capital. Every product made with Procter & Gamble's mock fat, olestra, is for sale. In addition to P&G, Frito-Lay and Nabisco are test marketing chips and crackers made with the fat substitute. Almost every grocer in Marion carries the chips and crackers. Purchases are recorded by scanners so marketers can track virtually every bag sold. Even Marion General Hospital hasn't been overlooked. Frito-Lay's olestra chips are sold in its cafeteria. How this community of 32,000 and other test cities react could determine the additive's fate.

The residents of Marion closely reflect the nation. The median household income in North Marion is $37,396 versus $38,783 nationally. The town's workforce is almost evenly split between white and blue collar. Some 42 ethnic nationalities are said to live in the area.

Consumers have been given every reason to "just say no" to olestra. First, products made with olestra are pricey. Chips with it cost about 40 percent more than regular chips—in part because P&G believes that consumers will pay a premium to keep pounds off. Chips and crackers made with olestra contain virtually no fat and about half the calories of regular salty snacks. Second, olestra is saddled with an ugly image problem. Products made from it must display the Food and Drug Administration warning: "Olestra may cause abdominal cramping and loose stools." P&G, however, has worked hard to convince consumers that olestra will not make them sick.

P&G is promoting olestra's benefits and touting it in test markets. P&G spent about $5 million in these markets to create an image for olestra that makes it sound as natural as the soybeans from which it often comes. P&G is going door to door to distribute thousands of cans of Fat Free Pringles. Nearly one-quarter of the population of central Indiana soon will have tried Fat Free Pringles. Convinced that women make up the key market, Nabisco purchased regional ads for Fat-Free Ritz in most major women's magazines sold in Marion. P&G estimates that more than 15 million one-ounce servings of olestra-containing chips and crackers were sold in the past 15 months in test cities. It appears nothing can stop olestra.

— *Test markets can show if consumers are willing to pay for a product's perceived benefits.*

Source: Bruce Horovitz, "Fake Fat's Big Test: Olestra," *USA Today,* June 19, 1997, pp. B1, B2.

Limitations of Test Markets

The most serious drawbacks of test marketing are that it is expensive and potential sales are lost because of delays in getting the product to the marketplace. In addition, it is difficult to interpret sales results because the products are new, and there are no standards of performance that can be used for comparison. Except for situations where sales are unusually high or low, test results may simply reflect the basic uncertainty that prevailed when the study was initiated. In addition, the small number of test cities used and the artificial nature of the testing process make it risky to project results into national sales figures. A compounding factor is the realization that some products succeed in test markets and then fail when introduced nationally, and vice versa.

For example, Holly Farms developed a roasted chicken to appeal to busy customers. This convenient precooked product scored well in a year of test marketing. Holly Farms found that 22 percent of Atlanta women had tried the roasted chicken and 90 percent said they would buy it again. Based on these enthusiastic results, Holly Farms built a $20 million plant to produce the chickens and spent $14 million in advertising to gain national distribution. Despite strong customer acceptance, the national rollout did not do well and the roasted chickens gained distribution in only 50 percent of U.S. stores. Holly Farms found that poor sales were due to the short (14-day) shelf life of the product and to the fact that it took up to nine days to get the chickens to the stores. Although grocery buyers described the product as outstanding, they were not reordering because of the limited time they had to sell it.

An even more insidious problem is the response that competitors can make to test market activity. One possibility is a direct attempt to sabotage the test by introducing price cuts or coupons that upset normal sales patterns. A more likely reaction is that competitors will audit your test markets and use the results to develop their own product. For example, a health and beauty aids firm developed a deodorant containing baking soda. A competitor observed the product in the test market and was able to create and roll out its own version of the deodorant nationally before the first firm completed its testing. To add insult to injury, the second firm successfully sued the product's originator for copyright infringement when it launched its deodorant nationally! The moral of the story is that firms that allow easily copied items to languish in test markets may find that competitors have stolen their ideas, their advertising copy, and their markets.

Test markets are also inappropriate for most industrial products and for items that require extensive tooling and unique production equipment. It is simply too expensive to test-market lift trucks, automobiles, and large appliances; alternative measures of customer acceptance must be developed for these items. One possibility is to prepare some test models and introduce them at trade shows. Chrysler's Viper, Prowler and Volkswagen's revitalized Beetle all started out as show cars and were later successfully introduced as the result of enthusiastic consumer responses from trade shows. Another approach is to try out new products with regional introductions. This involves promoting and selling the product in a few markets and then expanding distribution if the product is successful. Although regional introductions are more expensive than test markets, this method is less expensive than introducing a product nationally. Also, if successful items are moved quickly from regional to national distribution, competitive responses are likely to be weak and ineffectual.

Remember that test marketing is not a cure-all for product development problems. It is simply one of many ways to gather data on new items.

COMMERCIALIZATION

The last step in the product development process is the introduction of new items to the dealers and then to the ultimate buyers of the product. The objective of *commercialization* is to get the dealers to stock the item and persuade the ultimate consumer to purchase it for the first time. Previous stages have eliminated undesirable projects and have established the specifications, prices, and promotional arrangements most desirable for the new venture. Now you must weld these elements into a new product introduction plan that will achieve your objectives. Commercialization is concerned with implementing this plan.

The Importance of Timing

The success or failure of many products depends on when the product is introduced. Conventional wisdom suggests you should be first with new products to get the early adopters and establish a dominant market position. For example, Chrysler was first to sell minivans and they are still number one in this market. However, research has shown that sometimes the first to enter a market is the most successful and on other occasions late entrants dominate. A diagram showing the relationship between time of introduction and product performance of personal digital assistants (PDA) is provided in Figure 6-5. Personal digital assistants are small hand-held electronic devices that allow users to record notes and memos, organize appointments, and communicate with others. Most PDAs weigh about a pound and measure 5 by 7 inches. The three earliest entries to the market were the PenPad manufactured by Armstrad, the Newton made by Apple/Sharp, and the Zoomer produced by Tandy/Casio. These three PDAs were the smallest, cheapest ($700), and were targeted at a broad consumer market. The three late entrants included

APPLYING
...to
Durable
Goods
Marketing

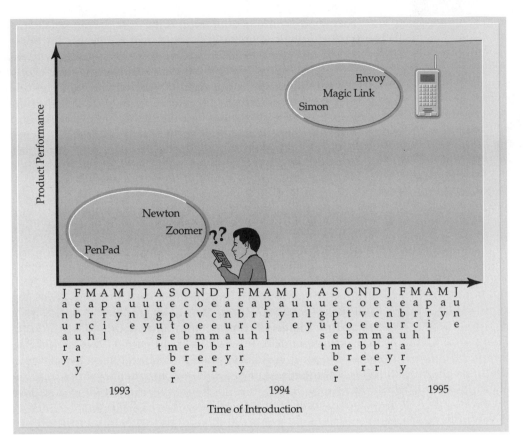

FIGURE 6-5   Relationship Between Time of Introduction and Product Performance (From Barry L. Bayus, Sanjay Jain, and Ambar G. Rao, "Too Little, Too Early: Introduction Timing and New Product Performance in the Personal Digital Assistant Industry," *Journal of Marketing Research,* **Vol. 34 [February 1997], p. 54.)**

the Simon developed by BellSouth, Magic Link designed by Sony, and Motorola's Envoy. These products were larger, heavier, and had some attractive additional features. They allowed the use of spreadsheets, word processing, pocket Quicken, and were equipped with fax/modems, fax receive, and two-way wireless. The late entrants cost a little more ($1,000) and were targeted at businesspeople. The data in Figure 6-5 show that PDAs like the Newton offered too little and reached the market too early to be successful. Products that came on the market later and offered more useful software and communications features like the Motorola Envoy prospered.

Although a few *market pioneers,* such as Coca-Cola, are long-lived market-share leaders, the first firm to sell in a new product category usually does not maintain this leadership very long—about five years. The firm known as the *early leader* (that is, the market share leader during the early growth phase of the product's life) is generally still the market leader today. For example, Trommer's Red Letter was the first light beer, but Miller Lite, introduced 14 years later, quickly became the dominant brand. Researchers believe that early leaders are successful because of their ability to spot a market opportunity and their willingness to commit large resources to develop the market.

One explanation of the *market development problem* may be found by revisiting the bell-shaped adopter category (Figure 3-4). Rather than the process being continuous, there may be gaps between the adopter categories as shown in Figure 6-6, especially for high-technology products. The gap between innovators and early adopters can occur when the

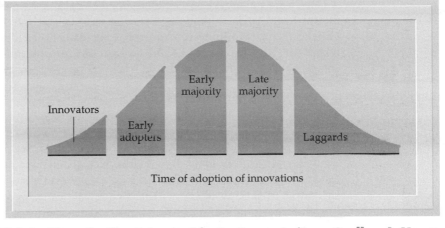

FIGURE 6-6 **Discontinuities Between Adopter Segments (From Geoffrey A. Moore,** *Crossing the Chasm* **[New York: Harper Business, 1995], p. 17.)**

excitement of the enthusiast cannot be translated into a compelling application, which would cause visionary early adopters to switch from established products. More critically, a very large gap or *chasm* can occur between early adopters and the early majority. Early adopters are willing to radically change how they do things in order to gain a major advantage over the competition. They are willing to accept some temporary minor defects or malfunctions of a breakthrough new product to gain major new benefits. On the other hand, the early majority wants properly working products that can be integrated into their organizations with minimal disruption. To be sure that they will get promised productivity benefits, they rely on good references and strong supplier support. The source of good references is typically other members of the early majority rather than early adopters. You must be careful not to mistake the early market for the desired emerging mainstream market. There can also be a gap between the early majority and the late majority. Whereas the early majority is willing and able to become technologically competent, the late majority is much less so. Consequently, a product must become even more user friendly at this point of market development or risk having the market stall prematurely.[13]

Cannibalization

APPLYING
. . . to
Consumer
Packaged
Goods
Marketing

Firms also have to be careful when introducing new items not to merely replace (cannibalize) sales of existing company products sold at the same prices. To avoid this problem, some firms develop new product ideas and then keep them in "cold storage" until they are needed.[14] This allows new items to be released at higher prices as interest in current products declines (product saturation) or when competitors come out with an innovation. Gillette faced this issue when they brought out their new MACH3 razor mentioned earlier. To make sure that the higher-priced MACH3 attracted enough buyers from their own and other companies' products, Gillette spent $300 million on introductory advertising the first year. Gillette also packaged the MACH3 blades in 4 and 8 packs compared with 5 and 10 packs for Sensor Excel to lessen the perception of high MACH3 blade prices. Commercialization of the MACH3 razor went well for Gillette. In the first week after introduction in July of 1998, the MACH3 became the largest selling razor in America. Also 25 percent of buyers switched from brands sold by other companies. By October of 1998, the MACH3 share of the blade market was 10.5 percent, only slightly behind Sensor Excel at 10.8 percent. This was remarkable given that stores were selling 10 Sensor Excel blades for $9.14 compared with $12.39 for 8 MACH3 blades. Consumers were paying $1.55 per blade for MACH3, a 70 percent premium over the $.91 Sensor Excel blade. Although 75 percent of MACH3 sales were cannibalized from other Gillette razors, profits were expected to increase because the gross margin on the new blades was three times as high. The MACH3 introduction managed to raise Gillette's share of the U.S. shaver and blade market from 65 percent in September of 1997 to 70 percent in 1998.[15]

Coordinating Product Introductions

Product availability is crucial during commercialization because goodwill and sales can be lost if the product fails to reach the market on schedule. The introduction of General Motors' Cavalier compact car provides a classic example of the problems that can occur. GM announced a spring availability date for the new car with a lavish advertising campaign. Customers were told to go to their dealers and test-drive it. When they arrived, however, there were no cars because last-minute production delays had greatly reduced the supply of engines. When the cars finally arrived months later, customers found them to be underpowered and first-year sales were far below expectations. In this case, failure to coordinate production and advertising cost GM millions in lost revenues.

MANAGING NPD

Surveys have shown that firms that use formal NPD processes and do not skip steps are more successful with new product introductions. The success rate for the Best firms in one study was 80 percent compared to only 52 percent for the Rest.[16] Best companies had lower mortality rates for new product ideas across all stages of the product development process. Higher success rates and fewer losses of product ideas gives the Best firms faster revenue growth and greater profits. Also best practice organizations expect 45 percent of their sales to come from products commercialized in the previous three years and were able to deliver 49 percent over a five-year period. This is twice the rate of the rest of the firms. In addition, best firms use multi-function development teams more extensively with less innovative new product ideas. Multi-functional NPD teams are made up of people from marketing, production, R&D, and finance. Having people from several business functions work together on a new product simplifies communications and coordination. Multi-functional teams use advanced stage gate evaluations in 69 percent of best firms compared with only 52 percent usage by the rest. The most common new product team reward for best firms is a project completion dinner followed by newsletter recognition. Best practice firms do not use financial rewards for NPD.

Careful management of NPD can create a number of advantages. A telecommunications company reorganized NPD and time to market plunged, products were better aligned with customer needs, and market share and revenue improved. Quality also rose and manufacturing costs decreased, substantially improving product margins. With the same resources, the company now has significantly more development projects under way. A study of 184 auto and computer firms in four countries revealed that the use of cross-functional teams and advanced design tools in NPD led to higher returns on assets, profit to sales ratios and sales growth.[17] These advanced design tools employ sophisticated computers and digital-imaging software to speed up the creation of new items. At General Motors all the various design and manufacturing activities use the same Unigraphics software package which turns every aspect of a vehicle into digital and mathematical models. Cars and trucks are designed on a computer screen, tested on screen, and then data are forwarded to manufacturing and suppliers. This saves money by eliminating the need for physical models, cutting down engineering changes, reduces lead times for ordering production tooling by 50 percent, and makes it possible to solve manufacturing problems in "virtual" factories instead of real ones. Computerized product design is expected to save GM $200 million on each new global car and truck program. Also the advanced designed tools improved engineering productivity 13 percent in one year and helped GM cut the time from project design approval to the start of production from 42 months to 24 months.[18]

SUMMARY

Product development is an exciting, creative process that converts ideas into commercially viable goods and services. Product development is also expensive. The likelihood of increasing sales and profits from new items is enhanced by careful attention to the organization and control of this activity. A key ingredient is a full-time director of product development to expedite and coordinate the many jobs and individuals necessary to produce new merchandise. In addition, the firm must foster a climate that is receptive to new ideas and develop screening criteria that are appropriate to its own objectives and resources. Also, new products need to be carefully tested so that they reflect the attributes and quality levels actually desired by the ultimate customer. This means concept tests to gauge customer reactions to product ideas, preference tests to select product attributes, and use tests to evaluate packaging and long-run customer acceptance. Where new products are radically different, sales tests may be needed to measure repurchase rates and alternative promotional appeals. Finally, products must be introduced to the marketplace so that dealers and customers will become aware of the new items and begin to purchase them on a regular basis.

NOTES

1. Rebecca Blumenstein, "Tough Driving: Struggle to Remake the Malibu Says a Lot About Remaking GM," *The Wall Street Journal* (March 27, 1997), pp. A1, A8.
2. Marvin L. Patterson, "From Experience: Linking Product Innovation to Business Growth," *Journal of Product Innovation Management* Vol. 15 (1998), p. 394.
3. Ron Winslow, "Missing a Beat: How a Breakthrough Quickly Broke Down for Johnson & Johnson," *The Wall Street Journal* (September 18, 1998), pp. A1, A5.
4. Barton G. Tretheway, "Everything New Is Old Again," *Marketing Management* Vol. 7 (Spring 1998), p. 8.
5. Cornelius Herstatt and Eric von Hippel, "Developing New Product Concepts Via the Lead User Method: A Case Study in a 'Low-Tech' Field," *Journal of Product Innovation Management,* Vol. 9, No. 3 (September 1992), pp. 213–221.
6. Michael J. McCarthy, "Slim Pickings: Food Companies Hunt for a 'Next Big Thing' But Few Can Find One," *The Wall Street Journal* (May 12, 1997), pp. A1, A6.
7. Christopher D. Ittner and David F. Larcker, "Product Development Cycle Time and Organizational Performance," *Journal of Marketing Research,* Vol. 34 (February 1997), p. 21.
8. Robert G. Cooper, "The NewProd System: The Industry Experience," *Journal of Product Innovation Management,* Vol. 9, No. 2 (June 1992), pp 113–127.
9. Mark Maremont, "How Gillette Brought Its MACH3 to Market," *The Wall Street Journal* (April 15, 1998), pp. B1, B8.
10. The MACH3 "Razor vs. the Rest," *Consumer Reports* (October 1998), p. 9.
11. Raju Narisette, "P&G Uses Packaging Savvy on Rx Drug," *The Wall Street Journal* (January 30, 1998), pp. B1, B11.
12. General Foods' Americana Recipe Vegetables (B) case written by Lawrence J. Ring, University of Virginia.
13. Geoffrey A. Moore, *Crossing the Chasm* (New York: Harper Business, 1995).
14. For some examples, see William P. Putsis, Jr., "Why Put Off Until Tomorrow What You Can Do Today?" *Journal of Product Innovation Management,* Vol. 10, No. 3 (June 1993), pp. 194–203.
15. Mark Maremont, "Gillette's Earnings Plummeted 99% in Third Quarter," *The Wall Street Journal* (October 16, 1998), p. B12.

16. Abbie Griffin, "PDMA Research on New Product Development Practices: Updating Trends and Benchmarking Best Practices," *Journal of Product Innovation Management,* Vol. 14 (1997) pp. 429–458.

17. Christopher D. Ittner and David F. Larcker, "Product Development Cycle Time and Organizational Performance," *Journal of Marketing Research* Vol. 34 (February 1997), p. 21.

18. Robert L. Simison, "GM Turns to Computers to Cut Development Costs," *The Wall Street Journal* (October 12, 1998), p. B4.

SUGGESTED READING

Cohen, Morris A., Jehoshua Eliashberg, and Teck H. Ho. "An Anatomy of a Decision-Support System for Developing and Launching Line Extension," *Journal of Marketing Research,* Vol. 34 (February 1997), pp. 117–129.

Mukhopadhyay, Samar K. and Anil V. Gupta, "Interfaces for Resolving Marketing, Manufacturing, and Design Conflicts," *European Journal of Marketing,* Vol. 32, No. 1/2 (1998), pp. 101–124.

Shankar, Venkatesh, Gregory S. Carpenter, and Lakshman Krishnamurthi. "Late Mover Advantage: How Innovative Late Entrants Outsell Pioneers," *Journal of Marketing Research,* Vol. 35 (February 1998), pp. 54–70.

Song, X. Michael, and Mitzi M. Montoya-Weiss. "Critical Development Activities for Really New Versus Incremental Products," *Journal of Product Innovation Management,* Vol. 15 (1998), pp. 124–135.

Urban, Glen L., John R. Hauser, William J. Qualls, Bruce D. Weinberg, Jonathan D. Bohlmann, and Roberta A. Chicos. "Information Acceleration: Validation and Lessons from the Field," *Journal of Marketing Research,* Vol. 34 (February 1997), pp. 143–153.

REFERENCES

Bacon, Frank R. and Thomas W. Butler. *Achieving Planned Innovation: A Proven System for Creating Successful New Products and Services.* New York: Simon & Schuster, 1998.

Clark, Kim B. and Steven C. Wheelwright. *The Product Development Challenge: Competing Through Speed, Quality and Creativity.* Cambridge, MA: Harvard Business School, 1995.

Crawford, C. Merle. *New Products Management.* Homewood, IL: Richard D. Irwin, 1996.

McMath, Robert M. and Thomas Forbes. *What Were They Thinking: Marketing Lessons I've Learned from Over 80,000 New Product Innovations and Idiocies.* New York: Time Books, 1998.

Meyer, Mark H. and Alvin Lehnerd. *The Power of Product Platforms.* New York: Free Press, 1997.

Smith, Preston G. and Donald G. Reinertsen. *Developing Products in Half the Time: New Rules, New Tools,* 2nd ed. New York: John Wiley & Sons, 1997.

Ulrich, Karl T., and Steven D. Eppinger. *Product Design and Development.* New York: McGraw-Hill, 1995.

QUESTIONS

1. For third quarter of 1998, Revlon reported profits of 7 cents a share instead of the 73 cents that analysts had been expecting, and the stock price dropped 44 percent. Low profits were partially due to Revlon's failure to launch its new ColorStay Compact in September. The new version of easy-to-apply foundation in a mirrored compact did not fare well in consumer tests and it was sent back to the lab for reformulation. What steps could Revlon have taken to make sure its new compact reached the market on time?

2. Chuck Mellon fell off a motorbike, tore a hole in his sweatshirt, and accidentally stuck his thumb through the hole. This suggested a new product where each cuff would be fingertip length and have a thumbhole, in effect a fingerless glove on the end of each sleeve. Pop your thumb out and the "glove" could be rolled up into a regular wrist-length cuff. After some false starts at selling this innovation, he managed to get a 20,000-unit order for JC Penney's catalog. The item sold out three days after the catalog was mailed. What does the product life cycle say about the need for product development activities at this firm in the future?

3. Suppose that you have a private firm recruit subjects for your new product focus groups at a central downtown facility. When you arrive for a session on cereals, you notice that your chief competitor has accidentaly left a box of a new cereal on the table in the room assigned for your use. Should you immediately return the box of the new cereal to your competitor or should you take it back to the lab and have it analyzed to see if it can be copied?

4. Panasonic introduced a $3,000, 36-inch, high-definition, cinema-style wide screen digital TV in the fall of 1998. The entire TV industry expected to sell only 10,000 digital sets in 1998 out of a total annual TV market of 23 million sets. Why did Panasonic introduce a digital TV before digital television signals and digital programming were available at a price four times the price of a similar analog TV set?

5. Philips Electronics, a Dutch firm, invented the audio cassette and co-launched the compact disk player. In 1991, they introduced a compact-disk interactive player that offered digital sound, picture, and graphics for games and education. The product was years ahead of its competition and easily attached to the back of a TV set. Operated by a hand-held remote control, the system plays easy-to-load standard music compact disks, photo compact disks, and interactive games. The machine was priced at $799 and had a limited number of game disks when it was introduced. Although Sony sold more than a million of its PlayStation game machines in less than a year, Philips sold only 400,000 of its CDi machines over five years. Philips is reported to have lost $1 billion on the CDi in the United States. What went wrong with Philips's CDi introduction? Could Philips have avoided the problems by conducting more focus groups and use tests? What changes should Philips make to its new product development process?

6. Four companies introduced electronic book reader to the consumer market in 1999. These devices store text downloaded from the Internet and reproduce it on screens for viewing by readers. Everybook comes in a two-screen color reader for $1,500. Softbook offered a device the size of a thick $8^1/_2$ by 11 inch notebook for $299 plus $19.95 a month, Nuvomedia has a paperback-sized device for $500, and Librius has a Millenium Reader in a paperback size for only $199. Liberius plans to target romance novels and best-sellers. One firm estimated electronic books will be a $2.5 billion market by 2002. The manufacturers of electronic books believe that book publishers will save so much money on paper, printing, shipping, inventory, and returns that they will offer substantial discounts for readers buying an electronic version of a book. Which of the electronic books has the best prospects for success? Is there room in this new market for four competitors? Is the success of this new product dependent on the cooperation of book publishers? If so, what should the manufacturers do to obtain this cooperation?

7. Japanese high school girls have been very useful to firms planning to introduce new products to the Japanese market. New items are shown to the girls in focus groups and they are asked for their opinions. Coca-Cola Co. asked a group of girls about a new fermented milk drink and they suggested a lighter smoother consistency than rival products, and a short stubby bottle with a pink label instead of a tall, skinny, blue-labeled bottle that Coke was considering. Shiseido asked some girls about a new line of cosmetics called Chopi. The girls told them to change the name to Neuve and change the color of the bottles from the usual black, white, or silver to beige. The high school girls also helped Dentsu Eye to talk up a previously unknown product at their schools. As a result, brand awareness increased to 10 percent of the target market, a result that would have cost $1.5 million in advertising expenditures. Why are focus groups so important in the development of new products? Why are teenage girls so helpful to companies marketing new products in Japan?

8. The development of a new low-cost microchip to act as the light gathering sensor in cameras has allowed Nintendo Co. to introduce a new accessory for its popular Game

Boy toy. The new filmless toy camera was priced at $49.95 and sold 800,000 units in six months. Does this mean that technology drives product development? How was Nintendo able to get their new digital toy camera to market seven months before Mattel Inc. introduced its Barbie digital camera for $69?

9. In 1998, Volkswagen introduced a new version of its original Beetle model that was designed in the 1930s. The New Beetle has front-wheel drive, a water-cooled engine, and was priced for about $16,000. Customer acceptance has been very good in the United States and Volkswagen expected to sell 50,000 Beetles in the first year on the market. What accounts for the success of this small cramped new model? Is it nostalgia or is it just clever marketing?

10. Campbell Soup Co. developed a new line of nutrient-fortified meals that research showed could actually reduce high levels of cholesterol, blood sugar, and blood pressure. The meals were called Intelligent Quisine and were test marketed in Ohio. After 15 months in the test market, sales were slow and Campbell dropped the new line at a cost of $55 million. Does the failure with IQ meals suggest that Campbell should reduce its expenditures on R&D? Do you think the problem was a lack of variety in meal options or was it a more basic problem that Americans resist long-term eating programs to improve their health?

11. Digital videodiscs (DVDs) were first introduced to the consumer market in 1997. DVDs offer sharper pictures than videocassette players but they cannot record movies or TV shows. DVDs sold slowly their first year on the market, because Hollywood studios released only a few films for DVDs and video rental stores did not promote them for fear they would hurt videocassette rentals. Sales picked up in the second year as video stores started to offer to rent DVD machines for five nights for $14.95 and the studios started to offer more films on disk. Why was it so important for the video stores to offer DVD rentals? Explain why new electronic devices catch on slowly.

7

BRAND MANAGEMENT

Nothing is more profitable than adding a few share points to an existing brand.

WILLIAM TRAGOS

*B*rand management is concerned with the supervision of brands of products and services from the time they are introduced until they are removed from the marketplace. Our focus is on the specific plans and strategies needed during each phase of the product life cycle to improve the competitive position of the firm. The objective is to show how marketing executives work to control the destinies of brands on a day-to-day basis.

You must first understand what brands are and how they fit into the offerings of your organization. In addition, you need to know the advantages of identifying products by national and store brand names. Finally, it is your job to decide when to rescue declining brands and when to bury them.

WHAT IS A BRAND?

A brand is a name, term, sign, symbol, or design intended to distinguish the goods and services of one seller from another. The idea with brands is to select a unique term for a product so that customers will be able to identify the item and find it in the marketplace. However, brands are more than just a product. The usual definition of a product is anything that can be offered to a market to satisfy buyer needs. This means products can be physical goods (cars), services (bank), retail stores, a person (member of Congress), place (Hawaii), or an idea (pollution control). A brand is a name attached to any of these product classes to help sell them to customers. In addition, a brand includes a summation of consumers' perceptions and feelings about a product's attributes. Marketers attempt to create appealing images around their products based on quality, shape, color, and lifestyle compatibility. These tangible and intangible image associations help marketing managers differentiate their brands from their competitors. Everyone knows the differences between Coke and Pepsi and many people have developed strong brand loyalty to each of these sodas. Brand loyalty means that a certain portion of buyers come back and buy your product again and again. When brands create repeat buyers, managers build value that can be turned into profits for the firm.

Brand Functions

Brands are found everywhere. Virtually all consumer products in America are identified by brands. In addition, many industrial products carry brand designations. For example, the "Intel

Inside" brand label we see on PCs identifies the Intel microprocessor chip that is built into Dell, Compaq, and IBM brands of personal computers. This suggests you need to understand the functions that brands perform that make them so valuable to buyers and sellers.

For buyers, a key attraction of brands is they simplify product decisions (Figure 7-1). Brands help buyers identify products, thereby reducing search costs and assuring a buyer of a desired level of quality. As a result the buyer's perceived risk of buying the product is reduced. In addition, buyers receive psychological rewards by purchasing brands that symbolize status and prestige. This reduces the psychological risks associated with owning and using the "wrong" product. Brands can be effective in signaling product characteristics and value to consumers for complex machines, insurance, and drugs. An example showing how effective brands can be is described in Marketing in Action box 7-1.

For sellers, brands make it easier for firms to promote repeat purchases and to introduce new products (Figure 7-1). Brands also facilitate promotional efforts and encourage brand loyalty across product categories. Brands make it easier to use premium pricing by creating a basic level of differentiation that should prevent the product from becoming a commodity. Brands facilitate market segmentation by allowing the seller to communicate a consistent message to a target customer group. Brands are useful in building brand loyalty in categories where repeat purchasing is common.

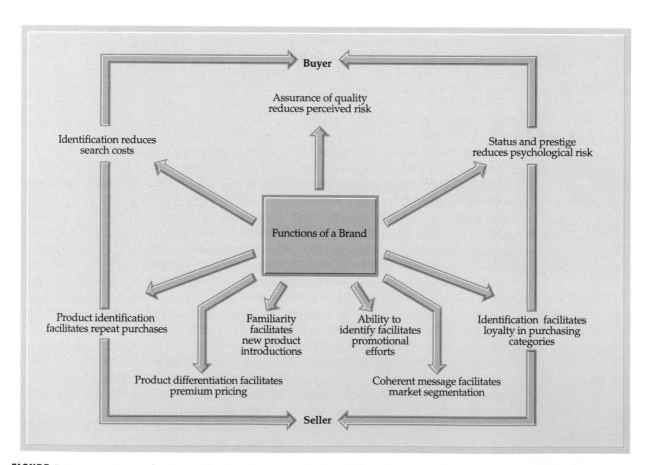

FIGURE 7-1   **Functions of a Brand for the Buyer and Seller (From Pierre Berthon, James M. Hulbert and Leyland F. Pitt, "Brand Management Prognostications,"** *Sloan Management Review,* **Vol. 40, No. 2 [Winter 1999], p. 54.)**

APPLYING
... to
Pharmaceutical
Marketing

MARKETING IN ACTION 7-1

Why Do Brands Outsell Generic Drugs?

Generic drugs are copies of national brands that are sold at lower prices. Brand name drugs are patented and when the patents expire, generic drug firms introduce imitations to try to steal market share from the original developer of the product. Although generic drugs are chemically similar to branded drugs and are sold at lower prices, they have not been able to grab a significant portion of the market. In 1997, brand name drugs had 92 percent of the dollar sales of pharmaceuticals in the U.S. Consumer preferences for brand name drugs is based in part on customer satisfaction and a concern that generic clones may not be manufactured with the same consistent high quality as the original. Also the larger pharmaceutical companies have done a better job of marketing their branded products. Name brand drug companies send out armies of sales reps to introduce new brands to doctors and provide them with free samples to give to patients. Once the samples run out, patients often end up on long term or lifelong prescriptions for the branded drug. They also advertise in journals directed at doctors, host medical seminars and pay marquee professors to laud their brands. In addition, brand companies spend heavily on direct consumer advertising to increase consumer awareness of their branded drugs. For example, the innovative Viagra brand male impotence drug received substantial direct consumer advertising and a great deal of news commentary because of its ability to improve the sex lives of older men. Generic drug companies are generally smaller than the brand drug firms and do not have the resources to build brand recognition with similar marketing programs.

— *Branded products can outsell generic copies.*

Source: Thomas M. Burton, "Bested Interests: Why Generic Drugs Often Can't Compete Against Brand Names," *The Wall Street Journal,* November 18, 1998, p. A1.

Other advantages of brands include the legal protection they offer for unique features. A brand can retain intellectual property rights, giving legal title to the brand owner. This allows the firm to protect its brands with trademarks and patents. Firms can then invest in a brand with the assurance they alone will benefit from its success. In addition, brands build goodwill that creates barriers of entry to keep competitive firms from entering the market. Further, companies can use brands to signal quality levels to satisfied customers.

Brand Personality

Many marketers believe that brands have human-type personalities that allow consumers to express themselves through the purchase of particular products. A brand personality framework is shown in Figure 7-2. The five dimensions in Figure 7-2 are based on consumer ratings of similarities between 114 personality traits and 37 brands of consumer products. The first brand personality dimension, sincerity, is described as wholesome, down-to-earth, and is typified by Hallmark cards. An excitement dimension is more daring, imaginative, and is associated with the MTV channel. Competence, the third brand personality dimension, is reliable, intelligent, and is represented by *The Wall Street Journal*. A fourth dimension, sophistication, is charming, upper class, and would be characterized by Guess brand jeans. The last brand personality dimension in Figure 7-2, ruggedness, is tough, outdoorsy, and is represented by Nike athletic shoes. Once a manager knows the dimensions of brand personality, they can be used to mold brand images to match desirable customer groupings. It is no accident that Nike advertising shows people climbing mountains and that ads for Mountain Dew focus on young sky divers and in-line skate daredevils.

BRAND EQUITY

Having described what brands are and why they are used in marketing, we now turn to an important concept called brand equity. Although brand equity has been defined in a variety

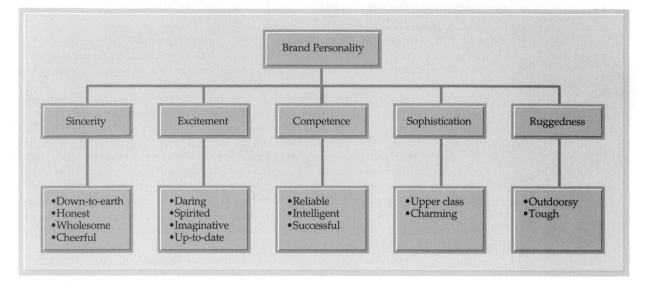

FIGURE 7-2   A Brand Personality Framework (*Source:* Jennifer L. Aaker, "Dimensions of Brand Personality," *Journal of Marketing Research,* **Vol. 34 [August 1997], p. 352.)**

of ways, we will focus our attention first on the word *equity*. When something has equity, it has value. This means that when firms invest in a brand they create added value or equity much like the cash prices assigned to stocks and bonds. If brands have value, then they can be bought and sold just like other financial instruments. For example, when Cadbury Schweppes bought Hires and Crush soft drinks from Procter & Gamble for $220 million, only $20 million went for the physical assets of the brands. This means Cadbury Schweppes paid $200 million for the brand equity associated with Hires Root Beer and Orange Crush soda. Similarly, when Newell Co. bought the floundering Rubbermaid Inc., they paid an astounding 49 percent premium over the closing price of Rubbermaid stock. Rubbermaid is the leading American manufacturer of consumer and commercial plastic products, and Newell paid billions to acquire Rubbermaid's brand equity.[1] In another case, when Volkswagen paid more than $700 million to acquire Rolls-Royce and Bentley cars from Vickers PLC, they were surprised when BMW paid $60 million to grab the rights to the Rolls-Royce brand name from Rolls-Royce PLC.[2] In this case, BMW paid $60 million for Rolls-Royce's car brand equity and Volkswagen was left with only the Bentley brand name and the Rolls-Royce car plants. All of these examples show that brand equity has value that can be measured in dollars and cents.

Customer-Based Brand Equity

Although the value dimension of brand equity is important, you should understand that there is a critical customer dimension as well. One definition of customer-based brand equity is the differential effect that brand knowledge has on consumer response to the marketing of the brand.[3] This suggests that brand equity arises when customers react more positively to one brand than to another. Second, differences in reactions are directly related to customer's knowledge of the brand. The more consumers know about a brand, the more lasting the brand's impression on a customer's memory and the stronger the resulting brand equity. Third, differential response is based on all elements of the marketing mix (advertising, pricing, promotional coupons, retail displays, etc.). Thus the source of brand equity is customer reactions in the marketplace and the result is added dollar value for the brand.

Brand Awareness

Brand equity occurs when customers have a high level of awareness of a brand and hold strong, favorable brand associations in memory. Knowing about a brand may be enough to trigger a positive purchase response for low involvement decisions where customers base choices on familiar brands. In more complex situations, brand associations can play a critical role in the differential responses needed to build brand equity. Brand awareness is developed by repeated exposure to advertising and promotion to build brand recognition. Brand recall is enhanced by strengthening associations with the right product category or consumption situations.

Brand awareness is amplified when marketers visually and verbally reinforce the brand name. One approach is to develop a slogan or jingle that matches the brand with the desired product category and consumption scenario. Other elements that can build awareness include logos, symbols, characters (the Energizer bunny), and unique packaging. Another way to intensify brand awareness is through careful matching of the brand with desired usage in a variety of communications alternatives. These may include featuring the brand or logo on race cars or sports teams, endorsements by celebrities on television, placement of favorable stories in magazines and newspapers, or prominent displays of the brand in movies or television shows. Anything that causes the consumer to experience the brand can magnify brand awareness.

Brand Image

Brand equity is reinforced when consumers have a positive image of a brand in memory. Brand images can be strengthened by marketing programs that link strong, favorable, and unique associations to the brand. Brand associations can be enhanced by direct experience (free samples and test drives for cars) and by word-of-mouth communications with friends. Another source of brand image information is nonpartisan data published by consumer testing groups such as *Consumer Reports*. These organizations describe product features of individual brands and list Web sites and telephone numbers so consumers can call in to get additional information on products they are thinking of buying.

Brand images are also influenced by the strength of brand associations. The more a person thinks about product information and ties it to existing knowledge, the stronger the ensuing brand affiliations. The key to building strong affiliations is to make sure the data are relevant to the individual and are consistent over time. In addition, brand images are intensified by presenting the brand in a context that is both familiar and provides cues for action. This means the models in the ads must match the ages of the target audience, the background scenery used for the ad should be familiar, and the text should build on such powerful motivators as better health, safety, or financial security.

BRAND STRATEGY

Brand strategy focuses on deciding which products should be branded and whether they should be sold under one's own label or under labels controlled by other firms. *Brands* include all names, terms, symbols, or designs that are used to identify and differentiate the goods of one seller from those of the competitors. Brands allow the customer to recognize products and increase the chances for repeat sales. Brands also encourage the use of preselling and reduce the need for personal contact at the retail level. In addition, brands facilitate the development of permanent price-quality images for products. Brands also simplify the introduction of new products and allow the manufacturer some control over the channel of distribution. Branding is easiest where identifying tags or symbols can be attached directly to the product and where the customer is willing to use brand designations to differentiate among products.

Umbrella Brands

Umbrella brands are groups of products sold under one label by a single firm. Heinz, Del Monte, and General Electric are companies that endorse a wide array of products with their own corporate name. Other firms, such as Procter & Gamble, prefer to use separate brand names for each product. Research has shown strong support for the idea that consumers transfer quality perceptions from one product to others sharing the same brand name. Consumer experience with one umbrella brand provides signals on quality and helps them reduce risks associated with the purchase of new items. These results suggest that providing free samples can help umbrella brands when the sample is perceived to be of high quality.

Umbrella brands have the advantage that advertising for one brand promotes the sales of all items carrying that particular label. Umbrella brands also make it easier to introduce new products to distribution channels and the customer. On the other hand, it is more difficult to create and maintain an identity for each item using an umbrella brand strategy. One possible compromise is to use separate brand names for each product and then tie them together with a unifying trade name. This is the strategy used by General Motors; cars are promoted under their own names, and the GM symbol is used as a common point of reference.

National versus Store Brands

There are basically two types of brands available to American consumers. National brands typically receive national advertising support, enjoy wide distribution, are sold at higher prices than other brands, and are frequently stocked by competing retailers. Store brands or private labels have more limited distribution, are often sold at lower prices than national brands, and are available only in stores that share a common wholesaler. The marketing of national brands is controlled by manufacturers that *pull* products through the channel of distribution with direct consumer advertising that emphasizes product quality. Store brands are managed by retailers that use shelf positions and low prices to attract customers to their brands.

Historically, national brands have outsold store brands because manufacturers have spent more money on advertising and product development. Store brands typically gain market share during economic slowdowns when customers are more price sensitive and are attracted to the less expensive store brands. However, the recent growth of mass merchandisers and the trend toward more mergers among grocery and drug retailers have strengthened the position of store brands.

Store Brands.   Store brand market shares vary widely across product categories. For example, store brands represent 65 percent of the sales of frozen green and wax beans and 25 percent of liquid bleach but only 1.1 percent of personal deodorants. One explanation for these differences is that the risks consumers accept when they buy private labels also varies widely across product categories. For example, if a consumer buys a $.98 package of private label frozen beans and is dissatisfied with its quality, the buyer is out only a small amount of money and there is little personal risk of embarrassment. However, when the consumer purchases a $6 private label deodorant and it is not effective in a social context, there is a higher dollar cost and a greater chance of humiliation in front of people that are important to the customer. Thus when perceived risk is high, buyers may prefer prestigious national brands with their strong reputations for performance. Store brands tend to do better in categories where they offer high quality comparable to that of national brands. They do much worse in categories where multiple national manufacturers are investing a lot of money in national advertising.[4] Where store brands were once positioned solely on the basis of price, many firms are having success using a "quality" focus. This is especially evident in Europe where retailers such as J. Sainsbury have achieved dominance over national brands in many product categories.[5] Indeed, researchers have noted that the price gap between national and store brands has no predictive power in determining store brand market share.[6] This means that the issue is really consumer perceptions of product quality.

Retailers have a number of advantages in their private label war with national brands. First they decide which national brands to carry in their stores, how much shelf space to devote to each brand, and the prices at which they will be sold. In addition, retailers can dilute the effects of manufacturers' promotions by not allowing full pass-through of trade discounts, promotional allowances, and slotting allowances to customers. Retailers also manipulate price gaps between store and national brands and shelf space elasticities of demand across product categories to earn higher margins on their own store brands. This means that store brands generate 10 to 15 percent higher margins than national brands and retailers can sell them for lower prices. For example, chain drugstores have been very successful selling store brand over-the-counter cold remedies alongside national brands. Store brands are also umbrella brands that help build store loyalty and help introduce new items.

National Brands. Although store brands have had success in some product categories, national brands have their own advantages. The key weapons for manufacturers are investments in high-quality production facilities, large advertising budgets, and the clever use of coupons and mail-in rebates to help strengthen brand equity. They also have more money for product development and packaging innovations. National brands have an enormous storehouse of brand preference with consumers. When *Consumer Reports* polled their subscribers, they found that 80 percent preferred national brands because they were perceived to be of higher quality. Thus national brands should not try to narrow the gap with store brands using trade promotions, but would be better off spending the money on brand advertising and new product development.[7] Sometimes national brands lose market share to store brands because the product category is losing favor with consumers. For example, the typical American breakfast is moving away from the traditional cold cereal and milk toward bagels and fruit that can be eaten on the run. This shift in preferences has had serious and long-term effects on national brand manufacturers of cold cereal. Kellogg has lost market share to store brands and has had to lay off employees to maintain profitability. Consumers who still eat cold cereal see fewer quality differences and are quick to pick up store brand cereals that sell for $2 a box less.

Mass merchandisers such as Wal-Mart and Target love to feature national brands in the weekly newspaper inserts to draw people to their stores. Once there, the retailers try to sell customers the higher-margin store brands. Even Sears has cut back on the number of its own Kenmore appliances and now features many popular national brands such as GE, Whirlpool, Kitchen Aid, and Sony. Sears purchases its Kenmore refrigerators from GE and Whirlpool and places them alongside of each other to promote the lower-priced Kenmore models. You should be aware that if the Worldwide Web becomes a significant channel of distribution, national brands will become more important as beacons to attract buyers to the Internet and as a way to assure consumers they are getting high-quality products.

New Brands versus Brand Extensions

When a new item is added to the firm's product line, you must decide whether to create a new brand name or use an existing name. For instance, when Coca-Cola first developed a diet cola drink, it chose to use a new name, Tab, rather than capitalize on its existing consumer franchise by using the name Diet Coke. However, when PepsiCo came out with Diet Pepsi, Coca-Cola countered with Diet Coke and phased out the Tab brand. Sometimes a firm will want to draw on its investment in a brand name and consequently will direct its product development to products that fit its existing image.

The various possibilities for products and brands are shown in Figure 7-3. When the firm simply adds another variant to an existing brand in an existing product category, the firm has a *line extension.* An example would be the addition of baking soda to Crest toothpaste. The new brand, "Crest with Baking Soda" is an extension of regular Crest toothpaste with the standard fluoride antidecay ingredient. The idea with line extensions is to use the customer's familiarity with a flagship brand, Crest, to gain acceptance of new brands that broaden a firm's product line by appealing to niche market segments. In this case "Crest with Baking Soda" joins other brands such as "Crest with Tarter Control" and "Crest Gel" to boost shelf facings for Procter & Gamble and increase total toothpaste sales. The use of a line extension by Duracell to fight the Energizer bunny is described in Marketing Strategies box 7-1.

Brand Extension.　　Using an existing brand name to enter a new product category is called brand extension or brand leveraging. For example, the brand name Healthy Choice was first used with a line of frozen dinners with reduced levels of fat and salt. The success of these items encouraged the manufacturer to leverage the Healthy Choice brand into a number of other food categories. Now we have Healthy Choice Soups and Healthy Choice Ice Cream.

Brand extension is potentially very attractive. It makes use of existing customer awareness and goodwill. As a result, the advertising expenditures needed to introduce the product to the market are minimized. Although the introduction of Always sanitary napkins, an entirely new brand name, cost Procter & Gamble about $100 million, the introduction of Liquid Tide cost a relatively modest $30 to $40 million because of existing name recognition.

Flanker Brands.　　When a firm markets a new brand in a category in which it already had a presence, the firm is protecting its market position and the product is said to be a flanker brand (Figure 7-3). A special case of a flanker brand is a fighting brand. When a firm has a

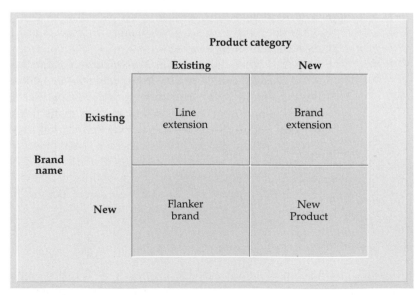

FIGURE 7-3　Types of Brands

MARKETING STRATEGIES *7-1*

Duracell Versus the Energizer

Duracell Inc., owned by Gillette, introduced a new line extension called Duracell Ultra in its increasingly bitter marketing war with Energizer brand batteries sold by Eveready Battery Co. Duracell says the Ultra batteries last up to 50 percent longer than its ordinary alkaline batteries in so-called high drain products such as flash cameras and compact disk players. These devices use up batteries far more quickly than low drain products such as wall clocks. The company says consumers can continue to use regular Duracell batteries for these applications. Duracell sells the new line extension alongside its existing range of alkaline batteries. The new Duracell Ultra batteries are priced 20 percent higher than its regular batteries and represent a first attempt to segment the alkaline battery market into distinct categories. When Energizer introduced its reformulated batteries, they simply replaced the old AA and AAA batteries with the new version. Duracell expects that the Ultra will eventually comprise about 20 percent of Duracell's AA and AAA alkaline battery sales. They also expect that one-fourth of Ultra's sales will be incremental, not just replacements for sales of other Duracell products. Thus the Ultra line extension should increase both Duracell's margins and their share of the alkaline battery market. In a direct challenge to the Energizer bunny, Duracell's head of sales and marketing says the Ultra batteries "give superior performance to any other alkaline battery on the market." When *Consumer Reports* magazine tested the new Ultra alkaline batteries, they found they performed as advertised. The strong brand awareness created by Energizer and Duracell ads claiming superior performance has allowed these two national brands to continue to dominate the alkaline battery market.

— *Line extensions can lead to increased sales and profits for the firm.*

Source: Mark Maremont, "Duracell Tactic Could Charge Battery Wars," *The Wall Street Journal*, February 18, 1998, p. B1.

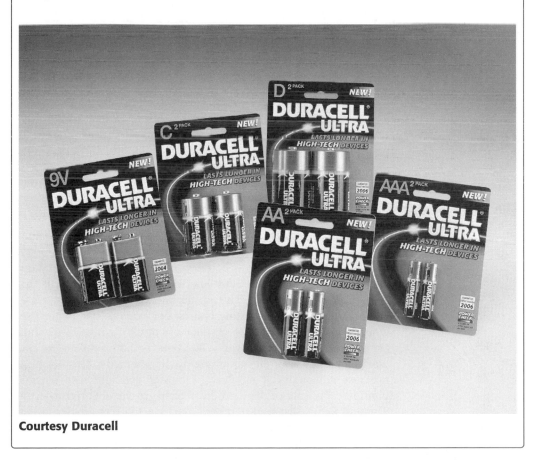

Courtesy Duracell

high relative market share, it is usually not in its best interest to cut price because it will be hurt most by the price cut if primary demand does not expand to offset the cut. This makes a dominant brand susceptible to having share sliced away by aggressive pricing by smaller firms. To discipline such firms, a fighting brand is created for which no money is invested in advertising, and the product is sold on price. Fighting brands are expendable and are sometimes discontinued after they have served their purpose of warning competitors to avoid predatory price competition.

APPLYING
. . . to Financial Services Marketing

American Express sells premium-priced products in the form of its green, gold, and platinum charge cards. Facing new entrants in the credit card business, such as AT&T, and intensified competition from veterans, including Visa and MasterCard, American Express brought out a credit card called Optima as a fighting brand.

You have to decide whether to bring out a new item as a line extension or as a new brand. Generally it is better to employ a line extension strategy when parent brand penetration is high and a new brand strategy when parent brand penetration is low. This is true even though a line extension will cannibalize parent brand sales much more than a new brand will. To maintain profit margins, a rule of thumb is that a new product must gain two share points for each point lost by the original company brand. Usually, half of the gain will come from users of competitors' products and half from new users being drawn into the market.

New Product Brands.   The most risky and expensive brand strategy is the creation of a new brand name for an item to be sold in a new product category (Figure 7-3). New product brands have no parent or flagship brands to help introduce them to customers and reduce consumers' anxiety about purchasing a new product. We mentioned earlier that it cost Procter & Gamble $100 million to introduce the new product brand Always. This was more than three times what it cost P&G to bring out a brand extension in the detergent market. New product brands are best used when the item is truly revolutionary and unique to the market. In this case the attributes of the new product are so powerful they overcome customer's unfamiliarity with the new brand name. An example of a successful new product brand is the PrimeStar direct satellite TV reception system. The PrimeStar system offered consumers in rural areas better TV reception, 150 channel alternatives, and the option to rent movies directly using their remote controls. Direct satellite TV offered so many advantages over regular cable or over-the-air reception that customers stampeded to sign up for the new service despite the fact that PrimeStar was an unknown brand.

APPLYING
. . . to Consumer Services Marketing

The Limits of Brand Proliferation

There are risks to using one brand name on many different products. The image conveyed by the brand name may become too diffuse as the specific customer benefit the brand name stands for is lost. Care must be taken not to extend the brand name to categories where it cannot provide its inherent customer benefit. The basic idea is that new brand extensions should be complementary. This means that a fresh use of a brand name should enhance the sales and reputation of existing brands. For example, the publishers of the U.S. auto magazine *Car and Driver* have licensed the use of the *Car and Driver* brand name to manufacturers of motor oil and antifreeze. While some brand loyal *Car and Driver* readers will buy the new brands of motor oil and antifreeze, these brand extensions clearly fail the complementary test. Although Car and Driver motor oil and antifreeze generates extra revenue for the publisher, the sale of these products damages the editorial independence of the magazine. The problem is that readers rely on the objectivity of articles in the magazine to help them select cars and products to purchase. Now that *Car and Driver* is selling motor oil and antifreeze, readers will no longer be able to believe the magazine's recommendations concerning these two critical automotive products.

An additional problem is that as the number of linked brands increases, the ability to reposition an individual item decreases. Finally, a bad product can tarnish the other products sharing a common brand name. Research has shown that inconsistent extension brands can dilute important consumer beliefs about individual products that carry the parent brand name.[8] This dilution of beliefs is more serious for line extensions where there are more company brands to be affected than with brand extensions where the firm is entering a new product category.

At some point, the number of brands and products in a category becomes greater than customers' need for variety and creates duplication. Too many sizes and too many me too products simply add to distribution costs. Consumers feel that they don't require 16 barbecue potato chip products to satisfy their need for variety. A Food Marketing Institute study found that retailers can reduce stock-keeping units (skus) by 5 to 25 percent without hurting sales or consumers' perception of variety offered by the store. As a result of the concern over brand proliferation, the prediction is that only the No. 1 and No. 2 brands will be assured of distribution. The No. 3 brand will probably need to go to value positioning to remain viable. Lesser-ranked brands will likely disappear. Even the leaders will need to rationalize the lines and reduce the number of skus. The U.S. leader in salty snacks, Frito-Lay, has dropped about 100 sizes and flavors.

Procter & Gamble has employed several strategies to accommodate retailers that want to consolidate the number of products. In detergents, P&G is continuing product innovation and differentiation even for secondary brands, reducing skus—mainly package sizes—rather than eliminating brands and strengthening secondary brands in regional markets. On the other hand, P&G has put Puritan cooking oil under the Crisco label and has discontinued the White Cloud toilet tissue brand by turning it into a Charmin extension called Charmin Ultra. The new tissue is 30 percent thicker than White Cloud and 50 percent thicker than regular Charmin, P&G's leading brand.

BRAND QUALITY

The ability of a firm or a country to compete is often influenced by the quality of the brands it offers for sale. Some American firms have been complacent about product quality deterioration, and their share of some markets has declined sharply. These changes are related to the ability of foreign firms to produce higher-quality products and sell them at lower prices in the United States.

Research has shown that most quality problems are a result of poor design (40 percent), errors in the manufacturing process (30 percent), and defective supplier goods (30 percent). Thus careful monitoring of customers' complaints and tough standards for suppliers can lead to improved quality. Moreover, high quality does not necessarily mean higher costs. The potential impact of higher quality on the performance of the firm has been shown by the Strategic Planning Institute. They examined 525 American business units and found that those with low relative product quality earned 17 percent; medium quality, 20 percent; and high quality, 27 percent. This suggests that continuous improvements in product quality can raise profits.

Quality is important, but how do you go about raising it? Many firms focus on *total quality management* (TQM). TQM calls for a comprehensive master plan for continuously improving quality in an organization. Concepts stressed in TQM are "continuous improvements," "zero defects," "do it right the first time," "faster is better," and "empowerment—employees closest to the situation know best how to improve it." Going further, a good approach is to adhere to a set of quality standards endorsed by more than 50 countries, including those of the European Community and the United States. The International Organization for Standardization has created a set of five standards, known collectively as *ISO*

9000, to offer a uniform way of determining whether manufacturing plants and service organizations implement and document sound quality procedures. To register, a company must undergo a third-party audit of its manufacturing and customer service processes, covering everything from how it designs, produces, and installs its goods to how it inspects, packages, and markets them. This is not cheap—it may cost $250,000 and take nine months to certify a plant. Nonetheless, ISO registration is rapidly becoming the passport to success in the international marketplace.[9]

APPLYING
. . . to
Consumer
Durable
Goods
Marketing

Our discussion of brand quality concludes with a story. Regina Company grabbed 11 percent of the U.S. vacuum cleaner market by heavy use of rebates, low prices, and an allocation of 20 percent of revenues for TV advertising. Unfortunately, it neglected product quality, and up to 20 percent of its vacuums were returned by customers for broken belts, handles, and beater bars. Meanwhile, their competitors (Hoover and Eureka) kept their returns at less than 1 percent of sales and remained profitable. Regina's profits plummeted, and the company was almost destroyed by the low-quality reputation of its vacuum cleaner brands.

BRAND WARRANTIES AND SERVICE

When customers are concerned about brand quality, warranties are often used to help reduce anxiety. Warranties represent commitments on the part of the seller to repair and adjust products that fail to perform after purchase. The main objectives of brand warranties and services are to encourage sales by reducing customers' worries about postpurchase problems and to build repeat business from satisfied customers. The linkages between consumers' attitudes about product performance and subsequent buying behavior were described earlier in Chapter 3.

Warranties Can Sell

Historically, warranties have been written statements that tell the buyer what steps the seller will take if the brand fails within a specific period of time. They were usually designed to limit the liability of the seller in case damage claims were filed by the buyer. In recent years, however, the courts have ruled that warranties do not have to be written and that they do not limit the liability of the seller. As a result, marketing managers have become more concerned with the promotional aspects of brand warranties. For example, a warranty that offers "double your money back" is clearly designed to boost sales by having the buyer try the product at little or no risk. Under these conditions, a warranty becomes a competitive tool designed to build customer confidence and to woo customers away from firms with weaker warranty policies.

After high-quality Japanese brands stole a significant portion of the U.S. car market, American manufacturers responded by offering longer warranties. When the standard Japanese warranty was 36 months or 36,000 miles, GM offered 60 months or 60,000 miles and Chrysler offered 70 months or 70,000 miles. The objective was to show buyers that American automakers had improved auto quality and stood behind their products. The evidence suggests that longer warranties helped Chrysler but did not increase GM's market share.

Service Strategies

Service strategies are concerned with establishing procedures for repairing merchandise after the brand has been sold to the customer. Over the years, product complexity and high wages for service personnel created service problems for many manufacturers. Consumers have found that it is difficult to get products repaired, and the cost is often out of proportion to the value of the product. As a result, consumers are now demanding and receiving better repair service from manufacturers. Many firms have expanded their regional repair centers and have installed "cool lines" so that customers can call directly when they encounter repair problems.

In the past, some manufacturers considered service a necessary evil and attempted to keep expenditures as low as possible. This raised profits in the short run, but eventually consumers began to rebel at the absence of local repair facilities. The failure of Fiat and Renault to penetrate U.S. auto markets is often attributed to the lack of adequate service facilities.

An alternative service strategy is to consider repair work as a profit-making opportunity. If most of the products owned by customers are out of warranty and require periodic repair, then the active solicitation of service work can be a lucrative business. Automobile manufacturers, for example, profit from the sales of fenders and other parts to their dealers and independent service facilities. However, too great a reliance on service profits may stifle product improvements and allow competitors to grow by introducing new items.

A more desirable market-oriented strategy for service emphasizes fast, economical repairs, with the objective of building long-run sales. Although a liberal factory service policy may cost more than other strategies, it can help protect the brand names owned by manufacturers and reduce problems caused by poor dealer service. Implementation of this strategy often requires extensive training of dealer repair personnel and the establishment of regional service centers run by the company. In recent years, the appliance industry has adopted a factory service policy of this type.

Manufacturers have used product service in a variety of ways to help promote the sales of merchandise. Sears, for example, emphasizes the nationwide availability of its service, so that even if customers move to another area, repair service will be available. Maytag, on the other hand, takes a more whimsical approach and shows its repair personnel with nothing to do, suggesting that Maytag appliances rarely break down. One of the most aggressive manufacturer service policies offers a lifetime of free service repairs. At the other extreme, service costs can be minimized by making the product disposable—for example, cigarette lighters that can be simply thrown away when they break or run out of fuel. These examples suggest that the choice of an optimum service strategy depends on the cost, complexity, and life expectancy of the brand; the importance of repairs to the customer; and the manufacturer's concern for maintaining a satisfied group of repeat buyers.

APPLYING
. . . to Consumer Durable Goods Marketing

EXPLOITING THE BRAND LIFE CYCLE

Most successful brands follow a life cycle that includes introduction, growth, maturity, and decline stages (Figure 7-4). At the start, brands are unknown, so the emphasis in the marketing mix is on promotion to acquaint customers with the brand and gain product trial. As sales increase during the growth phase, emphasis shifts to opening new distribution channels and retail outlets. When a brand reaches maturity, competition increases and marketing managers emphasize price, deals, coupons, and special promotions to draw attention to their merchandise.

The main danger during the growth and maturity stages of the brand life cycle is marketing inertia. If a firm becomes too complacent with its success, it may lose touch with its customers and ignore competition. Thus, when the market changes, the firm may fail to react quickly enough—or perhaps not at all—to the changed circumstances. An example of mature brand complacency is described for Campbell Soup in Marketing Strategies box 7-2.

One way of increasing customer interest during the growth and maturity phases of the brand life cycle is to expand product lines and offer greater variety. Another possibility is to follow a strategy of market segmentation and sell the product under a variety of brands owned by distributors or other manufacturers. A third alternative is to engage in clever promotional campaigns devised to catch the eye of selected groups of customers.

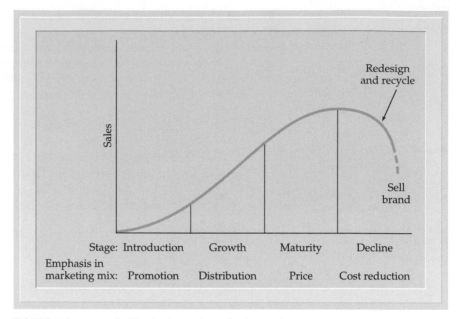

FIGURE 7-4   Brand Life Cycle and Marketing Mix

Brands in decline often need to be redesigned or reduced in cost so that they can continue to make a contribution to the company. When items become unprofitable, the company must decide whether the brand should be carried at a loss or sold to make room for more profitable lines. The effect of the brand life cycle on the marketing strategies of a toothpaste that periodically reenters the market with a "new and improved" version is illustrated in Figure 7-5.

Brand life cycles vary in length from a few weeks for fashion merchandise to up to 100 years for soaps, appliances, and food items. The amount of time a product stays in any one stage of the life cycle depends on customer adoption rates and the amount of new brand competition. Because businesses invest a great deal of money to gain consumer acceptance, it makes sense to extend the life of their brands as long as possible. Three methods that can be employed to stretch brand markets are (1) promoting of more frequent and varied usage among current users, (2) finding new uses for the basic material, and (3) creating new users for the brand by expanding the market.

Ciba-Geigy AG has extended the life cycle of its aging antiarthritis drug, Voltaren, by formulating a spate of new versions. To hold off the inevitable erosion caused by generic competition as its patents expire on the original tablet form of Voltaren, Ciba-Geigy now sells it in the form of eyedrops, as intravenous solutions, as time-release pills, and as emulgel—a cross between a cream and an ointment. The last product is so novel that it earned Ciba-Geigy a new 20-year cycle of patent coverage. As a result of these actions, Voltaren continues to be a blockbuster pharmaceutical.

BRANDS IN DECLINE

The brand life cycle suggests that brands are born, grow to maturity, and then enter a period of decline. The length of the decline phase is determined by changes in consumer preferences, activities of competitors, and the brand elimination policies of the firm. Although usually little can be done about basic shifts in consumer preferences and the entry of competitive items, the firm has a wide range of alternatives that can be exercised for brands with falling sales.

APPLYING
. . . to
Consumer
Food
Marketing

MARKETING STRATEGIES 7-2

Campbell Counters Declining Soup Sales

The Campbell Soup Co. derives 62 percent of its revenue from the sale of soups and sauces. Over the four years from 1994 through 1997, total canned soup sales in the United States declined every year and Campbell's sales decreased more than the category as a whole. In 1997, Campbell's soup sales dropped 3.5 percent compared to 2.4 percent for other soups. Sales of condensed soups fell another 2 percent in the fall of 1998. Campbell's market share for canned soups has fallen from 80 percent in 1992 to 74 percent in 1997. Shrinking soup sales led to lower profits in 1997 and 1998. In January of 1999, Campbell's stock price dropped 13 percent to reach a 52-week low as a result of the company's failure to reach profit goals. Most of the market share losses have been to lower priced store brand soups produced by H.J. Heinz Co. Consumers are also buying more ready-to-serve soup instead of the condensed soup primarily sold by Campbell. Progresso is a strong competitor in the ready-to-serve segment where Campbell's market share is only 55 percent. Reversing the decline in soup sales will not be easy because of changes in America's shopping and cooking habits. People are buying fewer canned foods of any kind. To counter this trend, Campbell has begun switching to glass jars for its ready-to-serve soup and aseptic boxes for its broth. Also the demand for "cooking soups" has declined. In the early 1980s Campbell sold as much as 40 percent of its tomato and other condensed soups to shoppers who used them as a cooking ingredient. However, today fewer people are preparing meat loaf and tuna-noodle casserole recipes that call for canned soup.

To help stem the declining sales of its Campbell brand soups, the company has made a number of changes in its marketing programs. In 1998, they did not take their usual 3 to 7 percent spring price increase. Customers were paying 20 percent more for Campbell brand soup compared to the prices of store brand soups and Campbell's battered brand equity would no longer allow them to raise prices every year to improve revenues. Campbell also planned to increase its soup advertising budget from 3.5 percent of sales to 8 percent of sales. Some of the new ads tout Campbell's soups as cooking ingredients and others will be run on children's shows. Also, hundreds of new recipes will be made available on Campbell's Web site. To cut costs, Campbell plans to end its long time practice of offering retailers rebates and steep discounts at quarter's end to entice stores to stock up on soup so Campbell can meet its sales targets. Basil Anderson, chief financial officer of Campbell Soup Co., blames the lack of enough new products for market share losses. He indicated that "Without significant innovation, any name brand tends to lose share to private label." The company is working on a number of new products.

— *Managers who fail to adjust mature brands to meet changing market conditions and consumer preferences can expect to lose volume to competitive brands.*

Source: Vanessa O'Connell, "Changing Tastes Dent Campbell's Canned Soup Sales," *The Wall Street Journal*, April 28, 1998, p. B1. Vanessa O'Connell, "Campbell Sees Profit Shortfall and Stock Gets Creamed," *The Wall Street Journal*, January 12, 1999.

Courtesy Campbell Soup Company

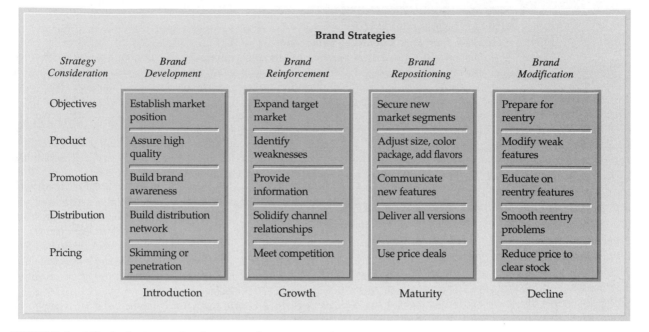

FIGURE 7-5   Life-Cycle Strategies for a Toothpaste Brand

Strategies for Reviving Brands

Perhaps the most important task of brand review procedures is to separate the items that can benefit from a redesign of the package or promotional plans from those that are on an irreversible downhill slide toward extinction. Often large sums of money are wasted in trying to save brands that have no future.

What Is the Problem?   The job of identifying candidates for rescue operations is not easy, and specific reasons for sales declines must be identified. The first step is to determine the contribution to the sales loss due to changes in the number of buyers versus the amount they buy. When customers are purchasing less of a brand and the number of buyers is holding up, the brand may be salvageable. The next step is to assess the underlying causes of such losses. If the quality is found to be inferior and customers are shifting to improved versions, there may be little hope for the brand. The best rescue situation occurs when most people have positive memories of the brand and the product still has a loyal group of fans.

The easiest solution to declining sales is to move the product into new foreign or domestic markets. This may require the addition of new distributors or the enlargement of the existing sales force. An alternative to greater breadth of market coverage is finding and promoting new uses among existing customers. Manufacturers of consumer products are particularly skilled at devising new uses for baking soda or bleach and coming up with new recipes that help extend the life of old brands. Since it costs millions to introduce a new brand, it can be cheaper to reformulate an existing product.

APPLYING
. . . to
Consumer
Food
Marketing

What Can Be Done?   A classic turnaround occurred with Kraft's Cheez Whiz. The processed cheese had been on the market for 36 years and was losing 3 to 4 percent of its sales each year. The marketing manager suggested repositioning Cheez Whiz as a sauce for the microwave oven. New ads were created emphasizing its use in microwave ovens, and the ad budget was tripled. Cheez Whiz was also repackaged in multipacks of 4-ounce cups designed for microwave heating. As a result of these activities, sales increased 35 percent.

Frito-Lay nearly dropped its Tostitos tortilla chip after sales slumped 50 percent from a peak. Instead, hoping to latch onto the Tex-Mex food craze, it reformulated Tostitos into a restaurant-style chip—doubling its size, changing its shape from circular to triangular, and substituting white corn for yellow. Packaged in a new clear bag with big, bolder graphics, Tostitos Restaurant Style Chips set new revenue records. This proves that consumers crave what's old and familiar. You just have to freshen it up. Another example of a brand revival is shown in Marketing Strategies box 7-3.

Despite the successful revivals that we have mentioned, however, not every aging brand can be saved. Also, spending money on weak products often takes energy and resources away from your leading brands. This suggests that fading brands such as Carnation powdered milk, Serutan laxative, and Del Monte canned peas do not warrant expensive new promotional programs. Marketing expenditures on declining products are risky and are justified only when there is good reason to believe that the item can be saved.

Strategies for Fading Brands

Perhaps the best strategy for poor performing brands is to sell them while they are still profitable so you can recoup some of the brand equity that remains. If you wait too long, no one will want the brand and you may be faced with paying significant costs to drop the brand from the product line. In 1998, Procter & Gamble reviewed its smaller and low-performing brands and sold off its Duncan Hines cake mix business which accounted for about 10 percent of its food sales. P&G also announced plans to sell the North American portion of its Attends incontinence-care business and Hawaiian Punch juice. Hawaiian Punch was profitable, but P&G wanted to focus its resources on brands with better growth prospects.[10] Hershey Foods also decided to sell its Ronzoni, Skinner, and San Giorgio brands of pastas.[11] Although these brands made Hershey the number-one pasta marketer in the United States with revenues of $400 million, sales declined 2 percent in 1998. Another reason Hershey wanted to sell the pasta brands is they produced operating margins of only 10 percent compared to 20 percent for candy. Hershey believed that by focusing resources on other brands they could generate a better return for their shareholders. Smaller firms that buy Hawaiian Punch and the pasta brands can make money because they require little promotion and no fixed investment in facilities. Sometimes a new buyer can expand a business through more aggressive marketing. Marketing Strategies box 7-4 describes what happened when IBM sold off its small printer division.

MARKETING STRATEGIES 7-3

Clairol Rescues Herbal Essences

*APPLYING
. . . to
Health and
Beauty Aid
Marketing*

Herbal Essences shampoo went from a moribund relic of the 1970s to the second largest shampoo brand in the U.S. thanks to a radical overhaul and a frisky ad campaign. The 1995 relaunch positioned the shampoo as an indulgence in the time pressed 90s, with a soothing scent and an ad campaign that touted it as a "totally organic experience." The campaign played on the "organic" tagline by showing women going delirious with pleasure while using the shampoo. One TV spot for the shampoo featured the well known sex therapist Dr. Ruth. The positioning and tagline continued into the launch of an Herbal Essences body wash in 1997. Clairol backed the Herbal Essences hair care brand with $34 million in ad support during 1998. As a result, Herbal Essences went from a market share of 2.1 percent in 1995 to 10.1 percent of the $1.68 billion market in 1998. Four percent of this growth was stolen from Procter & Gamble's market leading Pantene shampoo brand.

— *Creative positioning and great ads can revive lethargic products.*

Source: Mercedes M. Cardona, "Brands: In Trouble—In Demand," *Advertising Age,* February 22, 1999, p. 20.

APPLYING
. . . to
Industrial
Marketing

MARKETING STRATEGIES 7-4

IBM Sells Off Its Printer Business

As IBM struggled with its core computer businesses, they decided to focus on mid- to high-end printers and sold off their low-end desktop printer unit in 1991. Once free of IBM's bureaucracy, that business became Lexmark International Inc., a flourishing printer company based in Lexington, Kentucky. This left IBM with a niche role for its line of medium and large printers in the global printer industry. IBM's printer sales reached a peak of $935 million in 1994 and declined to $757 million by 1997. These declines were mainly due to new designs and aggressive marketing by rival printer manufacturers such as Xerox. Sales in the U.S. were particularly hard hit, declining by 27 percent. Since the printer unit produced only modest profits, IBM decided to sell out and buy any printers they needed from other firms.

— *Sometimes it pays to sell noncore business orphans.*

Source: Raju Narisetti, "IBM Is Seeking to Sell Its Printer Business," *The Wall Street Journal,* June 17, 1998, p. B6.

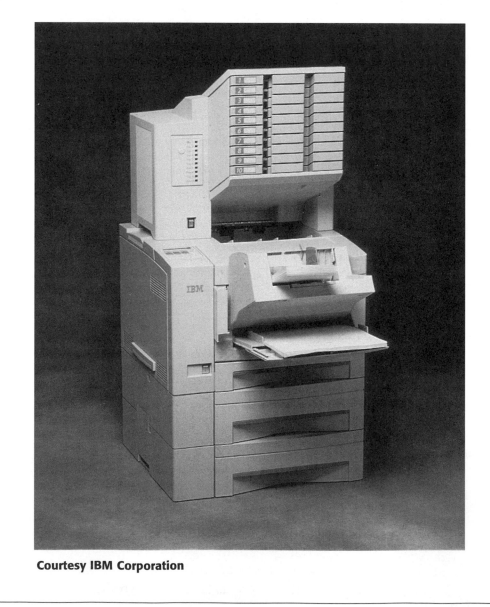

Courtesy IBM Corporation

Another successful strategy for fading brands is to drop all promotional activities and rely solely on repeated purchases from current customers. Where promotional expenditures have been substantial, sales are likely to decline slowly, and the savings from discontinued advertising can make the brand quite profitable in the short run. For example, when Chrysler introduced its new Jeep Grand Cherokee sport utility vehicle, they kept the outdated Jeep Cherokee model as a low-priced fighting brand. The boxy old model did not have air bags, a modern 4-wheel drive, or enough interior room, but Chrysler had written off all developments' costs for the brand so they could make money selling the Cherokees at low prices. This strategy was so successful that Chrysler sold enough Cherokees to pay for adding air bags and some other improvements.

Sharing the Risks.   Another useful strategy for declining products is to continue to sell the item but to contract with another company for manufacturing. An alternative is to continue to make the product but license others to sell it. A third possibility is to begin exporting the brand to foreign markets where it might be viewed as new and exciting. Sometimes brands that have worn out their welcome in one country can find new life when marketed in another. While cigarettes are viewed as unhealthy in the United States, American cigarette brands are still quite popular in Eastern Europe and China.

Helping the Dealers.   In situations in which nothing can save a declining brand, the firm should dispose of it with a minimum of inconvenience to the interested parties. This means notifying dealers in advance and helping them clear out old stock. Frequently, special discounts are offered to dealers to stimulate the sale of discontinued brands. It may even be necessary for the manufacturer to buy back the unsold merchandise. Dealers should also be informed about replacement brands that are being promoted to take the place of the discontinued items, which can help maintain consumer goodwill, and arrange to provide service and parts for recent buyers.

SUMMARY

In this chapter we have explained what brands are and the important concept of brand equity. We have also described the strategies used to manage brands over their life cycle. Brands are vulnerable to competitive pressures and you must know how to manipulate line extensions, brand extensions, umbrella brands, quality, promotions, prices, warranties, and repair services to optimize profits. Finally, a variety of strategies for brands with stagnant or declining sales have been explained.

NOTES

1. Steven Lipin, "Newell to Buy Rubbermaid for $5.8 Billion," *The Wall Street Journal*, October 21, 1998, pp. A3, A8.
2. Michelle W. Fellman, "Just the Name, Thanks: Why Beemer Bought Rolls," *Marketing News,* September 14, 1998, p. 6.
3. Kevin L. Keller, *Strategic Brand Management: Building, Measuring, and Managing Brand Equity* (Upper Saddle River, NJ: Prentice-Hall, 1998), p. 45.
4. Stephen J. Hoch, "Private Label a Threat? Don't Believe It," *Advertising Age,* May 24, 1993, p. 19.
5. P. Fitzell, *Private Label Marketing in the 1990s* (New York: Global Book Productions, 1992).
6. Stephen Hoch, "How Should National Brands Think About Private Labels?" *Sloan Management Review* (Winter 1996), pp. 89–102.
7. Steven J. Hoch, "Private Label a Threat? Don't Believe It," p. 19.

8. Deborah Roedder John, Barbara Loken, and Christopher Joiner, "The Negative Impact of Extensions: Can Flagship Products Be Diluted?" *Journal of Marketing Research,* Vol. 62 (January 1998), pp. 19–32.

9. Cyndee Miller, "U.S. Firms Lag in Meeting Global Quality Standards," *Marketing News,* Vol. 27, No. 4 (February 15, 1993), pp. 1, 6.

10. Tara Parker-Pope, "Procter & Gamble Mulls Selling Off Hawaiian Punch," *The Wall Street Journal*, November 12, 1998, p. B8.

11. Vanessa O'Connell, "Hershey, Faced with Limp Pasta Sales, Announces Plans to Sell Eight Brands," *The Wall Street Journal*, November 10, 1998, p. A4.

SUGGESTED READING

Aaker, Jennifer L. "Dimensions of Brand Personality," *Journal of Marketing Research,* Vol. 34 (August 1997), pp. 347–356.

Keller, Kevin L. *Strategic Brand Management: Building, Measuring, and Managing Brand Equity* (Upper Saddle River, NJ: Prentice-Hall, 1998).

REFERENCES

Aaker, David A. *Building Strong Brands* (New York: Free Press, 1995).

Aaker, David A. *Managing Brand Equity* (New York: Free Press, 1991).

Cortada, James W. *TQM for Sales and Marketing Management* (New York, McGraw-Hill, 1993).

Kapferer, Jean-Noel. *Strategic Brand Management: Creating and Sustaining Brand Equity Long Term* (London: Kogan Page Ltd, 1998).

Ries, Laura and Al Ries. *22 Immutable Laws of Branding: How to Build a Product or Service into a World-Class Brand* (New York: HarperCollins, 1998).

Shocker, Allen D., Rajendra K. Srivastava, and Robert W. Ruekert, Eds. "Special Issue on Brand Management," *Journal of Marketing Research,* Vol. 31 (May 1994), pp. 149–304.

QUESTIONS

1. Bausch & Lomb is the leader in the market for premium sunglasses costing more than $75, with an estimated 35 percent market share. Yet in 1997, the sunglass division lost $59 million on revenue of $492 million. In 1998, the company expected to make a small profit. Bausch & Lomb has hired an investment banker to help it decide whether to sell the sunglass division, enter a joint venture, or spin it off to shareholders. Why is a market leader considering getting rid of a business that provides 25 percent of its revenue?

2. Nabisco introduced a brand extension reduced fat cookie called SnackWell's at a premium price and they were an instant hit. In a few years sales mushroomed to more than $400 million per year. However, competitors rushed to bring out competitive brands and by 1998 sales had declined to only $150 million a year. In addition, Nabisco's total dollar sales fell 1.7 percent in 1997 while sales at rival Keebler Foods rose 7 percent. Nabisco responded by replacing the head of its biscuit unit with an executive from Pillsbury. What caused Nabisco to go from a successful SnackWell's marketer to an also-ran in the quest for cookie customers?

3. Dr Pepper/Seven-Up Inc. changed the formula of its 7-Up soft drink to be less sweet with a crisper lemon-line taste like its fast-growing competitor Sprite marketed by Coca-Cola Co. In 1997, Sprite was the fastest-growing soft drink in the United States with a market share of 5.8 percent. Meanwhile 7-Up's market share had declined from 3.2 percent in 1987 to 2.4 percent in 1996. In addition to changing the flavor of 7-Up,

the company is planning to increase promotion and advertising activities to try to revive the brand. Do you think 7-Up's sweeter flavor caused it to lose market share to Sprite? What marketing advantages does Coca-Cola have that helped it steal the lemon-lime soda market from 7-Up?

4. The Driscoll Strawberry Associates, Inc., of Watsonville, California, has been growing and shipping strawberries and raspberries since 1940. Given the success of Dole and Del Monte in branding fresh produce, should Driscoll launch branded berries for consumers? If so, how can they nurture the perception among consumers that their strawberries and raspberries are something different, something better? That is, suggest a positioning statement for them.

5. Several automobile manufacturers have had success with brand extensions into a new breed of vehicle that combines features from sedans and truck-based sport utilities. These light sport utilities are built on platforms from cars instead of truck platforms used for large sport utilities. The end result is a smaller, lighter, cheaper, and more easily handling vehicle such as Honda's CR-V, Toyota's RAV4, and Subaru's Forester. These small sport utilities are especially popular among women and young buyers. Why do manufacturers offer brands that attract single and young married customers? How can brand loyalty to these entry level products help them in the long run?

6. Are warranties primarily designed to protect consumers and manufacturers against loss or to boost sales of goods and services?

7. Parker Brothers introduced a new toy brand called Riviton that outsold any other toy the company had ever introduced. Children could use the plastic parts, rubber rivets, and riveting tool to assemble anything from a truck to a house. A total of 450,000 kits retailing for $15 to $25 were sold the first year, and sales were expected to reach $10 million in the second year. However, two children choked to death on the rubber rivets in the kits. Parker, which is a division of General Mills, decided to stop selling Riviton and ordered a recall. These steps were taken even though the product met all safety standards and was not under investigation by the Consumer Product Safety Commission. After three months, 370,000 kits had been returned at a cost exceeding $8.3 million. Do you agree with Parker's decision to recall the kits? Why or why not? Why did Parker move so quickly on the recall?

8. Research has shown that 91 percent of American women ages 18 to 39 advocate specific brands. Also women believe the brands they choose reflect their personality. Women also tend to advocate brands from a wide range of product categories. However, men advocate brands for only three product categories: cars, technology, and sports equipment. Do you believe this information would be useful to brand managers and if so, how?

9. Hughes Electronics Corp. introduced the first satellite-TV system in the United States carrying the brand name DirecTV. The digital system offered excellent reception, 150 channels, and employed a small 18-inch receiver dish. By 1998, DirecTV had 4 million subscribers and revenue rose 8 percent from the year earlier. However, Hughes lost $61 million on DirecTV due to costs of expanding coverage to Japan, the growth of digital cable alternatives, and competition from other satellite providers. Hughes hopes to break even in 1999. Should Hughes sell its DirecTV brand or try to find a way to rescue the brand? If they keep DirecTV, what steps do you recommend to make the brand profitable?

10. The Victoria's Secret chain is best known for flooding malls with provocative lingerie. It is now selling is own Victoria Secret's Cosmetics line through its stores. Assess this line extension.

11. The American Lung Association was launched almost a century ago to combat tubercu-

losis. The battle has largely been won. TB now kills about 1,000 people a year in the United States, compared with 150,000 in 1900. Lung cancer was a natural successor cause for the Lung Association, but other health-oriented charities had already adopted it. Meantime, the Lung Association's revenue machine, the annual Christmas Seal campaign, was losing its fund-raising wallop by failing to connect with a new generation of donors. The Lung Association decided to focus on asthma. Though a growing problem, among children and the urban poor, asthma has been a financial and public-relations flop for the Lung Association. Asthma has failed to excite the critical big-money donors. Simply put, the Lung Association does have a big scary disease anymore. What should the Lung Association do about its acute identity crisis?

CHAPTER 8

SERVICES MARKETING

> If you can sell green toothpaste in this country, you can sell opera.
>
> SARAH CALDWELL

*O*ne of the most important marketing developments in your lifetime has been the explosive growth of services in the U.S. economy. Today more than 75 percent of all businesses and personal consumption in the United States goes to purchase services. This growth is related to a decline in the manufacturing sector, additional wealth, an expansion in leisure time, and increases in the number of dual-career families. With their extra money, people are surfing the Internet, renting cellular phones, paying bills electronically, traveling more, and turning to a host of special cleaning and child-care services. Growth in services is not limited to the United States; many firms are finding new markets overseas. An example of the vast opportunities for growth in communication services is described in Marketing in Action box 8-1.

Now that the world is becoming more service oriented, it is essential for you to know how to sell these items. This chapter will acquaint you with the nature of services, their special characteristics, and show you how to manage service marketing activities.

NATURE OF SERVICES

Most physical products include some service elements as part of the offering. For example, a common service is the warranty to replace or repair durables such as compact discs, computer programs, or books that are defective. Goods with a low service component are positioned in Sectors 3 and 6 of Figure 8-1. Goods with a higher service component are shown in Sectors 2 and 5. Hotels are a classic example because, while rooms are a service, customers also consume food and take advantage of flower and gift shops that sell goods. Pure services such as mail delivery, medicine, and engineering are shown in Sectors 1 and 4 of Figure 8-1. Thus the service component of a product can range from very low to very high, and marketing programs vary for each type of product.

Recent Trends

A number of changes in the economic environment in the last few years have increased the importance of marketing in service industries.

Less Regulation.   Service industries have traditionally been highly regulated. Government agencies often mandated price levels, constrained distribution areas, and even regulated pos-

MARKETING IN ACTION *8-1*

Season's Greetings Using E-mail and Web Sites

An increasing number of Americans are now sending out greetings using e-mail and their own Web sites. Some people register their sites with a Web hosting service and use personal software to design it. This allows them to include an unlimited amount of pictures, family news, and musical accompaniment in their holiday message. Once they design their greeting, they tell their friends the location of the Web site using e-mail. Others buy a holiday letter, Web site, and e-mail package from companies such as Verio Inc. and Network Solutions Inc. After an initial payment, the quarterly fee is $59.95. Consumers who use e-mail and Web sites to send messages to their friends save enough on postage and the cost of cards to more than pay the costs of the electronic letters. The Internet division of Hallmark Cards Inc. offers a free service allowing people to go to Hallmark's site and design their own newsletter using preset formats and art. Another online card company, Blue Mountain Arts Inc. of Boulder, Colorado, offers a site that allows you to create and send personal greeting cards. Blue Mountain is now the 14th most visited site on the Web.

— *Creative marketing of new services can boost company sales.*

Source: Rebecca Buckman,"Season's Greetings From Our Web Site!" *The Wall Street Journal,* December 21, 1998, p. B1.

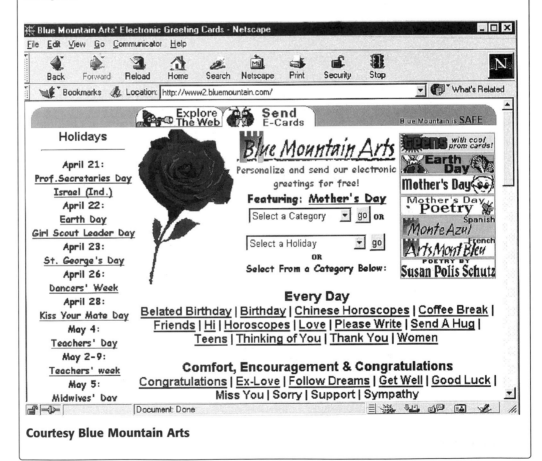

Courtesy Blue Mountain Arts

INTEGRATING *. . . with Information Technology, Production/ Operations Management*

sible product features. However, the trend in the United States and throughout the world is toward deregulation of major services. This means that there are fewer constraints on competitive activity in airlines, energy, railroads, trucking, banking, securities, insurance, and telecommunications. Barriers to entry by new firms have been dropped, geographical restrictions on service delivery have been reduced, and there is more freedom to adjust

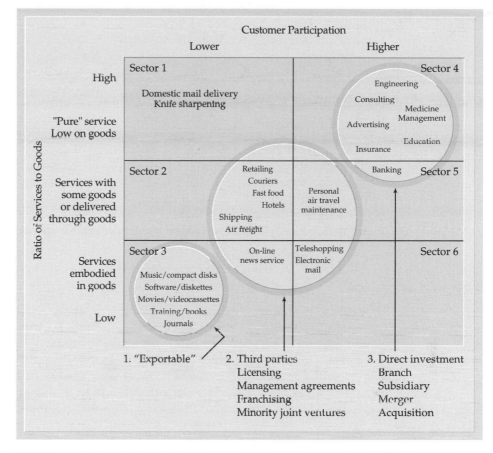

FIGURE 8-1 Service to Goods Ratios and Customer Participation (From Sandra Vandermerwe and Michael Chadwick, "The Internationalization of Services," *The Services Industry Journal* **[January 1989], pp. 79–93.)**

prices. Substantial relaxation of trade regulation of services is occurring in the European Union, and rules are being eased in Japan as well. The impact of deregulation on pricing of phone services in Germany has been dramatic. Viag Interkom, partially owned by British Telecommunications, cut some phone prices 60 percent. Deutsche Telekom responded by saying it would cut prices further to match the cuts by Viag, O.tel.O, and other German phone companies.[1]

A related trend has been a move to force professional associations to remove bans on advertising and promotional activities. Professions that now allow more competitive activity include accounting, architecture, medicine, law, and optometry. This has led to more use of informational advertising and more price competition.

Privatization. With the growth of government deficits, there has been a trend to return government-owned service industries to private investors. In England, France, Italy, and Japan there is a move to convert telecommunications, national airlines, and utilities to private ownership. Municipal governments are also selling airports and contracting with private firms to haul trash. The new result is more emphasis on cost cutting and more interest by new owners in meeting customers' service needs.

APPLYING
. . . to
Tele-
communications
Services
Marketing

Customer Participation

Services can also be classified by the amount of customer participation that is required. High-participation services shown in Figure 8-1 include banking and education; low-participation services include shipping and couriers. When you are having a couch reupholstered, you do not have to be present. This means that the upholstery firm can be located in an old building without a waiting room, while a dentist needs to offer a convenient location, comfortable seating, pleasant views, and soothing music. Marketing In Action box 8-2 shows how buyers work with an auction company to find new suppliers.

The degree of customer participation and the ratio of services to goods have an impact on international marketing strategies. Figure 8-1 groups products into three strategy clusters. Cluster 1 includes low-participation, low-service products that are best exported. Products with intermediate values in cluster 2 should be handled by third-party arrangements with overseas businesspeople through licensing or franchising. For pure services with high customer participation, you need to consider direct international investment in sales branches or subsidiaries.

Major Service Industries

A good way to understand the breadth of the service industry is to look at how the government classifies services for the Census of Business. Table 8-1 lists the major categories of service industries and gives examples. These include communications, consulting, educational, financial, health, household operations, housing, insurance, personal, and transportation. Note that retailing and restaurants are not considered to be major service industries even though they provide a service element in their product offerings.

Services Are All Around

One of the most striking things about Table 8-1 is how many services are routinely used by consumers and businesses. Consider a day in the life of Paula, an assistant product manager.

MARKETING IN ACTION 8-2

Bidding for Nuts and Bolts on the Net

APPLYING
. . . to
Industrial
Services
Marketing

A new Web company called FreeMarkets On Line Inc. helps firms get bids for parts from present and prospective suppliers over the Internet. FreeMarkets structures the auctions to maximize the psychological pressure on suppliers to offer their best possible price. First it prescreens the bidders to those acceptable to the buyer and arranges to have at least six to eight bids on each lot to assure brisk competition. Then it arranges for the first lots to have the most bidders. No bids of just a few dollars less than the last bid are allowed. Bidding is conducted on a secure computer network and the bidders are not told who they are bidding against. They also don't know the price the buyer paid for similar items in the past. FreeMarkets sends each bidder thick packages detailing the parts being sought and the buyer's quality requirements. In this type of online auction, the low bidder does not necessarily win. Sometimes buyers stay with incumbent suppliers even if their prices are higher because they have a good sense of their abilities. At an online auction session, United Technologies was hoping to identify potential savings of 15 percent on $7.3 million of simple machined parts. At the end of the day they saved 25 percent.

— *Internet auction services can help firms find low cost suppliers.*

Source: Timothy Aeppel, "Bidding for E-Nuts and E-Bolts on the Net," *The Wall Street Journal*, March 12, 1999, pp. B1, B4.

TABLE 8-1   Major Service Industries

SIC Code	Industry	SIC Code	Industry
48	*Communications*	49	*Household Operations*
	Telephone		Electrical companies
	Radio broadcasting		Sewer companies
	TV broadcasting		Laundries
73	*Consulting*		Cleaning
	Advertising agencies	65	*Housing*
	Outdoor advertising		Apartment buildings
	Direct mail		Rental agents
	Employment agencies		Hotels
	Testing laboratories		Trailer parks
	Temporary help	63	*Insurance*
	Auditing		Insurance agents
82	*Educational*		Life insurance
	Colleges & professional schools		Health insurance
	Libraries		Fire & casualty
	Technical institutes	72	*Personal*
60	*Financial*		Beauty & barber shops
	Banks		Motion picture theaters
	Savings & loans		Bowling alleys
	Credit unions		Skating rinks
	Commodity dealers	4	*Transportation*
	Security exchanges		Suburban transit
80	*Health*		Airlines
	Hospitals		Motor freight
	Medical laboratories		Automobile rental
	Physicians & surgeons		

When she wakes up in her rented apartment, one of the first things she does is switch on the lights to get ready for work. Soon she jumps in her leased BMW and turns on the radio to catch the traffic report. Parking the car in the pay lot at the subway station, she notices an outdoor ad for a movie she wants to see at a local theater. When she arrives at the office, she checks her e-mail and picks up the phone to talk with the advertising agency that handles one of her brands. Later that day, she calls her insurance agent about the liability coverage on her sailboat. On the way home, she stops at a teller machine to pick up some cash and then spends some of it on repairs for her watch. Back home, she flips on the TV to catch the evening news. As Paula prepares dinner, she checks a Web site, pays some bills, and arranges a vacation trip to Hawaii. After dinner she heads out to her marketing class at the local university.

All of this businesswoman's daily activities have involved contact with service organizations. But why did Paula select certain companies? The implication is clear. For service companies to succeed, they must understand how to market their benefits to customers. Marketing Strategies box 8-1 describes the ongoing battle to be the bill payer for American consumers.

SERVICE MARKETING CHARACTERISTICS

Services have special characteristics that affect how marketing programs are created and executed. These features include intangibility, perishability, inseparability, variability, and client relationships.

MARKETING STRATEGIES *8-1*

Paperless Bill Paying

The time is coming when most U.S. citizens will be able to pay their bills online with a click of a mouse. With current electronic bill payment systems, consumers get paper bills in the mail and pay them by typing out checks on their home computer that are then sent by a bank or outside processor such as CheckFree Holdings Corp. In the future, consumers will log on to a Web site and see a message telling them "You have bills." They would be able to scan the bills or pay them immediately with a click of their mouse. Paperless bill delivery is currently in limited use by a few American banks. However, with the potential for a multibillion dollar market up for grabs, a variety of financial, utility and technology firms are jockeying for position. Banks have a huge role to play if they are willing to capture it and a great deal to lose if they don't. As the trusted keepers of consumers' checking accounts, banks could become hubs of online financial activity. Also paper checks are expensive for banks to process, costing the nation $181 billion a year. Converting to electronic checks could save consumers 90 billion dollars. However, banks have been slow to cash in on this new online service and only 16 of the 35 largest banks offer even the old style electronic bill payment over the Web. Everyone is trying to figure out who is going to pay the start-up costs to convert to paperless bill paying even though savings for the country would be immense. Banks who have charged consumers extra for the new system have run into customer resistance. This has opened the door to firms like Intuit Inc. that allows its customers to view and pay bills online through its popular Quicken personal finance software. If banks fail to see the opportunity in paperless bill paying, brokers and Web outfits like Yahoo!, Inc. and America Online, Inc. could start delivering bills to consumers and steal away a huge market.

— *Banks stand to lose when the Web pays the bills.*

Sources: Rebecca Buckman, "Bills, Bills (Click), More Bills … A Race Is On for Best Paperless Payment System," *The Wall Street Journal*, November 19, 1998 p. C1; Lucinda Harper, "Americans Won't Stop Writing Checks," *The Wall Street Journal*, November 24, 1998, p. A2.

Intangibility

The most obvious problem with marketing services is that they are intangible. Buyers cannot touch, smell, see, taste, or hear services before they are purchased. When they buy goods, customers get something to take home. When they buy services, they receive only a ticket stub or a piece of paper. With services, consumers buy a performance rather than a physical product. As a result, intangibility of services raises the perceived risk of purchase compared with buying goods. Service buyers cannot effectively evaluate services prior to purchase and there is usually no way to try out services before purchase. The implication for marketers is that it is important to build and maintain high brand loyalty to make buyers feel secure about the higher risks they are taking with service purchases. For example, when customers purchase a home the cost of insurance is built into the monthly payment and stored in an accrual account at the financial institution making the loan. This is paid once a year by the financial institution directly to the insurance company. This means that customers may not know what they are paying for homeowners' insurance, so it is critical that brand loyalty is strong enough to overcome homeowner's fear that their insurance company may overcharge them.

Also the abstract nature of services means that marketers must find a way to dramatize the concept for the customer. Several clever solutions to this problem are offered in Figure 8-2. To overcome the lack of a physical product, marketers need to develop a tangible representation of the service. One of the best examples is the use of plastic cards to symbolize bank credit. Ads can then be created showing customers using their bank cards to pay for real products such as meals or souvenirs of exotic locations.

Another dilemma with intangibles is that it can be hard for buyers to grasp the idea of service concepts. One solution is to use physical symbols in the advertising that are more easily understood by the customers (Figure 8-2). For example, Travelers Insurance is well known for its umbrella. Insurance companies convey security by association with familiar rocks, hands, umbrellas, and blankets.

A third approach focuses on the service provider (actor, lawyer, professor), who is more tangible than the actual service (screen role, courtroom appearance, education). In this case, advertising emphasizes the skills and technical competence of the person who is in contact with the buyer. Insurance agents are shown as family counselors and loan officers as friendly neighbors; the Maytag repairman is depicted as someone with little to do. Thus, the service being offered becomes more tangible because of the fellowship with the provider.

Perishability

Services cannot be stored or carried in inventory. If they are not used when offered, they go to waste. The empty classroom or hospital bed represents revenue that is lost forever. Most of the problems with perishability are related to inaccurate forecasts of demand. When

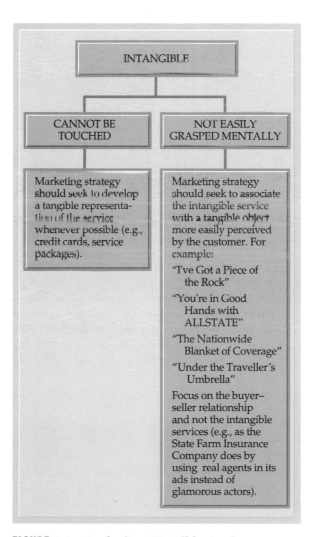

FIGURE 8-2 Marketing Intangible Services

demand is steady, service organizations are able to provide staff and equipment to meet customers' requests. However, unpredictable demand can lead to serious difficulties. For example, on a cold December day one of the author's cars broke down. He called AAA on his car phone to get a tow truck and was put on hold for 10 minutes. Then he was cut off and had to call back and was put on hold again. When he finally reached AAA, he was told it would take three to four hours to get a tow truck. Since it was 10 degrees outside, he flagged down an independent tow truck. In this case, AAA did not have enough people answering the phone and they did not have enough tow trucks under contract to provide the emergency services customers expected.

The best way to avoid service problems is to do a better job of matching supply with demand. This can be done by adjusting supply or by smoothing out demand. Some suggestions for supply-side management include the following:

- Perform maintenance at night when services are not in demand. Examples include airplanes and transit buses.
- Encourage customers to perform part of the service, such as filling out forms in doctors' offices or at the car rental counter.
- Hire temporary help to meet peak demands. An example is the use of Manpower and Kelly Services in offices.

Demand can be managed by the following methods:

- Differential pricing to shift demand from peak to off-peak periods. An example is low weekend rates at urban hotels.
- Advertising campaigns that focus on the solitude of island beaches during off-season periods.
- Offering complementary services to those who are waiting. Theaters sell popcorn and candy and rent videotapes to people waiting to see a movie.
- Reservation systems guarantee services to customers who cannot be handled during peak periods. These extra customers can be told of available service times and kept from going to competitors.

Inseparability

A tangible product is first manufactured by a firm; next, it is distributed to dealers who sell it; and finally, the product is consumed. With services, however, the sale comes first. Then the service is produced and consumed at the same time. For example, a customer buys an opera ticket; then, on the night of the performance, the opera is presented and viewed by the audience. Simultaneous production and consumption forces services to be delivered directly to the customer. This close relationship with buyers makes the image of the service provider more important in the purchase decision. In addition, services must be easily accessible to customers.

Outlet Accessibility.   Because services cannot be stored or transported, they have to be delivered to customers by local sales agents. This means that the revenue of service marketers is often limited by the number of service outlets they maintain. Although customers may be willing to drive 50 miles to an airport, they will travel only a few miles to go to a bank, dry cleaner, financial advisor, insurance agent, or bowling alley. Service marketers have to balance the revenues produced by additional outlets against the costs of maintaining the facilities. Service marketers have tried various strategies to reduce the costs of getting close to customers. H&R Block opens hundreds of temporary offices during the tax season

and then closes them. Century 21 uses a system of franchising local offices to expand its coverage and enhance revenues. One of the best ways to expand coverage is through the use of technology. Many firms now make airline and theater tickets available on the Internet. Also online service providers such as America Online and retailers like Amazon.com have agreed to share their revenues with computer manufacturers Compaq and Hewlett-Packard Co. In exchange, the PC makers have redesigned their keyboards to add "quick access" keys and to give prominent placement to the Web sites and services of their partners.[2] Ticketmaster has machines that dispense theater and sports tickets at locations accessible to customers. Banks have been very successful at providing low-cost services by placing teller machines in convenient sites that would not support a full-service outlet.

Image Is Important.   Since the buyer must be present to obtain certain services, marketers should be aware of the image projected by their facility. Doctors' and lawyers' offices are often luxuriously decorated to instill a feeling of confidence in the client. Attractive furnishings imply that the business is doing well and suggest professional competence.

The same concept applies to auto repairs. If you visit a shop and find the floor strewn with broken parts, tools, and pools of grease, you are likely to question the mechanic's ability to fix your car. Successful service suppliers maintain the quality of their customer contact facilities to attract repeat buyers.

Variability

Because most services are produced by people, service quality tends to vary considerably from one transaction to the next. Products, on the other hand, are produced in factories where inspectors can ensure uniformity from item to item. The lack of standardization by service providers means that you may be satisfied with your haircut, your dry cleaner, or your dentist on one visit and be dissatisfied on your next visit. Service buyers face greater uncertainty in the marketplace and try to reduce that risk. One result is that customers are more likely to seek a friend's recommendation when selecting a doctor than when buying a microwave oven.

A good way to reduce service variation risk is to provide warranties such as those used for physical products. One warranty program for auto repairs claims that if Ford doesn't fix the car correctly, the customer does not have to pay. Customers will be more willing to take their cars to Ford service departments if they know that the company stands behind its repair work.

One of the best ways to reduce variability in service delivery is through the increased utilization of technology. The expanded use of computers has led to greater standardization of services and less variation in the quality of service delivery. For example, ATMs and personal computer banking programs now allow consumers to transact their banking business without the use of tellers. CPAs now prepare tax returns using a sophisticated $1,000 computer program that reduces calculation and preparation errors. Other programs allow investors to trade stocks without a broker and gather instant information on securities they are considering buying.

Another way to reduce variability in services is to hire and train employees very carefully. For example, Disney World's success is clearly related to the enthusiasm and courtesy of its employees. Disney is selective in hiring and spends a great deal of time training its employees to deal with the public. If Disney can build a loyal and dedicated team of customer contact people, so can other service organizations.

Firms that expect to reduce service variability need to monitor service production to detect when problems exist. Information on customer satisfaction can be obtained through suggestion boxes, phone surveys, and mail questionnaires. Once a firm identifies rude, discourteous, and uninformed personnel, these employees can either be retrained or terminated.

Client Relationships

Relationships between service organizations and customers are often close and long-lasting. Under these conditions, service providers should work to develop client rapport. When you are dealing with clients, try to associate on a first-name basis and include customers in social activities (assuming this is appropriate to the culture). Clients are willing to deal on a first-name basis with the person who cuts their hair, buys stock for them, and creates their advertising. This means that service providers who are attempting to steal clients from competitors need to have a clearly superior product. Also, existing service customers need to be rewarded with extra perks and benefits. For example, it is not uncommon for stockbrokers to host cocktail parties and intimate dinner parties for clients. Even airlines have had success with "presidential lounges" for preferred groups of customers.

The objective of creating a client relationship is to make it easier to sell new services. The longer you provide a service to customers, the more confidence they will have in your recommendations. After all, it is easier for most people to consider new hairstyles, new investments, and new vacation ideas from those we like and respect. The task for the service company is to build an ongoing relationship so that customers will resist the blandishments of competitors and come back to buy again and again.

MANAGING THE SERVICE MARKETING SYSTEM

Services marketing is complicated because services are created and consumed simultaneously. This also means that you must produce services and sell them at the same time.

Service organizations usually have an operations person in charge of facilities, hiring, and customer contact personnel. As a result, marketing activities do not always get the attention they deserve. When marketing managers are employed, they usually advise staff on services development, pricing, promotion, and delivery. Thus service organizations often lack a strong marketing orientation that focuses on determining and filling customers' needs.

Systems for Service Marketing

A better structure for services marketing integrates the activities of the operations and marketing supervisors. The relationships between these two managers are highlighted in Figure 8-3. A service marketing system should consist of three interrelated parts: services operations, services delivery, and marketing support.

Services operations is responsible for facilities, equipment, and personnel. In a hotel, the operations manager runs the building and hires, trains, and supervises the employees. Only half of the services operations are visible to the customer. Hotel guests see the rooms and talk to the desk clerk and dining room personnel, but they do not come in contact with the kitchens, laundries, garage, and office areas behind the scenes.

Services delivery is concerned with the interface between the provider and the customer (Figure 8-3). The goal is to promote pleasant exchanges with customers so that they will return. Companies can encourage this trend by giving the marketing manager some control over service delivery. In a hotel, for example, marketing can oversee the reservation service, convention scheduling, and the information booth in the lobby. These activities solicit future business and take care of special needs of customers. If these tasks are handled efficiently, the flow of new business will be enhanced. Successful service delivery systems demand the coordinated efforts of marketing and operations personnel to make sure that customers are satisfied. A good marketing manager will handle inquiries and complaints to make sure that the quality of the services offered is maintained.

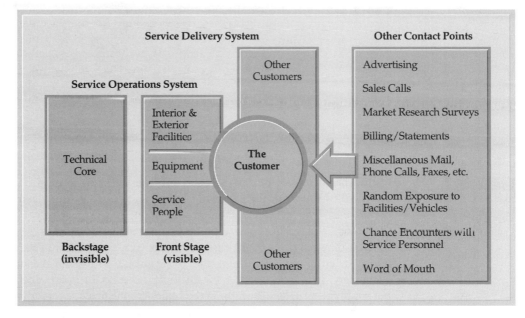

FIGURE 8-3   Services Marketing System (From Christopher H. Lovelock, *Services Marketing*, 3rd ed. [Englewood Cliffs, NJ: Prentice-Hall, 1996], p. 55.)

Customer Compatibility

Services frequently require that customers be present for service delivery (doctors, lawyers, dentists, cruises, concerts). This means that services are delivered in an environment where the customers interact with other clients. Note that Figure 8-3 highlights this relationship by showing one customer surrounded by other customers. There often is a direct connection between how a customer fits in with other clients and overall customer satisfaction. Successful service firms recognize this problem and are careful to segment their markets and group customers accordingly. For example, it would be foolish for a law firm to offer estate planning services and criminal law representation out of the same office. This would force wealthy customers interested in preserving their assets to sit in the same waiting room as clients seeking representation for robbery and theft. These two groups are incompatible and need to be serviced by offices located in separate buildings. The cruise ship industry is very good at ensuring customer compatibility by offering theme cruises targeted to bridge players, ballroom dancing enthusiasts, singles, and other groups.

Managing Service Quality

Firms that consistently deliver high-quality services can expect higher returns than organizations with poor customer relations. Table 8-2 shows how the top third of a sample of business units outperformed the bottom third in terms of service quality. These data reveal that high-service businesses were able to charge higher prices, grow faster, and make more profits on sales than their low-service competitors. Other research has shown that service quality is an antecedent of customer satisfaction. These results suggest that service organizations must pay attention to quality.

While it is easy to talk about delivering quality services, there are a number of problems that must be overcome. First, service quality is much more difficult to measure than product quality. Good service from a doctor is clearly a more subjective evaluation than whether a

TABLE 8-2   Service Quality and Performance

	Top Third in Service Quality	Bottom Third in Service Quality
Prices relative to competitors	7%	−2%
Change in market share per year	6%	−2%
Sales growth	17%	8%
Return on sales	12%	1%

Source: Phillip Thompson, Glenn Desoursa, and Bradley T. Gale, "The Strategic Management of Service and Quality," *Quality Progress,* (June 1985), p. 24.

INTEGRATING
. . . with Production/ Operations Management

dishwasher detergent cleans the spots off your drinking glasses. Remember, services are delivered by highly variable humans, whereas products are produced on assembly lines that are more easily checked and monitored.

Another problem is that customers often blame themselves for poor service delivery because they did not play their role correctly. If a garage fails to fix your car or a haircut is not right, customers often think they were unable to explain the malfunction or hairstyle adequately. In these situations, the customer does not complain about poor service quality, but simply goes to another shop in the future. Sophisticated service providers understand the presence of self blame and make a special effort to follow up by phone or mail to check on customer satisfaction.

To manage service quality successfully, you have to know what level of service customers expect. When clients call a securities firm, they do not expect to be put on hold for five minutes and bombarded with recorded excuses and Musak. Thus part of your job is to run surveys, analyze complaints, and review customer comment cards to determine exactly what buyers expect from service companies. Southwest Airlines is doing better than other airlines because customers know that Southwest planes are on time and offer low fares. Marketing Strategies box 8-2 shows how Southwest is moving its quality operation East.

Once you know what customers expect from a service company, you are in a better position to deliver. Frequently the easiest way to improve service quality is by providing front-line people with more training. This gives customer contact representatives a more solid background in solving problems and completing transactions more quickly. Another technique that can reduce human errors and improve quality is to provide additional automated equipment. Some firms have boosted their quality by adding Web sites and more toll-free phone lines, switching to 24-hour automated access to account data, and using computers to schedule doctors' appointments. Web sites are particularly attractive because of their ability to reduce customer errors and allow greater customization of services.[3]

INTEGRATING
. . . with Information Technology

The use of technology to improve service quality is demonstrated by Alaska Airlines, a Seattle-based carrier that serves the West Coast. Alaska was one of the first U.S. airlines to sell tickets on the Internet and to offer electronic ticketing. However, the company saw little consumer benefit if the traveler still had to queue for 20 minutes at the gate to obtain a boarding pass. So in 1996 it was the first U.S. airline to install self-service check-in computer kiosks for its e-ticket fliers. The machines verify the traveler's itinerary, pose security questions, sell upgrades, and dole out boarding passes, all in little more than a minute.

APPLYING
. . . to Transportation Services Marketing

Alaska plans to have 310 kiosks in place in 1999 and is starting to put them in remote sites such as airport parking garages and hotels. The company is also working on machines to automatically identify frequent fliers as they approach the counter and allow self-service baggage checking in an effort to make it easier for passengers to avoid lines and delays at airports. By offering better service than its competitors, Alaska expects to attract more customers.[4]

MARKETING STRATEGIES *8-2*

Southwest Moves East

Southwest Airlines, which began operations in Texas in 1981, has now expanded its high quality service to the Washington, Boston, and New York metropolitan areas. In each case, Southwest has chosen to land at small uncontested airports. To serve Washington, Southwest operates from Baltimore and the Boston market is handled by departures from Manchester, New Hampshire, and Providence, Rhode Island. These airports have lower landing fees and Southwest's planes do not have to enter the crowded Washington and Boston airspace. For New York, Southwest plans to operate out of Long Island's MacArthur Airport near Islip, New York. The addition of Islip will allow Southwest to compete in the lucrative market for direct flights to Orlando, Florida, Chicago, Illinois and Los Angeles, California. The secret of Southwest's success is to offer high departure frequencies, the best on-time record in the industry and low fares. The expected fare from Islip to Orlando is $160 compared to a standard fare of $259 and the fare to Los Angeles is only $302 while competitors charge $900. Southwest cuts its costs by operating only one type of airplane and skips amenities such as fancy meals. This allows Southwest to turn its flights around quickly at the small airports it uses and maximizes utilization of its fleet. At each of the secondary Eastern airports it has entered, average fares have declined sharply and passengers per day have risen dramatically.

— *Providing high quality services at economical prices improves sales and profits.*

Source: Scott McCartney, "Southwest Puts New York on Map," *The Wall Street Journal*, November 4, 1998, p. B1.

Courtesy Southwest Airlines

Managing Service Demand

Most services cannot be stored in inventory. When demand is high, there is usually no backup stock to help fill orders, and potential business is lost. When demand is low, service capacity is wasted. With manufactured goods, it is much easier to match production with demand and to draw down inventories when demand is unusually high. Service organizations need extra help to manage demand.

The first step is to list the major factors that affect sales. Does demand vary by the hour, day, week, or month? What are the underlying causes of demand changes? In some situations, service demand is affected by work schedules, pay dates, climate, and school schedules. Once managers know why customers use services, adjustments can be made to smooth fluctuations over time.

An example of the impact of demand variation on services is shown in Figure 8-4. In sector 1 of the diagram, demand exceeds maximum service capacity and customers are lost. When demand is greater than optimum capacity (sector 2), the quality of service deteriorates. This is undesirable because customers who wait in line for service may never return. With low demand (sector 3), service capacity is wasted and investors and customers may get the impression that the business is poorly run.

Inventorying Demand.   Although most services cannot be carried in inventory, astute marketers can inventory demand. The idea is to get customers to wait in line for services or to make appointments for a future slack period. Both of these approaches can help shift peak demand (Figure 8-4, sector 1) to periods with excess capacity.

The use of queues to manage demand is simplified if you know how long customers will wait. Amusement parks understand customer time constraints and sometimes use clocks to show how long it will take to get on a particular ride. They also provide covered ramps to provide shade and refreshment stands to make waiting easier. Other ways to make queues more enjoyable include providing seating, reading material, and numbered tags to show people their positions in line.

Inventorying Supply.   Although we have emphasized that many services cannot be carried in inventory, firms can carry inventories of required equipment. Thus car and truck rental

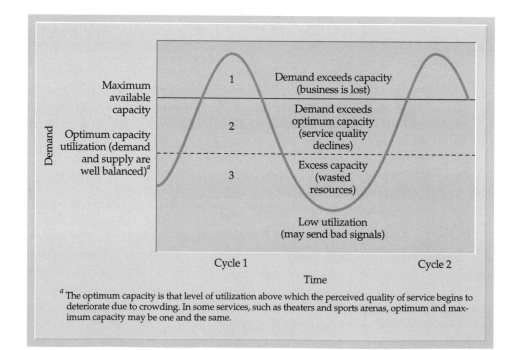

FIGURE 8-4   Impact of Demand Variation on Service Utilization (From Christopher H. Lovelock, *Services Marketing,* 3rd ed. [Englewood Cliffs, NJ: Prentice-Hall, 1996], p. 210.

firms can have storage lots of vehicles that can be quickly dispatched to areas of high demand. Also transportation companies maintain fleets of backup equipment that can be called in as needed. FedEx, for example, keeps 17 unused DC-10 aircraft stored on a desert field in Arizona so they can be phased into their fleet when demand is strong.[5]

Using Price.   A common method for balancing a limited service supply with varying levels of demand is through the use of pricing. The best approach is to set regular prices for high-demand periods and then offer special low prices to attract budget-minded customers to off-peak times. This procedure is used by ski resorts where special reduced-price lift tickets are offered for early and late season periods when snow conditions are less favorable. The advantage is that customers prefer paying lower prices during slow periods rather than paying higher prices when facilities are crowded. High regular prices help allocate demand and can increase profits at the same time. Also, special low prices attract customers during periods of low demand (Figure 8-4, sector 3). Because many service costs are fixed, special low prices can improve profits if demand is sufficiently elastic.

A good example of using pricing to manage demand is provided by the airlines. They charge high rates for inflexible business travelers and much lower rates for vacationers and people with limited resources. This successful strategy of pricing to shift air travel usage is based on a thorough understanding of the price elasticity of demand for each market segment. Service providers also have to ensure that the low-priced off-peak services do not attract too many peak customers. Airlines solve this problem by attaching enough restrictions to their excursion fares so that they cannot be used by full-fare business travelers.

Using Advertising.   Another effective technique to shift peak demand to slack periods is through advertising. Appropriate signs and advertising messages can encourage prospective customers to buy services during slack periods. Off-season promotions by resorts have been effective because some customers prefer vacationing when beaches are less crowded and there are no lines at the tennis courts. Suggestions to avoid the rush are also successful when aimed at movie theater and transit customers. When intermediaries such as travel agents are used, they can tell customers when the best slack-demand periods occur.

Overcoming Regulations with Technology.   When satellite TV service companies began to offer hundreds of channels and high-quality digital images for subscribers, Congress passed laws to protect broadcast and cable companies by limiting satellite access to local TV stations. Consumers could get hundreds of wonderful channels, but they could not get local news and weather. This blatant example of protective lobbying by the established TV industry slowed the growth of satellite TV in America and made it more difficult for satellite firms to manage demand. To avoid this regulatory problem, satellite TV firms have been signing marketing agreements with regional phone companies. This has allowed them to add a powerful new antennae to their satellite dishes to get local channels along with a package of phone, video, and high-speed data services. Many satellite customers are now enjoying more channels, better reception, and lower monthly costs than they were paying for cable. By using technology to overcome the restrictions on local TV access, satellite firms have now gained access to a much broader range of market segments for their direct satellite services.[6]

Managing the Mix of Service Customers

The selection of customers is much more important for service organizations than for manufacturers. While many manufactured goods are consumed in the privacy of customers' homes, service clients are often part of the product. In addition, service providers face fixed capacity constraints, whereas factories can easily schedule overtime to meet surges in demand. As a result, service managers must choose their customers with care.

Customer Profitability.   Service organizations have a high ratio of fixed to variable costs because of expensive facilities, equipment, and a cadre of full-time personnel. As a result, most of the costs of service organizations continue on and are not dependent on whether the hotel rooms are rented or the theater tickets are sold. Under these conditions, the firm does better by setting prices low enough to fill all available seats in a plane or sports arena. Generally the higher the usage rate, the greater the profit.

A common measure of performance in service firms is the percentage of capacity sold. Airlines talk of their "load factor" and hotels of their "occupancy rate." Although these percentages tell us something about how a company is run, they say very little about profits because the customers may have been obtained by aggressive price cutting. This suggests that success depends on knowing how much each customer segment will pay for services at different points in time.

INTEGRATING
. . . *with*
Accounting
Production/
Operations
Management

In pricing services, one measure of success compares the average price obtained per unit with the maximum price that might have been charged.[7] When this ratio, called the *yield percentage,* is multiplied by *capacity utilization,* the result is an index of *asset revenue-generating efficiency* (ARGE). Suppose that a hotel has 200 rooms with a posted price of $100. On a particular night, 80 rooms are sold for $100 and 40 for $70. The yield percentage would be:

$$\frac{\dfrac{(80 \times \$100) + (40 \times \$70)}{120}}{100} = \frac{\$90}{\$100} = 0.90$$

When this ratio is multiplied by the utilization factor of $120 \div 200 = 0.60$, an ARGE value of 0.54 is obtained ($0.90 \times 0.60 = 0.54$). ARGE can also be calculated by looking at the actual revenues relative to the maximum revenues that could be obtained:

$$\text{ARGE} = \frac{(80 \times \$100) + (40 \times \$70)}{(200 \times \$100)} = 0.54$$

These results show that the simple utilization ratio of 0.60 was lowered to a more meaningful *ARGE* of 0.54 by some price cutting. The ARGE ratio is a handy yardstick for evaluating how well a firm manages the desired customer mix.

Planning the Customer Mix.   One of the tricks of service marketing is recognizing the opportunity costs associated with accepting business from different groups of customers. For example, should a hotel book a block of rooms at a low price or hold them in case some transient guests show up to pay full rates? The answer might be that it depends on the probability of transient customers arriving. In reality, the solution is much more complicated. The reason is that customer demand is also influenced by personal selling and advertising. Since both of these factors are under the control of management, marketing managers must carefully plan how to allocate service capacity among different customer segments at particular times.

APPLYING
. . . *to*
Transportation
Services
Marketing

Perhaps the most successful *revenue management systems* are employed by airlines to allocate seats to different classes of passengers. American Airlines was the first to use a sophisticated computerized reservation system that allowed them to change seat allotments and prices as the flight time approached. For example, American might allocate 50 super-saver seats for a flight to Florida leaving in 60 days and 100 seats to higher-paying tourist customers. If they sold 30 super-saver seats in 20 days, they might cut the allocation to 40 seats with the idea of selling the other 10 seats to higher-paying tourist passengers as the departure time of the flight approaches. Airlines change the capacity allocations and prices

of airline seats on an hourly basis to make sure that their planes are as full as possible and revenues are maximized. The system is so refined that it automatically sends last-minute e-mail announcements of seat availability to people who have expressed interest in traveling certain routes.

Managing Productivity

Because service organizations are highly labor-intensive, many tasks are difficult to automate. This means that when wages increase, prices have to be raised and service growth tends to slow down. As a result, service managers are continually looking for ways to make operations more efficient.

The types of problems managers face are illustrated by employees answering customer-service calls at mutual fund companies. Phone reps are in relatively low-paid, low-glamour, high-turnover positions. A few years ago, a phone rep at Fidelity took 3 minutes and 188 keystrokes to complete a transaction. Now an advanced software package allows the transaction to be completed with 33 keystrokes in just 1 minute and 9 seconds. This allows Fidelity to handle more calls with fewer people and reduces customer waiting times. An even more advanced program is in the works that will allow phone reps to call up short bulletins on taxes, IRAs, and optimum fund allocations. These programs make it easier to train personnel, and phone reps will soon carry out most of the services offered by full-service brokers.

Another way to increase productivity in service industries is to move the work to lower-wage offshore locations. Recent advances in telecommunications technology and improved educational systems have made it easier to move backroom operations abroad. In Jamaica, 3,500 people work at office parks connected to the United States by satellite dishes. There they make airline reservations, process tickets, handle calls to toll-free numbers, and do data entry work. More than 25,000 documents a day are scanned electronically in the United States, and copies are transmitted to Montego Bay for processing. In Ireland, multilingual workers answer questions on computer software programs for customers in the United States and Europe. Metropolitan Life has 150 workers in Ireland analyzing U.S. medical insurance claims. Offshore service workers tend to be more productive and cost 35 percent less than U.S. workers do. In addition, foreign governments often grant tax concessions, and workforce turnover is usually very low.[8]

SUMMARY

Consumption of services is growing rapidly, so you need to understand how to market these intangible products. Marketing of services is tricky because services are perishable and often require the presence of a buyer. Since services are created and consumed at the same time, the delivery channel can be vital to your success. Other special characteristics of services include greater variability and stronger client relationships than for durables. Services have a high ratio of fixed to variable costs and require careful management to avoid losses during slack times. Successful managers know how to use reservation systems, pricing, and promotion to shift demand from peak to off-peak periods. Those who master the subtleties of service marketing are likely to satisfy customers, improve bottom-line performance, and reap financial rewards.

NOTES

1. "German Tele-Wars, Episode Umpteen," *The Wall Street Journal,* December 30, 1998, p. A6.

2. Evan Ramstad, "PC Makers Hunt for Gold in Internet Hookups," *The Wall Street Journal,* August 12, 1998, pp. B1, B4.

3. Leyland Pitt, Pierre Berthon, and Richard T. Watson, "Cyberservice: Taming Service Marketing Problems with the World Wide Web," *Business Horizons,* January–February 1999, pp. 11–17.

4. Susan Carey. "New Gizmos May Zip Travelers Through Airport Lines," *The Wall Street Journal,* January 4, 1999, pp. A13, A15.

5. Douglas A. Blackmon, "Will FedEx Shift from Moving Boxes to Bytes?" *The Wall Street Journal,* November 20, 1998, pp. B1, B8.

6. Leslie Cauley, "Antennae Attract Viewers to Satellite TV," *The Wall Street Journal,* December 3, 1998, pp. B1, B4.

7. Christopher H. Lovelock, *Services Marketing,* 3rd ed. (Englewood Cliffs, NJ: Prentice-Hall, 1996), p. 191.

8. Brian O'Reilly, "Your New Global Work Force," *Fortune,* December 14, 1992, p. 62.

SUGGESTED READING

Cross, Robert G. "Launching the Revenue Rocket," *Cornell Hotel and Restaurant Administration Quarterly,* April 1997, pp. 32–42.

REFERENCES

Fitzsimons, James A. and Mona J. Fitzsimons. *Service Management* (Boston: Irwin/McGraw-Hill, 1998).

Goncalves, Karen P. *Services Marketing* (Upper Saddle River, NJ: Prentice-Hall, 1997).

Kurtz, David L., and Kenneth E. Clow. *Services Marketing* (New York: John Wiley & Sons, 1997).

Lovelock, Christopher H. *Services Marketing,* 3rd ed. (Upper Saddle River, NJ: Prentice-Hall, 1996).

Payne, Adrian, and Malcolm B. McDonald. *Marketing Planning for Services* (Butterworth-Heinemann, 1993).

Zeithaml, Valarie A. and Mary Jo Bitner. *Services Marketing* (New York: McGraw-Hill, 1996).

Zimmerman, Jan, Michael Mathiesen, and Jerry Yanj. *Marketing on the Internet: A 7 Step Plan for Selling Your Products, Services, and Image to Millions over the Internet,* 3rd ed. (Gulf Breeze, FL: Maximum Press, 1998).

QUESTIONS

1. Alaska Air Group Inc. announced plans to enter a marketing arrangement with American Airlines and American Eagle commuter carrier. Why would Alaska, the nation's tenth largest airline, want a closer relationship with a giant service provider like American?

2. A marketing consultant to the legal profession has said: "Law firms are finding that the most effective way to get new business is to hire lawyers who already have it." Does this mean that the $45 million a year that lawyers spend on TV advertising is wasted? Should lawyers spend money on Yellow Pages advertising, entertainment, brochures, seminars, and newsletters?

3. Alltell Corporation Inc., a Little Rock, Arkansas, provider of local, long-distance, wireless and Internet access services has agreed to acquire Aliant Communications of Lincoln, Nebraska, for $1.4 billion. Why are we seeing so many mergers between local, long-distance, wireless, and Internet communications providers? What advantages do the combined companies gain?

4. An automatic teller machine (ATM) costs an average of $50,000 a year to service and maintain. This is twice the cost of a human teller. Why are banks and savings and loans installing ATMs, and how do they make them pay? Why do people use ATMs for withdrawals but not for deposits? How could this behavior be changed?

5. AT&T, historically America's largest long-distance phone carrier, has bought the largest U.S. cable TV company, TCI of Denver. They plan to use TCI cables to offer local telephone and high-speed Internet service circumventing the Bell company lines that AT&T must rely upon. Why is AT&T so eager to spend billions to get into local phone service?

6. Video rental is one of the fastest-growing departments in supermarkets. Sales are increasing 11 percent per year. Should supermarkets devote more space to the sale of other services?

7. Today 91 percent of U.S. hospitals have marketing programs costing more than $1.6 billion; about $500 million of which is spent each year on advertising. A survey of customers revealed that hospital advertising is considered boring, unclear, and uninformative. Respondents were turned off by "mushy" image-enhancing advertising slogans. Does this mean that hospitals should spend less on advertising? What would you recommend?

8. The cruise industry is attracting more passengers by adding exercise equipment, conference centers, small TVs in cabins, movie theaters, Las Vegas-style shows, financial seminars, shopping arcades, and casinos. They have also had great success with "theme" cruises that appeal to jazz enthusiasts, stamp collectors, bridge players, and pastry chefs. Does this mean that segmentation is the salvation of all service businesses?

9. The Canadian government has proposed legislation that would prohibit American magazine publishers from selling advertising space to Canadian firms. The intent of the law is to protect Canadian culture by reserving Canadian advertising dollars to Canadian publications. The United States objects to the law and says it will retaliate with tariffs on millions of dollars of trade with Canada. Since Canada has a free-trade agreement with the United States, it is fair for Canada to restrict U.S. sales of advertising services to Canadian firms?

10. You work for Media, Inc., which specializes in buying and selling airtime from radio and TV stations. Media, Inc., pays for airtime with travel, recorded jingles, and equipment and then resells the airtime to advertisers. You notice that Media, Inc., also routinely provides clients and prospects with cars, prostitutes, and envelopes filled with cash. Should you report these activities to your boss? the president of the company? the Securities and Exchange Commission? the police? Or should you remain silent?

11. Andrew Jackson Cooper was recently promoted to Vice-President of Marketing of an Atlanta region bank. When he moved into his new office, he found a very dated bank segmentation survey among the files there. Before throwing the survey away, he decided to have his summer intern reanalyze the data. If important relationships could be found, a new survey to update the information might be justified. The data is in the file bankdat.sav. It contains mainly categorical variables: reasons for choosing one's current bank, bank services used, media habits—especially radio listening—and sociodemographic characteristics.

9

PRICING

The art of pricing is to have the price be an equate to the value of the product to the customer—anything less than that represents a sacrifice in potential profits.

E. RAYMOND COREY

*P*ricing is a critical job in the successful operation of for-profit and not-for-profit organizations. Price is the primary element of the marketing mix that generates revenue. Many marketing executives are under great pressure to increase prices to boost short-term profits. Stock markets in the United States, for example, are sensitive to quarterly earnings reports, and managers often raise the prices of cash cows to maintain earnings growth. However, high earnings tend to attract competitors—and even investigations from government agencies. We discussed earlier how Campbell Soup once raised the prices of its condensed soups every spring until competitors began to steal the market with lower-priced private label soups and ready-to-eat soup.

Low prices can be used as a weapon to build market share. Prices that undercut competitors attract new customers and allow for greater utilization of facilities. However, low prices can squeeze contribution margins and may reduce net profits. Thus your challenge as a marketing manager is to find a pricing strategy that balances your need for sales growth against your demand for profits.

This chapter will answer three basic pricing questions: What are the basic ingredients for a successful pricing strategy? What pricing methods should be chosen? How and when should prices be changed?

FINDING THE RIGHT PRICE

Setting prices for new and existing products appears simple enough. All you apparently have to do is estimate your costs, add a margin for overhead and profit, and you have your selling price. However, this approach raises several important issues.

A first issue is that the amount you can sell varies with the price you set. Moreover, costs change with volume, so profits also depend on price.

A second issue is that some customers are value oriented and want to pay low prices for acceptable quality. At the other extreme are buyers who want high quality and are willing to pay more to get it. Thus your price must be congruent with the prospective buyers you choose to target.

A third issue involves competitors. The prices they set often limit what you can charge. Furthermore, when you sell several items, you have to consider how the price of one product affects the sales of others in your line.

Setting Pricing Goals

Your first pricing task is to select an overall pricing goal for the firm and then determine objectives for individual product lines. If your company is the first to enter a particular market with a patented product, you are in a good position to follow a premium pricing strategy. On the other hand, firms that enter later often use low prices to buy market share.

Profit Maximization.　Many organizations need profits to satisfy stockholders and provide funds for expansion and product development. To maximize profits, you need data on the number of units that can be sold at different prices plus estimates of fixed and variable costs. If these data are available, then it is fairly easy to calculate the combination of price and revenue that generates the highest profits. Unfortunately, many firms do not know enough about the shape of their demand curves to pursue a profit maximization strategy.

A variation of profit maximization occurs when a company starts with a high price to "skim" the market. This profit goal is often used with new products that cannot be easily copied. The idea is to charge high prices to early buyers and then slide down the demand curve with lower prices to capture successive layers of more price-sensitive buyers. The price-skimming goal tries to maximize profits and sometimes revenue by extracting the highest possible price from each market segment. For example, in 1999 television manufacturers were selling their new high definition TV sets for $6,000 each, while regular sets of the same screen size were selling for $600. These skimming prices will decline as more HDTV programming becomes available and unit costs decline with increased volume. The major problem with any profit maximizing goal is that high profits attract competitors, who try to steal away your customers with similar products offered at lower prices.

Revenue and Market Share Maximization.　An alternative pricing objective is to maximize revenue or market share. The usual approach is to lower prices to boost revenue while temporarily ignoring the impact on profits. Some managers who are looking for sales growth are willing to trade a little profit for higher volume. The lower prices associated with revenue or market share maximization are often employed to break into new markets or keep competitors out of a market. Some retailers demand that you obtain and keep a certain market share before they will stock your products. Revenue and market share maximization strategies are risky because the low prices required to achieve these goals typically lead to lower profit margins. This means that these strategies are usually employed for short periods or when firms have cash cows in other lines of trade.

An illustration of a firm pursuing a market share goal occurred when General Motors tried to improve labor efficiency at a key stamping plant in 1998. The United Auto Workers union saw this as a threat to their membership and the resulting strike shut down almost all of GM's North American assembly plants. Due to the shortage of cars and trucks, GM's market share dropped below 29 percent compared with the 31.2 percent share they obtained in 1997. After the strike was settled, GM offered consumers and fleet buyers generous rebates and price cuts in an effort to regain lost market share. By the end of 1998, GM had pushed its market share back up to 29.3 percent, but its profit margins suffered.[1] While Ford reported more than 5 percent profit on its sales in 1998, GM's drive to restore market share reduced profits to only 3 percent of sales.[2]

Quality Leadership.　Another pricing goal is to support an image as the quality leader in a market. Some customers seeking superior products use price as an indicator of quality. Buyers often prefer higher-priced products when price is the only information available, when they believe that the quality of available brands differs significantly, and when the price difference among brands is large. If customers believe that the quality is high, you can often charge a premium price. For example, Maytag builds very durable washing machines and advertises their lonely repairman. A survey by *Consumer Reports* showed that Maytag is the second-best company for repairs. The magazine also reported that Maytag washers are only average on washing performance, yet cost $140 more than the top-rated Sears washers. Maytag buyers are willing to pay more to get a repair-free washer.

Measuring Demand

Each price you charge for your goods or services is associated with a different level of sales. Assume that in the process of making price adjustments you have learned the general shape of the demand curve for battery-powered vacuum cleaners. This tells you how many units you can expect to sell at alternative prices (Figure 9-1). The basic relationship is negative: the quantity purchased increases as the price declines, and vice versa. When the price is set at $60, demand is 1,600 units and profits are maximized. If the price is cut to $25 per unit, demand expands to 3,000 units. When you know the shape of your demand schedules, you can set prices to reach any of a variety of goals. Today many firms have estimates of their demand schedules. The usual way to obtain these data is to vary prices in a laboratory or in the store over a short period of time and measure how much customers purchase.

Price Elasticity of Demand

The preferred way to express customer sensitivity to price is with a ratio known as the *price elasticity of demand.* This is obtained by dividing percentage changes in the quantity sold by associated percentage changes in price. The formula for price elasticity is

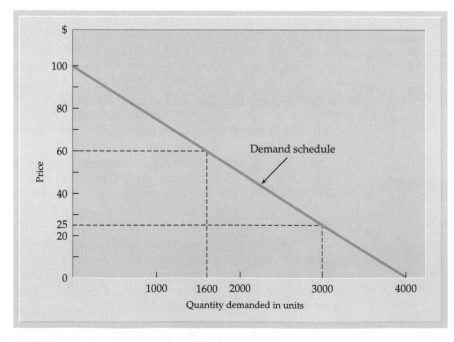

FIGURE 9-1   Demand for Vacuum Cleaners

$$\text{Price elasticity of demand} = \frac{\% \text{ change in quantity demanded}}{\% \text{ change in price}} \qquad (9.1)$$

The usual relationship between demand and price is inverse. When a relative change in volume is more than the relative change in price, demand is described as *elastic.* If the price is cut by 1 percent and demand increases by 5 percent, the elasticity is –5 (Figure 9-2). When demand is this sensitive to price, it almost always pays to cut prices. You will more than make up in volume what you lose in margin per unit. This, of course, should be verified by break-even analysis.

When a relative change in the quantity sold is less than the relative change in price, demand is said to be *inelastic.* Thus, if a price increase of 10 percent results in a 3 percent reduction in sales, price elasticity will be –0.3. In situations where elasticity is between 0 and –1, revenues increase as prices are raised (Figure 9-2). This suggests that when demand is inelastic, profits can be improved by raising prices. Demand is most likely to be inelastic when the product is infrequently purchased or it has few substitutes or competitors. Positive values for elasticity are unusual and signal that prices should be raised.

PRICING EXERCISE

A manufacturer observes that when the price of a $200 TV in the California market is cut $10, volume increases by 21,000 units. If the original volume was 300,000 units, what is the price elasticity of demand? What does the calculated value of price elasticity suggest should be done with the pricing for the TV set? Why?

You should understand that although an industry's price elasticity may be inelastic, an individual brand's elasticity is usually elastic. Thus, while the industry elasticity for gasoline is –0.3, the demand for Shell and Texaco brands across the street from one another is much more elastic. Brand studies have shown that the price elasticity of cars is –1.5; that of coffee, –5.3; and that of confectionery, –2.0.[3]

Price elasticities tend to vary over the product life cycle. Prices for brands often decline over time—even in the face of improvements to product quality. Products that are inelastic when introduced may become more elastic as they mature.[4]

An important part of your job as marketing manager is to make your brands less elastic, allowing you to charge higher prices. This can be done with advertising or by bundling your basic product or service with other products or services. For example, Technimetrics markets financial databases. It commands premium prices by bundling free consultations, research reports, and other services with its database products.

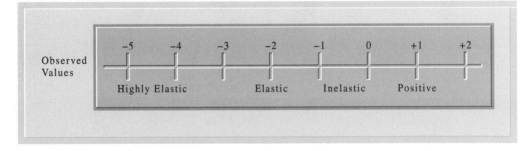

FIGURE 9-2   Range of Likely Values for Price Elasticity

Estimating Costs

Our discussion of demand provides a ceiling price that the organization can charge for goods and service. At the other extreme, costs determine the price floor. Organizations must charge enough to cover their total costs in the long run and have enough left over to reward the stockholders or buy replacement animals for the zoo.

INTEGRATING
. . . with Accounting

Types of Costs.   Costs come in two basic forms, fixed or variable. *Fixed costs* include expenditures for overhead such as plant, equipment, and executive salaries. These costs do not vary with the level of output. In the case of the battery-powered vacuum cleaner manufacturer, the fixed costs of tooling and other overhead amounted to $15,000 (Figure 9-3). These costs are the same at all output levels.

Variable costs represent the direct labor, materials, and commissions needed to produce and sell each unit of merchandise. The unit variable costs for the vacuum cleaner are $20. Variable costs are so named because their total varies with production levels (Figure 9-3). When you look at per unit costs, you notice that variable costs for this product are constant across different levels of production (Figure 9-4).

Total costs are the sum of the fixed and variable costs at various levels of output. Note that total unit costs for the vacuum cleaner decline sharply as the fixed costs are spread over more units of production (Figure 9-4). Most of the economies of scale that occur when plants are run at capacity are due to a decline in allocated fixed costs per unit. Although the unit variable costs in Figure 9-4 are shown as constant, they also may decline if volume purchases lead to quantity discounts on raw materials. Managers who have a decreasing unit-cost curve are in a strong position to lower prices to expand market shares.

Historically, American firms have looked at the product characteristics important to customers, estimated engineering and component costs, and added in a profit margin to give a selling price. The Japanese have taught us how to do it differently. They look at what the customer wants, check competitive prices, and come up with a planned selling price. Next,

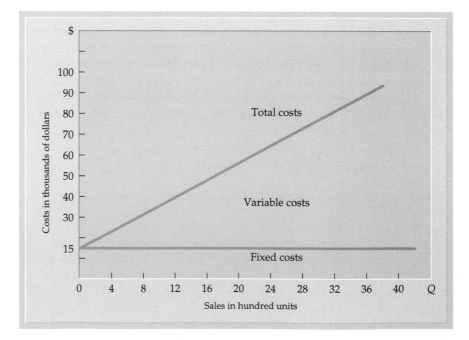

FIGURE 9-3   Cost Curves for Vacuum Cleaner Manufacturer

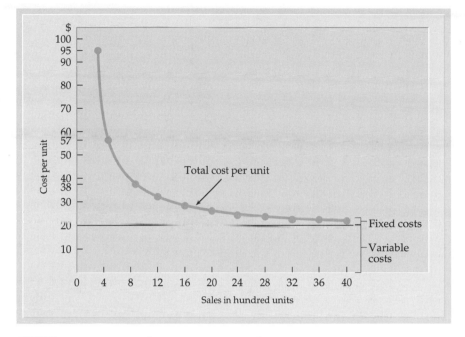

FIGURE 9-4   Vacuum Cleaner Costs per Unit

they subtract the desired profit to give a target cost. Then the product is designed and engineered to achieve the target cost. This system focuses on getting costs out during the planning and design stages. Careful attention to costs allowed Daimler Chrysler to cut the cost of their redesigned 1999 Jeep Grand Cherokee sport-utility vehicle by $250 even though it has an improved engine, a better climate control system, more interior space, and other luxury features.[5]

Costs and the Experience Curve.   There is convincing evidence that the cost of manufacturing products also declines as workers gain experience in their jobs. An example of an experience curve is shown in Figure 9-5.

There are two major sources of the cost reductions shown in experience curves. First, workers and managers learn how to do a better job through repetition. Assembly workers develop greater dexterity and better work routines, and machine operators learn how to adjust their equipment for the greatest output. Also, marketing managers learn through experience how to do a better job of introducing and promoting new products. A second source of cost reductions is technology. New production processes are introduced, and products are redesigned to save money.

Experience curves suggest that costs decline continuously over the entire product life cycle. This means that you have the ability to cut prices on a regular basis to meet competitive threats and to achieve sales objectives. For example, the learning curve allowed Ford to cut the price of its 1999 Taurus sedan $1,000 and the Taurus station wagon $1,800 in an effort to boost sales of this aging model.[6] Also, during introductory periods, it is common to set prices below current actual costs to help expand demand for the product. Firms expect profits to return later as costs fall faster than selling prices.

During the growth stage of the product life cycle, there is little incentive to cut prices. As a result, prices do not fall as fast as costs and profit margins grow fat (Figure 9-5). This price umbrella attracts new entrants who are able to make money despite high initial costs. The new firms survive by stealing market share from the market leader. Dominant organiza-

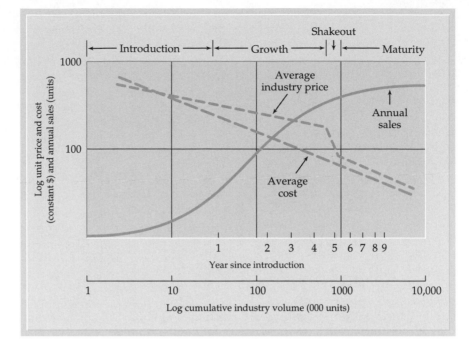

FIGURE 9-5   Experience Curves and the Product Life Cycle (From George S. Day and David B. Montgomery, "Diagnosing the Experience Curve," *Journal of Marketing,* Vol. 47 [Spring 1983], p. 51. Reproduced by permission of the American Marketing Association.)

tions that allow a price umbrella during the growth stage are actually trading long-run market share for current profits.

At the end of the growth stage of the life cycle, a shakeout occurs and prices drop sharply (Figure 9-5). This may happen because the market leader is attempting to stop the loss of market position or regain previous share levels. During the maturity phase of the life cycle, the margin between costs and prices erodes continuously, and cost savings are harder to find.

CHOOSING A PRICING METHOD

Now that you understand demand and costs, you are ready to select a price. Remember, prices should be high enough to produce some profit but not so high that customers refuse to buy. The primary external constraint on your prices is the actions of competitors. Any pricing procedure that you select must be in line with the prices set by competitors. Your task is to find a method that balances demand, costs, and competitive factors for an individual product.

Markup Pricing

Many organizations prefer pricing procedures that are easy to administer and require only limited assumptions about demand. Perhaps the simplest and most popular one is known as *markup pricing*.

With markup pricing, you add an amount to the cost of the item to yield a selling price. This amount is the markup designed to cover overhead expenses and produce a profit for the firm. Markups are stated as a percentage of the cost or selling price of the item. Setting prices with cost markups involves multiplying the markup percentage (expressed as a fraction) by the cost of the item and then adding the result to the cost. For example, if an item cost $5 to manufacture and the firm wanted a 300 percent markup on the cost, the markup would be 3 × $5 or $15 plus the cost of $5, giving a selling price of $20. This may be simplified by adding 1 to the markup percentage to create a cost multiplier.

Markups on selling price are more complicated because they cannot be multiplied directly by the cost to give a price. With these markups, costs are divided by 1 minus the markup percentage (expressed as a fraction) to yield the selling price. Thus, if a dealer wanted a 30 percent margin on the selling price and an item cost $7, the selling price would be

$$\text{Selling price} = \frac{\text{cost}}{(1 - \text{markup on selling price})} = \frac{\$7}{1 - 0.3} = \$10 \qquad (9.2)$$

Cost markups are always larger than markups on the selling price because of the smaller base. Note that markups on cost can be any amount, whereas markups on selling price range between zero and 100 percent. Traditionally, firms use *markup* (on cost) in internal operations and report *margin* (markup on selling price) in finanacial communications.

Markup pricing does not adequately handle demand when the same markup percentage is applied to different classes of goods. If you select this method, you should vary markup percentages according to customers' price sensitivities. For example, supermarkets use markups of 9 percent on baby food and 50 percent on the more inelastic greeting cards. This strategy of varying margins by price elasticities leads to greater profits.

APPLYING
. . . to
Retailing

Markup pricing was the most common technique reported in a study of small and medium-sized firms in England.[7] The method is easy to understand and the size of the markups can be set to accomplish a variety of objectives.

PRICING EXERCISE

If a retailer buys a dress for $40 and plans to use a 60 percent markup on the selling price, what will be the final purchase price for the customer? What is the dollar markup? A manufacturer calculates the cost of producing a lamp to be $25. To obtain a 400 percent markup on cost, what selling price should be set for the lamp?

Break-Even Pricing

Break-even pricing shows how many units must be sold at selected prices to regain the funds invested in a product. Suppose that the fixed selling, advertising, R&D, and tooling costs for a barbecue grill are $200,000 and the variable costs $6 per unit. At a factory selling price of $8, the break-even volume is

$$\text{Break-even volume} = \frac{\text{fixed costs}}{\text{price} - \text{variable costs}} = \frac{\$200,000}{\$8 - \$6} = 100,000 \text{ units} \qquad (9.3)$$

Profits are generated when volume exceeds the break-even point, and losses occur when volume fails to reach the break-even point. Break-even volumes for factory selling prices of $8, $10, and $12 are shown in Figure 9-6.

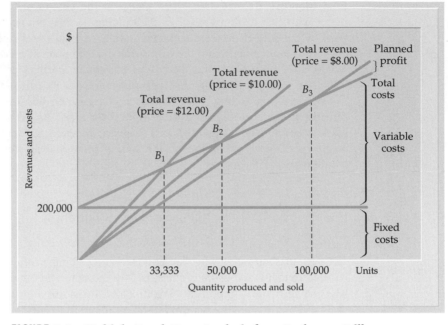

FIGURE 9-6   Multiple Break-Even Analysis for a Barbecue Grill

Although break-even pricing shows the volume needed to cover your costs, it makes some simplifying assumptions about demand. The total revenue lines in Figure 9-6 are straight, implying that larger volumes can be sold without lowering prices. This is unrealistic, and executives must be able to estimate the number of units that will be sold at each tentative price. Remember the prices shown in Figure 9-6 are factory prices and you have to add in margins for retailers to get accurate estimates of how many can be sold to consumers.

PRICING EXERCISE

The total fixed costs of producing a DVD player are $2.1 million and the variable costs are $80. If the manufacturer is considering factory selling prices of $150 and $200, what are the break-even volumes? What factory selling price do you recommend? Why?

Variable-Cost Pricing

Variable-cost pricing is based on the idea that the recovery of full costs is not always realistic or necessary for organizations. Instead of using full costs as the lowest possible price, this system suggests that variable costs represent the minimum price that can be charged. For example, assume that you have been able to sell 100,000 barbecue grills at $8.50 through your regular discount store channels. A supermarket chain offers to purchase 20,000 barbecue grills at $7 each. The buyer suggests that the grills carry the supermarket's label without the wheels found on the regular model. If the design changes reduce variable costs to $5.75, the order represents a potential profit of $25,000.

Should you accept the offer and price the modified grills at $7.00? Some would say that the order can *never* be approved because the price does not cover the full cost of $7.42 (Figure 9-7). Others would point out that if you cut prices to the supermarket, your regular customers may demand equally low prices. This could lead to losses, because it would be difficult to recover the fixed costs. The important point to remember is that the full cost to manufacture the grills is not constant, but in reality is quite sensitive to changes in volume (Figure 9-7), where unit costs decline as the fixed expenses are spread over a large volume. At a volume of 20,000 units the grills cost $16, but this cost declines to $7.42 at a volume of 120,000 units and to $7 at a volume of 200,000 units. This shows that very low prices can cover full costs if volume expands sufficiently. An example of variable cost pricing is described in Marketing in Action box 9-1.

Perhaps the most important issue in variable-cost pricing is whether the markets can be kept separate. If the supermarkets are in different geographic locations or service different income classes, then the additional business looks attractive.

Variable-cost pricing that focuses on *revenue management* is common where fixed costs comprise a large proportion of total unit costs. The airlines, hotels, and railroads are industries with high fixed costs that have made effective use of the volume-generating aspects of variable-cost pricing. For example, one summer American Airlines slashed fares on advance-purchase tickets by up to 50 percent to boost vacation business. These low fares were matched by other airlines, and within a few days, all the excursion seats on the major U.S. airlines allocated to these programs had been sold. This illustration shows that the demand for summer travel is very elastic and that low prices will fill seats on airplanes. However, the airlines had trouble keeping the special low fares out of the hands of their regular customers. Many people were able to exchange higher-priced tickets for the excursion fares, and others who had planned to pay regular fares rushed to take advantage of the low rates. Because of the size of the price cuts and their inability to restrict the low fares to new customers, all the major U.S. airlines lost money with variable-cost pricing that summer.

APPLYING
. . . to
Transportation
Services
Marketing

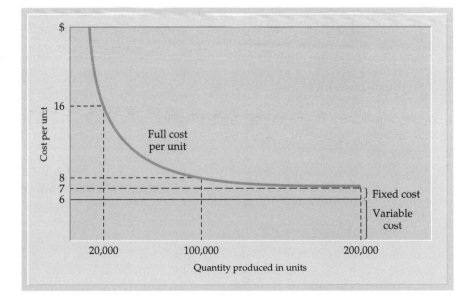

FIGURE 9-7   Effects of Volume on Unit Costs for a Barbecue Grill

MARKETING IN ACTION *9-1*

Lunch by the Minute

During a recession in Japan, a number of restaurants started charging by the minute for all-you-can-eat buffet lunches as a way to improve business. At the 43 Tohtenkoh restaurants the first 30 lunch customers get to pay by the minute. Customers are asked to punch in on a time clock so there is no haggling over the time spent in the restaurant. The price is 30 cents per minute and one customer was charged $5.70 for a 19 minute lunch. At Tohtenkoh the regular luncheon buffet cost $15.95. At a price of 30 cents per minute, the restaurant does not make a profit on the 30 lunches, but they do cover the variable cost of the food served. However, minute pricing has drawn more customers paying the regular price so total revenue has increased. The manager claims minute pricing is good publicity.

— *Innovative use of variable cost pricing can boost revenue.*

Source: Yumiko Ono, "We're Eating Out Tonight, So Please Bring a Stopwatch," *The Wall Street Journal*, December 23, 1998, pp. A1, A4.

Courtesy Tohtenkoh Company Ltd.

Since this fiasco, airlines have refined their computer programs that help them manipulate prices to maximize profits. Marketing Strategies box 9-1 explains how the new revenue management programs work at American Airlines.

PRICING EXERCISE

A golf course has a regular greens fee of $15 for play during the week and $25 on the weekend. Sixty women golfers ask for a special rate of $10 per person to play on a Thursday afternoon. The variable cost of handling this special group is estimated at $4 each. Should the golf course accept the proposal of the 60 women golfers? What other factors would influence your decision?

MARKETING STRATEGIES *9-1*

Using Computers to Optimize Airline Prices

Airline travel is a high fixed cost industry and the demand for leisure travel is very elastic. Under these conditions, profits can be increased by cutting ticket prices for tourists to fill empty seats. American Airlines computers combine historical data bases on ridership with up-to-the-minute bookings to predict how many business customers will want seats on a particular flight. Business clients typically buy unrestricted tickets at the last minute and are charged higher fares than tourists who must book weeks ahead and stay over a Saturday night. For example, American's Flight 2015 from Chicago to Phoenix has its 125 coach seats divided into seven classes with prices ranging from $238 for the lowest priced tourist fare to $1404 for a last-minute unrestricted fare. In the weeks before each Chicago to Phoenix flight, American's revenue management programs constantly adjust the number of seats available in each price class, taking into account tickets sold, historical ridership patterns, and the number of connecting passengers likely to use the route as one leg of a longer trip. If advance bookings are slim, American adds more low-fare seats. If business customers buy unrestricted fares earlier than expected, the computer takes seats out of the discount class and preserves them for last-minute bookings. With 69 of 125 coach seats already sold four weeks before one recent departure of Flight 2015, American began to limit the number of low priced seats. A week later, it totally shut off sales for the bottom three tiers. One day before departure, with 130 passengers booked for the 125 seat flight, American still offered five seats at full fare because its computer indicated 10 passengers were likely not to show up or take other flights. Flight 2015 departed full and no one was bumped. Also American's computers make price changes instantly available to other airlines and this tends to dampen price cutting by competitors. Computerized pricing of tickets has allowed airlines to raise their percentage of seats filled to over 70 percent and increase profits.

— *Revenue management programs can set prices to correspond with elasticities of different buyers.*

Source: Scott McCartney, "Ticket Shock: Business Fares Increase Even as Leisure Travel Keeps Getting Cheaper," *The Wall Street Journal,* November 3, 1997, pp. A1, A6.

Courtesy American Airlines

Nonlinear Pricing

Nonlinear pricing is based on the observation that the second, third, and additional units of a product or service have a lower value to the customer than the first purchase. An illustration is provided by a movie theater that offered discounts for successive visits within a month. The number of visits is monitored by a free card that is issued at the first visit. The plan requires that the theater owners know how much different customer groups are willing to pay for successive visits. Revenue generated by offering a uniform price can then be compared with sales produced by offering lower prices for second, third, and more visits. Since virtually all costs of a movie theater are fixed, revenue projections provide a good estimate of the profit impact of nonlinear pricing. Profit improvements from nonlinear pricing can range up to 50 percent because marketing managers are reaching more segments of a demand curve (see Figure 9-1) than they would get with a uniform price.

Price Bundling

Bundling involves selling two or more products at a price that is less than the sum of their individual prices. With pure bundling, only the package of products is offered. In a mixed bundling strategy, the individual products are sold separately as well. Bundling is widely used in the sale of fast food, automobile option packages, tourism, and telecommunications. An example of a successful mixed bundling strategy for automobile options is shown in Figure 9-8. The manufacturer was considering offering comfort, sports, and safety packages. A study revealed that buyers were quite sensitive to the discounts for the option bundles as compared to the price of options if purchased individually. Bundling was attractive to the

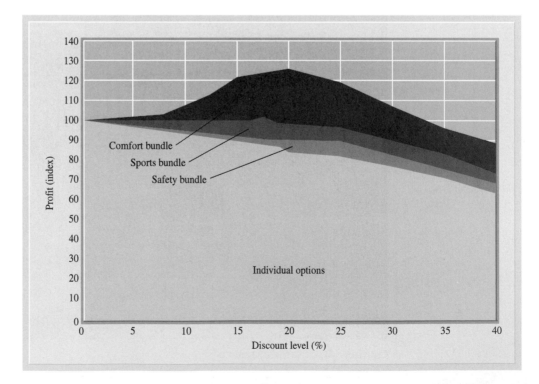

FIGURE 9-8   Profits Associated with Option Bundle Discounts (From Hermann Simon and Robert J. Dolan, "Price Customization," *Marketing Management* [Fall 1998], p. 16.)

manufacturer because it lowered the cost of the purchased components and reduced complexity in logistics and auto assembly. Figure 9-8 shows the relation between profits and the discount level to be offered on the three discount packages. As the discount on the packages increases, the profit generated on individual options declines as customers switch to the bundles. However, overall profit increased because of the growth in the total number of options sold. In this example, the maximum profit was reached with a bundle discount of 21 percent.

The key to successful bundling is to find combinations where willingness to buy varies across products. For example, in America the popular $1,000 air-conditioning option is often bundled with less popular options such as cruise control, power door locks, and power windows. Customers who want air conditioning have a choice of buying it as a separate option for $1,000 or in a package where they pay $800 and get 20 percent off the price of cruise control and the other options in the price bundle. Enough buyers who want air conditioning are attracted by the discounts offered in the package to make a mixed bundling strategy the most profitable for the manufacturer. Typically price bundling increases profits by 14 to 25 percent.[8]

New-Product Pricing

One of the more complex pricing issues that you must resolve is setting prices for new products. These decisions are complicated by the frequent lack of information on demand and costs. Because new products have not been sold before, price elasticity cannot be estimated from an analysis of historical data. Asking consumers if they are interested in buying a new product at a particular price is not very helpful. Also, the desire to prevent competitors from learning about new products may prevent the firm from using test markets to obtain elasticity data. Even the simple expedient of copying a competitor's price is not a practical alternative for new products. Despite these problems, marketing managers must find a price that will sell the product and still contribute to the profits of the firm.

Value-in-Use Pricing.   This approach stresses understanding price from the customer's point of view. Business buyers are often more interested in the total value of the product or service than they are in the initial price. These buyers are concerned with how long products last, availability of repair parts, length of warranties, timeliness of delivery, and other operational or financial benefits. In addition, you have to know what costs customers incur beyond the price of the product. These costs may include order handling, freight, installation, and training. Customers also have other costs, such as the fear of late delivery, the need for custom modification of the delivered product, or the impact of product failure on organizational productivity. Thus, you must understand the customer's possible applications of the product. Once a firm assesses customers' benefits and costs in terms of the complete usage system, it is in a position to set the price.

The importance of value-in-use-pricing was made clear to one of the authors who had to replace a national brand PC due to early hard drive failure. When I took the American brand PC to the shop, I was surprised to find that the machine was assembled overseas from components manufactured by offshore companies. When the shop owner offered to configure a computer with an American hard drive and a full two-year warranty on all new parts, I accepted even though I could have bought a name brand PC at a lower price. In this case, doubling the length of the warranty and access to local repair service provided more value over the expected life of the product than the seductive allure of a low initial price.

APPLYING
. . . to
Consumer
Durable
Goods
Marketing

Skimming Prices.   Research has shown that the more innovative a new product is, the less sensitive customers are to price.[9] This suggests that high skimming prices should be used for new products and then gradually reduced over time. This situation is described by the downward-sloping curve *DD* in Figure 9-9. The high initial price (P^1) is designed to skim off the

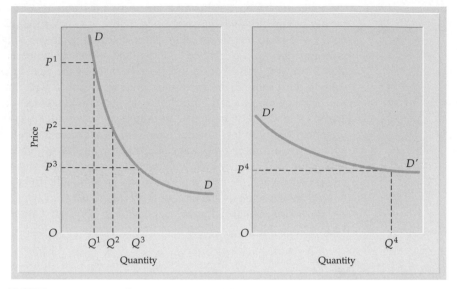

FIGURE 9-9   **Demand Curves Assumed by Skimming and Penetration Price Strategies**

segment of the market that is insensitive to price, and subsequent reductions (P^2, P^3) broaden the market by tapping more elastic sectors of the market. The logic of the skimming price strategy is supported by the observation that many new products have few technical substitutes and that the price is not as important as it is for more established products.

A successful application of a skimming price strategy occurred with the microprocessor chips that control personal computers. Intel is the leading supplier to this market and it regularly introduces new more powerful microprocessors at high initial prices of $500 or $600. Over time, these prices are periodically reduced to expand sales to lower prices segments of the PC market. Older versions of its Pentium processor are now sold under the Celeron label with prices as low as $71.[10]

The main disadvantage of a skimming price policy is that high margins attract competitors into the field. This suggests that a skimming price is best used when the product has strong patent protection or when there are other barriers to entry, such as technical knowhow or high capital requirements. Although skimming prices can increase short-term profits, they may not be sustainable in the long run. An example of price skimming in the toothbrush market is described in Marketing Strategies box 9-2.

Penetration Prices.   A penetration price is set below current costs and is designed to open mass markets quickly. This pricing strategy is based on the assumptions that (1) there is little prospect of creating or maintaining product superiority, (2) there are few barriers to entry by competitors, and (3) demand is highly elastic (curve $D'D'$ in Figure 9-9) and low prices will significantly expand the market. In addition, penetration pricing assumes that the high volume associated with a low introductory price (P^4 in Figure 9-9) will reduce costs, so that a profit can be made during the growth phase of the product life cycle. Penetration prices are encouraged by the experience curve and declines in unit costs over the product life cycle (Figure 9-5). One of the most successful examples of penetration pricing in recent years was Chrysler's introduction of its small Neon cars.

Why do managers set high prices on new products when it is often in their long-run interests to set the price low to keep competition out? The answer seems to be that current profits are needed to fund growth in production capacity, R&D, and market development activity. Also, the reward system for managers often emphasizes immediate profits. Remem-

APPLYING
. . . to
Industrial
Marketing

MARKETING STRATEGIES *9-2*

Pricing Toothbrushes

Gillette Co.'s Oral-B Laboratories has introduced the most expensive mass market toothbrush ever at a list price of $4.99. The new CrossAction brush will cost the consumer 50 percent more than any of its high end rivals. Oral-B has the largest share of the U.S. toothbrush market and their new brush is designed to strengthen this position. Bristles on the CrossAction don't stand up straight, but are set in three rows of bristles of varying sizes angled in opposite directions. This allows the new brush to remove 25 percent more plaque than competitive brushes. Also the CrossAction has a fat ergonomic rubberized handle and denser bristles at the tip to clean behind back teeth. Gillette test marketed the new brushes at $3.99 and $4.99 and found no significant difference in sales. Since many customers are willing to pay $7 to $12 for replacement heads for electric toothbrushes, Oral-B decided that a skimming price of $4.99 for the new CrossAction brush was feasible. One of the authors bought a Cross-Action brush to see if it worked as claimed. The fat grippy handle made the brush easier to maneuver and the dense tip bristles did clean better behind back teeth. Also, the angled bristles seemed to scrub adeptly at the gum line. Looks like Gillette has a winner at $4.99.

— *Skimming prices for innovative products can raise profits.*

Source: Mark Maremont, "New Toothbrush Is Big-Ticket Item," *The Wall Street Journal*, October 27, 1998, pp. B1, B6.

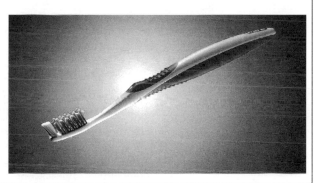

Courtesy The Gillette Company

ber that if you are or can become the low-cost producer, low initial prices are often the best way to build market share and long-run profits.

PRICING EXERCISE

Extensive research has led to the development of an innovative new digital phone with longer battery life and greater range than its competitors. The manufacturer is considering either a skimming price of $190 or a low penetration price of $99. The variable cost of producing the new phone is $70. First-year sales at the $190 price are estimated to be 500,000 units and 2,069,000 units at the $99 price. Which price should the firm use? Why?

Multidimensional Pricing

With multidimensional pricing, firms break up prices into two or more components. When companies buy steel, sulfuric acid, and industrial gases, they pay a flat rate per pound or gallon. Each customer pays the same price. One supplier in the industrial gas market introduced a multidimensional price program that charged customers a daily rental fee for the steel cylinder and a reduced price per pound for the gas. With the new system, customers who use the gas quickly pay a lower total price than those who use it slowly do. Success with multi-dimensional pricing requires that the seller take a great deal of care to make sure the two prices are set correctly.

An example of effective multidimensional pricing is shown by German Railroad Corp.'s introduction of a two-dimensional scheme for passenger travel. In the past, the company set prices for passenger tickets as a simple multiple of a rate times the distance traveled. Unfortunately, this scheme led to prices that were higher than the cost of driving for many potential riders. To attract more business, the company introduced a new BahnCard at a cost of $300 per year for first class and $150 per year for second class. Travelers with these cards could buy tickets at 50 percent off the standard per kilometer price. Once purchased, the BahnCard is a sunk cost and the car or train decision depends on the marginal price per kilometer. With the marginal cost of train travel now below the cost of driving for many customers, German Rail was able to attract 3.5 million loyal card holders. The net result of multidimensional pricing in this case was an increase in profits of $200 million per year for the German Railroad Corp.[11]

APPLYING
. . . to
*Transportation
Services
Marketing*

WHEN SHOULD PRICES BE CHANGED?

Once you have selected a basic price for your goods and services, there are a number of situations in which adjustments have to be made to account for unique market conditions.

Responding to Competitive Cuts

One of the most difficult challenges you will face as a marketing manager is responding to price cuts by competitors. This situation is fraught with danger no matter what you do. If you play it safe and maintain your prices to keep short-run profits up, you risk losing market share and long-run profitability. If you match competitive price cuts to maintain market share, short-term profits and the price of your company's stock will plummet. Price wars with competitors appear to be a no-win situation. An example of a price war in the mature beer market is described in Marketing in Action box 9-2.

Brand loyalty does not last forever when competitors cut prices. If you expect to survive a price war, you must keep your costs under control so that you can continue to make money when prices are pushed down. Some firms are able to avoid price wars by differentiating their products and focusing on customers in niche markets. It is also desirable to have some "fighting brands" available to do battle when price competition heats up. Another approach is to develop computer models to help predict what will happen when competitors cut prices. For example, Research International offers its PriceSolve model to help you plan pricing strategies for the future.

Geographic Pricing

There is often money to be made by charging different prices to customers located in separate geographical areas. These adjustments reflect variation in transportation costs and price elasticities. The most common geographic pricing system is known as *FOB pricing*.

FOB Pricing.   With FOB pricing, the manufacturer places goods *free on board* a carrier, and the buyer pays the freight to the destination. The system is fair because customers near the plant pay the lowest freight charges and those farthest away pay the highest charges. With FOB pricing, buyers tend to purchase from the closest supplier. The main problem with FOB pricing is that it is difficult to build market share by selling in distant markets.

MARKETING IN ACTION 9-2

Beer Price Wars

Per capita consumption of beer has been declining in America. Under these conditions, the best way to increase revenue is to take market share from competitors. Miller, a distant No. 2 to Anheuser-Busch, started a price war in 1997 and was initially successful. Anheuser-Busch didn't immediately follow, and Miller was able to increase their market share from 20.6 percent to 22.4 percent while Anheuser-Busch's share dropped from 46.6 percent to 43.8 percent. When Anheuser-Busch found out the size of its market share decline, it started to cut prices and by the end of the fourth quarter of 1997 its share had soared back to 47.5 percent and Miller's dropped back to 20.9 percent. The heavy discounting hurt beer profits and Miller's revenue per barrel fell $2.60 from 1996 and Anheuser-Busch's fell $0.54. As a result of the price war, the combined market share of Miller and Anheuser-Busch rose 1.2 percent at the expense of smaller brewers. Coors Brewery and Stroh Brewery stayed out of the price war and managed to increase revenues. Stroh decided to give up some market share to maintain profits. As it turned out, Anheuser-Busch's 1 percent price cuts led to a 4 percent increase in sales while Miller's 2 percent price cuts actually led to a 1 percent decline in revenue.

— *Those who start price wars do not always win them.*

Source: Rekha Balu, "Big Brewers Find Price War Seems to Have No End," *The Wall Street Journal*, July 2, 1998, p. B6.

Courtesy Anheuser-Busch Companies

Delivered Pricing. Firms that want to expand into other markets often set prices on a delivered basis. Under this plan, an average freight charge is added to the factory price, and everyone pays the same delivered price. This is the system used by American automobile manufacturers to set retail selling prices for their vehicles. A delivered price strategy favors distant customers and allows the use of a single nationally advertised price. However, customers close to the factory pay higher prices, and they may buy from local competitors who use FOB pricing. Delivered pricing tends to sacrifice sales nearby to gain business from more distant buyers.

Zone Pricing.   Under a zone pricing system, markets are divided so that all customers within a zone pay the same price. Zone pricing is often used to take advantage of differences in price elasticity across markets. In the United States, the most common example of zone pricing is the sale of national brands of gasoline. Large manufacturers divide states and even cities into pricing zones so they can charge different prices in each area. This makes it easier for them to prevent damage from the spread of gasoline *price wars.* When low prices hurt profits in one area, manufacturers can charge higher prices in other higher income areas where demand is more inelastic. Zone pricing works for gasoline because the franchised independent dealers are obligated to buy from their national brand supplier and it is not practical to pump out the gasoline from the tanks of one dealer and haul it to higher-priced markets for resale. Also consumers are not likely to drive 50 miles to buy gas and take advantage of lower prices in other pricing zones.

Zone pricing has the disadvantage that price disparities across zones may become large enough to catch the attention of dealers and customers. In Indiana, for example, gasoline prices may vary as much as $.15 a gallon over a distance of only 50 miles. Clearly a differential this large is not related to the cost of hauling gasoline to the dealers. Rather it reflects an effort on the part of manufacturers to maximize profits. Some independent Indiana franchised Shell dealers have sued their supplier claiming that Shell's zone pricing is discriminatory. Independent dealers usually own stations in one town and often feel they are treated unfairly when other dealers in nearby zones are able to buy gasoline at lower prices. Although zone pricing may appear to be discriminatory in some situations, courts of law have ruled that zone pricing for competitive products like gasoline is perfectly legal.

A more serious problem occurs when zone pricing is used for high-value products that are easily shipped. When price differentials become large enough to pay for shipping, independent dealers will start buying products in low-priced zones and haul them to high-priced markets for resale. These parallel importers, as they are called, can quickly destroy the profit maximizing appeal of zone pricing. *Parallel importing* is common with cameras, watches, liquor, and cigarettes. This suggests that zone prices must be set carefully if border disruptions are to be kept to a minimum.

Discounts and Allowances

To help field representatives close sales, many firms offer special discounts and allowances.

Cash Discounts.   The most common incentive is a cash discount for paying bills early. For example, an organization might offer terms of "2/10, net 30," which means that the buyer can deduct 2 percent of the price if the bill is paid by the tenth of the month; otherwise, the whole amount is due on the thirtieth. A 2 percent discount may not seem like much incentive, but it encourages buyers to pay 20 days early, and this amounts to 36 percent on an annual basis. Cash discounts improve the cash flow for the seller and reduce collection costs.

Seasonal Discounts.   Consumer purchases in industries such as toys and swimwear are highly concentrated, leading to underutilization of labor and factories in the off-season. To help control this problem, many firms in these industries offer seasonal discounts to encourage buyers to place orders early. Seasonal discounts are often substantial and can be thought of as an example of variable-cost pricing.

Allowances.   Allowances for price reductions are designed to compensate buyers for certain activities. Promotional allowances, for example, include cash or free merchandise designed to get dealers to advertise or build in-store displays to promote products. Trade-in allowances are another incentive offered on durable goods to help reduce down payments and get customers to buy. To be legal, discounts and allowances must be made available to all competing channel members.

Product-Line Pricing

When there are several items in your product line, prices must be set to maximize profits for a whole array of products. This may be difficult because margins vary and some items have interrelated costs. A further complication is that the sales of one product may be influenced by the price charged for a second product. This can be measured by calculating values for *cross-price elasticity.* Suppose that when you raise the price of Bayer Aspirin 5 percent in your store, sales of Tylenol increase 10 percent. In mathematical terms,

$$\text{Cross-price elasticity} = \frac{\% \text{ change in sales of Tylenol}}{\% \text{ change in price of Bayer Aspirin}} = \frac{+10\%}{+5\%} = +2 \quad (9.4)$$

The positive cross-price elasticity of +2 indicates that consumers considered the two items to be substitutes. A negative cross-price elasticity would indicate that the products were complementary and typically were sold together.

A study of egg pricing revealed that the price elasticity for large eggs was a very elastic −3.3. This means if you raise the price of large eggs, customers will start to buy medium or private label eggs. Cross-price elasticities among the three types of eggs were all positive, indicating consumers considered them to be substitutes. Thus, a consideration of price elasticities and cost data can lead to the most profitable price level for each brand sold by the company. The results suggest that total profits would increase if you consider cross-price elasticities when you set prices for different sizes and brands of eggs. When price elasticities can be measured, marketing managers no longer have to rely on rules of thumb for product-line pricing.

Price Discrimination

Price discrimination is an attractive pricing strategy that can boost volume and profits by taking advantage of differences in customers' price sensitivities. For example, you can segment your market on age and offer lower-priced admission tickets to children. Another approach is to vary price by time. Customers who want to play golf on weekdays are offered low prices, whereas weekend players are charged high prices. A third way to segment customers is by location. Theater managers and sporting events promoters charge higher prices for front-row seats than for seats in the balcony.

Price discrimination works best when customer segments have different elasticities. Also, a low-price customer must not be able to resell the product to the high-price segment. Moreover, the cost of segmenting and policing the market should not exceed the benefits of price discrimination. You must make sure that the form of discrimination employed is not illegal.

SUMMARY

Pricing is a key component of the marketing mix, and it is essential that you understand the different pricing options that are available. Prices must be set that are consistent with your product's positioning and appropriate for your target market segment. Effective pricing is impossible without a keen awareness of price elasticities. When demand is inelastic, you can increase profits by raising prices. When demand is elastic, lower prices increase revenues. You also need to understand markup procedures to help set prices for wholesalers and retailers. No pricing analysis is complete without a review of the fixed and variable costs associated with different product alternatives. Sometimes prices should be set below current full costs to expand markets and keep out the competition. At other times multidimensional and bundle pricing should be used. The ideal pricing system combines estimates of costs and price elasticity to maximize the discounted stream of profits of the firm. Finally, no pricing scheme can last unless it considers the actions of competitors and is within the law.

NOTES

1. Gregory L. White, "Sales of Cars, Light Trucks Rose 7% in December," *The Wall Street Journal,* January 7, 1999, pp. A3, A4.
2. Fara Warner and Joseph B. White, "Ford Plans to Reduce Costs by Another $1 Billion," *The Wall Street Journal,* January 8, 1999, pp. A3, A6.
3. Dominique M. Hanssens, Leonard J. Parsons, and Randall L. Schultz, *Marketing Response Models: Econometric and Time Series Analysis* (Boston: Kluwer, 1990), pp. 187–191.
4. Philip Parker, "Price Elasticity Dynamics over the Adoption Cycle," *Journal of Marketing Research,* Vol. 20 (August 1992), pp. 359–367.
5. Gregory L. White, Fara Warner, and Joseph B. White, "Bumper Crop, Competition Rises, Car Prices Drop: A New Golden Age?" *The Wall Street Journal,* January 8, 1999, pp. A1, A8.
6. Ibid., p. A1.
7. David Carson, Audrey Gilmore, Darryl Cummins, Aodheen O'Donnell, and Ken Grant, "Price Setting in SMEs: Some Empirical Findings," *Journal of Product & Brand Management,* Vol. 7, No. 1 (1998), p. 78.
8. Hermann Simon and Robert J. Dolan, "Price Customization," *Marketing Management,* (Fall 1998), p. 16.
9. Ronald E. Goldsmith and Stephen J. Newell, "Innovativeness and Price Sensitivity: Managerial, Theoretical and Methodological Issues," *Journal of Product & Brand Management,* Vol. 6, No. 3 (1997), p. 168.
10. Dean Takahashi, "Intel Introduces 2 Low-End Chips, Cuts Some Prices," *The Wall Street Journal,* January 5, 1999, p. B5.
11. Simon and Dolan, "Price Customization," p. 13.

SUGGESTED READING

Hamilton, Will, Robert East, and Stavros Kkalafatis, "The Measurement and Utility of Brand Price Elasticities," *Journal of Marketing Management,* Vol. 13, No. 4 (May 1997), pp. 285–298.
Simon, Hermann, and Martin Fasfnacht. "Price Bundling," *European Management Journal,* Vol. 11 (December 1993), pp. 403–411.

REFERENCES

Cross, Robert G. *Revenue Management* (New York: Broadway Books, 1997).
Dolan, Robert J. and Hermann Simon. *Power Pricing: How Managing Price Transforms the Bottom Line* (New York: Free Press, 1997).
Holtz, Herman. *Priced to Sell: The Complete Guide to More Profitable Pricing* (Upstart Publishing Company, 1996).

Monroe, Kent B. *Pricing: Making Profitable Decisions* (New York: McGraw-Hill, 1990).

Nagle, Thomas T. and Reed K. Holden. *The Strategy and Tactics of Pricing: A Guide to Profitable Decision Making* (Upper Saddle River, NJ: Prentice-Hall, 1994).

Wilson, Robert B. *Nonlinear Pricing* (London: Oxford University Press, 1997).

QUESTIONS

1. Since 1997, Fuji Photo Film Co. of Japan and Eastman Kodak Co. have been engaged in a furious price war for the U.S. consumer photographic film market. In 1998, Fuji stunned Kodak by offering a four-pack of 24-exposure rolls for $4.99 through Wal-Mart and other mass merchants. Kodak responded with a rebate promotion at Sam's Club stores with a six-pack for $5.99, a new low of 4 cents a snapshot. The average price per roll has fallen 9.6 percent for Fuji and 7.3 percent for Kodak, hurting profits for both firms. Why is Fuji with 15 percent of the market going after Kodak which holds 73 percent of the market? How should Kodak respond?

2. If a retailer has product costs of $42 and plans to make a 40 percent margin on its selling price, what price would it charge?

3. Some stores are selling replacement blades for Gillette's new MACH3 razor for 70 percent more than the cost of blades for the Sensor Excel razor that it displaced. Should Gillette allow this price gap to continue? Why are consumers willing to pay a premium to get the new blades?

4. A retailer notes that a line of woks is selling at a rate of 100 per week. When the price is cut from $40 to $35, sales increase to 106 per week. What is the price elasticity of demand? What happens to revenue? What price should the retailer place on the woks?

5. Florida's attorney general has charged 10 large paper companies with conspiring to fix the prices of toilet paper sold to schools, hospitals, prisons, hotels, and other commercial customers. The suit notes that while the price of wood pulp (which is used to make toilet tissue) has dropped 18 percent, the price of tissue has risen 41 percent. Why do large firms conspire to fix the selling prices of toilet paper, citric acid, and other basic commodities?

6. Matsushita announced an introductory price of $1,000 for a digital compact cassette deck. DCC machines boost quality by storing sound digitally instead of in the analog format used in conventional cassettes. The new players will also play conventional cassettes, but without enhanced sound quality. Why has Matsushita set the DCC price so high?

7. A shortage has developed for a popular model of automobile, and customers must now wait two months for delivery. A dealer has been selling these cars at list price. Now the dealer prices this model at $500 above list price. Is this acceptable behavior or is it unfair?

8. Advanced Micro Devices was able to grab a large piece of the microprocessor market for PCs selling at under $1,000 by offering chips for $100 or less. Intel, the high-priced market leader, responded by offering similar chips for as low as $71, causing AMD to lose money in 1998. What should AMD do to start making profits?

9. A grocery store has several months' supply of peanut butter in stock which it has on the shelves and in the storeroom. The owner hears that the wholesale price of peanut butter has increased and immediately raises the price on the current stock of peanut butter. Is this acceptable or is the grocer unfairly taking advantage of his customers?

10. The manager for a brand of margarine wondered how sensitive the total market was to changes in margarine and butter prices. Using the data in the file margarinedat.sav, calculate margarine's own-price elasticity and butter's cross-price elasticity. Hint: If you first compute the natural logarithm (LN) of each variable and then run a linear multiple regression on the transformed variables, the regression coefficients of the variables can be interpreted as elasticities.

SELECTING DISTRIBUTION CHANNELS

> The art of getting rich consists not in industry, but in a better order, in timeliness, in being at the right spot.
>
> RALPH WALDO EMERSON

A critical task for marketers in the new millennium is the efficient movement of goods and services from the point of production to the points of consumption. Distribution costs between 25 to 35 percent of the value of most products and it is your job to get products to customers quickly and at the lowest possible expenditure. Your job is complicated by the vast array of distribution alternatives available. Some firms sell directly to customers through the use of the Internet, telephone, mail order, or calls by company salespeople. Others use marketing intermediaries such as wholesalers, distributors, and retailers to get their goods and services to buyers. Another approach is to use agents who search for customers and negotiate sales but do not take title to the goods they handle. Each approach has its advantages and disadvantages. In this chapter, we explain how distribution networks are created and adapted to changing market conditions. The key tasks are selecting the best channels for each firm and finding ways to operate them efficiently.

DISTRIBUTION ALTERNATIVES

There are hundreds of ways goods and services can be distributed to customers. No one distribution system can satisfy the needs of every firm, and many organizations use several distribution channels to reach different market segments. A paper mill, for example, may contact large users directly and service small customers through independent wholesalers.

When Should Intermediaries Be Used?

Industrial firms sell to relatively few customers and usually contact these buyers directly. Intel, for example, set up a Web site in July to take orders and by November of that year was booking $1 billion in orders a month over the Internet. This amounted to about half of the company's total revenue. It has been estimated that by the year 2007, 100 percent of business-to-business sales will be over the Internet.[1] However, consumer products need wider distribution than industrial goods and have traditionally been sold using channel intermediaries such as wholesalers and retailers.

For many firms, the cost of owning a consumer channel of distribution can be prohibitive. Ford has a network of 5,300 dealers who sell its cars in the United States. To own this channel, Ford would have to spend billions of dollars. Rather than invest this huge amount, Ford initially used franchising so that the cost of setting up its distribution network was borne by the local independent dealers. More recently, Ford has been buying up dealerships in local markets and creating networks of superstores under the brand Auto Collection. By 2003 Ford expects to have expanded its ownership to 25 percent of its dealers.[2]

Another distribution problem occurs when your product is part of an assortment. Mars M&M candies are sold along with other brands of candy in supermarkets, drugstores, theaters, vending machines, and convenience stores all over the world. Instead of owning all these businesses, Mars has decided to work with established wholesalers and retailers.

Selling Through the Internet

The newest and most rapidly growing channel of distribution is the sale of goods and services using Web sites on the Internet (Figure 10-1a & b). Customers log on to the Internet using their computers and then call up Web sites for products in which they are interested. The sites function as electronic catalogs that provide pictures, information, and prices on merchandise that is available for sale. Interested customers complete a purchase by typing in a credit card number and then have the goods shipped to an address by mail or UPS delivery services. Web shopping allows customers to easily compare an unlimited breadth of offerings from a wide variety of suppliers and quickly order items they want. Web selling is attractive because it offers a fast way to reach customers without paper record-keeping, bricks and mortar shops, and piled-up inventories.

You must understand that some Web sites are owned and operated by manufacturers or service providers (Figure 10-1). Merchandise sold on these sites represents *direct* sales from the producer to the final consumer. Other Web sites are owned by intermediaries that buy products from a number of manufacturers and resell to final users. These Web sites function as electronic retailers (Figure 10-1a). An example showing how the largest Web retailer of

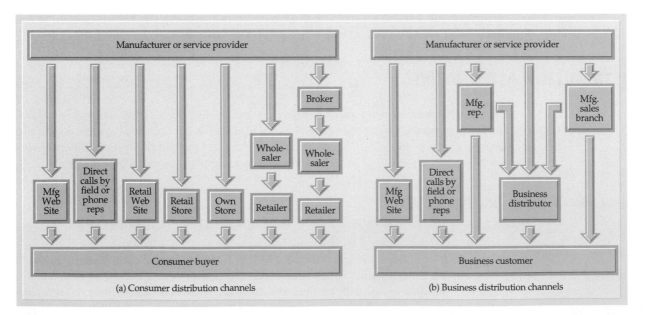

FIGURE 10-1   Consumer and Business Channel Alternatives

consumer items, Amazon.com, operates on the Internet is described in Marketing in Action box 10-1.

What Sells on the Internet?   If you define Internet commerce broadly to include all business-to-business purchasing, all Web site advertising, and all consumer on-line shopping, the total has been estimated to be $200 billion in 1998 and could rise to a trillion by 2002.[3] Consumer on-line shopping alone was $13 billion in 1998 and is expected to rise to $60 billion by 2002 (Table 10-1). The most popular items are travel and computer hardware with more than half of all Web sales. In third place is the sale of securities with 11 percent of Web business. Given the huge sales of computers and related hardware on the Web, it is not surprising that software provides 8 percent of Web sales. Clothing ranks seventh on the Internet with 4.6 percent of the business. This can probably be explained by the problems buyers sometimes encounter with fit, colors, and fabrics when they order electronically. Also it is understandable that groceries account for only 2 percent of Web sales given consumers' preferences to select food to meet their nutritional and freshness needs.

APPLYING
. . . *to*
Industrial
Marketing

One of the most successful and profitable Web site direct sellers is Cisco Systems. Cisco sells routers that shuffle data from one computer to another over the Internet and the software to go along with these machines. Customers can easily download their software purchases direct from the company Web site. In 1998, Cisco's web sales were $14.9 million a day or 64 percent of the company's total revenue of $8.5 billion. Part of Cisco's Internet success is due to its policy of paying its field sales representatives commissions on Web-driven sales. Reps make money on Web sales and they encourage their customers to gather information and check orders at the Cisco Web site.[4]

MARKETING IN ACTION 10-1

Selling on the Internet

INTEGRATING
. . . *with*
Information
Technology
Management,
Production/
Operations
Management,
Logistics

Amazon.com Inc. has become one of the largest retailers of consumer products over the Internet. The company began selling books over the Internet and has now expanded into music and videos. In the third quarter of 1998, Amazon.com reported revenues of $153 million and its music sales of $14 million surpassed those of its two rivals N2K Inc. and CDnow Inc. Amazon.com's success is due to its convenience (open 24 hour a day, 365 days a year) and its huge assortment of titles. Where a Barnes & Noble bookstore and a Tower Records store offer a combined 275,000 titles, Amazon.com had 3 million titles. However, Amazon.com keeps very few of these titles in stock. When Amazon.com receives an order, a computer determines if the book is on hand or must be ordered. Amazon.com relies on quick delivery of books, CDs, and videos from publishers or wholesalers to fill most of its orders. The company maintains one distribution center in Seattle and another in Delaware. These centers are run 24 hours a day and most of the items received in the morning are sent out by the end of the day. While Amazon.com is growing rapidly, its two major competitors, Barnes & Noble and Borders, both reported net losses in profits in the third quarter of 1998 on their combined Internet and retail store book sales. However, the higher combined sales of Borders and Barnes & Noble may enable them to undercut Amazon's prices in the long run.

— *Distribution channels are constantly tested by new networks and only the strong and the innovative survive.*

Sources: Paula L. Stepankowsky, "Amazon.com Gets Real at Distribution Site," *The Wall Street Journal*, November 16, 1998, p. B7G. Kara Swisher, "Amazon.com Posts Wider Period Loss, But Tops Forecasts," *The Wall Street Journal*, October 19, 1998, p. B8.

TABLE 10-1   Internet Sales in the United States in 1998

Product Categories	Percentage of Sales
Travel	30.5%
Computer Hardware	20.3
Stocks	11.3
Software	8.2
Books	7.1
Content (pay-per-use sites such as stock quotes)	4.7
Clothing	4.6
Groceries	2.0
Music	1.2
Other	5.2
	100.0%
Estimated total revenue	$13.0 billion

Source: Adapted from material presented in Rebecca Quick, "Internet Retailing May Drum Up $13 Billion in Revenue This Year," *The Wall Street Journal*, November 18, 1998, p. B6 and Christina Lourosa, "Change in Store," *The Wall Street Journal*, November 18, 1998, p. R28.

APPLYING
. . . to
Consumer
Financial
Services
Marketing

Another product that seems to be made for distribution over the Internet is the buying and selling of securities. More than 80 brokers now offer Web site trading and online business now accounts for over 30 percent of all trades by individuals. High-speed transactions are important to investors, and the Internet offers almost instant execution of buy and sell orders. Also the transactions are recorded electronically and there are only a few pieces of paper to deliver to the customer. The main problem with online trading is the conflict between expenditures needed to build brand strength and relentless price-cutting by competitors. The number-one and number-two online brokerage firms (Charles Schwab and E*Trade) have lost market share to firms that charge as low as $7 to $10 a trade. Thus E*Trade, which was able to make a profit in 1998 on revenues of $215 million by charging $14.95 a trade compared to Schwab's $29.95 fee, had to spend heavily to keep its number-two position. E*Trade spent $150 million on advertising in the latter part of 1998 and 1999 to maintain its market share in the online trading market. These massive expenditures were expected to produce losses for several quarters and the firm projected marketing costs would eventually decline to 25 to 35 percent of revenues.[5]

APPLYING
. . . to
Consumer
Durable
Goods
Marketing

Although not reflected in the numbers shown in Table 10-1, the Internet is becoming quite popular with automobile buyers. Surveys have shown that 25 percent of new car buyers shop on the Internet and this number is expected to increase to 50 percent by the year 2000. A popular site is Autobytel.com Inc. which offers dealer cost data for cars and helps match buyers with dealers that are willing to negotiate prices online. Autobytel.com's success has prompted General Motors, Ford, and Chrysler to upgrade their Web sites.[6] GM's BuyPower program at www.gm.com will eventually make it possible for customers to get a price for the specific vehicle they want (with optional equipment), find the vehicle in dealer inventories, and arrange for a test drive. Where Autobytel.com charges dealers for customers referrals, GM's BuyPower program will be initially offered to dealers free of charge.

Is the Web Profitable?   Although many firms are jumping on the Web site selling bandwagon, only a few are making good profits. Amazon.com Inc., for example, has been selling millions of dollars' worth of books, CDs, and videos over the Internet for years, yet profits are elusive. In the third quarter of 1998, Amazon.com reported record sales of $153 million compared with $37 million in the year earlier period and loss of $45 million.[7] The problem is that it is expensive to set up Web sites and it takes low prices (30 to 40 percent off list for best-sellers) and high advertising expenditures to grow a Web site business. Amazon.com spends 23 percent of sales on marketing expenses alone, and analysts project it will not be profitable until 2001. If Internet retailers require margins of 25 to 30 percent of sales to operate, they are not going to drive supermarkets and Wal-Mart out of business on the basis of lower prices. These conventional retailers can make a profit on gross margins of 22 percent of sales.

In addition, Internet buyers have powerful search engines available to find the lowest price available anywhere on the Net. This makes it difficult for Internet retailers to raise prices. Thus while the two larger chain bookstore retailers, Barnes & Noble and Borders, have opened Web sites to compete with Amazon.com, they do not know when the sites will break even. A further problem for Web buyers is that although advertised prices may appear to be low, customers are often charged a "handling fee" of several dollars plus postage to ship the merchandise to their homes. This means that many consumers would save money by stopping by their local Borders' stores to pick up a book on the way home from work. Despite all the problems we have mentioned, Internet shopping is growing rapidly because it is so "convenient." Buyers can shop the Internet from their homes or offices and avoid the driving, parking, walking, and standing in line at check-out counters at conventional retail stores. Innovations in the sale of postage stamps over the Internet are described in Marketing in Action box 10-2.

APPLYING
... *to*
Consumer
Services
Marketing

MARKETING IN ACTION *10-2*

Selling Stamps on the Internet

The U.S. Postal Service began testing the sale of postage over the Internet in 1998 and expected the business to expand rapidly starting in 1999. To buy stamps, customers link up to their Internet postage vendor and establish electronic links to their bank accounts to draw on when needed to buy digital postage. Stamps are printed on envelopes when customers type in a recipient's address and the required postage. Software then generates an intricate checkerboard of coded data that contains the letter's source, its destination and the current date. This information can be read by a scanner and appears below a more traditional postage mark. Electronic postage appeals to small businesses who want the convenience of printing postage on demand. The new delivery system is expected to steal business from traditional postage meters sold by Pitney Bowes Inc.

— *Internet distribution can threaten traditional channels.*

Source: George Anders, "It's Digital, It's Encrypted—It's Postage," *The Wall Street Journal*, September 21, 1998, p. B1.

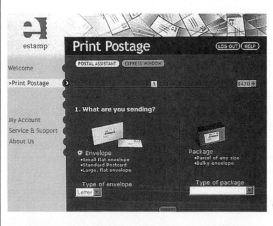

Courtesy E-Stamp Corp.

Selling by Phone, Catalogs or Sales Reps

Direct channels of distribution also include phone contacts by telemarketers and sales calls by field representatives (Figure 10-1). Sales reps are widely used to sell insurance and complex industrial products where buyers need tailored presentations and personal attention. Field sales calls are also used to sell Electrolux vacuum cleaners direct to consumer buyers. Because of the high cost of field calls ($400 to get a sale) and because phone sales cost considerably less than field calls, many firms are hiring telemarketers to contact consumer and industrial buyers over the phone. An amazing amount of business is conducted by telemarketing. Many people trade securities, buy flowers, books, seeds, CDs, and clothing using toll-free phone numbers offered in catalogs and direct mail advertising. Fifty-four percent of Americans buy from catalogs they receive in the mail, spending about $90 billion each year.[8]

In the past, marketers believed that only simple, standard items such as tickets and tapes could be sold direct. Today, however, cars and even complex computer equipment are being sold over the phone. For example, one of the authors responded to a newspaper ad and bought a Honda Civic over the phone with a credit card. Many firms are running print and television ads featuring toll-free 800 phone numbers to encourage customers to buy direct over the phone.

Customers are offered money-back guarantees and toll-free service lines to encourage sales. The result has been an explosion in the amount of business conducted over the phone. Michael Dell was the first to see that computers had become a commodity that could be sold direct using phone reps. Now Dell is a $20 billion company and a leading player in the U.S. computer market. Marketing Strategies box 10-1 describes how Michael Dell revolutionized the mail-order sale of computers with toll-free numbers. Direct marketing is discussed in more detail in Chapter 12.

Adding Retailers

Retailers have been a part of distribution channels for hundreds of years (Figure 10-1). They provide shopping convenience, local inventories, exchange services, and repairs. The use of retailers has proved effective and efficient for both consumers and manufacturers of food, clothing, tires, video rentals, hardware, dry cleaning, pharmaceuticals, furniture, office supplies, and auto sales.

**APPLYING
. . . to
Retailing**

The most exciting recent changes in retailing have been the growth of chain stores in the sale of pharmaceuticals, video rentals, hardware, and office supplies. Small family-run pharmacies, hardware stores, video rental stores, and stationers are vanishing under the onslaught from giants like CVS, Home Depot, Blockbuster, and Office Depot. The new larger pharmacy chain stores sign contracts with big health care providers for exclusive pharmaceutical coverage and patients buy liquor, paper goods, aspirin, and other items while they are waiting for their prescriptions to be filled. Hardware superstores like Builder's Square and Home Depot offer huge selections, low prices, and seven-day-a-week access.

The Blockbuster chain has become the number-one video rental store by offering broad selections of titles and multiple copies of new movies. Blockbuster signed new agreements with Hollywood studios that allows them to get movies for $6.50 each plus a 40 percent share of rental income instead of the usual $65-purchase price. This arrangement allows them to stock up to 400 copies of hits such as *Titanic* and helped slow the growth of the independent competitors. Within a year Blockbuster's revenue was up 16 percent and the greater availability of titles made it easier for them to compete with direct-to-home satellite services that allow customers to choose from an assortment of movies from menus on their TV screens.[9]

MARKETING STRATEGIES *10-1*

Dell Sells Direct

One of the most successful direct sales organizations in the history of American business is Dell Computer. In the past, complex, high-priced items that required after-sale service were thought to be inappropriate for mail-order distribution. Virtually all major PC manufacturers elected to sell through storefront dealers that allowed customers to touch and feel the machines and provided repair service. Michael Dell was the first to realize that PCs were a commodity business. Dell's strategy was to cut out the middleman and sell his computers directly to consumers via heavy advertising in the computer press, toll-free numbers, and Internet purchasing. He eliminated the uncertainties of mail-order purchasing by offering next-day, on-site service as well as phone and online technical support. Dell also offers factory integration of proprietary hardware and software, leasing and installation, warranty coverage, and an online superstore with 30,000 complementary items from industry leading companies.

Some people assume that Dell's success is simply due to its low prices. While Dell's prices are lower than those of its major competitors, they are not the lowest in the industry. Dell succeeds because it builds a quality machine and backs it with the best service in the country. In addition, Dell builds its computers to meet the needs of individual customer orders. This allows Dell to stay abreast of changing market conditions and greatly reduces inventory carrying costs.

Dell is a very efficient manufacturer and distributor of computers. Its selling and administrative costs are dramatically lower than those at Compaq, Apple, and IBM. Dell's sales organization includes thousands of telephone sales representatives. About 30 percent of Dell's sales are now made over the Internet.

The highest praise of Michael Dell's genius is that *all* of his major competitors (IBM, Apple, and Compaq) have instituted direct sales operations. Dell will be remembered as the greatest computer marketer of the twentieth century.

— Technical products can be sold successfully over the phone and Internet.

Source: Dell Publications, 1999.

Courtesy Dell Computer Corporation, 7/99

Selling to Business Buyers.   Many medium-sized and smaller firms buy computers and office supplies from large chain retailers. Currently the 1,940 office superstores run by Staples, OfficeMax, and Office Depot dominate the office supply business in the United States. These stores were initially in large towns, but now they are opening units in towns as small as Lebanon, New Hampshire, with only 12,000 people.[10] These stores succeed because their long hours of operation, broad assortments of supplies and computer equipment, and low prices can blow away their small independent competitors.

Another recent trend is for some of the giant direct selling PC manufacturers to strengthen their relationships with retail dealers. Dell gets 75 percent of its revenue from large corporate buyers, and about 15 percent of these orders are configured and installed by computer dealers. Gateway 2000 Inc., the number-two direct seller of personal computers, gets only 30 percent of its sales from corporate buyers and has begun opening retail stores to give them better access to this market segment. Gateway uses dealers as order and installation points and does not let them carry inventories of finished units.[11]

What Is Retailing's Future?   Some people believe that the rapid growth of telephone and Web site selling will lead to declines in the business done by traditional retailers. Although this may be true for some categories of merchandise, there are clear limits to what can be bought over the phone and Internet. Some consumers will always buy their food from supermarkets because they want to inspect the meat, produce, and packaged goods to see that they are fresh and meet their needs. Also, large grocery chains such as Kroger now offer bigger stores with one-stop shopping for food, banking, liquor, pharmaceuticals, video rentals, books, and take-out prepared foods.

Another service advantage of local dealers is highlighted by a mail-order purchase of some tires by one of the authors. I bought a set of tires over the phone from a low-priced magazine ad and they were delivered in two days. I had them mounted and threw away the old tires. The new tires were fine around town, but when I took the car out on the freeway I noticed an annoying vibration in the steering wheel at 65 miles per hour. When I called the phone tire dealer, I was told I would have to drive 250 miles to their office to have the tires checked with no assurance the tires could be exchanged unless they found them defective. My dilemma was that since I dumped the old tires, I could not mail the new tires back, I did not want to drive 500 miles to have them checked, and I did not like the vibration in the steering wheel. After having the tires rebalanced several times to no avail, I replaced them with another brand from a local dealer. My substantial loss on this phone purchase suggests that for products that require service, local retailers are unlikely to vanish from the channel of distribution anytime soon.

Using Wholesalers

When products are sold in many different types of retail stores scattered throughout the country, wholesalers may be needed to help transfer the merchandise from manufacturers to retailers (Figure 10-1a). Wholesalers are dealers that buy in volume and resell to retailers in small lots. They provide retailers with assortments of merchandise, backup stocks, credit, delivery, promotional assistance, and may stock the shelves. Organizations use wholesalers to get maximum exposure when direct contact with retailers is not justified because of low volume or lack of resources. For example, magazines and paperback books are stocked on display racks in newsstands, drugstores, discount stores, and supermarkets by specialized wholesalers. A few years ago there were 180 of these wholesalers in the United States. However, large supermarkets and discount stores have reduced the number of wholesalers they deal with to improve efficiency, and now there are fewer than 60.[12] The new larger wholesalers have better information systems and can help retailers fine-tune their displays and cut unprofitable titles. Ralph's Grocery, a West Coast supermarket chain, found that when it cut the number of titles from 1,100 to fewer than 500, overall magazine sales increased.

While wholesalers are a standard component of many distribution systems, they are currently losing market share to factory outlets, mail-order catalogs, warehouse clubs, and mass merchandisers that buy directly from manufacturers. Research suggests that wholesalers'

INTEGRATING
. . . *with*
Information
Technology
Management,
Production/
Operations
Management,
Logistics

share of producer shipments will fall to 36 percent by the year 2000.[13] Mergers have increased sharply among food and pharmaceutical wholesalers as more and more retailers and hospital chains are buying direct. If the 300,000 mostly small wholesalers in the United States expect to survive in the future, they will have to find ways to cut costs and improve customer benefits.

Agents and Brokers

Some manufacturers use brokers and independent representatives to sell goods in a channel of distribution (Figure 10-1). Reps are specialized agents who neither own nor take possession of the merchandise they sell to wholesale, distributor, business, or retail customers. They operate on commission in specified territories and sell where manufacturers cannot handle the job. For example, small food packers with a limited product line often lack the resources to hire their own sales force. By using a rep, the manufacturer avoids the high fixed costs associated with salespeople and branch facilities and gains the benefits of the contacts the rep has already established with the wholesale and retail trade.

APPLYING
. . . to
Business-to-
Business
Marketing

Although reps are a common element in distribution channels, they have begun to lose clout in many markets. Large retail chains like Wal-Mart, the cataloger Fingerhut, and K-Mart's Builder's Square no longer deal with reps in favor of direct negotiations with executives of supplier organizations. If this trend continues, reps may be relegated to special situations and employment by small manufacturers. This change suggests that distribution channels are rarely permanent and that you must continually search for new ways to lower costs and improve service to customers.

Channel Ownership

Some organizations can sell their goods and services through their own retail outlets. When an organization extends its activities to the wholesale and retail levels, it has a *vertically integrated channel.* This method of distribution can improve efficiency by eliminating promotion and selling expenses that normally occur between the organization and the wholesaler and between the wholesaler and the retailer. With a completely integrated channel, the main job for marketing executives is to increase demand among the final buyers and to coordinate the activities of different units in the channel. The primary advantage of this system is that it gives maximum control over the selection of products sold in the channel, their prices, and the promotional activities designed to sell them to the final consumer. Examples of completely integrated distribution channels are provided by Sherwin-Williams, which operates 2,000 paint stores; Hart Schaffner Marx, which owns more than 200 clothing stores; and Japan's Bridgestone which owns 1,500 Expert and Firestone tire stores in the United States. Although the completely integrated channel offers manufacturers the most control over the distribution of their products, it also requires the greatest financial investment and good managers to operate the facilities efficiently.

Franchise Distribution

Franchising is a system of distribution whereby independent business managers are given the right to sell products or services in exchange for a fee or agreements on buying and merchandising policies. The main advantage of franchising is that it offers the parent organization a low-cost way to expand rapidly. For example, when Prudential Insurance Company opened a chain of real estate agencies, the franchisees put up most of the money and the business was profitable from the start. Prudential estimates that it would have cost more than 10 times as much to open its own outlets. Ashland Oil chose franchising to

APPLYING
. . . to
Consumer
Services
Marketing

expand its quick-lube business. Ashland wanted to grow from 178 outlets to over 2,000. Since each unit cost more than $500,000, growth by franchising saved Ashland over $1 billion.

In the case of franchised ice cream stores, franchisees pay an initial fee ranging from $10,000 to $30,000 and then put up between $80,000 and $675,000 to get the business started. Local outlets also pay a royalty and advertising fee of 2 to 9 percent of sales. This shows how franchisees pay to expand a distribution network for you and then subsidize the advertising needed to make it successful.

A revolution in the ownership of some franchised outlets is shifting power away from manufacturers and service providers to corporations that own large numbers of franchised outlets. Historically franchisees were family owned, but today they are often controlled by big business. The most conspicuous example is Republic Industries, which owns 350 car and truck franchises in 18 states. The company is operated by former Blockbuster video executive Wayne Huizenga. Republic also owns Alamo Rent-A-Car, National Car Rental, and 39 AutoNation USA used car superstores. By grouping car franchisees together, Republic expects to cut costs 30 percent on such things as advertising, insurance, and the costs of borrowing money. Dealers in the same area can share ad campaigns instead of running separate promotions. Republic has become America's largest car dealer with sales in 1997 of $6.1 billion and an operating loss of $68.4 million. Critics point out that although the average auto dealer made a profit of 1.7 percent of sales in 1997, Republic reported losses of 1.1 percent of revenue. While General Motors, Ford, and Chrysler have supported Republic's growth, Toyota and Honda have gone to court to try and stop Huizenga from buying up their dealers. These maneuvers have not deterred Republic, and it seems determined to continue expanding and eventually break even.[14]

APPLYING
. . . to Consumer Durable Goods Marketing, Retailing

CHANNEL CHOICE

Distribution channels are designed to give customers ready access to goods and services at a minimum cost. Thus you have to balance the costs of employing different types of channels against the revenues generated. Using a wholesaler, for example, reduces the manufacturer's sales and communication costs and can increase profits. Some customers, however, may want to buy direct. A model of the channel selection process is shown in Figure 10-2. The choice of distribution method begins with a decision on planned market coverage. Depending on the product and the number of customers, the organization must decide whether it wants broad distribution or more selective coverage with a few dealers.

Intensive Distribution

The intensive distribution approach is used for convenience goods when the firm wants the product available in as many retail outlets as possible. Intensive distribution can be achieved by recruiting large numbers of jobbers and wholesalers to cover every market area. Candy, photographic film, and cigarettes are made available in thousands of stores for easy access and more impulse sales.

Selective Distribution

With selective distribution, several dealers in each area are designated to handle the product, but the merchandise is not made available to every retailer. The idea is that restricted availability will increase the volume per dealer and make the brand more important to them. Also, selective distribution is used when dealers require extensive training and carry large stocks and parts inventories. Selective distribution is common with automobiles and branded

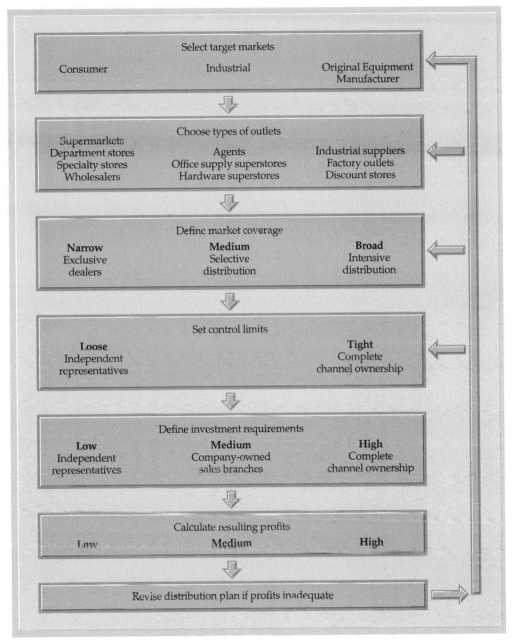

FIGURE 10-2   Choosing Distribution Channels

clothing. For example, designer jeans and Liz Claiborne-dresses are available in department and specialty stores but are kept out of K-Mart.

Exclusive Distribution

With exclusive distribution, the organization appoints a single dealer in each local market area to handle branded goods or services. Exclusive distribution has been used in the sales of luxury automobiles, Schwinn bicycles, Midas mufflers, and soft drink concentrate. By granting dealers local monopolies, the firm expects to gain cooperation on price maintenance, promotion, and inventory levels. Exclusive distribution helps dealers build customer loyalty and allows the dealers to charge higher markups. In addition, the use of exclusive territories allows dealers that invest in marketing activities to capture all the customers who want to buy the firm's goods and services.

Multiple-Channel Distribution

When an organization is new, it is common to concentrate its efforts on a single channel of distribution. As the firm grows, however, there are strong incentives to add channels to reach new market segments and to accommodate changes in customer shopping preferences. As a result, many companies distribute goods and services through several channels at the same time. Sometimes the addition of new channels creates morale problems with existing dealer networks. Firms face the terrible dilemma of choosing between the slow growth offered by traditional distribution channels and faster growth via new channels, which in turn, may cause regular dealers to drop the product.

**APPLYING
. . . to
Business-to-
Business
Marketing**

One solution pursued by Pella, a manufacturer of premium windows and doors, was to introduce a special ProLine of lower-priced items for sale in home supply stores such as Payless, Cashways, and Home Depot. To keep its regular distributors happy, Pella designated them as quality assurance representatives for all ProLine products sold in their territory. Distributors now train local retailers and help with installation and customer service. Pella distributors also earn a commission on every ProLine window the chain outlets sell. As a result, Pella's stagnant sales and profits have improved.

International Distribution

Once the firm has established distribution channels for domestic markets, emphasis often shifts to finding ways to sell in foreign countries. Because of the high costs and risks associated with international distribution, most firms start by making arrangements with foreign dealers to handle their products. For example, joint ventures have helped a number of American firms to enter the Japanese market. Black & Decker, the leading U.S. manufacturer of power tools, has been losing market share in the domestic market to Mikita Electric. Its response has been to sign an agreement with Shin-Daiwa Kogyo to market Black & Decker's tools in Japan. The idea is to take advantage of Shin-Daiwa's extensive sales force, distribution network, and service operations.

**APPLYING
. . . to
Consumer
Durable
Goods
Marketing**

Careful attention to building strong distribution networks is often the key to successful foreign sales. The Germans, for instance, have grabbed 76 percent of the imported car market in Japan due to their strong local dealers. Volkswagen sells its cars in Japan through Yanase & Company, the largest group of foreign car dealers in the country. BMW purchased its own dealer network in Japan and then expanded it. BMW has also set up a service and parts system so that Japanese buyers do not have to worry about repair problems. The lesson from these examples is that you cannot ignore distribution problems if you expect to win overseas sales.

MANAGING THE CHANNEL

Once you have a distribution network, the emphasis shifts to finding ways to improve performance. This is an ongoing process of evaluating results, modifying dealers' incentives, and replacing weak players.

Dealer Incentives

Independent wholesalers and retailers are in business to make money and are interested in stocking and promoting items that will increase *their* profits. Organizations that sell through these dealers must design products and marketing programs that are equal to or better than competitive offerings if they expect to gain support of these entrepreneurs. The most common dealer incentives are price concessions granted for volume purchases, advertising support, and seasonal orders. Other, more indirect methods for building dealer excitement include display materials, training programs, sales literature, and the hiring of in-store demonstrators. Perhaps the most enduring technique used to gain dealer cooperation involves the extension of credit. This may take the form of loans to finance inventories of display merchandise, loans for fixtures and equipment, or cash to finance customer purchases.

Another way to encourage dealers' cooperation is to give them exclusive rights to sell particular brands or models. Although Michelin sells a few lines of tires through K-Mart discount stores, its premium tires are available only through its traditional independent dealers. Dell has expanded its distribution channels to include retail outlets and has tailored its Precision line of computers for warehouse stores such as Sam's Club and Price Club. In a similar fashion, Hallmark sells Ambassador cards through supermarkets and reserves its own name cards for sale through its franchised independent outlets.

Disincentives that damage dealer relations include delayed delivery, shipment of unwanted products, slow warranty claims, and high prices. Firms that discuss their strategies with dealers and those that make simple requests are able to gain dealer agreements on inventory levels, participation in special programs, number of salespeople, and advertising expenditures. On the other hand, companies that make threats, promises, legalistic pleas, or specific recommendations have a negative impact on dealer cooperation.

Channel Power

Power in a distribution channel is the ability to get people to do things they might not otherwise want to do. Manufacturers and service providers who own their distribution channels have the power to set price, inventory, and promotion levels as they see fit. However, many firms distribute their products through independent dealers, so there are limits to what they can be forced to do. Firms that exercise too much channel power are likely to lose shelf space and dealers, be sued, or face additional legislation designed to protect channel members.

An example of a power struggle between food manufacturers and grocery stores developed over slotting allowances. In the old days, large manufacturers could bully grocers into carrying their products, and the manufacturer could dictate prices. However, supermarket chains consolidated into regional giants with immense distribution clout. Supermarkets used their control over shelf space to ask for slotting allowances of $15 to $1,000 per store to place new items on their shelves. Manufacturers were told that they had to pay cash to gain retail distribution they once purchased with consumer advertising. Manufacturers grew tired of this game and began to push food sales in discount stores, warehouse clubs, and superstores that were not so greedy. As a result, the share of the food business handled by traditional supermarkets has declined. This example suggests that firms that abuse their power in distribution channels may lose in the long run.

Gray Market Distribution

One of the most difficult distribution control problems facing multinational firms is the so-called gray market issue. The *gray market* is a system in which retailers import branded goods from foreign countries without approval of the product's manufacturer. These importers purchase branded goods from wholesalers in countries with low taxes and markups and then resell them in countries where markups are high. Gray market goods typically sell for 25 to 40 percent less than imports handled through regular distribution channels. Common gray market merchandise includes cameras, watches, fragrances, cosmetics, electronics goods, liquor, and tires made overseas.

Gray market (or parallel) importation develops when multinational firms sell products at higher prices in one country than in another. Firms often use larger markups in new markets to help attract wholesalers and pay for advertising and sales promotion activities. Although high markups help build a strong distribution network, they also attract gray market importers. The problem with gray markets is that the regular distribution network supplies inventory backup, spare parts, repairs, and promotional support that are not provided to customers who buy through gray markets. Thus, the gray market grows under an umbrella of services provided by the regular channel. Parallel importation can seriously damage authorized dealers by siphoning off sales.

The best way to eliminate gray markets is to reduce price differentials across countries that allow parallel importation to exist. Another solution is to buy up the merchandise brought in by gray marketers to protect your regular dealers. This approach could become expensive if it encouraged dealers to bring in even more merchandise. The U.S. Supreme Court has ruled that gray market importation is legal, so the problem is likely to exist for many years.

ORGANIZING DISTRIBUTION

For many products, distribution costs can be 30 percent of a product's cost. Firms that learn how to cut these costs can sell at lower prices and steal market share from their competitors. Amazing changes are taking place in physical distribution systems, and this area may be a key profit area for marketing in the twenty-first century.

Using Scanner Data

INTEGRATING
... *with*
Information
Technology
Management,
Production/
Operations
Management,
Logistics

The engine fueling the revolution in distribution efficiency is improved information on customer purchases. These data are gathered by optical scanners in retail stores that read bar codes on product packaging. Whenever a customer buys anything, data on the purchase goes directly—in real time—to the retailer's central computer and on to the manufacturer's plant. Computers prepare a manufacturing schedule and instructions on when, how, and where to ship. This type of system is used by the largest retailer in the United States—Wal-Mart. By tying point-of-sale terminals to suppliers' factories, Wal-Mart has made several cost savings. Most of the cost of distribution involves keeping inventory in three warehouses: the manufacturer's, the wholesaler's and the retailer's. With Wal-Mart's system there is no need for factory buffer stock, because the goods are made to order and shipped immediately. Also, some of the orders go directly to the stores, reducing the need for wholesale inventories. Since store shipments replace stock already sold, Wal-Mart needs less safety stock at the store level. Wal-Mart allocates only 10 percent of its square footage for inventory compared to 25 percent at other stores. Another area for savings is reduced order cycle time. Because of direct computer linkages, communication delays are eliminated and it takes less time to get merchandise into Wal-Mart stores. This means that fewer people are needed to process the orders, and quick delivery cuts out-of-stock conditions and boosts sales.

INTEGRATING
... *with*
Suppliers

Wal-Mart's direct information ties with suppliers has allowed it to reduce its expense ratio to only 15 percent of sales. This compares with expense ratios of 23.8 percent at J.C. Penney Co., 21.6 percent at Sears, Roebuck & Co. and explains how Wal-Mart is able to use low prices to become the world's largest retailer.[15] No traditional retailer, no supermarket, and no catalog store can compete with Wal-Mart on price. Wal-Mart has successfully employed advanced information technology to achieve a sustainable competitive advantage in distribution costs.

Although the use of scanner data to automatically reorder merchandise has lowered distribution costs, the systems are not perfect. This was shown by the experience of one of the authors who went to a Target discount store to get some cat food and cat litter on a Sunday afternoon. Target was out of one flavor of cat food that I wanted and did not have my preferred brand of cat litter in stock. I went to a K-Mart store and found the chicken-flavored cat food, but they were out of the Arm & Hammer cat litter. Walking through the store I noticed that many of the shelves were depleted of merchandise. I asked the service person at the front of the store when they would have more cat litter. She indicated that the store received merchandise Monday through Friday. This meant that the reorder system did not provide enough inventory to get the store through the weekend. Thus while Target's and K-Mart's automated reorder systems improve distribution efficiency, they do not always take care of Sunday afternoon shoppers. In my case, I found Arm & Hammer cat litter at a Kroger supermarket that was open 24 hours a day, 7 days a week, suggesting their system was better able to keep products in stock. The cat litter was priced 10 percent higher at Kroger, however, suggesting I could save money by adapting my shopping trips to coincide with Target and K-Mart's restocking cycle.

Are Warehouses Necessary?

INTEGRATING
... with
Information
Technology
Management,
Production/
Operations
Management,
Logistics

In the past, inventories were carried at factory warehouses, wholesale warehouses, and retail warehouses. Today the question is whether they are needed at all. Firms that produce to customers' orders and sell directly do not have to operate any warehouses. Dell Computer, for example, takes orders over the phone, builds machines to these specs, and then ships directly to customers via UPS. Inventories and warehouses are not required in this distribution system. Any storage in the channel is maintained by the shipping company.

Other firms are also finding ways to reduce the need for warehouses. In one medium-sized supermarket chain, half of the merchandise goes directly from manufacturers to stores. The other half still goes through company warehouses, but it is not held there: the merchandise is shipped to stores within three hours. These warehouses are *switching yards* instead of storage bins. Any retailer that stores only half of its goods for three hours in a warehouse is saving a great deal on inventory carrying costs.

Firms that serve many small customers requiring warehouse distribution have found ways to operate their remaining warehouses more efficiently. Helene Curtis, for example, has built a highly automated and computerized warehouse that can handle twice the volume of the six older warehouses it replaced. The new system helped Helene Curtis cut distribution costs by 40 percent. These savings allowed the company to cut prices to the consumer by 10 percent and increased market share. Mervyn's has built four new automated distribution centers to serve its 247 department stores. These centers cut the average time merchandise spends moving from vendor to store from 14 days to less than 9 days. The results have been spectacular. Mervyn's sales have grown 50 percent, but inventory carrying costs have remained the same as they were five years ago. Manufacturers and retailers that refuse to buy into computerized information systems will have trouble competing in the future.

SUMMARY

This chapter has discussed selecting channels of distribution and designing systems to move goods and services efficiently to the point of final consumption. You have to decide whether to sell direct over the Internet or to organize a channel made up of independent brokers, wholesalers, or retailers. This choice is influenced by customer preferences, the supply of independent distributors, and by the amount of money and sales volume the firm has to support its own distribution network. If independent dealers are selected, you must find ways to care for and nourish channel members to ensure their continued cooperation and survival. A common problem today is finding ways to keep your regular dealers happy as you add new distribution channels to build market share.

The last frontier of marketing efficiency is finding ways to reduce the costs of distribution. Some of the most spectacular savings have been achieved by linking optical scanners in retail stores to factories. Others have had success by automating field warehouses and using intermodal transportation systems. American distribution systems are undergoing radical changes, and firms that do not pay attention may not survive.

NOTES

1. William M. Bulkeley, "Peering Ahead," *The Wall Street Journal* (November 16, 1998), p. R4.
2. Fara Warner, "Ford Motor Files for 'Shelf' Stock to Buy Dealers," *The Wall Street Journal*, (November 16, 1998) p.B2.
3. Ken Auletta, "The Last Sure Thing," *The New Yorker* (November 9, 1998), p. 41.
4. Julie Schmit, "Cisco Embraces 'Internet Economy,'" *USA Today* (September 23, 1998), p. 3B. Melanie Berger, "New Sales," *Sales & Marketing Management* (April 1998), p. 90.
5. Michael Schroeder, "SEC Is Stuck Refereeing Big Board, Web-Trade Spat," *The Wall Street Journal* (September 24, 1998), pp. C1, C17. Rebecca Buckman, "Brokerages Spend Big on Web-Site Ads," *The Wall Street Journal* (September 11, 1998), p. C22.
6. Gregory L. White, "General Motors to Take Nationwide Test Drive on Web," *The Wall Street Journal* (September 28, 1998), p. B4.
7. Kara Swisher, "Amazon.com Posts Wider Period Loss, But Tops Forecasts," *The Wall Street Journal* (October 29, 1998), p. B8.
8. *Newsweek* (October 19, 1998), p. 8.
9. Eben Shapiro, "Blockbuster Seeks a New Deal with Hollywood," *The Wall Street Journal* (March 25, 1998), p. B1. David Segal, "Blockbuster Thrives on Deals with Studios," *Herald-Times*, September 20, 1998, p. G2.
10. William M. Bulkeley, "Office Supply Superstores Find Bounty in the Boonies," *The Wall Street Journal* (September 1, 1998), p. B1.
11. Evan Ramstad, "Gateway Unit to Bolster Ties to PC Dealers," *The Wall Street Journal* (April 20, 1998), p. B1.
12. G. Bruce Knecht, "Rack or Ruin," *The Wall Street Journal* (May 26, 1998), p. A1.
13. Michael Selz, "Firms Innovate to Get It for You Wholesale," *The Wall Street Journal* (July 24, 1993), p. B1.
14. Fara Warner, "Republic Extending Auto Nation Brand to New Car Sales in Bid to Build Chain," *The Wall Street Journal* (September 24, 1998), p. A4. Kerry Pipes, "Used-Car 'Superstores' Fail to Dominate Market," *Car and Driver*, (November 1998), p. 36. Oscar Suris, "Honda Sues Republic Industries in an Effort to Limit Franchises," *The Wall Street Journal* (May 12, 1997), p. B1.
15. Robert Berner, "Moving the Goods," *The Wall Street Journal* (July 16, 1996), pp. A1, A6.

SUGGESTED READING

Dant, Rejiu P., and Patrick L. Schul. "Conflict Resolution Processes in Contractual Channels of Distribution," *Journal of Marketing*, Vol. 56 (January 1992), pp. 38–54.

Frazier, Gary, and Raymond C. Rody. "The Use of Influence Strategies in Interfirm Relationships in Industrial Product Channels," *Journal of Marketing*, Vol. 55 (January 1991), pp. 52–69.

Keep, William W., Stanley C. Hollander, and Roger Dickinson. "Forces Impinging on Long-Term Business-to-Business Relationships in the United States: A Historical Perspective, *Journal of Marketing*, Vol. 62, No. 2 (April 1998), pp. 31–45.

Siguaw, Judy A., Penn M. Simpson, and Thomas L. Baker. "Effects of Supplier Market Orientation on Distributor Market Orientation and the Channel Relationship: The Distributor Perspective," *Journal of Marketing*, Vol. 62, No. 3 (July 1998), pp. 99–111.

REFERENCES

Coyle, John J., Edward J. Bardi, and C. John Langley, *The Management of Business Logistics,* 6th ed. (St. Paul, MN: West, 1996).

Rosenbloom, Bert, *Marketing Channels,* 5th ed. (Chicago, IL: Dryden Press, 1994).

Stern, Louis W., Anne T. Coughlan, and Adel El-Ansary, *Marketing Channels,* 5th ed. (Englewood Cliffs, NJ: Prentice-Hall, 1996).

QUESTIONS

1. Twenty-five automobile dealerships in the Northwest settled Federal Trade Commission charges in 1998 that they threatened to boycott Chrysler Corp. unless it restricted the number of vehicles allocated to Dave Smith Motors of Kellogg, Idaho. Smith Motors offers lower preset prices over the Internet to attract buyers. Why did the 25 dealers try to boycott Chrysler and how should they respond to Dave Smith's Internet program?

2. PepsiCo has announced plans to acquire one of its largest independent franchised bottlers for an estimated cost of $275 million. Independent bottlers buy syrups from PepsiCo, package beverages in cans and bottles, and deliver the products to retail stores. Why would PepsiCo want to buy up its bottlers and how will they justify the $275 million purchase to their stockholders?

3. SuperValu, Inc., of Minneapolis, Minnesota, has purchased Wetterau, Inc., of Hazelton, Missouri, for $643 million. The combined firm is the nation's largest food wholesaler. Before the merger, SuperValu serviced 2,600 independent grocery stores in 31 states plus 105 of its own stores, including its deep-discount Cub Foods stores. Wetterau owned 160 retail stores and distributed to 2,800 independent grocers. Why are mergers taking place among America's wholesalers?

4. Avon Products Inc. is one of the largest direct sellers of cosmetics and other products in the world. It has a corps of over 400,000 sales representatives who sell to customers in their homes and workplaces. The company has announced plans to open its first ever retail outlet in the United States. Why is Avon making this move? Won't the stores steal sales from the field sales reps?

5. The media giant Time-Warner is planning to become a Web retailer, selling an array of products such as Madonna compact disks, Batman videos, books, and Tweety Bird socks on the Net. Why is Time-Warner opening a Web store that is likely to cannibalize sales from its 185 Warner Brothers Studio Stores and its current direct-mail businesses?

6. The Jones Company was trying to decide whether to continue using independent sales reps or to replace them with company salespeople. The firm produced a line of ceramic dinnerware that was sold by 15 rep organizations employing 55 salespeople to contact 12,100 retail stores. Management felt that the reps were not giving Jones's dinnerware enough attention, particularly in the large department stores. Annual sales of the Jones Company were $5.2 million. The company liked to have its retail accounts contacted every six weeks. The reps were paid 10 percent of sales, although 12 percent was typical for this type of merchandise in other firms. Compare the advantages of reps over company salespeople for making personal contacts. How many company salespeople

would be needed to call on the retail accounts? Should Jones switch to company sales-people? If not, what should it do to improve the performance of the present reps?

7. General Motors has announced plans to open 75 regional distribution centers across the United States with large inventories of cars and light trucks. Some of the centers will carry as many as 2,000 vehicles. This plan will move some of the dealer's inventory, which GM subsidizes to the new regional centers. With 75 new regional distribution centers, GM's inventory interest charges will increase. How will the new centers help the retail dealers and how will they help GM?

8. Hewlett-Packard and Motorola have traditionally sold their high-powered workstations directly to engineers and technicians or to value-added resellers that market complex packages of computer equipment, software, and service. They recently agreed to sell workstations through mass market dealers MicroAge and Intelligent Electronics, which sell PCs to businesses. Explain why they are making this change in their distribution channels.

9. A manager of a large cola bottling company in the United States was charged with paying bribes to an employee of a U.S. military installation to gain sites for soda vending machines on the base. Why was the bottler trying to gain distribution of its products on the base? What can manufacturers do to prevent managers from paying bribes and kick-backs to customers who ask for them?

10. The German pudding-with-topping market is dominated by four national competitors: Gervais-Danone (a subsidiary of the French BSN group), Dr. Oetker (part of a highly diversified firm), Chambourcy (a subsidiary of the German Nestle group), and Elite (belonging to the German Unilever concern). The remainder of the market is shared by approximately 30 locally or regionally operated competitors. One of these regional companies, Ehrmann, is attempting to broaden its geographic reach. Annual data on sales (1000 tons), advertising (1000 DM), price (DM), and distribution penetration (%) are available for four years. In addition, a dummy variable for distinguishing between national (1) and regional/local brands (0) has been created. Pooling the data, i.e., combining cross-sectional and time-series data, from the file puddingdat.sav, assess the marketing mix of a prototypical brand. Use the $\alpha = 0.10$ level of significance. *Hint:* If you first compute the natural logarithm (LN) of each variable and then run a linear multiple regression on the transformed variables, the regression coefficients of the variables can be interpreted as elasticities. Because regional brands do not advertise and the natural logarithm of zero is minus infinity, you must add one to ALL advertising values before taking the logarithm, i.e., ladv = LN[adv+1]. Also, do not take the natural logarithm of the dummy variable.

11

PERSONAL SELLING AND SALES FORCE MANAGEMENT

> In the world of business, it is useless to be creative unless you can sell what you create. Customers cannot be expected to recognize a good idea unless it is presented by a good salesperson.
>
> ANONYMOUS

Marketing communications encourage customers to buy goods or services. The three principal means of communications, in order of the strength of their relationship with the customer, are the sales force, direct marketing, and advertising. Supporting activities include sales promotion and public relations. These communication methods interact to build sales. They must be carefully coordinated so that they conform with the brand platform and reinforce brand values—giving rise to the term *integrated marketing communications* (IMC). While the basic concept of IMC is not new, the information age has made its implementation feasible.

Marketing depends on personal contacts made by sales representatives, and these calls represent a key channel of communication for the firm. Personal selling accounts for more than 50 percent of the marketing budget, and it costs more than $456 to close each sale.[1] Thus you need to manage sales resources effectively if you expect to have a successful marketing program.

Your first job is to come up with a selling strategy and a plan of action. Then you have to locate target customers and recruit, train, motivate, compensate, and organize a field sales force. You also have to manage the interactions between customers and salespeople very carefully. This dialogue is influenced by the buyer's needs and the salesperson's skills. The results of successful salesperson–customer interactions are orders, profits, and repeat customers. An example of an effective sales manager at work is shown in Marketing in Action box 11-1.

THE ROLE OF PERSONAL SELLING

Sales managers help define the role that personal selling plays in marketing programs. In some door-to-door companies, such as Avon, personal selling dominates the marketing program almost to the exclusion of other forms of promotion. At the other extreme, book clubs and mail-order firms rely entirely on advertising and employ no field salespeople at all.

MARKETING IN ACTION *11-1*

Turning It Around in Cleveland

When Frank Pacetta took over the Cleveland district sales office for Xerox, turnover was high, and revenue was the lowest in the region. Customers were complaining about erratic service and slipshod billing. Pacetta knew he had to build relations with customers, so he hired seven more sales reps. This reduced the number of large customers per rep so important customers got more attention. Pacetta spent lavishly on promotional campaigns and customer parties.

In the office he created a fraternity atmosphere with parties and pep rallies and recognition for birthdays and anniversaries. He showered reps with plaques and praise for jobs well done. He created elaborate sales contests with some winners getting $2,500 to $3,000 extra per year. Pacetta also weeded out employees who failed to meet his pumped up sales targets.

Pacetta believes sales reps should be well groomed. He hands out shoe polish, asks overweight reps to slim down, and requires that shirt collars be heavily starched. He even demands clean-shaven faces. His dress code and management style did not appeal to everyone, but in his first year the Cleveland district soared to No. 1 in the region and No. 4 among Xerox's 65 districts.

Source: James Hirsch, "To One Xerox Man, Selling Photocopiers Is a Gambler's Game," *The Wall Street Journal,* September 24, 1991, p. 1.

Pacetta's Selling Tips

- Prepare customer proposals at night and on weekends.
- Never say no to a customer—everything is negotiable.
- Make customers feel good by sending cards for birthdays, etc., take them to lunch and ball games.
- Meet customers' requirements even if you must fight your own bureaucracy.
- Do things for customers you don't get paid for, like solving billing problems.
- Know competitive products better than they do.

THE DOCUMENT COMPANY
XEROX

Courtesy Xerox Corporation

Thus, you must decide how to balance personal selling with direct marketing, advertising, and sales promotion to achieve the goals of your organization. Next, you have to determine the source of field sales help.

Reps Versus Own Sales Force

Your first decision as sales manager is whether to hire your own sales force or to hire salespeople from independent rep organizations. Some firms adopt a strategy of spending all available cash on product development and promotion, so field sales work is left to independent representatives. Because reps are paid a percentage of sales, the companies pay only when sales are made, thereby avoiding the fixed costs of hiring, training, and supervising their own sales force. Furthermore, the firm can capitalize on the reps' already established relationships with the trade. The advantages and disadvantages of independent sales reps are summarized in Table 11-1.

TABLE 11-1 Comparing Company Salespeople with Reps

	Advantages	*Disadvantages*
Company Salespeople	1. Sell only your products 2. Can be directed to specific accounts 3. Can train them to sell by company guidelines 4. Sell full product line 5. Can be paid lower wages	1. High fixed costs 2. Takes time to hire them 3. Takes time to train them 4. Costs more initially 5. Sales grow more slowly
Independent Reps	1. Paid straight commissions so fixed costs are low 2. No need to hire or train reps 3. Produce sales quickly 4. Have established relationships with customers	1. Sell for several firms 2. Cost more as sales grow 3. Tend to push popular items 4. Only call on best accounts 5. More difficult to control

The use of a company sales force offers several advantages. For example, firms can exert more control over the activities of their own field personnel and can train them to sell according to fixed guidelines. In addition, inexperienced people can be hired and paid relatively low salaries, and these fixed costs help to keep expenses down as sales increase over time. A company's own salespeople spend all their time selling the firm's products rather than dividing their efforts among the products of several firms.

The choice between a rep strategy and a hire strategy is made on the basis of costs and benefits. When a firm is small, with limited financial and personnel resources, it may make more sense to hire independent reps. This approach conserves cash and provides more flexibility for growth. As your product line grows, however, the firm eventually reaches a point where it is more cost-effective to hire and train your own salespeople. Thus sales managers must choose between the variable costs, flexibility, and special services offered by reps and the fixed costs and greater control offered by a company sales force.

The Selling Job

Personal selling is a sequence of eight tasks (Figure 11-1). Most organizations do not have enough customers, and it is the responsibility of the field sales force to go out and discover who may need your products so as to identify new prospects. Once they are located, they must be qualified to make sure that they can use what you are selling and have the financial resources to pay for it. Then salespeople have to prepare what they will say to the prospect during the sales call. Next, the salesperson must overcome the obstacles erected by receptionists, secretaries, and assistants to gain an audience with the person with buying authority. At this point, the salesperson should try to find out something about the customer's needs. Sometimes information can be gleaned from trade gossip or talks with shop personnel. The salesperson should deliver a sales presentation tailored to fit the special needs of the prospect. This is called *adaptive selling*.

Because every sales presentation encounters objections from the prospect, the salesperson must be prepared with counterarguments. Salespeople frequently fail to try to close a sale after they have made their presentation. Salespeople do not want to be turned down, and customers can't be expected to volunteer orders. This means that sales managers must train salespeople to ask for the order. The average number of calls needed to close a sale is four, so managers need to encourage salespeople to go back again and again to get the order.

After-sale service is important in cementing relations with customers. Service work is designed to help customers solve problems related to the goods and services sold by the firm. This includes such activities as expediting orders, obtaining repair parts, setting up displays, stocking shelves, taking inventories, and training dealer personnel. Equipment salespeople, for example, often help customers rearrange machinery and personnel to improve

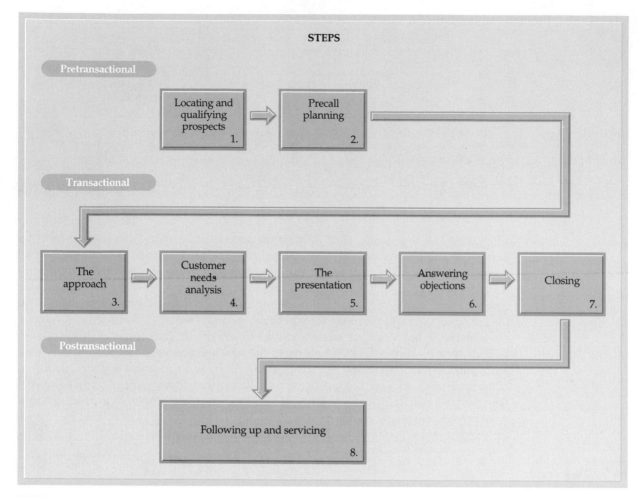

FIGURE 11-1   The Selling Job

efficiency. After the role of personal selling has been determined, managers must decide on how many salespeople to hire.

HOW MANY SALESPEOPLE?

Finding the right size for a sales force is complicated by variations in salespeople and customer needs. However, a rough idea of the personnel needed can be obtained by looking at costs and the number of customers.

What Can I Afford?

The size of the sales force is often a compromise between what the firm can afford and the total number of people needed to call on all existing and potential customers. An example of the "What can I afford?" approach suggests that a firm with $20 million in annual volume might be able to allocate 10 percent for field sales, or about $2 million a year. If supervisory expenses amounted to about 15 percent of selling costs, the firm would have $1,700,000 to hire salespeople. Assuming that salespeople cost $70,000 a year each for salary, commissions, bonus, benefits, and expenses, the company could afford to acquire 24 field salespeople. The size of the sales force is thus a direct function of the amount budgeted for field selling. The main problem with this approach is that it does not consider market potential or customers' needs.

The Workload Approach

The workload method of determining the size of the sales force is based on decisions regarding the frequency and length of calls needed to sell to existing and potential customers. An estimate of the total number of salespeople required using this approach can be made with this formula:

$$\text{Number of salespeople} = \frac{\left(\begin{array}{c}\text{number of}\\\text{existing}\\\text{customers}\end{array} + \begin{array}{c}\text{number of}\\\text{potential}\\\text{customers}\end{array}\right) \times \begin{array}{c}\text{ideal}\\\text{calling}\\\text{frequency}\end{array} \times \begin{array}{c}\text{length}\\\text{of call}\end{array}}{\text{selling time available one salesperson}} \qquad (11.1)$$

For example, if you had 3,000 existing customers and 2,250 potential clients to be called on five times a year for two hours (including travel time) and available selling time per salesperson was 1,500 hours, the size of the sales force would be

$$\text{Number of salespeople} = \frac{(3,000 + 2,250) \times 5 \times 2}{1,500} = 35 \qquad (11.2)$$

Note that the number of salespeople based on workload estimates is larger than the number derived using the percentage of sales method. This points out the biggest weakness of the workload approach: its failure to consider the costs and profits associated with different levels of customer service. Because ideal call frequencies are based on executive judgment, you never really know if you have set the number of calls to maximize profits.

Setting Sales Force Size at Loctite

An example showing how one firm set the size of its sales force is shown by Loctite, an industrial adhesives firm. In a push to improve profits, Loctite allowed its sales force to decline through attrition, and hired telemarketing people to fill in the gaps. Although profits increased, Loctite's reps were unable to provide adequate service to existing customers and sales growth stalled. Adhesives require a lot of technical support that could not be provided over the phone by telemarketers. The solution in this case was to hire 30 new salespeople over a one-year period; soon afterward sales began to grow. The moral of this story is that sales growth is often tied to the number of salespeople operating in the field.

Sales Force Turnover

The size of the sales force is also influenced by the problem of personnel turnover. If salespeople are constantly leaving, then unfilled territories make sales goals hard to reach. Turnover is calculated by dividing the number of separations during a year by the average size of the sales force. Thus, if 15 people leave or are fired each year and the size of the sales force is 150, then the turnover rate is

$$\text{Turnover rate} = \frac{\text{separations per year}}{\text{average size of sales force}} = \frac{15}{150} = 10\% \qquad (11.3)$$

Turnover is important because customers prefer to establish long-term relationships with suppliers. When they have to deal with a new salesperson on every contact, they are less likely to continue working with these organizations. In addition, a constant turnover of salespeople may indicate poor management supervision and cause buyers to lose confidence in a supplier. Also empty territories mean lost sales, and high turnover raises hiring and training costs. For example, assume that it costs $25,000 to recruit and train each sales force replacement. This means that a turnover of 30 percent in a sales force of 150 people would cost the firm $1,125,000 (0.30 × 150 × $25,000 = $1,125,000).

When turnover costs $1 million a year, sales managers seek ways to reduce separations. Turnover can be cut by balancing territories and by improving the financial rewards paid to salespeople. Another way to lower turnover is to offer a variety of nonfinancial rewards such as trips, prizes for sales contests, plaques, trophies, and recognition awards. All these techniques are designed to make salespeople feel better about their jobs and to reduce the attractiveness of outside offers.

We have discussed the problems of high turnover, but turnover can be too low as well. For instance, when a sales force has no turnover, it could mean the salespeople are happy with their job. There is immediate suspicion, however, that the salespeople may be resting on their laurels, overpaid, or both. A lack of turnover may also signal that salespeople are all of the same age. The situation can be serious because they are likely to retire at the same time, and the firm will have to recruit and train an entirely new sales force. The ideal situation is to have salespeople of various ages so that a few retire each year and new recruits can be added on a regular basis. For example, if the average sales career spans 20 years, then 5 percent of the sales force would retire each year. Because some salespeople leave before they retire—because of promotions, resignations, or dismissals—a turnover rate of 10 to 15 percent a year can be considered normal. Beyond the issues of size is the problem of how to build an efficient sales organization.

INTEGRATING
... with Human Resource Management

ORGANIZING THE SALES FORCE

In small firms with only a few employees, the sales force usually reports directly to the president of the company. However, when firms grow larger, there is often an opportunity to raise productivity by adding sales managers. An example of a line sales organization employing two regional and six district sales managers is shown in Figure 11-2. In this case, 12 salespeople report to each district sales manager. This span of control can vary from 6 to 1 to 14 to 1 or more, depending on the type of product. Narrow spans of control are used for expensive technical products and wider spans of control are used for simpler consumer products.

As sales organizations grow larger, it is often necessary to hire additional staff personnel. For example, Figure 11-3 shows staff recruiters, trainers, and sales analysts reporting to a national sales manager. These staff specialists act as advisers to the general sales manager and interface with the regional and district sales managers.

Field salespeople are usually organized around geographic control units. Each salesperson is given an area, and these areas are grouped into districts and regions headed by sales managers. In a straight geographic orientation, salespeople sell all products to all customers in their territories (Figure 11-3, Western Region). Geographic organization produces the smallest territories and is the most economical way to structure a sales force. Only one person calls on each customer, and there is no cross-travel.

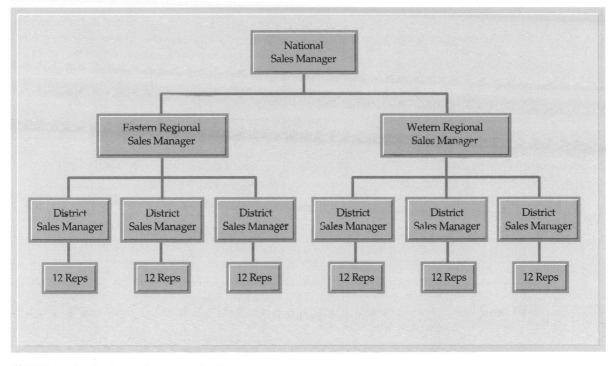

FIGURE 11-2   A Line Sales Organization

Organizing salespeople around customers makes sense when customers have unique purchasing requirements (Figure 11-3, Central Region). For example, one computer company uses a customer approach, with one sales team selling data entry systems to banks and a second group selling to other retailers. When companies have a diverse, highly technical product line, it may be desirable to hire salespeople to sell groups of products (Figure 11-3, Eastern Region). Under this plan, salespeople are product specialists, so it is unlikely that buyers will become bored during sales presentations. Salespeople who focus on groups of customers or products tend to work larger territories, and the resulting cross-travel increases selling expenses. To help control costs, customer and product salespeople often operate out of district sales offices that are organized on a geographic basis. Geographic-, product-, and customer-oriented sales forces have all been used successfully, and some firms switch back and forth, depending on the needs of the times.

RECRUITING AND SELECTING SALESPEOPLE

After you have decided on the dimensions of the sales force, you have to hire salespeople. Basically, two recruiting strategies are available. You can recruit experienced salespeople who can be placed in the field immediately, or you can hire inexperienced people and teach them product knowledge and sales skills. Although experienced salespeople must be paid higher wages, they begin producing orders sooner and in larger amounts than new trainees. Small firms selling technical products often hire experienced people because they lack the time, personnel, or facilities to train new employees. Larger companies, on the other hand, have the resources to train new salespeople to follow directions and act in a prescribed manner with customers. One of the risks of hiring experienced sales personnel is that they have changed jobs in the past and are more likely to be hired away by competitors. The advantages of hiring experienced reps is shown by Information Systems of America, which sells

APPLYING
... to
Business-to-
Business
Marketing

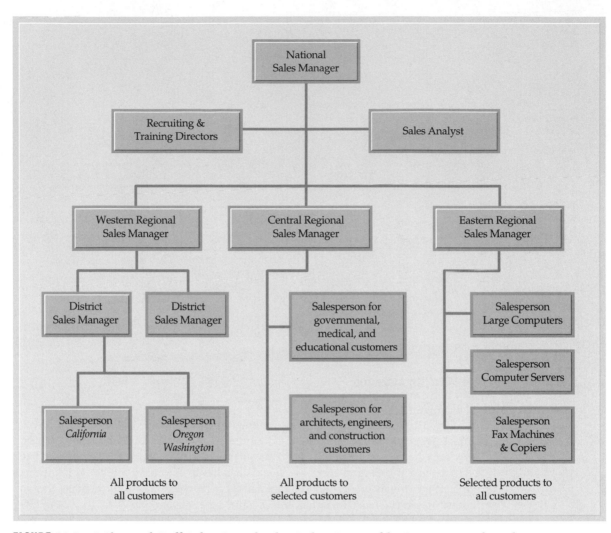

FIGURE 11-3　A Line and Staff Sales Organization Using Geographic, Customer, and Product Specialization

financial applications software. People with related selling experience are able to master the product line quickly and training costs have been slashed to $3,000 per person.

Screening Procedures

Once you have accumulated a pool of candidates from Web site announcements or searches, newspaper ads, visits to schools and colleges, and employment agencies, the next step is to select and hire the best salespersons (Figure 11-4). This job is complicated by a need to fill open territories quickly and by the fear that poorly selected salespeople may damage your firm's relations with important customers.

As a result, companies spend more time screening applicants for sensitive industrial sales positions than they do for more routine selling jobs. In the case of retail delivery people, door-to-door salespeople, and insurance agents, turnover is high, and it doesn't pay to spend a lot of time searching for the perfect candidate. With these jobs, the best policy is to place recruits on the job as quickly as possible and let the "sink or swim" policy identify those with the most potential.

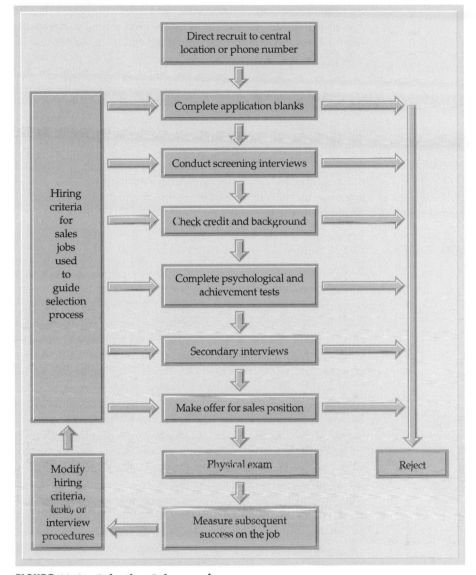

FIGURE 11-4   Selecting Salespeople

There are no hard-and-fast rules guaranteed to match job requirements with the best candidates. You have to weigh the job qualifications against the background of the applicants and make a decision. The best approach is to have candidates fill out application blanks, go through a series of interviews, have references checked, and complete aptitude and psychological tests (Figure 11-4).

Application blanks are a standard screening device for sales positions because it is essential that salespeople be able to read and write. They also provide useful background information on educational level and experience that can be explored during personal interviews. However, federal regulations prohibit questions related to age, sex, race, marital status, financial position, national origin, and other subjects. As a result, sales managers tend to place more emphasis on testing and personal interviews to screen sales candidates. Hiring tests are widely used, but they have to be validated to show a correlation between test scores and job performance.

Another way to evaluate sales candidates is to send out candidates with a regular sales-person to see how they react to actual field selling conditions. In one insurance company, candidates selected after exposure to conditions in the field were much more successful than salespeople selected by other methods.

MOTIVATING AND COMPENSATING SALESPEOPLE

INTEGRATING
...*with*
*Human
Resource
Management*

Salespeople are rewarded with compensation and other incentives to help inspire them to do a better job. The ideal compensation plan motivates salespeople to achieve both their own goals and the company's objectives at the same time. Sometimes the desire of salespeople to make money for themselves conflicts with the firm's need to control sales expenses. Thus you have the difficult task of designing compensation programs that motivate the sales force without financially ruining the company.

Straight Salary

Perhaps the simplest reward system for salespeople involves paying a fixed amount each pay period. *Straight salary* rewards people for time spent on job responsibilities and was used by 7 percent of the firms reported in Table 11-2. The major benefits of salary are more control over wage levels and generally lower compensation for field salespeople. For example, senior sales reps on salary make an average of $64,900 compared with $122,900 for those on straight com-mission.[2] With a salary plan, wages are a fixed cost to the firm, and the proportion of wage expense tends to decrease as sales increase. Another advantage of salary is that it allows maxi-mum control over salespeople's activities. Salaried employees can be directed to sell particular products, call on certain customers, and perform a variety of nonselling jobs for customers.

APPLYING
...*to*
*Industrial
Marketing*

Because a salesperson's income is not tied to the volume of business done with specific cus-tomers, it is easier for the sales manager to divide territories and reassign salespeople to new areas. Further, salaried salespeople exhibit higher loyalty to the firm than employees under other plans. Salary plans are common in industrial selling, where service and engineering skills are important. Salary is also effective when salespersons spend their time calling on retailers to set up displays, take inventory, and arrange shelves. Pharmaceutical detail people, for example, are not expected to make direct sales and are paid a salary to strengthen relations with doctors and pharmacists. Because pay is not tied directly to performance, salary systems are often crit-icized for failing to provide incentives for extra effort.

Commission Plans

Ten percent of firms pay salespeople a percentage of the sales or gross profits that they gen-erate (Table 11-2). The straight commission plan rewards people for their accomplishments

TABLE 11-2   Use of Compensation Plans

Method	Percentage of Companies Using
Straight Salary	7
Straight Commission	10
Salary Plus Bonus	34
Salary Plus Commission	21
Salary Plus Bonus Plus Commission	24
Commission Plus Bonus	4
Total	100%

Source: Donald W. Jackson, John L. Schlacter, and William G. Wolfe, "Examining the Bases Utilized for Evaluating Salespeoples' Performance," *Journal of Personal Selling & Sales Management,* Vol. 15, No. 4 (Fall 1995), p. 59.

rather than for their time. Also, salespeople who are paid commissions typically make more money than with other wage programs. Higher wages tend to attract better-qualified applicants and provide a strong incentive to work hard. For example, most new car salespeople in the United States are paid a 20 to 25 percent commission on the gross profit produced on each car sold. This plan encourages salespeople to sell cars at prices as high as possible to maximize returns to the dealer and the salesperson.

The advantages of a commission plan are shown in Figure 11-5. Notice that when sales per person are low, the costs of the commission plan are low. In contrast, the fixed-cost salary plan ($32,000) gives higher costs when sales are low. Companies that want to minimize their financial risk can choose variable-cost commission plans. Firms that want to minimize compensation costs as sales grow use fixed-cost salary programs. Thus, in Figure 11-5, when sales are less than $400,000 per year, the commission plan results in lower total costs for the company. But when sales exceed $400,000 a year, the straight salary plan costs less. Thus small firms use the commission plan to get started and then tend to shift to the salary plan as they grow larger.

Despite some obvious advantages, straight commission has a number of drawbacks. The major problem is that sales managers have little control over commission salespeople, and nonselling activities are likely to be neglected. Commission salespeople are tempted to sell themselves rather than the company, as well as to service only the best accounts in their territories. Because salespeople's wages are directly related to sales to particular accounts, salespeople are often reluctant to have their territories changed in any way.

Combination Plans

The most common compensation plan, used by 79 percent of firms, combines a base salary with a commission and/or bonus (Table 11-2). The base salary provides salespeople with

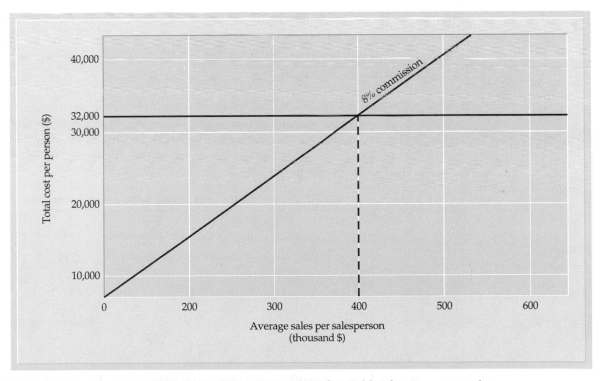

FIGURE 11-5   Comparing Salary and Commission Plans for Field Sales Representatives

income security and the commission and/or bonus give added incentives to meet the company's objectives.

These plans allow wages to be tailored to the needs of a particular firm. If an organization wanted a modest incentive, the plan could be designed so that 80 percent of the compensation was salary and 20 percent was earned by commissions or bonuses. Firms that needed more *push* to move their products could raise the incentive portion to 40 percent or more.

Some firms start paying commissions on the first dollar of sales; others establish base points or quotas that must be reached before commissions or bonuses are paid. Many organizations vary commission rates by sales volume or by the profitability of groups of products. For example, one industrial fastener company pays a base salary of about $30,000 a year, plus a commission that varies from 0.3 to 1 percent of sales and a discretionary bonus for reps who show good sales increases.

When products are largely presold by advertising, like many consumer items, it does not make sense to pay a salary plus a commission to push for added volume. Procter & Gamble spends more money on advertising and promotion to *pull* its detergents, diapers, and tissues through the channel of distribution than any other packaged goods company in the United States. Under these conditions, a salary plus a bonus is enough to get the job done.

Sales managers can obtain guidelines about current pay levels by reviewing surveys published by the Dartnell Corporation, the Conference Board, and trade and industry associations. For example, Table 11-3 shows typical pay levels for combination plans in sales organizations in 1996. Note that the highest pay goes to top sales executives followed by regional sales managers. First-level field sales managers ($83,700) earn more than the key account reps ($71,200). However, sales managers may earn less than the top rep in their district. Also other studies suggest that the relatively low pay of telesales reps ($33,900) can lead to morale problems and high turnover. On the other hand, having positions such as key account rep in the middle of the compensation range provides incentives for trainees and telesales reps to move up the promotion ladder. Although sales trainees start with a base salary of $28,800, they usually get a car, an expense account, and an opportunity to earn a bonus.

DESIGNING EFFICIENT SALES TERRITORIES

Dividing customers into geographic territories improves both market coverage and customer relations. Territories encourage salespeople to get to know their customers' needs and allow managers to evaluate sales performance more easily. Sales territories are constructed from

TABLE 11-3 Compensation Levels for Firms Using Salary Plus Incentives, 1998

Position	Salary ($000)	Incentive ($000)	Total Compensation ($000)
Top Sales Executive	$91.0	$29.0	$119.9
Regional Sales Manager	74.5	21.9	96.4
National Account Manager	72.2	26.0	98.2
District Sales Manager	64.5	20.3	84.8
Key Account Rep	57.4	22.3	80.3
Senior Sales Rep	47.5	26.0	73.5
Intermediate Rep	36.1	15.3	51.4
Entry Level Rep	29.7	13.4	43.1

Source: Sales Force Compensation Survey (Chicago: Dartnell Corporation, 1999), p. 28.

APPLYING
... to
*Industrial
Marketing*

groups of present and potential customers and assigned to individual salespeople to help ensure adequate customer contact, minimize selling costs, and simplify control. Territory design is a never-ending task because customers, products, and salespeople change regularly and territorial boundaries must be adjusted to meet the new conditions.

The Buildup Method

The most popular technique used to create sales territories is the *buildup* method. This approach follows a five-part decision process:

1. Select a geographic control unit.
2. Decide on allocation criteria.
3. Choose starting points.
4. Combine adjacent control units.
5. Compare territories on allocation criteria.

Geographic control units usually are counties, but they can be states, zip code areas, or census tracts. Control units must be small enough to allow flexibility in setting boundaries, yet not so small that the areas lose their identity. States, for example, are often too large for effective combination into sales territories, and census tracts may be unnecessarily small. The selection of appropriate control units for individual companies depends on the availability of data on population, sales, and prospective customers in each of the areas.

Allocation Criteria: An equitable way to group control units into territories would be to divide the market to minimize differences in the number of present customers and the amount of sales potential per territory. Equal opportunity territories can lead to better morale and greater incentive to earn a better living. In addition, similar territories make it easier for the sales manager to identify and reward outstanding performance. If territories are essentially the same, differences in productivity can be attributed to individual effort.

Combining Control Units: Suppose that you have the problem of dividing a territory that has become too large for one person to handle. A map of the territory is shown in Figure 11-6a, with the numbers of present accounts in each county labeled. The salesperson currently assigned to the territory lives in Brockton. A logical home base for the second salesperson is Hillsdale, located in the west center of the territory. If these cities are used as starting points, new territories can be constructed by adding and subtracting adjacent counties until all the counties are assigned and the number of customers is the same for both territories.

One solution to this problem is shown in Figure 11-6b. Note that the heavy concentration of customers in the Brockton area has produced one small territory in the eastern region and one very large territory in the west. Although the two new territories have the same number of customers (225), the western territory requires considerably more travel because the customers are more scattered. In addition, the western territory is likely to have greater sales potential than the small eastern territory.

Designing Territories by Computer

Computer are now routinely used to help design sales territories. Sales managers can save a great deal of time by building territories with computer programs. The simplest computer programs display territory data on computer screens and allow the manager to use the buildup method to create improved sales territories. More sophisticated design programs are also available that allow managers to balance territories optimally using several factors and minimize drive time. MapInfo advertises a ProAlign program that automatically optimizes sales territories and shows the results on a computer screen. The heart of this program is a TerrAlign algo-

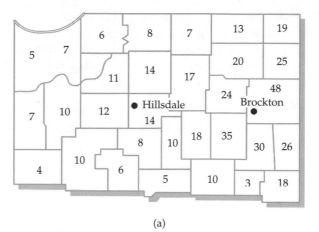

(a)

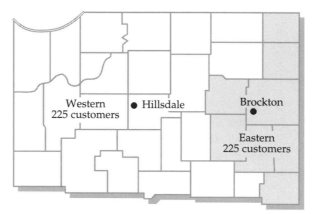

FIGURE 11-6   Dividing a Large Territory

rithm that searches out the optimum realignment solution.[3] Computer programs have been successfully used to build territories for pharmaceutical reps and for salespeople who call on supermarkets. Sales managers are generally pleased with the computer territories; they feel the solutions are imaginative, realistic, and relieve them of a major clerical burden.

ALLOCATING SELLING EFFORT

Careful scheduling of sales calls can minimize travel time and expenses. One firm has reported that an analysis of driving patterns reduced the travel of salespeople by 15,000 miles a year and allowed each salesperson to make eight more calls a week. Techniques used to schedule and route salespeople have received considerable attention from management scientists, and the issue has become known as the *traveling salesman problem.* The dilemma is usually stated as a search for a route through the territory that visits each customer and returns to the starting point with a minimum expenditure of time or money.

A variety of techniques can be employed to search for the best routes for salespeople, including linear programming, nonlinear programming, heuristic programming, and branch-and-bound methods. They all appear to provide good solutions. One disadvantage of these methods is that they require complicated manipulations of travel costs between cities to find the optimal route. A simpler way to find the best sequence of calls is based on a consideration of the location of points in two-dimensional space.

Four basic rules should be followed when designing routes through a sales territory:

1. Tours should be circular.
2. Sales tours should never cross.
3. The same route should not be used to go to and from a customer.
4. Customers in neighboring areas should be visited in sequence.

The idea of circular tours is reasonable because salespeople usually start at a home base and then return at the end of the sales trip. Also, if sales tours cross, the salesperson knows that a shorter route was overlooked.

EVALUATING SALES PERFORMANCE

Evaluation is a complex task because salespeople and territories are all different, and field reps spend most of their time away from their supervisors. In addition, salespeople perform a vast array of jobs, and there are a host of control measures that can be used to monitor their activities. Traditionally, managers have relied on qualitative measures such as product knowledge, selling skills, communication skills, number of calls, and number of days worked to evaluate salespeople. Research has suggested that there is a trend away from input based measures and an increase in output factors such as sales to quota, sales growth, orders secured, size of order, and gross margin per sale.[4] It is your job to design a performance evaluation system that looks at all the dimensions of the salesperson's job and helps the firm achieve its objectives. A computer program that can help managers monitor salespeople is described in Marketing in Action box 11-2.

Sales by Territory

Territorial sales at Bear Computer are shown in Table 11-4. At first glance, things look good because dollar sales are up in all four territories. Also, overall growth is 8.3 percent in the current year, which compares favorably with the performance achieved in 1999. The largest dollar increases in sales were achieved in territories 1 and 3, and the weakest performance was in territory 4. However, these results take on a different meaning if you look at the sales potential of the four territories.

If actual sales in territory 1 of $825,000 are divided by planned sales of $943,000, the sales manager finds that this territory is running about 13 percent below expectations. Territory 3 has not achieved planned sales even though it has the largest potential of all (32 percent). Territory 4, which had the lowest dollar increase, was still able to sell 102 percent of the sales plan. Thus, the two territories with large dollar increases in computer sales actually were the two weakest territories when sales are related to potential. The best performance

TABLE 11-4 Analyzing Territorial Sales in the Eastern Division of the Bear Computer Company, 1999–2000

Territory	Sales 1999 Jan–Sept ($000)	Sales 2000 Jan–Sept ($000)	Dollar Change ($000)	Market Potential Index (%)	Planned Sales ($000)	Percentage of Plan Achieved	Sales Variance ($000)
1	$750	$825	+$75	26%	$943	87%	−$118
2	500	570	+70	15	543	105	+27
3	1025	1110	+85	32	1160	96	−50
4	960	1000	+40	27	977	102	+23
Total	$3235	$3505	+$270	100%	$3623		

MARKETING IN ACTION *11-2*

Using Computers to Eliminate Paperwork

APPLYING
. . . to Business-to-Business Marketing

INTEGRATING
. . . with Information Technology

Sales departments are often the last area in an organization to take advantage of computers. After reviewing sales statistics at RealWorld Corporation, the national sales manager realized that the sales force was becoming stagnant. Further research revealed that salespeople were buried in mountains of paper, with lists and tickler files everywhere. The company decided it was time to introduce a computer system for field sales reps. The objective was to make the salespeople more efficient so that they could make more calls and keep better track of existing proposals and accounts. They also wanted the sales managers to have more control over the field reps.

RealWorld looked for a computer program that included tickler reports, lists, a calendar, personal notepad, word processing, calculator, activity reports, proposals, and the ability to generate orders. Existing packages were unable to fill the bill, so RealWorld developed its own system. Next, it ran a field test and found that reps using the new program increased sales 16 percent compared to salespeople operating with the old manual system. This success prompted RealWorld to equip all 35 reps with laptop computers.

Since the new computer system was installed at RealWorld, the volume of contracts, number of proposals, and dollar sales have increased 10 to 20 percent due to better organization. Leads are handled more rapidly and are no longer lost in the shuffle. Also, sales managers are better able to track the productivity of each rep and to print reports and graphs to monitor results.

— *Giving salespeople laptop computers can increase efficiency.*

Source: Sam Licciardi, "Paper-Pushing Sales Reps Are Less Productive," *Marketing News,* Vol. 24, No. 23, November 12, 1990, p. 15.

Courtesy RealWorld Corporation

was achieved in territory 2, which had the smallest potential in the division and was third in terms of dollar sales growth. These results suggest that you should consider cutting the size of territory 3 and giving some of this potential to the salesperson who is currently handling territory 2. This change should increase total sales of the division, for the salesperson in territory 3 is not covering this large market adequately.

TABLE 11-5　Analyzing Sales by Product Line, Bear Computer Company

Product Line	Industry Sales Ratio (%)	Actual Sales ($000)	Bear Sales Ratio (%)	Forecast ($000)	Variance ($000)
Computers	60%	$18,200	70%	$18,816	−$616
Accessories	20	5,200	20	5,000	+200
Software	20	2,600	10	3,064	−464
Total	100%	$26,000	100%	$26,880	−880

Sales by Products

Breakdowns by products are also useful in evaluating sales performance (Table 11-5). Industry figures suggest that Bear Computer should sell 60 percent of its volume in basic computers, 20 percent in accessory equipment, and 20 percent in computer software. Actual sales figures in 2000 show that Bear is selling 70 percent computers, 20 percent accessories, and only 10 percent in the software category. This heavy emphasis on machine sales can lead to long-run problems, because customers will not have enough programs to use their computers effectively. Perhaps existing commission rates encourage salespeople to push the sales of higher-priced machines rather than lower-priced software.

Another breakdown that provides valuable information for the sales manager is based on the number of units sold (Table 11-6). Unit sales are useful when inflation and other price changes distort dollar sales figures. For example, dollar sales of Bear computers went from $16.8 million in 1999 to $18.2 million in 2000. However, unit sales actually declined from 560 to 520 over the same period, meaning that the average price of a Bear computer went from $30,000 in 1999 to $35,000 in 2000. Although some of the 17 percent increase in computer prices was due to inflation, some other factor is contributing to this change. The data suggest that the sales force is trading customers up to the most expensive computers in the line. Another breakdown of unit sales by individual models of Bear computers would tell you what items are being ignored. Unit sales growth is desirable because it keeps production lines and employees busy.

A somewhat different situation exists with Bear's line of accessory equipment (Table 11-6). Note that dollar and unit sales both increased between 1999 and 2000. Unit sales grew much more rapidly than dollar sales, however, and the average unit price dropped from $1,200 in 1999 to $1,100 in 2000. These results suggest that the sales force is cutting prices to boost unit volume. This push for market share is to be applauded as long as profit margins are not completely destroyed.

Cost Analysis

Although a sales analysis provides useful data on the operation of a field sales force, it does not tell the whole story. Sales figures show general trends, but they do not reveal the effects

TABLE 11-6　Sales by Products and Units for Bear Computer Company, 2000 versus 1999

Product Line	1999 Sales Thousands of Dollars	Units	Average Price per Unit	2000 Sales Thousands of Dollars	Units	Average Price per Unit
Computers	$16,800	560	$30,000	$18,200	520	$35,000
Accessories	4,800	4000	1,200	5,200	4727	1,100
Software	2,400	1200	2,000	2,600	1280	2,031
Total	$24,000	5760		$26,000	6527	

INTEGRATING
... with
Accounting

of price cutting or the differences in selling costs, potential, and saturation that exist across products or territories.

An example of a territorial cost review is shown in Table 11-7 for the Bear Computer Company. The analysis begins with net sales for each territory, from which the cost of goods sold and sales commissions are then subtracted. The resulting contribution margin is greatest in territory 4, even though territory 3 had the highest sales. Note that territories 1 and 4 had high contribution percentages compared with territories 2 and 3. Salespeople in territories 2 and 3 are apparently pushing low-margin products and are cutting prices to gain volume.

Another selling cost issue is raised by the activities of the salesperson in territory 1. This territory produced almost as much contribution margin as territory 3 and had an outstanding contribution percentage, but the resulting profit contribution in territory 1 was $7,700 less than that generated in territory 3. The explanation for this difference lies in the various expense categories. Although the salary of the salesperson ($42,000) seems reasonable, the amounts spent on travel, food and lodging, and entertainment appear to be high. Although salespeople in the other three territories averaged $9,700 for these expenses, the person in territory 1 spent $17,400. The typical response of a sales manager to expenditures of this size would be to pressure the salesperson to cut back so that the profit contribution will increase. These above-average expenditures might explain why territory 1 was generating a 40 percent contribution margin on sales. The salesperson is apparently entertaining customers so effectively that they are buying high-margin computers at list price, although it is possible that the salesperson is using the expense account to offer customers under-the-table discounts on the computers. If these travel, food, and entertainment expenditures are legitimate, the manager might consider asking the other salespeople to increase their spending on these items.

Jones Versus Smith

An example comparing the performance of two sales reps is presented in Table 11-8. The data show that although Pete Jones had high sales, Ann Smith worked more days, made more calls, had lower expenses, and landed more orders. As a result, Smith made one more call per day and had a 50 percent batting average (orders per calls). Although Jones closed the sale on only 40 percent of his calls, he had a high average-order size. Thus, despite lower values for days worked, calls per day, and batting average, Jones obtained larger orders and the highest total sales volume.

TABLE 11-7   Analyzing Costs and Profits of the Southern District of the Bear Computer Company

	Territory Performance ($000)			
	1	*2*	*3*	*4*
Net Sales	$825	$570	$1110	$1000
Less: CGS and commissions	495	428	777	660
Contribution margin	330	142	333	340
Contribution margin as a percentage of sales	40%	25%	30%	34%
Less: Direct selling costs				
Sales force salaries	42.0	25.0	45.0	55.0
Travel	8.5	4.1	5.5	5.0
Food and lodging	6.5	4.0	4.2	4.5
Entertainment	2.4	0.3	0.5	1.0
Home sales office expense	4.5	2.0	4.0	4.5
	$63.9	$35.4	$59.2	$70.0
Profit contribution	$266.1	$106.6	$273.8	$270.0
Profit contribution as a percentage of sales	32%	19%	25%	27%

TABLE 11-8   Evaluating Individual Performance

Performance Factors	Peter Jones	Ann Smith
Sales	$1,000,000	$650,000
Days worked	210	225
Calls	1,200	1,500
Orders	480	750
Expenses	$22,000	$14,300
Calls per day	5.7	6.7
Batting average (orders per calls)	40%	50%
Average order	$2,083	$866
Expenses per call	$18.33	$9.53
Expenses per sales	2.2%	2.2%

In this case, you might be tempted to encourage Ann Smith to increase the size of her average order. Larger orders should increase total sales but would probably result in fewer and longer sales calls and a reduction in her batting average. Fewer calls per day produced larger orders in Jones's territory, but it is not clear that this strategy would work as well for Smith. The differences in performance may be due to the presence of many large firms in Jones's territory and mostly small companies in Smith's area. The data in Table 11-8 suggest that managers need to understand differences in selling styles and character of each territory when evaluating performance data.

Performance Rankings

INTEGRATING
. . . with
Human
Resource
Management

One way to simplify sales force comparisons is to convert performance results into rankings. The rankings can then be added up to give an overall measure of efficiency. For example, Table 11-9 shows how five salespeople ranked on 10 different control factors. Sales per person is a good overall measure, but it can be deceiving. Note that Ford had the highest total sales but was last on sales-to-potential, suggesting that his volume was due to a large territory. Gold, on the other hand, had low volume and high sales-to-potential, indicating good coverage of a limited market. Sales-to-quota is also popular, showing primarily a salesperson's ability to increase revenue. Sometimes attainment of quotas qualifies salespeople for special commissions or bonuses.

Sales per order is important because many firms have found that small orders are unprofitable. Thus, salespeople who sell large quantities to each customer are viewed as the most efficient. Ford, for example, achieves a high sales volume by making a large number of calls and selling small amounts to each customer (Table 11-9). The ratio of orders to calls

TABLE 11-9   Ranking Salespeople on 10 Input/Output Factors

Ranking Factors	Ford	Bell	Shaw	Mann	Gold
Dollar sales	❶	2	3	4	5
Sales to potential	5	3	4	2	❶
Sales to quota	5	4	2	❶	3
Sales per order	5	❶	4	3	2
Number of calls	2	5	❶	3	4
Orders per call	4	2	5	3	❶
Gross margin percent	5	❶	3	4	2
Direct selling costs	4	3	5	❶	2
New accounts	❶	4	2	5	3
Number of reports turned in	4	3	❶	5	2
Total of ranks	36	28	30	31	25

measures the ability of the salesperson to convert prospects into buyers. Sometimes called the *batting average,* this ratio shows how successful salespeople are at closing sales presentations.

The gross margin percentage achieved by salespeople shows how good they are at controlling prices and selling the right mix of products. Table 11-9 suggests that Ford's low margins are the result of price cutting to open new accounts and boost sales. Direct selling costs usually vary with the size of a territory, and salespeople have only limited control over these costs.

The performance of the five salespeople in Table 11-9 varied widely across the 10 factors, and each person ranked first on two criteria and last on at least one factor. If all of the criteria are considered equal in importance, then the ranks can be added down to give a measure of overall performance.

This procedure shows that Bell, Shaw, and Mann had total performance scores close to the expected value of 30 points, whereas the scores of Ford and Gold were different enough to warrant special attention. Note that although Ford had the highest sales volume, he actually had the worst overall record, whereas Gold was doing an excellent job despite low sales volume. The most obvious change suggested is to shift some of Ford's territory to Gold, giving Gold more to do and providing better coverage for some of Ford's customers. Also, Ford should be encouraged to work for larger orders and told to stop cutting prices.

SUMMARY

Selling is a personal encounter between the salesperson and customers, and the firm must understand how this relationship works. If salespeople with certain characteristics are more successful than others, it may pay to select or train field representatives to fill these needs. The optimum size of the sales force is obtained by hiring salespeople until the marginal profit from an additional salesperson is equal to the marginal cost of adding another person. In the absence of sales response data, the firm can set the size of the sales force on the basis of what it can afford or the actual workload. The creation of equitable territories for salespeople is important for building morale and improving the efficiency of the sales organization. Sales territories are usually created by combining geographic areas, and the computer has proved to be a great help in speeding up this tedious, recurring task. Once sales territories have been created, you must decide how to deploy the sales force to cover different customers and product lines. In addition, the careful scheduling and routing of salespeople through their territories can reduce expenses and increase the number of calls that can be made. Salespeople also must be rewarded for their services, and the design of compensation plans is one of the most creative jobs performed by sales managers. The idea is to provide a blend of salary, bonuses, commissions, and noncash incentives that stimulates the salespeople to work hard, maximizing the profits of the firm at the same time. This requires decisions on what factors measure success and the subsequent inclusion of these criteria in a sales reporting system that is both easy to use and economical to operate.

NOTES

1. The average intermediate salesperson on salary plus incentives costs $75,014 in wages, benefits, and expenses per year. Since they make about 660 calls per year and it takes 4 calls to close a sale, the cost is ($75,014)/(660) = $114 × 4 = $456 cost to close. (*Sales Force Compensation Survey* [Chicago: Dartnell Corp., 1999], pp. 20, 50.)
2. Christen P. Heide, *Sales Force Compensation Survey* (Chicago: Dartnell Corporation, 1999), p. 49.
3. *Sales & Marketing Management* (May 1998), p. 23.

4. Jackson, Donald W., John L. Schlacter, and William G. Wolf, "Examining the Bases Utilized for Evaluating Salespeoples' Performance," *Journal of Personal Selling & Sales Management,* Vol. 115, No. 4 (Fall 1995), p. 64.

SUGGESTED READING

"The 25 Best Sales Forces," *Sales & Marketing Management* (July 1998), pp. 32–50.

Bollinger, Caroline. "Building a Sales Force from Scratch," *Sales & Marketing Management* (February 1998), pp. 26–28.

REFERENCES

Brooks, William T. *Niche Selling: How to Find Your Customer in a Crowded Market* (Homewood, IL: Business One Irwin, 1992).

Churchill, Gilbert A., Neil M. Ford, and Orville C. Walker, Jr. *Sales Force Management,* 4th ed. (Homewood, IL: Irwin, 1990).

Dalrymple, Douglas J., and William L. Cron. *Sales Management: Concepts and Cases,* 6th ed. (New York: John Wiley & Sons, 1998).

Stanton, William J., and Rosann L. Spiro. *Management of a Sales Force,* 10th ed. (Chicago: Irwin, 1999).

QUESTIONS

1. Precision Cutting Tools manufactures industrial products for a national market. Until recently, they employed 12 salespeople to call on accounts. Dissatisfied with the results, the sales manager discharged all 12 in favor of 9 independent manufacturer's representatives. (Manufacturer's reps are not employed by the company; usually they sell for a number of companies.) The rep in this case sold other industrial products along with the Precision line to the same customers. Immediately, sales began to increase, old business was retrieved, and new accounts were acquired. What possible reasons might explain this? What are the advantages and disadvantages of manufacturer's reps compared to an in-house sales force?

2. Phil Tumminia, director of the Glassboro State College Development Fund in southern New Jersey, made a cold call on a local industrialist in 1990, and asked for and received a gift of $1,500. On succeeding calls, he got $3 million for the library, $20 million for the business school, and finally $100 million for a new engineering school. Why did personal sales calls work better than direct mail, phone calls, or media advertising for this tiny college's development program?

3. A district sales manager said, "I have a rule I never break. I only hire salespeople who are in their thirties, married, with three or more kids, and carrying mortgages as big as the Ritz. That way, they'll need me more than I'll need them, and I know they'll be back on the job each and every morning." Comment on this statement. Are there other ways to minimize turnover of the sales force?

4. Suppose an office supplies dealer has 750 large customers that need to be called on each month, 1,500 medium-size firms that should be called on every six weeks, and 3,000 small organizations that need to be serviced once every quarter. Given that salespeople make 10 calls per week, how many salespeople are needed?

5. Although insurance agents rarely have exclusive territories, insurance companies are finding that mapping programs are quite useful. Sales managers load demographic data, policies in force, and agent locations on computerized area maps. How would a manager use this information?

6. You are the district manager and have all the accountability that comes with the job. You have the feeling that your salespeople are not following many of your instructions. Are you becoming paranoid? John seems to be the informal leader of the salespeople in his district. Deliberately or not, he seems to have become very influential. Although John is also one of your top salespeople, district sales overall are dropping. Is there a connection? You must correct the situation soon, and you do not want to lose John because he is a valuable salesperson. Why did an informal leader emerge? How do you handle John? What can you do to prevent a recurrence?

7. A car salesperson spent three hours selling a new Nissan Maxima for $800 over cost. The dealer kept the first $600 of the gross profit and split the remaining $200 with the salesperson on a 75 percent/25 percent basis. This left the salesperson with only $50 for three hours' work, which he had to divide with another salesperson who talked with the customer over the phone. Is this system beneficial for the dealer? For the salesperson? What changes would you recommend?

8. Merck & Company, one of the largest pharmaceutical companies in the United States, uses a forced distribution of a bell curve to reward its employees. This means that the high-performing reps are paid considerably more than average or below-average reps. The strong emphasis on individual quantitative performance measures has met some resistance from those who believe in promoting group cooperation. Merck has responded to these concerns by offering a 100-share stock option grant to all employees. Staff turnover is running at a low 5 percent per year. How should Merck measure the performance of reps who call on doctors but rarely take orders? Should Merck's plan be used by other firms? Why or why not?

9. Sears has cut the base hourly pay of its salespeople who sell big-ticket items and increased their commission rates. Why has Sears made this change, and how well do you think the new plan has been received by the salespeople?

10. Julie has the talent and experience to greatly improve sales in her territory. A veteran salesperson, 15 years with the company, Julie has been a top performer in the past, but just gets by now. Her husband is a doctor and their children are on their own, so Julie's financial needs are fully met. Julie's sales volume is third in the district of five people, so it's not that she doesn't sell; it's just that her sales volume has not increased much in the past three years and you believe there is opportunity for greater sales out of her territory. Your company has recently downsized and budgets are tight. It's time to do something about Julie. How would you address this situation without losing a strong salesperson?

11. The CEO of Vanstar Corporation found that one of his top sales reps came to the office early every morning and called customers' voice mail and left messages with her opening ideas for them for the day. When she called later, the customers always took her calls personally to respond to the ideas she had left on their machines. Should the CEO incorporate this activity in the company's sales performance evaluation system? How would you measure performance on this activity?

12. You are a sales manager for an industrial manufacturer. The performance of one of your salespeople, James Weber, has slipped; he has achieved only 75 percent of his quota for the past six months. The average sales quota achievement in your district is 90 percent. Weber has worked for your firm for six years and has a bachelor's degree in business administration. Jim's territory is above average in potential but requires considerable travel. At the recent company picnic, Weber seemed depressed and spent his time drinking rather than interacting with the other salespeople. Weber is divorced, and his ex-wife lives in another city with their three children. You have decided that it is time to call in Weber for a conference. Develop a script for a meeting with Weber that will motivate him to work up to his potential.

13. A United Technologies employee has charged that the company's Sikorsky Division offered two Saudi princes a "bonus" of 3 to 5 percent of a $130 million portion of a $6 billion potential Blackhawk helicopter order. The employee is seeking $100 million in damages from United Technologies. What seems to be the motive of the employee in reporting the attempted bribe? Why are such "commissions" so common in foreign sales agreements? How should the company handle these demands for special favors?

14. The product manager for industrial cleaning products in the inorganic products division of a large German chemical company is concerned about the performance of the company's sales force. Information is available for 19 sales territories on the sales revenue, number of calls made, and number of inhabitants (a measure of potential). To properly appraise the performance of field representatives, the sales of giant buyers were eliminated because they dealt directly with territorial managers. Using the data in the file indchemdat.sav, assess salesforce performance. *Hint:* If you first compute the natural logarithm (LN) of each variable and then run a linear multiple regression on the transformed variables, the regression coefficients of the variables can be interpreted as elasticities.

CHAPTER *12*

DIRECT MARKETING

irect marketing allows you to speak directly to the people who are most likely to buy your product.[1] You ask them to take an immediate action in the form of an order, a donation, an inquiry, or a store visit. You want to establish an ongoing customer relationship. You focus on the profit generated *over the life of the customer.*

Direct marketing usually involves building a database of respondents. Hence the term *database marketing* is often used. A survey of packaged goods marketers found that two-thirds were compiling and using consumer databases. Among those building databases, mail-in premium offers and sweepstakes are the most commonly used methods of information collection, followed by trackable coupons and rebates. More than two-thirds of those using database marketing enhance their data with outside demographic and lifestyle information. Sophisticated database methodologies identify high-potential prospects. Marketing resources are concentrated on these select-list segments.

Strategic decisions in direct marketing include program scope (test versus rollout or full program), the basic offer (product, incentives, and premiums), the concept and theme, versioning and/or personalization, and media selection. We begin by addressing targeting.

TARGETING

Your starting point must be "Who is my customer?" One way to answer this question is to collect your own data. HoneyBaked Ham Co. of Georgia has been collecting the telephone numbers of its customers for $3^1/_2$ years. The resulting database, with addresses and buying habits of those customers, now numbers about 1.5 million people in the Southeast. The database is the foundation of HoneyBaked Ham's catalog and its business-to-business line as well as being a critical tool for its retail side. The database represents about 25 percent of its marketing budget. HoneyBaked Ham, which doesn't share its customer list with other marketers, focuses on its customers' buying patterns, showing what times of the year they make purchases, what they buy, and how much they spend. It can do targeted mailings, whether going to formerly faithful customers or to frequent buyers. Customers are sent coupons and other offers. HoneyBaked Ham has had 25 percent of volume from a sales promotion driven completely by direct mail where three to four percent is usually considered successful.[2]

Custom data providers are another source of data. For example, National Decision Systems segments the population into 50 subgroups based on demographic factors weighed against national averages. Some examples of these subgroups are given in Table 12-1. One

TABLE 12-1 Selected National Decision Systems U.S. Segments

A Good Step Forward
Typically 22- to 34-year-olds living in non-family households with one or two people. Two-thirds are renters, with very high per capita income. Only 14 percent of households have children. Twice as likely as U.S. average to have a bachelor's or graduate degree; almost 80 percent have white-collar occupations. Second most likely to listen to classic rock radio.

City Ties
Adults who tend to be between 50 and 59 years, with children in the 10- to 17-year-old range. More likely than average to be a single-parent household, very often with five or more residents. More than 75 percent of households are African-American. Per capita income is 25 percent below average. They are 24 percent more likely than average to not have a high school diploma. Six percent more likely than average to own their home, with a property value 14 percent lower than average. Twice as likely to take public transportation to work. Most likely to have call waiting, call forwarding, and automatic call return. Listen to urban contemporary radio stations.

Country Home Families
Typically married adults, between 40 and 54, with children between 10 and 17. Average median household income 12 percent below average. Nineteen times more likely than average to work in blue-collar occupations, and rank first in precision production and crafts. Among most likely to have only a high school diploma. More than 80 percent own their homes, and almost 15 percent live in mobile homes. Almost 50 percent more likely than average to live in relatively new homes. Tend to own motor homes, boats, rifles, and fishing equipment.

Family Ties
Families with children, living in suburbs. Adults typically between 35 and 44, children between 5 and 17. Forty percent more likely than average to have three to six people in the household. Median household income 19 percent above average, but large number of household members drops per capita income 6 percent below average. Rank third in having attended some college and having received an associate degree. Like to go boating, camping, bowling, or golfing. Most likely to have unsecured line of credit and to use the phone to transfer funds.

Great Beginnings
Younger adults, typically between 22 and 34 years old. Thirty-one percent of these households have children, with most younger than 4. Median household income is 8 percent above average, and they are 56 percent more likely to be renters. Tend to drive alone to work in a sub-compact car, play pool, drink Coors beer, have overdraft protection, and listen to album-oriented rock stations.

Home Sweet Home
Typically married couples between 50 and 69, with one or no children at home. Rank in the top 15 nationwide in household income, and eighth in the percentage that receive retirement income. Almost 80 percent own their homes, with property value 60 percent above average. Typically have two or more vehicles, drive alone to work, and have an average commute time of just under 22 minutes. They get their carpets professionally cleaned and are likely to have recently had a home energy audit. A relatively high percentage finance home improvements with a home equity line of credit.

Mid-Life Success
Typically between 40 and 54 years old, with a median income 68 percent above average. Thirty-six percent have children. A majority own their home, which has an average value three times the norm. Primarily work in white-collar occupations such as sales, executive, and managerial positions. Very likely to own a PC and access online services. Typically save more than $5,000 a year and buy stock from discount brokers.

Movers and Shakers
Typically, households include two working adults between 35 and 49, with no children. Median household income is 46 percent above average. Twice as likely to have a bachelor's or postgraduate degree, and rank fourth in working in white-collar occupations. One-third are renters, who pay almost 50 percent more in rent costs than average. Twice as likely to dine at upscale restaurants, own a PC, and use a full-service stockbroker.

Upper Crust
Highest income of the 50 subgroups, with a median household income almost three times the average. Adults primarily between 45 and 59 years old, and 38 percent have children at home. Three-fourths are married, and almost 80 percent live in the suburbs. Rank first and second in bachelor's and post-graduate degrees. Highest percentage of children enrolled in private schools. More than 40 percent more likely to own their home, with property values four times the national average. Most active in using financial services. Large contributors to PBS (Public Broadcasting System), most likely to own a notebook computer, and home fax machine.

service it provides is a market profile report, which shows what type of consumers live where.[3] An example is given in Figure 12-1 for the five-mile radius around Lenox Square, Atlanta's largest mall.

MEDIA SELECTION

Our focus is cost-effective media selection for the product and situation. Telemarketing and direct mail are two media that traditionally have been used for direct marketing, although

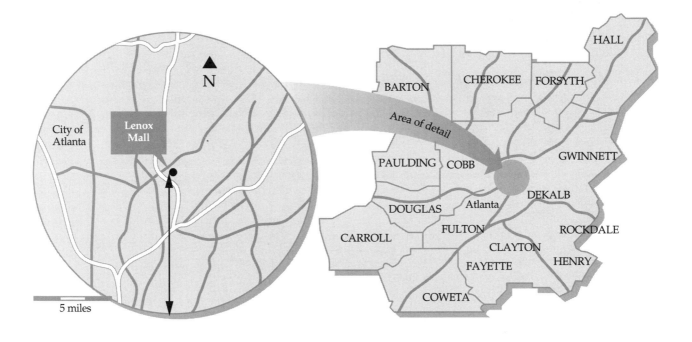

Lenox Square 5-mile radius

Total households: 113,124

16-county metro Atlanta area

Total households: 1,357,472

The five top profiles for this area comprised more than 80% of all residents.

profile	households
A Good Step Forward	41,612
Movers and Shakers	19,896
Great Beginnings	15,853
Upper Crust	8,624
Midlife Success	5,343

The six top profiles for this area comprise more than 44% of all residents.

profile	households
Country Home Families	148,992
A Good Step Forward	116,233
Great Beginnings	104,634
City Ties	99,389
Family ties	66,942
Home Sweet Home	66,740

FIGURE 12-1   Lenox Square Mall Market Profile (From "Here's What Companies Know about Your Habits," *Atlanta Journal-Constitution.* **[October 12, 1998], p. E6)**

general mass media can be used as well. The Internet is the newest medium and opens up the possibility of *interactive marketing.*

Telephone

The telephone is the third largest medium in the United States with more than 18 million calls being made each day. Telephone marketing uses communication technology as part of a marketing program that prominently features the use of personal selling. Telemarketing works because it is personal, urgent and deadline-driven, interactive, and flexible, generates immediate response, allows for constant improvement through testing, and is cost-effective. You can take the initiative in contacting your customer (outbound operations) or you can let your customer contact you (inbound operations).

Outbound Operations With the average cost of business-to-business sales call costing more than $300, many firms are turning to telephone marketing where the average cost per contact is only $7. A major advantage of telephone marketing over other direct marketing approaches is *flexibility.* Scripts can be changed as events unfold in real time (see, for example, Marketing Strategies box 12-3).

The acceptability of telephone marketing varies by type of product or service being offered. A recent survey shows customer reactions to telephone marketing: 62 percent terminate call before or during presentation, 32 percent listen to the entire presentation, and 6 percent comply with request. When asked what was the impression of your last phone call: 42 percent said it was an unpleasant experience; 39 percent a pleasant experience; and 19 percent said neither or don't know. Another survey followed up calls placed 30 days earlier and found: 72 percent didn't mind the call while 2.8 percent objected to all calls. Overall, 95 percent said relationship was unchanged or better. Reasons for a call being unpleasant are poorly trained caller, computer message, inconvenient timing, and poor targeting/no need.

Inbound Operations The telephone can be used to take customer-initiated orders, requests for information, and complaints. You have to decide whether you want a lot of calls that are free to the caller (800 numbers) or fewer, but more qualified calls, for which the caller has to pay (900 numbers). The telephone is one way to listen to your customers, what they like about you, what they don't like. The Buick Division of General Motors handles 30,000 calls monthly through an 800 number for customer assistance.

Telecommunications technology lets you know the telephone number of a caller before actually picking up the phone. With Automatic Number Identification (ANI), the caller's telephone number is sent along with the call. When ANI is coupled on a real-time basis with reverse directory match, customers can be given more personalized service. With the help of some software, you can have displayed on a computer screen not only the customer's name and address, but also the record of past purchases, credit history, and other information.

Direct Mail

More than 60 billion pieces of mail, from fashion catalogs to ads offering pizza coupons, arrive at American homes each year. About 68 percent of all magazine subscription are sold through the mail and 25 percent of all charitable contributions are raised in the same fashion.

Direct mail involves sending a sales proposition to targeted respondents through the mail. The aim is to create a direct response to the mailing, whether it be by mail, phone, or personal contact. This response can be measured. A 2 percent response rate represents success if the target market is enormous and undifferentiated. One key to improving upon this rate is the targeted mailing list. The targeted list makes it possible to establish relatively personal relationships with potential and existing customers.

Mailing Lists   Target marketing depends on qualified list choices. If you are selling a product for children, the most significant qualifier in a list selection process would be the presence of children on the list. On the other hand, if your product is geared to the agricultural market, you would want lists of farmers and suppliers to the agricultural community. 3Com, a maker of computer network adapters, targeted LAN coordinators and MIS managers for its Etherlink II adapter (Marketing Strategies box 12-1). In any case, be sure to test your assumptions about who your customer is. One conservative organization was convinced that medical doctors would contribute to its cause. An order was put in for a 5,000-name test list. The prospect package cost 55 cents to mail out, but only raised 10 cents per name mailed!

Lists may be classified as internal or external. An internal list, called a *house file,* is an organization's own file which may include buyers, former buyers, subscribers, lapsed sub-

APPLYING
. . . to
Not-for-Profit
Marketing

APPLYING
. . . to
Business-to-
Business
Marketing

MARKETING STRATEGIES *12-1*

Business-To-Business Direct Mail

3Com, a leader in computer network solutions, launched a new adapter board, EtherLink III. The company's biggest challenge was the commoditylike nature of the network adapter market. Adapters from competing manufacturers often offer price as their only distinguishing feature. In addition, the network adapter market is traditionally a low-involvement category in which purchases are not based on brand name. The value-added reseller (VAR), who installs the board and tests it for hardware and software compatibility, recommends adapters. 3Com's objectives were to persuade VARs to recommend 3Com network adapters over the competition and to encourage end users to try 3Com boards.

EtherLink III used direct mail and sales tools featuring bright, colorful visuals and headlines that focused on the benefits of the product rather than technical features. In this marketing effort, Ether-Link III adapters were christened "SuperBoards." The initial direct mailing to resellers used short copy, bright colors, and sophisticated illustrations to make the point that EtherLink III network adapters are faster than the competition, yet competitively priced. The resellers were asked to fill out a business reply card or call an 800 number to receive a free sales kit. A direct mail piece sent to LAN coordinators and MIS managers at Fortune 2000 companies used a series of humorous cartoon vignettes to drive home key points about the product and the technology, and to grab the prospect's attention.

This product launch elevated EtherLink III above other entries in the crowded 16-bit board market. End users began requesting the board by name.

— *Creative, nontechnical approaches can be developed to market even the most technical products.*

Source: Marcia Kadanoff, "Nontechnical Approach to Marketing High Tech Has Benefits," *Marketing News,* April 26, 1993, p. 10.

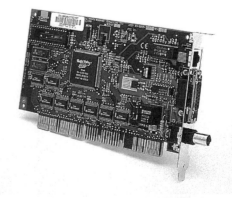

Courtesy 3com

scribers, donors and former donors, prospects, inquiries, employees, salesperson contacts, warranty card respondents, stockholders, and so on. External lists include compiled and direct response lists. *Compiled lists* do not necessarily represent people who have bought by direct mail, but who do have common relevant characteristics. There are compiled lists that cover most of the households and businesses in the United States. Households can be selected by demographic, geographic, or other identifiers. Businesses can be selected by Standard Industrial Classification code, number of employees, net worth, and many other factors. Some sample records from one list company are shown in Figure 12-2. In addition, there are compiled business lists of executives by names—including chairmen, presidents, and treasurers—which can be selected by line of business and other important characteristics. *Direct response lists* contain the names of past direct mail purchasers. These lists are possible because many firms make the internal mailing lists available to noncompeting firms. Obviously, the most responsive list is the house file. Maximum financial return comes

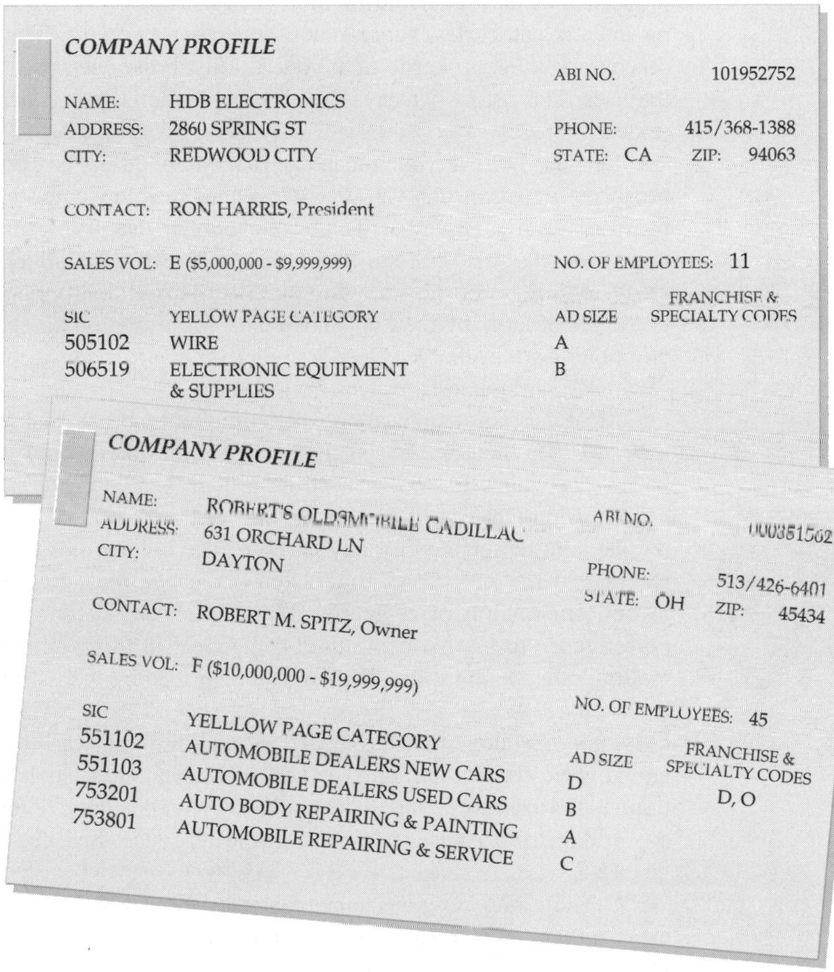

COMPANY PROFILE

		ABI NO.	101952752
NAME:	HDB ELECTRONICS		
ADDRESS:	2860 SPRING ST	PHONE:	415/368-1388
CITY:	REDWOOD CITY	STATE: CA	ZIP: 94063

CONTACT: RON HARRIS, President

SALES VOL: E ($5,000,000 - $9,999,999)   NO. OF EMPLOYEES: 11

SIC	YELLOW PAGE CATEGORY	AD SIZE	FRANCHISE & SPECIALTY CODES
505102	WIRE	A	
506519	ELECTRONIC EQUIPMENT & SUPPLIES	B	

COMPANY PROFILE

		ABI NO.	000351562
NAME:	ROBERT'S OLDSMOBILE CADILLAC		
ADDRESS:	631 ORCHARD LN		
CITY:	DAYTON	PHONE:	513/426-6401
		STATE: OH	ZIP: 45434

CONTACT: ROBERT M. SPITZ, Owner

SALES VOL: F ($10,000,000 - $19,999,999)

NO. OF EMPLOYEES: 45

SIC	YELLLOW PAGE CATEGORY	AD SIZE	FRANCHISE & SPECIALTY CODES
551102	AUTOMOBILE DEALERS NEW CARS	D	D, O
551103	AUTOMOBILE DEALERS USED CARS	B	
753201	AUTO BODY REPAIRING & PAINTING	A	
753801	AUTOMOBILE REPAIRING & SERVICE	C	

Key: Ad size   Key: Franchise code
      A - Regular listing   D - Cadillac
      B - Boldface listing   O - Oldsmobile
      C - In-column ad
      D - Display ad

FIGURE 12-2   Sample List Records (from American Business Information)

from taking into account the recency, frequency, and dollar amount of past purchases or gifts.

The use of *overlays* has surfaced as a value-added marketing technique. This involves matching the house file against the 85 million households, which are classified by key demographic, socioeconomic, housing, and ethnic characteristics. The measurement units are then clustered into groups with similar demographic and lifestyle characteristics and applied against the internal file. The result is a profile of customers and products. When you need an external list, you could do your own list research, which may involve some creativity. The Sierra Club gathers the names of environmentally aware young people with tabletop displays at rock concerts, setting up voter registration booths on college campuses, and marketing an affinity credit card to college students. Such diverse direct marketing activities attracted 45,000 members at a cost per thousand (CPM) of $9.70 and these members had a net dollar value to the Sierra Club of $18.80. In contrast, while direct mailings yielded more members, 105,000, the CPM was $27.60 and the net dollar value only 40 cents.

APPLYING
. . . *to*
Not-for-Profit
Marketing

Getting names yourself is time consuming and expensive, so why do it when there are thousands of lists available? Within each list, there are segments that can be selected based on interest categories, geographics, and other elements. Thus, you will probably want the services of a list broker to help you. The list broker serves both parties—the list owner and the user. The list owner pays the broker's commission (usually 20 percent of the list rental price).

Because not everyone on an external compiled list is a prospect, you want to reach your prospects economically. You will need to develop a model or *overlay* to identify your prospects from a larger list. To do so, enough offers or appeals must be mailed to an nth of a large compiled list with appended data to assure a statistically viable response group. This means doing systematic sampling with perhaps 100,000 pieces. Respondents are compared to the file at large by their appended data—information on spending or giving, lifestyle, and any other data available. Once a model for your organization is determined, you can mail sections of compiled lists using your overlay.

Most list transactions are on a onetime rental basis. List rental transactions are priced on a per M (per thousand basis). List rental prices are biased toward mailers that mail entire lists and penalize those that need more narrow selects of lists. The rental of lists involves certain important conditions. First, the names are rented for onetime use only. No copy of the list is to be retained for any purpose. The only names that can be retained are those that respond to the specific mailings. Second, usage must be cleared in advance with the list owner. The mailing piece approved by the list owner is the only one that can be used. Third, no reference to the list being used can appear in the promotional package. And finally, the mailing must be made on the mail date approved by the list owner.

Catalogs   Catalog sales have been increasing rapidly in the United States in recent years and now exceed $50 billion. The very large catalogers, such as JC Penney and Spiegel, continue to perform well, and niche marketers have uncovered audiences for catalogs devoted to everything from African violets to barbecue sauce. See, for example, Marketing Strategies box 12-2.

Catalog marketing has some characteristics of both direct mail and retail selling. However, unlike most direct mail, customers rarely make an immediate decision based on impulse; rather they wait until something triggers a buying impulse. Response to many solo mailings comes in just three weeks, whereas response to a typical catalog comes in over many weeks, perhaps up to six months later. Unlike retail selling, a catalog does not provide an opportunity to touch and feel the merchandise or ask questions of a salesperson (although this last issue can be addressed by an inbound telephone operation).

Catalogers often have multiple catalogs as a way to reach another market segment without compromising their image. Spiegel entered a partnership with Johnson Publishing's

MARKETING STRATEGIES *12-2*

APPLYING
. . . to
Apparel
Retailing

Limited Too: A Catalog for the Preteen Girl Segment

Preteen girls are a lucrative market these days. The over-300-store Limited Too chain sells clothes mostly to 10- and 11-year-old girls, though some of its customers are as young as seven. While households receive over 100 catalogs a year on average, very few are addressed to preteen girls. The Limited Too is launching a catalog to pitch its products, such as trendy embroidered jeans and shimmering body lotion. The catalog is to be mailed directly to preteen girls, not their parents. Catalogs aimed at teens already exist but most 10-year-old girls would find themselves too small for what is offered in the Delia's, Wet Seal, Alloy Designs, and Just Nikki catalogs. The Limited Too's target audience will top out at age 14, an age when girls start getting interested in teen catalogs.

Targeting such a narrow age range means a lot of shuffling of catalog-mailing lists, for preteen girls grow quickly into teenagers. The company hopes that the girls who get initial catalogs will show them off to friends at school, quickly boosting the mailing list.

Moreover, while many girls aspire to wear the same cutting edge fashions as older teens, the clothes must appeal to parents, who typically do the buying. Thus, a crew of in-house designers has been trying to adapt the latest teen fads for younger girls, while running elaborate reality checks to see if parents will object. For example, the Limited Too carries white cardigans, with matching tank tops cut close to the neck and arm—made with thick material so they aren't see-through.

One challenge for the Limited Too catalog is to replicate the superstimulating atmosphere in its stores. In addition to loud pop music and flower-shaped tables spilling with sample makeup bottles, the retailer has been adding things to try to get girls to linger in stores. One example is an instant-photograph machine that prints your picture onto 16 tiny stickers for $3.00.

— *You have to explore alternate ways of reaching your customer.*

Source: Yumiko Ono, "Limited Plans a Preteen Cataloging Blitz," *The Wall Street Journal*, August 25, 1998, p. B8.

Ebony magazine to create a new catalog targeting black women. Market research indicated that, on average, black women have distinct fit and proportion needs and prefer better tailored clothing. The new catalog, called E Style, contained 64 pages showing a complete line of apparel and accessories along with selected merchandise for the home. To promote E Style, Spiegel ran a print ad in an issue of *Ebony* that resulted in the largest response to a single print ad in its history. E Style is also promoted through ads for Spiegel's big book and with cards inserted in the company's other catalogs.

Interactive Media

APPLYING
. . . to
Personal
Computers
Marketing

The Internet is not just changing where people buy (see Chapter 10, "Selecting Distribution Channels") but how they buy. The customer is in charge of the sale. What the customer wants to buy is what counts. Dell Computers and Micron Computers have been highly successful selling computers by direct mail. The Internet only serves to enhance this type of buying experience. Dell, Micro, and others provide the buyer with detailed information at their Web sites. This makes it possible for customers to build computers to suit their needs without talking to anyone. Live customer service representatives are available, if necessary. But they are facilitators, not salespeople; their role is to assist and answer questions. Dell consistently receives top honors for its record of high-quality customer satisfaction.

The real power of marketing over the Internet comes when an organization offers meaningful interactive services that create a relationship with the customer. Amazon.com, the poster child of Internet commerce, built a "community" around the product. Amazon publishes customer reviews as well as those by staffers and outside reviewers. You can build an online community to sell almost anything—for example, seeds and garden tools (Garden Escape). Developing a Web presence that engages the customer with individually tailored content and services is what differentiates the Internet from other direct marketing media. Amazon maintains records of customer preferences (books, authors, and genres) and tells you what new books have come out since you last logged on that might be of interest to you. Amazon's collaborative filtering software program tells you what other people of similar tastes liked.

You have to do everything possible to draw prospects into your "web-net" until they decide that it is a place to do business. You may have to spend heavily on traditional advertising to establish your brand. Effective banner advertising on the Internet asks questions. For example, one dry cleaner seeking off-season clothing storage business used a banner that asked, "Need more closet space?" You want to make alliances and exclusive agreements with related sites to do "syndicated selling." Amazon has arrangements with approximately 30,000 sites. When consumers visit StarChefs.com to check out recipes from celebrity chefs, for example, they can click a button to let them order a cookbook from Amazon. Don't simply: sell, sell, sell. Be an information source. Useful, helpful information establishes confidence.[4]

Mass Media

Direct response marketing makes use of mass media—print and broadcast—to make initial contact with customers, especially for single product appeals, and to support other media approaches. Cable shopping channels and infomercials demonstrate mass media's important role as a primary direct response medium.

Print   Print, or space, media include magazine ads and free-standing inserts (FSIs). Magazines help you efficiently reach groups of people with special interests, such as tennis players or gardeners. See Marketing in Action box 12-1. Newspaper costs-per-thousand CPMs are often a fraction of the cost of magazines or direct mail. Direct response print ads provide a way for your customer to respond by incorporating a clip-out coupon, coming with a bind-in reply card, or giving an 800 number.

Broadcast   Broadcast media include radio, cable, and broadcast television. A key feature of broadcast is speed. When coupled with a toll-free telephone number, results can be known in a matter of hours rather than having to wait several weeks as in the case of direct mail. This provides you with an opportunity to adjust, fine-tune, and improve a broadcast campaign while it is being conducted.

Although the price of a direct mailing is relatively stable, broadcast time fluctuates widely market by market and even day-to-day. Because broadcast time is a perishable commodity, a station will frequently reduce prices on unsold inventory. This means you must continually assess the cost of the broadcast.

You can use broadcast as support for another medium or as the primary sales medium. A radio or television spot commercial can tell your prospect to "Watch for your mailing," or "Look for your ad." In this supporting role, broadcast works more efficiently with print media, with their more predictable delivery dates, than with direct mail. With direct mail you have to run announcements over an extended period of time to bracket anticipated delivery dates. Cable shopping channels and infomercials are two specialized ways of using broadcast as a primary direct response medium.

Cable Shopping Channels   The home shopping industry has annual sales of more than $2 billion in the United States. It is drawing name retailers, including Saks Fifth Avenue, which sells merchandise on the home shopping network QVC.

> ┌───
>
> **MARKETING IN ACTION** *12-1*
>
> ### Reader's Digest Targets Patients by Their Ailments
>
> Health data was long considered off-limits to direct marketers because it was so private and difficult to get. Then *Reader's Digest* mailed out a survey to its 15 million U.S. subscribers asking them to disclose medical information about their families. The cover letter accompanying the survey said, "In every issue of *Reader's Digest,* we give you medical information to help you stay healthy. Now we'd like to give you information and product news that specifically addresses those medical conditions that directly affect your household. But to do that we need your help." *Reader's Digest* asked about specific illnesses:
>
> 1. I or someone in my household:
>
> | | Suffers from | Wants more information on |
> |---|---|---|
> | Arthritis | ◯ | ◯ |
> | Asthma | ◯ | ◯ |
> | Bladder Control Problem | ◯ | ◯ |
> | ⋮ | ⋮ | ⋮ |
>
> The survey also asked respondents to tick off prescription medicines in use in the home. The letter said, "some of the information in this survey may be shared with healthcare companies." The survey came with a sweepstakes offer, with prizes of $45,000 or a new Cadillac Coupe de Ville.
>
> *Reader's Digest* sorted the responses and created mailing lists of sufferers of diseases and medical conditions. The magazine in 1998 had about nine million names on file, about 800,000 arthritis sufferers, 700,000 people with high blood pressure, 600,000 with high cholesterol, 400,000 with frequent heartburn, 200,000 with osteoporosis, and 500,000 smokers. Now the magazine could send these people something extra with their magazine: a booklet filled with articles and prescription drug ads, all about the very ailment each subscriber has. Each booklet carries four pages of ads from a single drug-company sponsor. For example, SmithKline Beecham, maker of Tagamet acid blocker and Nicorette gum, initially sponsored two booklets.
>
> ━ *You can collect and use even sensitive personal data to target customers.*
>
> *Source:* Sally Beatty, "*Reader's Digest* Targets Patients by Their Ailments," *The Wall Street Journal,* April 17, 1998, pp. B1, B3.
>
> └───

APPLYING *... to Publishing, Healthcare Products Marketing*

Who shops by TV? Deloitte & Touche conducted a national survey of home TV shoppers. People who shop regularly by television are younger than previously thought. Almost half of home shoppers are in the 25 to 44 age range. Their household income was lower than the market average, the number of children living in their households higher. They are more likely to watch sporting events but less likely to exercise. These shoppers are more interested in fashion than in value or comfort.

Infomercials   An infomercial is a 30-minute (typically) TV commercial that incorporates an 800 number for viewer response. The emphasis is on reality-based commercials with real, live people. Originally associated with kitchen gadgets, beauty products, and "get-rich" schemes on late-night TV, most products and services can be sold in the format and at virtually any time thanks to cable and independent networks. Infomercials are typically run in off-hours because the rates are lower. Even though H.U.T. (households using television) rates are lower at off-hours, the return on investment is greater. From a marketing perspective, an infomercial is long-form, direct response advertising that pays for itself.

APPLYING
... to
Tele-
communications
Marketing

GTE, a leading-edge telecommunications company, launched a new package of services with an infomercial. The services included Personal Secretary, a person's own voice-messaging system for important reminders, and Smart Ring, a service for distinguishing rings on different lines into the same place so that you always know for whom the call is intended. The 30-minute length gave GTE an opportunity to educate and inform its customers on what these services were all about. The day after the first program ran, GTE knew it had a winner.

INTEGRATED DIRECT MARKETING

Adding media to a marketing program will raise total response more effectively than simply increasing the level of activity in a single medium because different people are inclined to respond to different stimuli. When a mailing piece that might generate a 2 percent response on its own is supplemented by a toll-free 800-number ordering channel, response typically rises by 50 percent. A skillfully integrated outbound telemarketing effort can add another 50 percent lift in response. Integrated direct marketing builds synergies.

APPLYING
... to
Financial
Products
Marketing

For example, one of Citicorp's primary goals is to break down the traditional geographic restrictions on financial institutions to expand its business and consumer customer bases. The keystone product of one campaign was a fixed-rate home equity loan. Bank research indicated that the same target market segment would also be interested in a flexible revolving credit line vehicle. Thus, more than the immediate sale of a financial instrument was at stake. Each completed transaction produces a new, geographically remote customer for continued solicitation in an ongoing banking relationship. To assess how to market the home equity loan product to territories outside the area where the corporation maintains a branch banking presence, Citicorp tried four test packages involving increasing levels of integration starting from a common direct mail package. The impact of each was carefully tracked with the results shown in Table 12-2. Based on these figures, Citicorp decided to roll out the fourth package—the combination of all media tested. At a 1 percent higher cost than the third test package, the fourth package produced a 15 percent higher market share. An illustration of integrated direct marketing for a nonprofit organization is given in Marketing Strategies box 12-3.

TABLE 12-2   Citicorp Integrated Marketing Test

Test Packages	Accounts Opened	Revenue per Account	Cost Decrease per $1000 Loaned
Basic *control* package: a direct-mail piece with a lengthy application to be filled out and mailed to the bank.	Baseline	Baseline	Baseline
The same mail piece with the addition of an 800 number inviting the customer to call, ask questions, and have the application completed by phone.	+7%	+30%	−63%
The same mail package with 800 service plus a business reply card for requesting further information. People who returned the card received a follow-up telephone call.	+13%	+19%	−72%
Newspaper ads featuring an 800 number were run in the test market. These ads were timed to coincide with the mail drop.	+15%	+23%	−71%

Source: Ernan Roman, "Integrated Direct Marketing," in *Resource Report* 506.03A, New York: Direct Marketing Association, July 1989, p. 3.

MARKETING STRATEGIES *12-3*

Financing the America³ Team

For the Defender Selection Trials for America's Cup, the financing of the America³ Team, the American challenger skippered by Bill Koch, depended largely on individual donations. This was in contrast to competitor Dennis Connor, who relied on major corporate funding to compete. To encourage current members of the America³ Foundation to upgrade their memberships to higher levels of giving, selected members were invited to become charter members of the Foundation's newly created Masthead Society. As part of the overall marketing strategy, an integrated direct marketing program was executed. Direct mail, a video, and a personal call as a follow-up were used.

Each person first received a letter telling them to watch for a 10-minute, fast-action videotape—featuring live footage of the America³ yacht entries, *Jayhawk* and *Defiant*—in their mail within the next week. They were also given an 800 number to call in case the tape was never delivered. Enclosed with the video was a four-page letter, introducing the Masthead Society, and inviting the member to be a guest at the Defender Trials by joining at one of three levels. Each level or "club" offered various benefits based on its value. The highest level, the Skipper's Club, entitled the member to two, four-day Defender Selection Trial passes, deluxe double accommodations for four nights, two invitations to a formal Masthead Society Reception, and a personalized commemorative America³ yacht identification flag. Approximately one week after the member received the video, a telephone marketing firm called on behalf of the Foundation to personally invite them to the Defender Trials. The script was straightforward and benefit driven. The member was offered the option of paying by credit card or invoice. If they chose to be billed, they were sent an invoice accompanied by a personalized letter, acknowledging the phone conversation, thanking them for becoming members, and restating the many benefits of their membership. Even when members were unable to attend the Defender Trials, they were extremely impressed with the video and that the Foundation would personally call with an invitation. The success of the program went beyond dollars and cents to reinforce the loyalty of the members to the organization.

Subsequently the Foundation decided to take advantage of the enthusiasm of the races by launching an emergency, last-minute fund-raising campaign during the week of the America's Cup. Members were telephoned starting the day of the first race. Throughout the scripted presentation, communicators referenced the race, specific happenings, and the outcome, adding timeliness, excitement and authenticity to the appeal. In fact, during the days when the race was actually taking place, a supervisor monitored the race on the cable television sports channel, ESPN, and made up-to-the-minute script changes as events transpired. As a result of this flexible scripting, the Foundation was able to convey its own enthusiasm and engage in a knowledgeable interaction with the member over the phone. [The America³ Team won the America's Cup, four races to one against the Italians.]

— *Integrated direct marketing is a powerful marketing approach.*

Source: TransAmerica Marketing Services, Inc.

Courtesy America3 Foundation

SUMMARY

As lifestyle changes have created the need for convenient, time-sensitive, and reliable ways for people to shop and as increased competition segments the market into every more-distinct niches, traditional mass marketing has become less efficient. Marketing funds are being shifted to database-driven direct marketing. Direct marketing creates a dialogue between you and your customer. The key to exploiting this relationship is the use of a customer database to maintain up-to-date information on your customers and your exchanges with them.

Integrated direct marketing emphasizes the coupling of diverse marketing media to create powerful media interrelationships. Although integrated direct marketing increases your upfront investment, more customers are contacted and more orders per thousand contacts are produced.

NOTES

1. Major portions of this chapter have been taken from materials provided by the Direct Marketing Educational Foundation at their Direct Marketing Institute for Professors.
2. Mickey H. Gramig, "Mailbox Marketing Mania," *The Atlanta Journal-Constitution* (October 12, 1998), p. E6.
3. Check out the specifics of the demographic profile for your ZIP code at National Decision Systems Web site. Go to *http://www.natdecsys.com/* and then click on "Lifestyle Game."
4. Clint Willis, "Does Amazon.com Really Matter?" *Forbes* (April 6, 1998), pp. 55–58; Steve Ditto and Briggs Pille, "Marketing on the Internet," *Healthcare Executive* (September/October 1998), pp. 54–55; John R. Graham, "Capturing the Cyber Customer," *American Salesman* (November 1998), pp. 9–15.

SUGGESTED READING

Blattberg, Robert C., and John Deighton. "Interactive Marketing: Exploiting the Age of Addressability," *Sloan Management Review,* Vol. 33, No. 1 (Fall 1991), pp. 5–14.

FURTHER READING

Berry, Michael J. A. and Gordon Linoff. *Data Mining Techniques: For Marketing, Sales, and Customer Support* (New York: John Wiley, 1997).
Direct Marketing Educational Foundation Inc. *Resource Reports* (New York: Direct Marketing Association, 1989).
Hughes, Arthur M. *The Complete Database Marketer* (Chicago: Probus Publishing, 1996).
Magliozzi, T. L., and P. D. Berger. "List Segmentation Strategies in Direct Marketing," *OMEGA,* Vol. 21, No. 1 (January 1993), pp. 61–72.
Muldoon, Katie, and Anne Knudsen (Eds.). *How to Profit Through Catalog Marketing* (Lincolnwood, IL: NTC Business Books, 1996).
David Shepard Associates, Inc. *The New Direct Marketing* (New York: Irwin, 1995).
Stone, Bob. *Successful Direct Marketing Methods* (Lincolnwood, IL: NTC Business Books, 1997).

QUESTIONS

1. Federated Department Stores, parent of stores such as Bloomingdales, Macy's, and Stern's, announced that it was buying Fingerhut, a big direct marketer. Federated's core customer base is middle- to upper-middle-income households. Fingerhut, which sells everything from cookware to gift baskets through its core catalog business, caters mainly to low-income customers who usually can't get credit elsewhere. Federated has about 60 million credit card accounts. Fingerhut has a database of more than 30 million current and former customer names. Fingerhut has developed its own Web sites and and has bought stakes in a number of other Internet retailers. Traditional retailers have circled warily around Web sites and electronic malls fearful that online sales would cannibalize those in their own stores. Why do you think Federated bought Fingerhut? Would you have?
2. CVS Corp., America's second-largest drugstore chain, uses prescription information to send mailings to its own customers. Drug makers fund some of these mailings. For exam-

ple, a diabetes sufferer received a letter from a CVS pharmacy. The letter, paid for by Warner-Lambert Co., touted the company's new diabetes drug, Rezulin, as a "breakthrough option" that could eliminate their injections completely. What is your opinion of CVS's practice of doing these mailings?

3. A "cookie" is a file that Web sites install on your computer's hard drive when you visit a site that offers cookies. They are very small files. Cookies are used for Web-site tracking, delivering targeted advertisements, storing IDs, personalization, and target marketing. For example, online vendors, such as Amazon.com, can read the user's cookie and match it with a stored profile that would contain credit card information, so that the user won't have to enter the information each time. Cookies enhance the Web experience for the user by limiting the repetitiveness of advertising and increasing the level of relevant content on the Web. There is the possibility that unscrupulous Web sites might take your information and sell it to offline marketers. Should a Web site be allowed to use cookies?

4. Most healthcare organizations recognize the importance of bonding with the people they serve. How could a hospital use the power of the Internet for deepening consumer relationships? Focus on the case of consumers expecting their first baby.

5. Magazine subscription businesses use frequent and repeated mailings to promote sweepstakes to encourage the purchase of merchandise. Their marketing practices are sometimes borderline. For example, customers of the Publishers Clearing House have received letters from contest representatives urging them to make purchases to "avoid embarrassment" when the PCH shows up at their door with the big money prize. Whose responsibility is it to protect the elderly, disabled, retired, and homebound from suffering major financial losses by spending heavily on merchandise?

6. Why is getting someone to buy something via telemarketing, through the mail, from a catalog, or over the Internet considered the ultimate test of branding?

7. Some direct marketing organizations collect names of prospects from obituaries published in newspapers. Family members are called by phone and asked to buy burial urns and artificial flower arrangements to place in cemeteries for deceased relatives. Other firms clip out obituaries from newspapers and mount them in plastic. These mementos are mailed to family members with a request for contributions to a charity. Are these direct marketing activities ethical? Why or why not?

8. The credit card division of a large western bank wants to forecast applications received (and eventually new accounts opened). Three factors drive applications: marketing spend, annual maintenance fee (AMF), and annual percentage rate (APR). Accounts opened is subject to a lag effect, in as much as two to three weeks pass from the time an application is received. Therefore, applications received is considered to more accurately reflect the effects of marketing spend and pricing options offered, assuming the bank's credit policies remained unchanged throughout the period. Marketing spend used the cost accumulated in the functional area "Credit Processing and Account Acquisition Expense." Costs that appeared related to processing of incoming applications and to ongoing department operations have been removed. The bank's prices are not considered in a vacuum but are considered relative to competing products. Market prices were estimated from data in *American Bank Management* magazine. Information is available for 12 months (July–June) and is given in the file creditcarddat.sav. Estimate the response function (assuming that there is no substantial temporary promotion during the period by major card issuers). Does marketing spend have an effect? Which is more important, annual maintenance fee or annual percentage rate? *Hint:* First compute relative AMF and relative APR by dividing bank prices by market prices. As always, if you compute the natural logarithm (LN) of each variable and then run a linear multiple regression on the transformed variables, the regression coefficients of the variables can be interpreted as elasticities.

CHAPTER
13

DESIGNING ADVERTISING PROGRAMS

> Associating meanings with products in order to turn products into brands is the real value of effective advertising.
>
> CHARLES YOUNG
> MICHAEL ROBISON

Advertising communication expenditures have a variety of purposes: enhance the image of the organization, build brand preferences, promote the sale of particular items, announce a special promotion or sale, and encourage participation in causes. Advertising is employed around the world because it is a very cost-effective method of communicating ideas to mass audiences. It works for promoting disease prevention as well as for selling soap.

In your role as marketing manager, you will need to identify the appropriate target market segments and uncover the relevant buying motives. You then must make a series of decisions that establish the scope and direction of your advertising program. These include

- Select advertising objectives.
- Develop advertising budget.
- Develop campaign themes.
- Pick appropriate media.
- Monitor results.

These decisions are shown in Figure 13-1 and are explained in more detail in the following sections. These decisions are part of an ongoing process and the market results feed back into the next round's decisions. In making these decisions, you must have an appreciation of when and how advertising works. Thus, this chapter begins with a discussion of the foundations of advertising.

THE FOUNDATIONS FOR ADVERTISING

To avoid wasting advertising expenditure on ineffective campaigns, you should understand when advertising works and the predominant theories of how it might work.

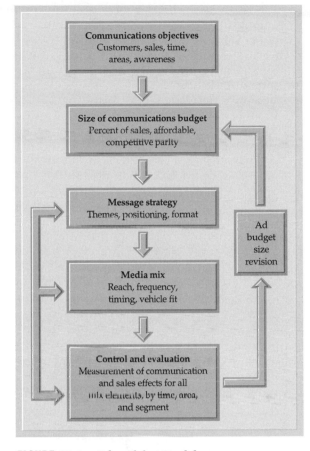

FIGURE 13-1   Advertising Decisions

When Advertising Works

Before setting budgets and other advertising planning, you must decide whether you should do any advertising. The Hershey chocolate bar, for example, became a leading product in the United States on the basis of extensive distribution gained through the use of salespeople, and not as the result of consumer advertising. Even so, Hershey now spends heavily on advertising. A product's brand equity may suffer if there is a long hiatus in its advertising. This happened to Heinz ketchup as discussed in Marketing in Action box 13-1.

An appraisal of the opportunity for advertising begins with an assessment of potential for stimulation of demand. The ability to increase demand with advertising varies across product categories. To assess opportunities for advertising, you must understand the factors that account for these differences. Four of the more important factors are that

- The trend in primary demand is favorable.
- Product differentiation is marked.
- Hidden qualities of the product are important to customers.
- Funds for advertising are available.

The social and environmental factors that underlie the basic trends in product demand are often more important than the amount of advertising expenditures. Advertising can accelerate an expansion in demand that would have occurred without advertising or, correspond-

MARKETING IN ACTION *13-1*

Heinz Seeks to Reestablish Dominant Ketchup Position With Heavy Ad Spending

For five years in the mid-1990s, H. J. Heinz did not advertise ketchup on television. During this period, Heinz ketchup maintained its position as market leader, with more than double the sales and volume of its nearest competitor, ConAgra's Hunt's ketchup. However, Heinz saw its market share erode from more than 50% to about 47%. Price competition was stiff due to private-label brands. Meanwhile the ketchup category also suffered from a change in consumers' eating habits. Consumers were snacking more on munchies, especially chips with salsa. Salsa has a healthy, veggie image.

Ketchup is present in 97 percent of U.S. households. Unfortunately, it has a problem that many staples have: people don't use it as often as they might. For example, about 60 percent of ketchup is eaten on hamburgers, hot dogs, and french fries. Although these three food dishes are the most-eaten for kids and adults, they are eaten with ketchup less than 40 percent of the time. Children consume more ketchup per capita then adults. In particular, children three to 11 account for 5.4 percent of the U.S. population but 24 percent of the ketchup-eating occasions.

Heinz responded with a $20 million advertising campaign timed for the barbecue season. The new ads began by showing a gaggle of healthy looking tomatoes squeezing themselves into a ketchup bottle. Next came a shot of someone pouring ketchup onto a hamburger and a child biting into it with glee. The tag line was "Mine's Gotta Have Heinz."

— *No matter how powerful a brand is, if you stop advertising, there will be erosion of brand equity.*

Source: Rekha Balu, "Heinz Ketchup Readies Super Bowl Blitz," *The Wall Street Journal*, January 5, 1998, p. B6.

Heinz trademark and tag line are owned by The H. J. Heinz Company and used with permission.

ingly, might retard an adverse trend. A reversal of a trend by advertising alone, however, is most unlikely. You are better off repositioning your product through advertising than fighting the tide as illustrated in Marketing Strategies box 13-1. You should also realize that the elasticity of advertising is believed to decline over the product life cycle.

When demand is expanding, there are frequent opportunities for selective advertising appeals. These selective appeals are more effective if the product has "special" attributes. Product differentiation facilitates the establishment of brand preference, and this preference enables the product to have a larger gross margin than might have been possible with an undifferentiated product. In turn, a larger gross margin provides more funds for advertising. The firm must have sufficient resources to make an impression on the customer, however, and high advertising costs are a barrier to entry in some markets.

How Advertising Works

You need to understand how advertising affects consumers in order to formulate more effective advertising strategies. Two views of what takes place when a person receives an advertisement have been put forth: accumulation and replacement.

Accumulation   Desirable response tendencies increase with advertising exposure and compete with undesirable or incorrect response tendencies, such as positive attitudes toward competing products or misinformation. New information is combined with existing concepts. From an information processing perspective, then, product positioning and message consistency are critical. This model implies it is necessary to measure the strength of both desirable and competing responses.

Replacement   Existing concepts are replaced in memory by new concepts with increasing exposure to advertising. This theory implies that you can capture your product category by

---

**APPLYING
. . . to
Consumer
Food
Marketing**

MARKETING STRATEGIES *13-1*

Special K Changes Advertising Strategy

Kellogg's launched Special K in 1955 as a weight-control product targeted at women. Advertising messages emphasized "thinness is everything." For example, some commercials showed women trying to "pinch an inch" on their waists. In the process, Special K became one of the top ten global cereal brands. However, this strategy began to wear thin in the United States as "baby boomers" started to reject the emphasis on perfection—and Special K's market share slid.

A Kellogg survey found that more than two-thirds of women believed TV ads and fashion magazines influenced society's image of ideal height and weight, which few felt that they had attained. For baby boomers, careers and sports had much more relevance to how they viewed themselves than did having a perfect body. Indeed, a 1995 poll by *USA Today*/AdTrack found that nearly 30 percent of women ages 25–54 actually disliked Special K's advertising campaigns.

Kellogg decided to change its long-time advertising strategy accordingly. Kellogg felt a self-esteem message would resonate more strongly with contemporary women. Its advertising agency, Leo Burnett, created a new campaign centered on the theme "Reshape your attitude." In one TV commercial, a fellow on a barstool asks an unseen interviewer, "Do I look fat?" Another man wonders aloud if his posterior is too big. A third sighs and says, "I have my mother's thighs. I have to accept that." The commercial's parting shot was "Men don't obsess about these things. Why should we?"

— *You must recognize when market changes require that your consistent-theme advertising have a new theme.*

Source: Rekha Balu, "Special K Ads Flip-Flop on Body Attitude," *The Wall Street Journal*, August 12, 1998, p. B7.

delivering more messages than your competitors. You would want to have the highest "share of voice."

With this backdrop, various theories of how advertising works have been suggested. Psychological *learning* theory states that a *new* stimulus first has to be grasped then seen to be relevant before it is accepted or rejected. This reasoning fostered the notion that advertising can be strongly persuasive and play a key role in brand building. The learning theory approach to advertising is known as the hierarchy-of-effects theory.

The Hierarchy of Effects   The hierarchy-of-effects hypothesis states that advertising guides the consumer through a sequence of steps which culminates in purchase. Consumers can be classified into seven groups. The first group contains potential purchasers who are *unaware* of the existence of the product. The second group contains consumers who are merely *aware* of the product's existence. The third group contains consumers who *possess* knowledge of the product and its benefits. The fourth group contains customers who *like* the product. The fifth group is those who have developed a *preference* for the product over all other possibilities. The sixth group contains consumers who are *convinced* that they should buy the product. The final group contains consumers who *purchase* the product. Variants of this hierarchy-of-effects theory include AIDA and ATR.

Awareness-Interest-Desire-Action   The *AIDA* theory asserts that advertising is a *strong* market force that propels the prospect through a sequence of steps which culminates in purchase. Advertising works by changing consumer attitudes about brands. The emphasis is on brand image. The theory focuses on *new* buyers of a brand and does not say much about former buyers of the brand. Your job would be to develop a brand position that was appealing and unique. A different view of advertising is given by *ATR* theory—one that does not require an attitude shift prior to purchase.

Awareness-Trial-Reinforcement   The *ATR* theory contends that advertising is a *weak* market force that is suggestive rather than strongly persuasive. ATR says that advertising can only exert influence at each stage of the process. First purchase for a frequently purchased consumer good is viewed as a trial purchase. Consequently, advertising plays a role in reducing cognitive dissonance and reinforcing satisfaction. Given brand switching, advertising rekindles brand awareness and retrial by lapsed users. You want to reassure heavy users and remind light buyers. Thus, the *R* in ATR theory stands for *reminder, reassurance,* and *retrial* as well as *reinforcement.* The process is diagrammed in Figure 13-2. The emphasis is on *brand salience* (or presence). Brand salience refers to which brands consumers think about rather than what they think about the brands. The order in which brands come to mind, for example, top-of-mind awareness, is crucial. Your job would be to register your brand name with the public.

Advertising spending could be directed toward improving both brand salience and brand image. The reality is that many businesses do not have adequate advertising budgets to have a large impact on brand image; it is easier to change brand awareness. Moreover, most advertising is not about learning but about reminding. Most consumers are already *familiar* about what is being presented in ads for established products.

APPLYING
. . . to
Consumer
Services
Marketing

Consider the U.S rent-a-car market. Car rental is an established service category with companies that spend "moderately" on advertising—typically $50 million or less per year. Tracking research has shown a strong relation between the amount of money a car rental company spends on advertising and its share of market. A further analysis showed that awareness measures (brand salience) accounted for approximately 70 percent of advertising's effect and content-related measures (brand imagery) about 30 percent. Finally, highly recalled themes and slogans, such as "We try harder," were most likely to be supported by not only well-funded campaigns but also long-standing ones.[1]

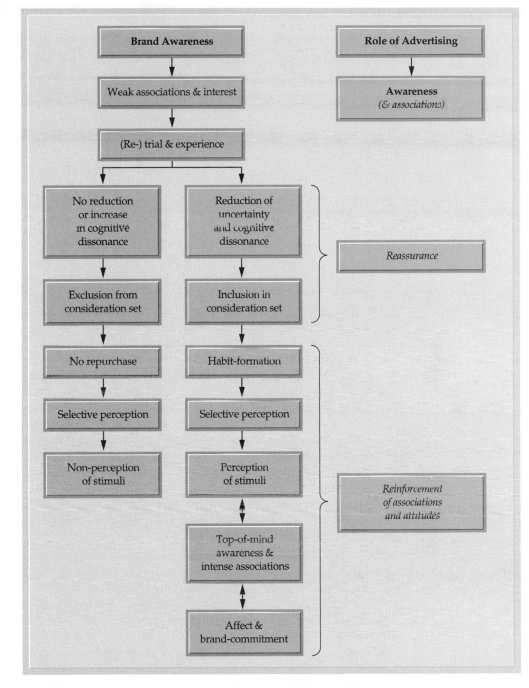

FIGURE 13-2   Brand Awareness and the Role of Advertising (From Giep Franzen, *Advertising Effectiveness,* **[Henley-on-Thames: Admap Publications, 1994], p. 214.)**

ADVERTISING OBJECTIVES AND GOALS

Under most conditions the primary objective of a firm is shareholder value. This usually means that you should select the advertising alternative that generates the highest present value for long-term profits. Nonprofit organizations focus on net benefits rather than on profits.

Setting Advertising Objectives

Advertising objectives for a product will depend on the stage of the life cycle that the product is in. New product advertising makes the customer aware of the existence of the new product, forces distribution of the new brand, and provides the customer with a reason for buying the product. Established product advertising is aimed at maintaining the product's market position.

The task of advertising is also a function of the product category. For more expensive products such as cars and appliances, the decision process of the buyer is deliberate and occurs over a comparatively long time horizon. Most buyers would be able to identify various brands even when labels are removed. In contrast, many packaged goods such as soaps and detergents are almost physically identical, and these products are often of low interest to buyers. Consequently, manufacturers of these products seek to achieve top-of-mind awareness among buyers. Ideally, they attempt to associate their brand name with the generic product category. An example would be Kleenex and facial tissue.

Advertising can increase the number of customers or increase the usage rate among current customers or both. More customers come from converting customers from competing brands, from holding current customers by developing brand loyalty, and from expanding the total market for the product class. Greater usage comes from reminding customers to use the brand and from telling them about new uses. Encouraging loyal customers to use your brand more often is sometimes called "frequency marketing." Advertising is also aimed at intermediaries in the distribution channel. This advertising seeks to encourage the wholesaler and retailer to stock and promote the advertiser's brand.

Advertising objectives should be coordinated with the objectives set for the other marketing variables. For instance, advertising can be used to solicit sales leads, and salespeople can then contact these prospects. In cases in which the product is too complex to explain in an ad, advertising might be used to presell the salesperson rather than the product.

In sum, advertising objectives can be described as "demand pull" or as "demand push" advertising. Pull advertising is designed to sell the final user of the product so that the user will go to the distributor and ask for the product, and in effect pull the merchandise through the channel of distribution. Most brand name advertising falls into this category (Timken bearings, Hagger slacks). Push advertising, on the other hand, is directed at brokers and distributors and is intended to presell the dealers on the merits of the product. It is more common to use push advertising with industrial products and stress direct mail, trade journals, and display materials rather than broadcast media.

Defining Advertising Goals

Advertisers should specify their advertising objectives and subsequently measure the results. The idea is to measure performance in terms of achievement of a quantitative statement of performance. A goal for a new brand might be to attain 80 percent brand awareness within six months after introduction. This provides a benchmark against which to measure accomplishment. Advertising performance should be measured in terms of sales whenever possible because of the simple accounting equation that relates sales to profits.

Under the AIDA model, the consumer moves through a sequence of steps from awareness of a brand to action. The role of advertising in moving consumers from one group to another in this process tends to vary. A panel survey can provide the data necessary to assess the economic value of causing consumers to change groups. This means that immediate sales results might not be the major criterion for measuring advertising effectiveness. Simply measuring the consumer's progress through the intermediate steps may provide a better indicator of the long-term effects of advertising.

The danger with defining advertising goals for measured results (*DAGMAR*) is that rather than defining your goals first and then determining how to measure the results, you might be tempted to decide what can be easily measured first and then set your goal. Moreover, if you select some intermediate measure of performance, you have to assume that your measure ultimately drives sales—and it may not.

THE BUDGET

Various procedures are used to determine the size of advertising expenditures. The efficiency of these procedures often depends on a firm's ability to measure the effectiveness of advertising. Judgment-oriented techniques include the subjective approach, the affordable approach, and the fixed guidelines approach, while data-oriented techniques include the competitive parity approach, the objective and task approach, the experimentation and testing approach, and the modeling and simulation approach. Selection among these methods depends on the extent to which returns from advertising can be identified.

The Subjective Approach

The subjective method sets budgets on the basis of executive judgment and experience. The executive generally has the task of allocating a fixed budget between advertising and other marketing costs. When direct customer contact is viewed as the most important element in the marketing mix, advertising needs are often subordinated.

The Fixed Guidelines Approach

A fixed guidelines approach involves setting the advertising budget in terms of a percentage of sales, a fixed sum per unit, or competitively with other firms. Many companies determine their budgets as a percentage of the sales volume forecasted or anticipated for the period that the advertising budget will cover. A variant of the percentage of sales method sets the budget as a fixed sum per unit. In this approach, the appropriation for advertising is determined by multiplying the projected unit sales volume by a certain number of dollars, euros, or yen per unit. The method is used primarily for consumer durables. When applied to convenience goods, the method is called the case rate method. One problem with the judgment-oriented approaches is that when a firm is under pressure to lower costs, advertising is usually cut because of the absence of hard data to support the need for promotion.

Competitive Parity Approach

The competitive parity approach sets spending in line with major competitors. To some degree it reflects a belief in collective industry wisdom. The focus is on share of voice. Information on competitive spending comes from sources such as Nielsen Ad Tracker. This system automatically monitors the commercial content of network, national cable, spot TV, and national syndicated programs by recognizing the unique programs signal of each commercial broadcast. Local cable spending is estimated.

The Objective and Task Approach

The task approach involves setting objectives, translating these objectives into a series of communication-specific tasks, then determining the necessary appropriation. Firms using this approach begin by setting specific and measurable objectives for their advertising. The Texasgulf Company provides a useful case history.

Texasgulf supplies phosphoric acid to fertilizer manufacturers. Before advertising began, Texasgulf had a market share of about 5 percent, and about six large customers accounted for most of the sales. A short-term advertising goal was set to increase the awareness of Texasgulf's superior phosphoric acids by 10 percent in a one-year period. The campaign that was employed emphasized that Texasgulf acid products had fewer impurities than those of the competition, and had a distinctive green color. The acid products were always referred to as being "clean and green," and the overall campaign theme was "Texasgulf has changed things."

A before-and-after research study found the following: (1) an increase from 15.3 to 35.1 percent in the number of respondents who recognized that Texasgulf made a clear, green acid; (2) an increase from 3.6 to 16.3 percent in the number of respondents who associated Texasgulf with the theme "(Blank) has changed Things"; (3) an increase from 9.4 to 24.3 percent in the number of respondents who thought that Texasgulf made an "above-average" acid. The results indicate that the advertising campaign met the objectives that were set.

Experimentation and Testing

The experimentation and testing approach involves controlled field experiments. The impact of spending and weight variations in test markets is compared to baseline results from controlled markets.

An example of a controlled field experiment is Du Pont's evaluation of its advertising for Teflon coatings for cookware. Du Pont was following a pull strategy in which it hoped that advertising could create sufficient consumer demand so that cookware manufacturers would be forced to coat the inside of their utensils with Teflon. Advertising was varied in selected markets to determine the best level of Teflon advertising expenditures between zero and $1 million. There appeared to be a threshold effect at which $500,000 had little impact, but $1 million gave significantly greater sales. The million-dollar expenditure was known to be profitable, but not necessarily the most profitable level. Another experiment was conducted in which much higher levels were tested. This second experiment permitted Du Pont to set the advertising level so that the marginal profit from the sale of Teflon was just greater than zero.

Today controlled market testing often involves split-cable markets or electronic test markets and scanning data. This process is illustrated in Figure 13-3. Traditional split-cable heavy up tests often fail to show a significant sales response to large increases in advertising spending. The reason may well be that heavily exposed groups are already beyond their saturation limits. Once customers decide that they have enough information to make a purchase, they will tend to ignore more information.

Modeling and Simulation

Econometric methods can be used to estimate the unknown parameters of an advertising sales response function from historical data. Once estimation is complete, the estimated sales response function can be used to answer "what if" questions.

A simulation is the representation of the behavior of one system (in our case, the "real world") through the use of another system (i.e., a computer program designed for that purpose). Typically a planner can input alternative advertising levels to assess their impact.

In conclusion, research has shown a significant movement by medium- and large-size companies toward more professional approaches to advertising budgeting. The objective and task approach, and to a lesser extent experimentation and testing, are being adopted by advertising managers. If you use a data-oriented technique, remember it generates only suggestions and must be tempered by your judgment. "What you can afford" seems to play an important role in determining the degree to which the prescriptions of these more sophisticated techniques can be implemented. The budget-setting process in many organizations is a *political process.*

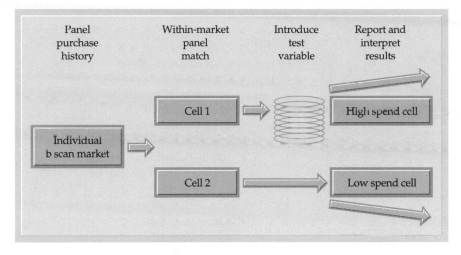

FIGURE 13-3   Split-Cable TV Market Test

MESSAGE CONTENT

The message content of a marketing communications strategy typically falls into one of three broad categories. The first approach stresses product features and customer benefits. The focus is on "demonstrable differences" or the "unique selling proposition." For instance, Mrs. Butterworth's Lite Syrup advertises itself as "The only Lite syrup made with Grade A Butter." A brand personality is developed in the second approach. The focus is on "image," "goodwill," "brand franchise," and "brand equity." An example would be Pillsbury's use of the "doughboy." The third approach positions the product through the great idea. The focus is on "strategy." For instance, 7-Up positions itself as the "Un-Cola."

Advertising Strategies

Under the assumption that advertising works by changing brand attitudes, as in AIDA theory, you have several advertising strategy options:

1. Influence the choice criteria that govern product class selection.
2. Change the relevance of a product attribute (create a salient attribute).
3. Change the ideal amount of an attribute that a brand should possess.
4. Change the perceived amount of an attribute held by the firm's brand.
5. Change the perceived amount of an attribute held by a competitor's brand.

Note that these advertising strategies are substrategies of the more general marketing strategy of positioning.

APPLYING
. . . to Consumer Durable Goods Marketing

Strategy 1 attempts to stimulate primary demand by modifying the individual's motivation and choice criteria. Usually, this involves accelerating an environmental trend, such as the use of margarine instead of butter. Compaq encouraged demand for multimedia personal computers using a print advertisement having the headline "Just because you learned the hard way doesn't mean your kid has to." Strategy 2 can take several forms. Sometimes an existing attribute can be made more prominent. At one time, all appliance manufacturers had wheels as an optional feature for their refrigerators so the homemaker could move the appliance in order to clean under it, but none of the firms advertised this feature. One com-

APPLYING
*. . . to
Consumer
Packaged
Goods
Marketing*

pany with a history of noninnovation decided to advertise this attribute. After the campaign, image studies revealed that the consumer viewed the firm as innovative! Sometimes a new attribute is added to extend the life of a mature product. The low-suds detergent market in Great Britain is dominated by Procter & Gamble with its Ariel, Bold, Fairy, and Daz brands and Lever Brother with its Persil, Surf, and Wisk brands. During the 1980s, Lever lost share to P&G. To reverse this trend, Lever launched Radion in late 1989. Advertising introduced the concept of odor removal as the ultimate test of a detergent's cleaning power and conferred ownership of this property on Radion. This odor-removal proposition was based on a Unilever patented technology, a unique deo-perfume system that deodorizes clothes rather than merely masking odor. Advertising worked to position Radion to complement other Lever brands. The impact of Radion's launch upon brand images in the low-suds sector is shown in an image map by Millward Brown (Figure 13-4). The communication of odor removal placed Radion in the modern/efficient quadrant of the map. Moreover, Radion was differentiated from the Lever portfolio, market leader Persil in particular.

APPLYING
*. . . to
Consumer
Beverages
Marketing*

The remaining three strategies involve positioning the firm's brand in relation to ideal and competing brands by moving the ideal toward its own brand position (strategy 3), by moving its brand toward the ideal (strategy 4), or by moving competitive brands away from the ideal (strategy 5). Croft Original pale cream Spanish sherry employed strategy 3. When Croft Original was launched, all sweet or cream sherries, including market leader Harveys Bristol Cream, were dark in color. Croft Original's advertising presented paleness as a positive product attribute while also establishing Croft Original as the superior pale cream sherry. Creative executions were based on P. G. Wodehouse's characters, Jeeves and Wooster. The relationship between the likable but basically inept Wooster and his butler Jeeves, the arbiter of good taste and discernment, provided the platform for projecting the quality of Croft Original and the stylish sophistication of its drinkers. Jeeves leaves no doubt as to the discerning quality of Croft Original: "One can tell a great deal, sir, just by looking at things. Your Croft Original, for example, with its light delicate color. One glance at the sherry tells one all one needs to know about the quality." The concept of paleness was later expanded, associating it with modernity (and dark with old-fashioned). The success of this

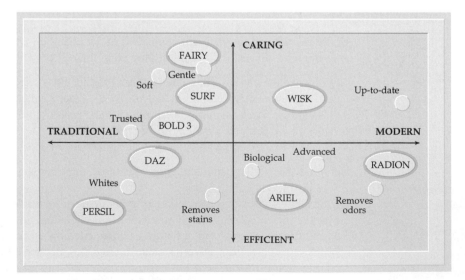

FIGURE 13-4   Detergent Brand Image Map (From "The Case for Radion Automatic: A New Brand in the Lever Portfolio," in *Advertising Works 6,* Paul Feldwick, ed. [Henley-on-Thames: NTC Publications, 1991], p. 220.)

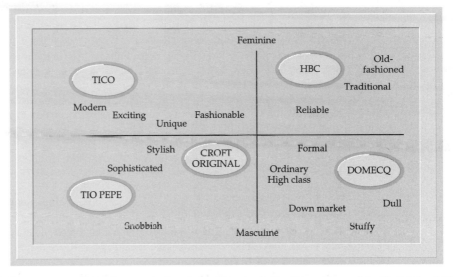

FIGURE 13-5 Spanish Sherry Market Brand Personality Map (From "Croft Original 'One Instinctively Knows When Something Is Right'," in *Advertising Works 6*, Paul Feldwick, ed. [Henley-on-Thames: NTC Publications, 1991], p. 41.)

communication strategy is evidenced by the correspondence map by MAS shown in Figure 13-5.

Strategy 4 can be illustrated by L&M cigarettes. Liggett & Myers decided that their L&M brand of cigarettes was not properly positioned and that it must be repositioned into the full-flavor category. Although L&M was reformulated so that it had a new tobacco blend and a new cork filter, the primary repositioning effort was a massive advertising campaign. The first print advertisements showed a rugged, powerfully built man clearing an area and building a cabin in the wilderness. Liggett & Myers was trying to move its brand closer to Marlboro, which was already in the full-flavor category. Rather than repositioning toward a competitor, it is more likely that you would want to differentiate yourself from your close competitors as illustrated by Marketing in Action box 13-2. An example of the strategy 5 is a china ad that reads "Royal Doulton, the china of Stratford-on-Trent, England versus Lenox, the china of Pomona, N.J." Thus, Royal Doulton is repositioning Lenox china, a brand that many consumers believed was imported. This advertisement resulted in a 6 percent gain in market share for Royal Doulton.

Product Line Positioning

Creative strategy plays a crucial role in product line positioning. Kraft was interested in a multibranded, segmented positioning approach that would maximize its opportunity within the ice cream category. Kraft had been marketing an ice cream called Breyers in the northeastern region of the United States. Breyers ice cream does not contain any kind of artificial flavoring, added coloring, stabilizers, or emulsifiers. Kraft wanted to take this premium ice cream national by capitalizing on its all-natural positioning through an advertising claim that Breyers was "*The* All-Natural Ice Cream." The only problem was that Kraft already had premium quality ice cream, Sealtest, on the market. Blind product testing showed that Sealtest compared favorably on taste with ice cream parlors' ice cream. Given that Sealtest cost only half, or less, of what these hand-packed ice creams cost, Sealtest offered the consumer real value. Sealtest was positioned as "The Supermarket Ice Cream with That Ice Cream

MARKETING IN ACTION *13-2*

Repositioning Kronenbourg 1664

Les Brasseries Kronenbourg is a unit of the French DANONE Group. City sophistication is at the core of Kronenbourg's new British campaign with its humorous take on famous French sayings. Premium lager Kronenbourg 1664 has gone for Parisian sophistication in its new television campaign, abandoning the rustic image the brand used to share with arch-rival Stella Artois. Three 30-second executions feature vignettes of city life, with a humorous twist on French expressions. "C'est la Vie" shows a young clubber failing to pick up a girl by buying her a Kronenbourg 1664, when she makes off with both their drinks and joins her female lover. In "Déjà Vu" a young woman poses as a lost tourist to get men to buy her a beer in the local cafe. And "Savoir-Faire" features a young man jumping the queue at a crowded bar by using his mobile to place a telephone call to himself. "The proposition is to bring Kronenbourg 1664 to life as the best-loved premium beer in France."

The shift to the city is intended to put a bit of distance between the brand and Stella Artois, which projects a rural image in its long-running TV campaign, originally based on the film *Jean de Florette.* Kronenbourg commercials last year also featured the French countryside, with two old men in a vineyard bemoaning people's growing preference for beer. Kronenbourg is one of Scottish Courage's three core brands, with Foster's and John Smith's, all supported by substantial advertising campaigns. Its Frenchness is belied by the German-sounding name: it actually originated in the 17th century in Strasbourg, straddling the French-German border.

Premium lager is the fastest growing sector of the beer market, as younger consumers seek out quality. Kronenbourg 1664 is the second largest premium draught brew with 18% market share compared to Stella's 28%, and Carlsberg Export and Heineken Export each with under 10%.

Kronenbourg has enjoyed year-on-year growth of around 20%, and the current TV and cinema push is part of a 10 million spend aimed at keeping the momentum going. It benefited from a press campaign during the World Cup in France, including a guide to areas where matches were being played. "We are trying to increase brand saliency on a national basis. Premium lager is biased toward the south of the country where it continues to do well, but northern sales are growing faster from a smaller base."

The focus on women in two of the three commercials has been viewed as a conscious attempt to win over female drinkers to what has traditionally been seen as a male product. The company says that while this was not an active part of its strategy, it recognizes female purchasers are a growing sector of the market. That applies especially to the off-trade, as women often do the buying for their partners or for parties, and can be influenced to purchase a familiar brand even if they are not themselves regular beer drinkers.

— *You can use advertising to differentiate your product.*

Source: Robert McLuhan, "Kronenbourg's Urbane Tales," *Marketing*, December 17, 1998, p. 17.

Parlor Taste." This appeal was not in conflict with Breyers' natural ingredient appeal. In the first five years after the start of the new advertising campaigns, total sales of packaged ice cream only rose about 5 percent, but Sealtest sales increased 23 percent and Breyer's sales jumped 50 percent. Each brand established its own niche in the marketplace.

Appeals by Target Segment

Where a product's image is important, psychographics are critical. Cosmetic firms, for example, use psychographics to make sure that the image of their products and ads is in sync with their customers' self-image. Marketers tend to reflect their own lifestyle in marketing communications without adequate attention being paid to the lifestyle target group. You have to make sure it's your customers, not yourself, to whom you are talking.

Many firms make different appeals to different segments. AT&T Long Lines segmented its residential long-distance market and found a group of prospects with reasons to call long distance, but who didn't because of a perceived price barrier. As a result, AT&T augmented its successful emotional appeal, its "Reach Out and Touch Someone" campaign, with a pragmatic appeal, a "Cost of Visit" campaign.

Message Creativity

Message creativity often is a deciding factor in the success of an advertising campaign. For example, one year California raisins had the most popular ads on television despite a budget of only $6.8 million. McDonald's spent a total of $385 million on TV ads in the same year and only ranked third in popularity. The difference was the appeal of the animated dancing raisins dreamed up by the agency Foote, Cone, and Belding. This campaign was so successful that the California Raisin Board received millions of dollars in licensing fees from the sales of toy raisin figures.

Copy Pretesting

Focus groups are frequently used to evaluate rough commercials. The purpose is to ensure communication objectives are met—that the message you want to send is the same one being received. This screening procedure prevents spending money on flawed commercials.

A variety of commercial copy-testing services test finished commercials. They differ in whether they conduct on-air or off-air tests, use a pre/posttest design or posttest-only (matched-group) design, provide a single exposure or multiple exposures (reexposure), and other details. A major concern you should have in using one of these services is whether their audience corresponds to your target market.

Copy-testing measures fall into six general categories: measures of persuasion, brand salience, recall, communications (playback), overall commercial reaction (liking), and commercial diagnostics. Representative examples are given in Table 13-1.

The ARF Copy Research Validity Project studied five pairs of commercials for established packaged goods that had produced significant sales differences in split-cable copy tests. The pairs were commercials that had not previously aired from advertisers making minimal use of print in the test markets. The commercials were the only ones in use during the tests. At least six months of sales data were available. The Validity Project found that copy testing is helpful in identifying commercials known to be generating incremental sales. The most surprising finding is a strong relationship between likability of the copy and its effects on sales. On the other hand, the IRI "How Advertising Works" study found that the relationship between standard recall and persuasion scores and the sales impact for established brands is tenuous, at best.

TABLE 13-1 Copy-Testing Measures

Measure	Example
Persuasion	Overall brand rating
Brand salience	Top-of-mind awareness
Recall	Recall brand from category cue
Communications (playback)	Main point communication
Commercial reaction (liking)	Impression of commercial (average)
Commercial diagnostics	Told me something new about the product that I did not know before

MEDIA SELECTION

The objective in media planning is to select the set of TV and radio programs, magazines, newspapers, and other media vehicles, including online Web (i.e., banner ads), that will maximize profits within a given budget. Your problem is that the optimum allocation tends to vary for each individual organization. Computer models have been developed to help evaluate media and audience data. The success of these models depends on understanding the appropriateness of media vehicles and on knowledge of how media are matched with markets.

Reach Versus Frequency

The total impact of an advertising campaign can be measured by counting the number of exposures that result from *reaching* different people and multiplying by the average *frequency* of ad exposure per person. Thus, we have

$$Total\ exposures = Reach \times Frequency$$

This implies that high total exposure can be obtained by reaching a large number of people with a few ads or by exposing a small number of potential buyers to many ads. Your problem is to decide which combination of advertising reach and frequency is best for a particular product at a point in time.

When an advertiser has a message that has to be heard only once, a media schedule that maximizes reach is used. The idea is to have every exposure appeal to a different potential buyer. Most of the retail advertising that emphasizes special sales and prices falls into this category. Also, many of the direct-mail promotions used for book and record clubs are designed to make a sale on the first impression and reach is crucial to their success. In addition, reach can be important when introducing new products to the marketplace. This is especially true when cents-off coupons are offered to encourage trial use and the firm wants each potential buyer to get only one coupon. When emphasizing reach, duplication is an issue. *Duplication* in advertising occurs because some of the individuals exposed to an ad in one vehicle will also see the ad in a second vehicle. This suggests that the more media vehicles you buy, the greater the chance for duplication and the more likely you are to have diminishing returns to advertising.

Continuity in advertising is used to keep the name of the product in the buyer's mind so that when a purchase is planned, the company's brand will be remembered. *Recency* is particularly important for frequently purchased consumer goods for which brand loyalty is low. Reminder ads can also be used to promote the sale of products and services that are bought infrequently. Funeral homes, insurance agents, and car dealers all employ continuity in their advertising so they will be considered when the buyer is ready to make a purchase. Given budget constraints that most firms face, continuity requires that reach be stressed.

Alternatively, some advertisers must repeat ads frequently to get the buyer's attention and bring about attitude changes that precede purchase. In these situations, the emphasis is on the number of exposures per person rather than the reach of the campaign. This approach is based on research, which shows that recall of ads and purchase intentions increase with the number of exposures per person. For many consumer products, the best exposure frequency, called the "effective frequency," seems to be at least two, and perhaps three, exposures within a purchase cycle. Given budget constraints that most firms face, effective frequency requires that advertising be pulsed.

Because of differences in products and market conditions, it is probably foolish to generalize about the optimum combination of reach and frequency for an advertising campaign. However, managers usually have better data on the reach of media vehicles than they have on duplication and the effects of repetition on sales. This suggests that media selection will often emphasize reach, with a more subjective adjustment made for frequency.

Media Vehicle Appropriateness

Media vehicles are not passive conductors of messages and can often influence the effectiveness of the message. Factors that determine the appropriateness of media vehicles include editorial climate, product fit, technical capabilities, comparative advertising strategy, target population receptiveness, and the product distribution system.

A vehicle has an image and personality that can add to or detract from a message. *Sunset* is regarded as an expert source and *Vogue* as a prestige source. The relative value will depend on the campaign objectives (awareness versus attitude change versus image creation), the target segment, the campaign tactics (image versus reason-why advertising), and the product.

Media are believed to work in different ways. At each state in the purchase process, one medium may be superior to another. In relation to TV commercials, print advertisements are less able to command attention, are more able to arouse personal involvement, and are more likely to cause conscious, discrete attitude change.

Consumers can pay *no* attention to a print advertisement or deliberately expose themselves to one. They do the latter when they are seeking information for decision making. Consumers can concentrate longer on an advertising theme and thereby make more personal connections with it. This means they can become more personally involved in print advertisements for products that possess intrinsic interest. Because attention is voluntary, the consumer is more likely to be consciously influenced. Attitude change under conditions of high involvement occurs through the process of dissonance resolution.

Even when customers do not watch a TV commercial, they usually listen to it. Their involvement is low and they are unaware that their attitudes are slowly being modified by the onslaught of repeated exposure to the message. Their attitudes may change more rapidly later when the source of the message is forgotten. This phenomenon is called the *sleeper effect*. When the consumer ultimately faces a purchasing situation, these shifts in attitude move to a more conscious level.

These differences suggest that print and TV advertising may be used most effectively in combination. One may be more suitable than the other for a particular step in the intermediate process. Thus, you need to match the media with company goals. Next, the manager must match the media with the target audience.

Matching Media with Markets

Advertisers prefer media whose audience characteristics are closest to the profile of market characteristics of their customers. Characteristics by which the target population may be identified include demographic, psychographic, and purchase behavior variables. Matching takes two forms: direct matching, in which media are matched to product usage variables from syndicated product-media research services, and indirect matching, in which media are matched to demographics or psychographic profiles. The latter is useful when target markets are defined using a company's market research survey, and media usage is obtained from a syndicated research service. Managers also need methods to help them select media that show the best combination of cost and exposure value.

MEASURING ADVERTISING EFFECTIVENESS

A firm's ability to measure the effectiveness of its advertising is crucial to developing more efficient advertisements, to determining the level of expenditures, and to allocating available funds to media. As soon as the relationship between advertising pressure and effectiveness is known, a firm can calculate the advertising budget size, compare various media, and select vehicles within the same medium.

The four most commonly used measures of advertising effectiveness are changes in sales, number of inquiries received, increases in knowledge of the product, and attitude changes. In the case of online advertising, the measure is click-throughs, the number of times a banner ad was actually clicked on by a guest. Although the intermediate measures of effectiveness can provide helpful insights, sales is the best criterion to evaluate advertising results.

The analysis of the influence of advertising on the sales of a product or service is a complex undertaking. The methods available for measuring advertising elasticity include controlled experiments and econometric procedures. Controlled field experiments can provide good data, but they are expensive. Econometric methods are more popular for studying the impact of advertising on the sales of existing products. We begin with a discussion of the effects of advertising on demand.

Effects of Advertising on Demand

Advertising can increase the demand for a particular brand within a product category or raise per capita consumption—that is, encourage customers "to choose" or "to use." The competitive activity generated when brands attempt to increase their own sales may result in an increase in total demand.

At an operational level, advertising is measured in monetary units and we talk of advertising expenditures or *adspend.* After all, you need this number to budget and to calculate your profits. But this is an internal measure. You also need an external measure that expresses advertising *delivery* to prospects. Here we speak of opportunity-to-see (OTS), television rating points (TVR), or gross rating points (GRP). GRP is calculated by multiplying a program's audience share by the number of times an ad is run. If an ad is shown 14 times a week on two programs, you will get

4 showings in a time slot with a 12 rating =   48 GRPs
10 showings in a time slot with a 9 rating =   <u>90</u> GRPs
Total for the week   138 GRPs

Since ratings are expressed as percentages, the average person will be exposed 1.38 times. Of course, some people will not see the ad at all and others could be exposed 14 times. Depending on the media mix employed, the same adspend could generate quite different GRPs. A further refinement comes when we do household-level measurement of the actual number of advertising *exposures* received by each household.

The impact of advertising is often spread over several periods. Not everyone who sees an advertisement in a particular week will buy in the same week. Consequently, we allocate advertising delivery in part to when it actually happens and distribute the rest in decreasing amounts to subsequent periods. This new advertising variable is called *adstock.* An example of this process is shown in Figure 13-6.

The sales response function for advertising may be S-shaped. At low levels of advertising, sales response may be negligible. The advertising does not have sufficient weight to break through the clutter of advertisements. At some *threshold,* sales response begins to increase at an increasing rate. Finally, additional advertising produces further sales, but at a decreasing rate. This is the region of *diminishing returns to scale.* Empirical evidence shows that this is the region in which most major brands operate.

The sales response functions for two brands in the same product category are shown in Figure 13-7. These are important brands in a very large package-goods category. Data are from the 20 largest U.S. markets covering 1.5 years of weekly scanning and media data. The horizontal axis shows television gross rating points (GRPs or TVRs) that have been adjusted for adstock. The vertical axis is a sales index scaled so that 1.0 corresponds to no advertising. For example, a continuous delivery of 100 GRP stock for Brand A corresponds to about

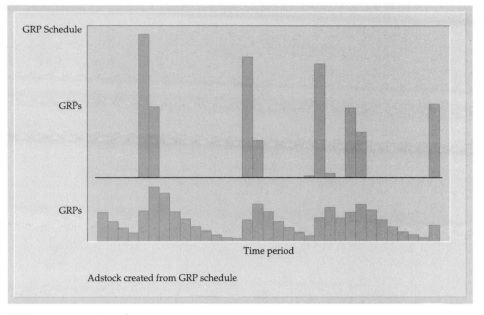

FIGURE 13-6 Adstock

an index of 1.15. This level of stock will increase sales 15 percent over what sales would have been with no advertising. Brand A shows diminishing returns to advertising.

One way to measure the impact of advertising is by calculating advertising elasticities. The formula is

$$E_{adv} = \frac{\% \text{ change in sales}}{\% \text{ change in advertising}}$$

A representative advertising elasticity for a fast-moving consumer good is probably on the order of 0.10. This means that doubling the advertising spending will only increase sales volume by 10 percent. Research has shown that advertising elasticities typically range in value from 0.03 to 0.25.

Tracking

Consistent theme advertising maintains the saliency of the mental connections that constitute the brand. You should then track the advertising memories that people associate with brands. One company that does this is Millward Brown.

APPLYING
. . . to
Consumer
Packaged
Goods
Marketing

Andrex toilet paper is closely associated with the benefits of being "soft, strong, and long." These associations were developed, maintained, and enhanced from advertising. Andrex has used a series of "puppy" ads. One specific advertisement was known as "little boy" and featured a young boy sitting on the toilet and watching a puppy run off with the toilet roll. Millward Brown tracked this advertisement in Great Britain as the ad consolidated the traditional associations and added some more emotional strands. One question they ask consumers is, "when you think of all the advertising you've seen for Andrex, what if anything, do you particularly remember from it?" The results are shown in Figure 13-8. Notice how heavy media weight gradually brings images from the "little boy" ad into people's minds in connection with Andrex. This approach gives us information about when the communications job is done. Often measures of brand loyalty and brand equity are included

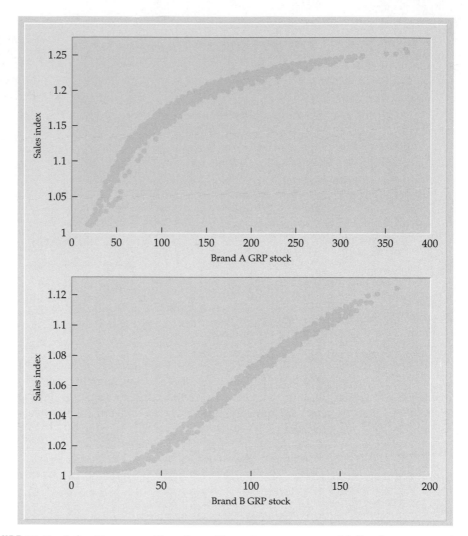

FIGURE 13-7   Sales Response Functions (From Laurence N. Gold, "Let's Heavy Up in St. Louis and See What Happens," *Journal of Advertising Research,* Vol. 33, No. 6 [November/December 1992], pp. 34–35.)

in tracking studies and improvements in these measures are taken as indicators of advertising's success.

Qualitative research in the form of before-and-after brand image maps can indicate whether or not your advertising is working as desired. Silentnight launched a new bed in the United Kingdom. Unfortunately, a serious industrial dispute that hampered production mired the launch down. After the industrial dispute was ended, Silentnight needed to relaunch an improved version of the product. The ultimate Sleep System was a unique combination of mattress and base that offered individual support for two sleepers no matter what the differential in weight, support right up to the edge of the bed to eliminate roll off, and a posturized zone of extra springs in the central third to provide extra support where the body weight was the greatest. The creative advertising solution for communicating these features was a unique product demonstration that was sufficiently novel to overcome customer apathy and to convincingly communicate the product's principal benefits. The stars of this demonstration were a hippo and a duck! Consumers reacted enthusi-

APPLYING
. . . to
Consumer
Semi-
Durable
Marketing

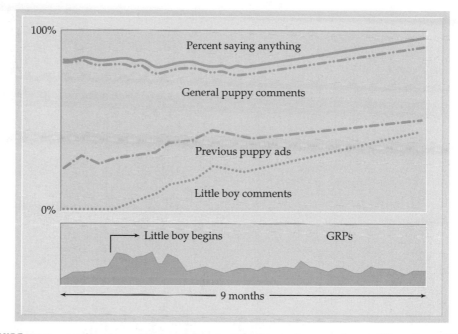

FIGURE 13-8 Andrex Long-Term Ad Awareness (From Jeremy Green, "How Repetition and Consistency Build Mental Connections," in *People, Brands & Advertising* [Millward Brown, 1992], p. 48.)

astically. The establishment of Silentnight's differential positioning is tracked over 18 months in Figure 13-9*a,* while the improvement in perception of the brand is tracked over 24 months in Figure 13-9*b.*

Experimental Methods

Successful users of field experiments include AT&T, Nabisco, and Campbell Soup. AT&T used a dual-cable television system in conjunction with its own long-distance usage tracking system to test the impact of a new "Cost of Visit" campaign against the existing "Reach Out" campaign. Households in test markets are connected to either an "A" or "B" cable in checkerboard fashion. This allows different ads to be sent to each group. The experimental design executed by AT&T is shown in Table 13-2. The test results indicated that, over a five-year period, the "Cost of Visit" campaign would generate some $100 million more than the "Reach Out" campaign.

RJR Nabisco was resigned to slow growth from its biscuit division because it was in a mature industry. Nabisco experimented with saturation advertising aimed at small population segments and found that the whole cookie and cracker business was underpromoted. Nabisco advertised heavily for its 40-year-old Ritz crackers, in six different geographical markets, representing 3.2 percent of the adult population in America. The buying behavior of this group in the face of heavy TV and store promotions was monitored for one year. The purchases of a control group were also recorded. The experimental group had a 16 percent increase in sales. Nabisco modified its promotional strategy in light of its experimental findings.

Campbell Soup has conducted a series of experiments and subsequent analyses that have shown that budget levels generally had little or no impact on sales of well-established brands. Changes in copy strategy, media selection, media mix, and targeting had a substantial payout. Products studied included Campbell's Condensed Soup, Chunky Soups, Franco-American, V-8, and Swanson.

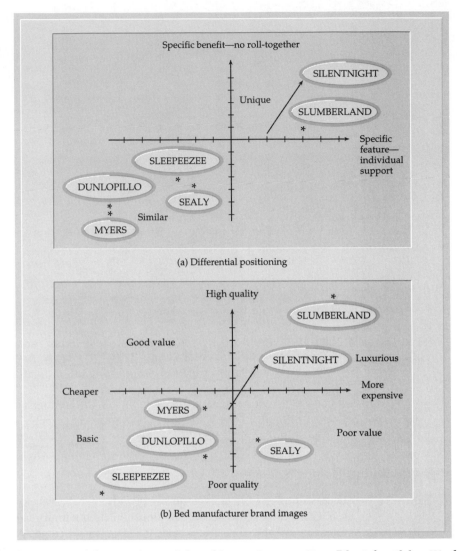

FIGURE 13-9   Brand Maps (From "The Ultimate Success Story," in *Advertising Works 6*, Paul Feldwick, ed. [Henley-on-Thames: NTC Publications, 1991], pp. 59–60.)

ADVERTISING VERSUS DIRECT MARKETING

While general mass media advertising allows you to target your audience somewhat, ultimately your customers self select themselves while remaining anonymous. Direct marketing, on the other hand, sells to identifiable customers at their location. As discussed in Chapter 10, direct marketing has the added benefit of delivering your product directly to the customer's door. Advertising is often used as part of direct marketing to generate

TABLE 13-2   AT&T Field Experiment

Study Phase	5-Month Preassessment	15-Month Test	6-Month Reassessment
Cable A	"Feelings"	"Reach Out"	"Reach Out"/local company
Cable B	↓	"Cost of Visit"	↓

TABLE 13-3 **Comparison of Direct Marketing and General Mass-Marketing Advertising**

Direct Marketing	General Mass-Marketing Advertising
Selling to individuals, with customers identifiable by name, address, and purchase behavior (personal, targetable, ability to vary the message by segment, measurable, ability to capture data).	Mass selling, with buyers identified as broad groups and sharing common demographic and psychographic characteristics (cost efficient where identity of customers is unknown).
Products have the added value of distribution to the customer's door as an important product benefit.	Product benefits do not typically include distribution to the customer's door.
The medium is the marketplace.	The retail outlet is the marketplace.
Marketing controls product all the way through delivery.	The marketer typically loses control as the product enters the distribution stream.
Uses targeted media.	Uses mass media.
Is hard for competitors to monitor—the stealth factor.	Can be monitored by competitors using syndicated services.
Advertising is used to generate an immediate inquiry or order, with a specific order.	Advertising is used for its cumulative effect over time in building awareness, image, loyalty, and benefit recall. Purchase action is deferred.
Repetition is used within an ad or mailing.	Repetition is used over a period of time.
Consumer feels a high perceived risk—product bought unseen, distant recourse.	Consumer feels less risk—has direct contact with product and direct recourse.

Source: Adapted from DMA's Direct Marketing Institute; and Jim Kobs, *Profitable Direct Marketing* (Lincolnwood, IL.; NTC Business Books, 1991), p. 13.

inquiries and orders. A comparison between direct marketing and general mass marketing advertising is laid out in Table 13-3. The main distinction between direct marketing—and especially interactive marketing—and general mass marketing is that of a dialogue versus a monologue.

SUMMARY

Advertising can assume an important role in building awareness and providing information about goods and services. Advertising begins with the determination of objectives and goals. Next you need to set the size of the advertising budget. This can be done using percentage-of-sales methods, the task procedure, or normative approaches. Given a budget, you need to develop appropriate themes and campaign materials. The next step is to pick an appropriate set of media vehicles. Advertising agencies are often employed to help with this work. Finally, you need to measure the effects of advertising expenditures.

NOTE

1. Stephen Miller and Lisette Berry, "Brand Salience versus Brand Image: Two Theories of Advertising Effectiveness," *Journal of Advertising Research,* Vol. 38, No. 5 (October 1998), pp. 77–82.

SUGGESTED READING

Achenbaum, Alvin A. "Reversing the Advertising Productivity Crisis," *Marketing Management,* Vol. 1, No. 3 (1992), pp. 22–27.

Gold, Laurence N. "Let's Heavy Up in St. Louis and See What Happens," *Journal of Advertising Research,* Vol. 33, No. 6 (November/December 1992), pp. 31–38.

REFERENCES

Broadbent, Simon. *Accountable Advertising* (Henley-on-Thames: Admap Publications, 1997).

Duckworth, Gary. *Advertising Works* 9 (Henley-on-Thames: NTC Publications, 1997).

Forker, Olan D., and Ronald W. Ward. *Commodity Advertising: The Economics and Measurement of Generic Programs* (New York: Lexington Books, 1993).

Franzen, Giep. *Advertising Effectiveness* (Henley-on-Thames: Admap Publications, 1994).

Jones, John Philip. *When Ads Work* (New York: Lexington Books, 1995).

McDonald, Colin. *How Advertising Works* (Henley-on-Thames, NTC Publications, 1992).

Millward Brown International Plc. *People, Brands & Advertising* (London: 1992).

Randazzo, Sal. *Mythmaking on Madison Avenue* (Chicago: Probus Publishing, 1993).

Vakratsas, Demetrios, and Tim Amber. "How Advertising Works," *Journal of Marketing,* Vol. 63, No. 1 (January 1999), pp. 26–43.

QUESTIONS

1. The Gillette Company fosters a unified strategic position for its men's shaving products by advertising that it's the "Best a man can get." Develop an advertising theme for positioning its women's shaving products—one that would position Gillette's products as an essential part of a woman's beauty regime and as the key to being physically and psychologically ready for anything.

2. The Internet is the most-hyped and fastest growing medium yet invented. Ironically, Internet Service Providers (ISPs) must use traditional media to attract more customers. Construct a media strategy to help an ISP gain customers.

3. The network television business is built around the belief that advertisers covet youth. Programming emphasizes sassy sitcoms and steamy soap operas that appeal to 18- to 49-year-olds, and especially adults under 35. The premise is that this group is free spending, impressionable, and trendsetting. Meanwhile, the growing number of older viewers is more affluent than ever. They are the best customers for luxury cars, cold and allergy medicines, food, toothpaste, detergents, computers, travel, medical services, financial services, and entertainment. Can the networks and advertisers continue to justify their devotion to youth?

4. Off-price shopping is not unlike a treasure hunt. Shoppers can find designer and name-brand clothes, shoes, crystal, and jewelry for 20 to 60 percent below some department store prices. When off-price retailer TJX Cos., known for its TJ Maxx chain, bought its rival Marshalls, Marshalls' sales were falling and profits were nonexistent. TJX's solution was to slash Marshalls' ad spending from 2.5 percent of sales to 1.5 percent of sales—this when many retailers spend 5 to 10 percent of sales. What do you think of TJX's turnaround strategy? Marshalls' ads had frequently featured new shipments of clothes or highlighted the price of a number of products, noting how much of a discount

they represented. Do you think TJX should change Marshalls' advertising message appeals? If so, why and how?

5. September is always a blockbuster month for women's fashion magazines. One study found readers of *Harper's Bazaar* would have to slog through 127 pages before they got to the first feature article; for *Elle* it was 140 pages, and for *Vogue* it was 128 pages. Indeed, 77 percent of the pages in *Vogue*, America's top-selling women's fashion magazine, were advertisements; and *Elle* ran 32 ad pages before its table of contents page! Why would advertisers continue flock to these magazines? How does an advertiser stand out?

6. With the threat of an AIDS epidemic, public health organizations ran massive media campaigns to stress the seriousness of AIDS and that everyone was at risk. These campaigns created a high level of awareness and generated anxiety. However, for health organizations to maintain publicity at a high intensity was impossible. When the publicity died down, people believed the threat of AIDS had lessened. The swing from alarm to complacency needs to be addressed. Construct a media campaign for preventing HIV/AIDS slipping off the public agenda and for encouraging sexually active heterosexuals (demographically 16 to 34-year-olds with two or more sexual partners in the last 12 months) to use condoms. This target group has already forsaken the sensible advice of abstinence outside of marriage.

7. Consumers discovered that boxes of Dassant's New England Pumpkin Spice Bread & Muffin Mix were not made in New England and did not contain any pumpkin. Is this an example of deceptive advertising?

8. The economic turmoil in Asia generated a new experience—recession—for most professionals in that region. What is the primary role of advertising during an economic downturn? To what extent should the advertising budget be adjusted?

9. What responsibility does an advertiser have to ensure that advertisements meet the mores of society? To ensure that the editorial contents of media vehicles in which advertisements are placed meet these mores? Who determines the mores of society? Are marketers contributing to the decline of moral values in society?

10. The brand manager for a salad dressing would like to assess the impact of advertising versus price on the brand's sales. She first removed the impact of temporary promotions. She wants to focus on the impact of base price and brand awareness on base sales. These data can be found in file dressingdat.sav. To be able to do "what if" simulations, she decides a linear regression should be estimated. What would be the incremental base sales volume from a $0.10 base price decrease? an awareness increase of 200?

14 SALES PROMOTION AND PUBLIC RELATIONS

*E*ach element in the basic marketing mix is supplemented by a group of marketing instruments whose main purpose is to induce immediate buying behavior by strengthening the basic mix elements for a short period of time. This group of instruments is called the *promotion mix.* Specific support activities are often classified as either sales promotions or public relations. *Sales promotions* have been defined as "action-focused marketing events whose purpose is to have a direct impact on the behavior of the firm's customers."[1] Sales promotions involve such activities as specialty advertising, rebates, couponing, temporary price reduction labels, bonus packs, samplings, premiums, point-of-purchase material, trade allowances, sales and dealer incentives, trade shows, exhibits, and demonstrations. *Public relations* are actions that promote goodwill between a firm and its customers. Public relations involve activities such as customer service, crisis management, consumer education, publicity, special events, and sponsorships.

Companies make considerable investments in sales promotion as a strategy for building and maintaining brand dominance. Although you might believe most of a company's promotion budget is spent on media advertising, the various sales promotion activities taken as a whole involve much larger expenditures. Product marketers in the United States spend about 25.1 percent of their promotional budgets on media advertising, 49.5 percent on trade promotions, and 25.4 percent on consumer promotions. Trade promotion passed media advertising as the leading category in the mid-1980s. The relative importance of some components of promotion is indicated in Figure 14–1. Sampling, particularly in-store, continues to grow in popularity. Companies try to weave sales promotion into their marketing strategies in a way to create a "brand experience" among consumers. We begin by discussing the elements of the sales promotion mix in more detail.

SALES PROMOTION MIX

The sales promotion mix can be described in the same terms as the marketing mix. The instruments that support each element of the marketing mix are shown in Table 14–1.

TABLE 14-1   Promotion Mix

Mix Element Supported	Instruments Used
Product	Samples, bonus product, premiums
Price	Coupons, temporary discounts, temporary price reduction labels, refunds, slotting fees, temporary favorable terms of payment and credit, end-of-season sales
Distribution	Trade promotions, point-of-purchase materials
Communications	
Personal selling	Temporary demonstrations, trade shows, exhibitions, sales force contests
Mass	Customer contests, sweepstakes
Publicity	Special events, press bulletins, press conferences, tours by journalists

Source: Based on Walter van Waterschoot and Christophe Van den Bulte. "The 4P Classification of the Marketing Mix Revisited," *Journal of Marketing.* Vol. 56, No. 4 (October 1992), pp. 83–93

Product

The main type of product promotion is the *sample.* A sample is a free trial of a product. A sample is usually smaller than the actual product and is given away at no charge. About 90 percent of sampling is for new products.

There are a variety of ways to deliver a sample: instore, direct mail, on doorknobs, and in plastic bags along with newspapers. The most effective way to get product trial is to mail or distribute free samples directly to customers' homes. This is illustrated in Marketing in Action box 14–1. Sampling efficiently requires precise target market information. Since buying Carol Wright from Donnelly Marketing in the mid-1990s, CoxDirect has revamped the mailing list to identify more promotionally responsive households. It created a 25-million-name, household mailing file from sources including retailers, manufacturers, personal

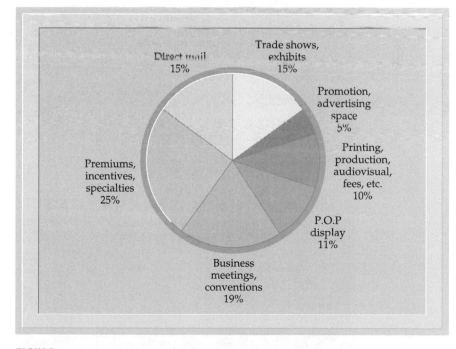

FIGURE 14-1   Importance of Sales Promotion Methods

Sampling with Co-Op Mailings

The best place to sample herbal tea drinkers is in a soothing setting, like their own living rooms. That was the thinking of Thomas J. Lipton Co.'s Canadian division when it looked for trial of its new Bedtime Blend flavor. "Those who drink it tend to drink a lot of it. It's very important to find those

(continues)

Courtesy Lipton, a Division of UL Canada, Inc.

people." Lipton turned to direct mailer ICOM to locate the niche target and reach them with a test offer. ICOM surveys Canadians with detailed questionnaires deriving household-level information on buying behavior. Surveys go to one out of every four households every six months, and the company receives a better than 20 percent response. "Their survey showed who the heavy users were." A Lipton sample was sent out to medium and heavy users and competitive users in co-op mailing with other offers. Lipton paid $150 per thousand to be in the co-op mailing, not including the cost of the samples. The tea sample, plus a 75 cent coupon, appeared in 255,000 of the 550,000 envelopes in the mailing. Initial response was positive based on coupon redemptions and calls through an 800 number.

"When you do a mass sampling for niche categories there is a tremendous amount of waste, even if you consider demographics," said ICOM. "Our mailing is based on purchase behavior." Lipton estimated it would have cost 15 times more to reach each 1,000 people in-store.

— *Direct mail zooms samples to select user segments.*

Source: "Pushing the Envelope," *PROMO,* September 1998, p. 51.

computer sellers, and pet shop owner lists. "We wanted this mailed to families with children who own a house with an average income of $52,000. They spend more money on everything." It then plotted neighborhoods around the top 50 food, drug, and mass merchant retailers in 160 markets.

Research has shown that 75 percent of the homes will try the free samples and 25 percent of these will buy the product. Up to 20 percent more users can be obtained by including a coupon with the free sample. Sampling should be used if the product exhibits a demonstrable superiority, if the concept is difficult to convey by advertising, if a sizable budget is available for a broad usage category, or if product class dominance is sought.

Sampling can be expensive but it does ensure that people will try the product and it has proved to be one of the most powerful promotional devices available to marketing managers. Moreover, the *cost per customer converted* is much lower than any other promotion because there is no barrier to trial.

Another product promotion is to give all persons making a purchase a free gift, known as a *premium*. For example, Frito corn chips has employed a promotion in which they attach flower seeds to packages of the product. A variation on the gift idea is the offer of merchandise at low prices to customers who send in labels from packages. These *self-liquidating premiums* are one of the least expensive of all promotional devices because the revenue derived from customers usually covers most of the costs of the promotion. The "self-liquidating" feature is made possible by volume purchases and the elimination of the normally high retail margins on premium-type merchandise. The most desirable premiums are showy items that inspire retailers to build off-shelf displays and encourage usage of the product by the consumer.

Price

The primary consumer price promotion is the *coupon*. Where promotional funds are limited, "cents-off" coupons can be an effective means of getting product trial. The average coupon face value in the United States is about 70 cents. In addition, retailers earn an 8-cent handling fee per coupon. U.S. manufacturers of consumer packaged goods distribute about 250 billion coupons a year. The largest coupon vehicle in the United States is the free-standing insert (FSI), the glossy coupon-in-a-print ad typically distributed in Sunday newspapers. The coupons are also sent by mail, appear in magazine and daily newspaper ads, are attached on pack, or enclosed in pack. The number of coupons returned is one measure of the impact of the promotion.

The typical coupon shopper in the United States is a middle-aged married working white woman who has a household income of $29,000 and who knocks $6 off her weekly $74 grocery bill by using coupons. Lower-income families aren't exposed to as many coupons because the vast majority of coupons are distributed through newspapers and magazines and such families spend less than average for reading materials.

A slight variation is to offer the consumer a package with a special *temporary price reduction (TPR) label.* A "cents-off" designation indicates the amount the regular retail price is supposedly reduced during the special promotion. Although the manufacturer may lower the price to the dealer, there is no assurance that the retailer will pass the savings on to the consumer. Manufacturers have encountered sharp trade resistance to "cents-off" packs because retailers resent handling problems and duplicate inventories. The inability of the manufacturer to adequately control "cents-off" promotions makes this technique less desirable than couponing. On-pack instant coupons have largely replaced it.

Because coupons suffer from misredemption problems, some manufacturers prefer cash *refunds* or *rebates.* Although these refunds carry higher values, a much lower redemption rate may be expected. Many people buy with the intention of sending in for the refund, but never get around to it.[2]

Distribution

Point-of-purchase (P-O-P) displays can increase sales markedly. Numerous studies have proved having P-O-P at retail will increase sales 5 to 15 percent above normal movements. The key is to get the retailer to use them. Stores are inundated with P-O-P, especially during certain times of the year. Stores often have no idea what to do with many of the P-O-P materials they receive, so they get left sitting in the back room. If manufacturers emphasize retail compliance—ensuring that stores and merchants put up all the P-O-P they receive, sales increases can soar as high as 40 percent.[3] See Marketing in Action box 14–2.

Communication

Manufacturers frequently try to build customer interest and sales volumes with *contests, sweepstakes,* and other games of chance. The idea is to attract consumer attention by offering substantial merchandise and cash prizes to a few lucky winners. Entry blanks and lottery tickets are dispensed at the retail level to tie the promotion to the sales of the product. The main objective of most contests is to stimulate sales with in-store displays of the product rather than produce a large number of entries. For on-line merchandisers, however, encouraging visits to their Web pages is important as discussed in Marketing in Action box 14–3.

The activities that have been discussed represent only a few of the many techniques that can be used in creating a promotional strategy for the firm. The only real limit to the variety of promotions is the depth of the imagination of the managers in charge.

TYPES OF PROMOTIONS

Promotions can be directed at intermediaries in your channels, in which case they are called trade promotions, or they can be directed at the ultimate buyer, and are called consumer promotions. These two kinds of promotions are usually used in concert, especially for new product introductions.

Trade Promotions

Trade promotions are designed to improve dealer cooperation, and they include such things as training sessions for sales personnel to familiarize them with the goods and services of a

MARKETING IN ACTION *14-2*

APPLYING
. . . to
Consumer
Automotive
Products
Marketing

Winning the P-O-P Compliance Game

Mobil used an outside merchandiser, Professional Inventory Management and Merchandising Services (PIMMS), to effect a huge retail tie-in for its "Mobil Oil Tour" concert series starring country music stars Reba McEntire and Brooks & Dunn. PIMMS asked store personnel of automotive chains and mass merchandisers to make island or endcap case displays of Mobil 1 motor oil and use concert-related P-O-P to recommend the product to customers. Stores were supplied with a standee promoting the tour's stars plus window posters, counter cards, and take-one pads affixed with offers to win concert tickets and CDs.

Mobil was worried about its ability to track the fate of all that P-O-P. "The number of personnel available for monitoring the campaign came down to seven. There was no way seven field reps could cover a promo of that size. We needed a special promotion force to give us information from the field." With the tour running from February through the end of the year, PIMMS sent mystery shoppers into several participating retail chains to verify and reward promotion compliance. Mobil's chief concern was to find out if stores were putting up the P-O-P displays and if sales staffers were recommending the designated products, which was part of the commitment retailers had made to the company.

Once mystery shoppers began working a particular city, store managers would call other stores to tell their peers that compliance prizes were being handed out. In addition to mass merchants, PIMMS mystery shoppers visited automotive aftermarket retailers including AutoZone, Discount Auto Parts, Grand Auto, and VIP Discount Auto. The secret merchandisers checked out a total of 1,000 stores coast to coast, hitting on an average of 25 stores per major market.

Posing as average shoppers, the PIMMS spies first determined that the proper window signage and P-O-P displays were in place. Then, working from three prepared scenarios, they asked retailer personnel several questions about choosing a motor oil. When store employees made an endorsement for Mobil, the mystery shoppers gave them vouchers for free concert tickets.

The campaign was a complete success, with a compliance rate of 100 percent scored by stores visited by the shoppers, including stores that had no advance notice of the shoppers' arrival.

— *You need to get serious about getting your displays up.*

Source: Richard Sale, "The Display Police," *Promo*, March 1999, pp. 80–81, 84.

Courtesy Mobil Oil Corporation

MARKETING IN ACTION *14-3*

Web Promotions

CDNow Inc., a leading Internet music store, was once called by *USA Today* "the most recognized e-commerce brand." CDNow ran the first million dollar promo on the Internet and the prizes ranged from phonecards to instant cash to cruises. CDNow Million Dollar Music Mania! instant-win sweepstakes awarded more than 60,000 prizes, as well as a chance for customers to win a $1 million grand prize. The contest was offered to hundreds of thousands of participants in 26 countries. With each online purchase, the CDNow customer received an electronic "Scratch & Win" game card that showed instantly if the participant had won anything. Since chances were one-in-five, there were many repeat players. Each time a customer made a purchase, he was automatically entered in a weekly vacation sweepstakes for eight world-class destinations such as Paris, London, and Rome.

For CDNow the value of the promo lay in the way it built the CDNow brand. "Brand exposure is one of our goals and, no matter what, the repeated exposure is absolutely crucial. The aim is also to have fun, to make winning a game, and make the game part of an explicit bargain—rewarding customers for engaging in a dialog with CDNow." When visitors repeat, they feel more at home at the site, can move around better, and view more frequently the offers from CDNow and the merchants and retailers with whom CDNow partners for its marketing campaigns.

CDNow's more recent music trivia promotion, the Honorary Roadie Sweepstakes, produced the greatest outpouring of letters praising the brand. CDNow got comments saying, "We love your store," or "You give away great prizes." CDNow wanted to reinforce itself as the music authority on the Net. To do this, they needed content. By setting up a trivia game about music, CDNow could much more quickly take the customer through the store to learn about its product range, including which bios of musical figures were available or which record jackets offered vital music information. And it did all this in the guise of testing the consumer's knowledge of the field. (Did you know that the Grateful Dead was originally called Mother McCree's Uptown Jug Champions?) Ian Plimsoll, the "world's greatest roadie" character featured in CDNow radio and television ads, acted as guide for game players. Correct answers won entry in an Honorary Roadie Sweepstakes that offered top prizes of airplane tickets to any destination in the continental United States or Canada.

CDNow measures traffic and session time on their site, as well as the purchase behavior of repeat visitors. The trivia contest changes each week to ensure that players return. "We have huge customer loyalty. At least 50 percent of players are repeat customers."

CDNow is starting to partner with big, established brands. The Plimsoll roadie character was created solely to blend CDNow's offline and online branding effort. The company just completed a holiday promotion with Coca-Cola in which Coke linked its Web site with CDNow in an offer of a special Christmas CD from EMI Music. It also hooked up with Prodigy to offer new customers of the Internet service provider $10 gifts at CDNow.

— *Real promotion strategies and tactics can be applied to online marketing.*

Source: Scott Thurm, "CDNow," *Promo,* January 1999, pp. 30–32.

---

particular company. A related procedure is to give dealer salespeople special gifts or bonuses when they push the sale of certain products. Dealer interest can also be improved by providing attractive point-of-purchase (P-O-P) materials. As an added incentive, prizes are frequently offered to the merchants who construct the best displays utilizing the product and promotional materials. Perhaps the most popular promotional device directed at distributors is the "deal" or special reduced price offer. "Deals" are short-run discounts designed to build dealer stocks and to stimulate retail sales. They may be expressed in terms of lower prices or as "free" merchandise offered for minimum orders. Another effective promotional technique is a sales contest for distributors. Dealers who sell the most merchandise during a certain period are rewarded with vacations in Hawaii, mink coats, and cash bonuses. All promotional efforts are designed to raise sales, but most dealer programs have the goal of improving relations with those who sell the product to the final consumer. Better dealer relations can increase the number of distributors willing to carry the product, enlarge display areas, and gain acceptance of larger inventories and new items.

Trade promotions have been increasing—reflecting the increasing power of the retailer. A survey of product marketers found that 87 percent implemented account-specific promotions for key retail customers. Information Resources, Inc. analyzes a number of trade promotions annually and finds that very few of them pay out—IRI estimates it is less than 20 percent. We will return to this point shortly.

Consumer Promotions

Consumer-oriented promotional activities are designed to induce consumers to try products. A proportion of those introduced to a product will become steady customers. Moreover, brand switching is a fact of life for low-cost, frequently purchased products. You want to gain more customers than you lose in this churn. Thus, getting back former customers through encouraging retrial is very important. The relative importance of alternative consumer promotions is shown in Figure 14-2.

Price promotions may have a "mortgaging" effect as consumers purchase for inventory. When the brand returns to regular shelf price, sales may be initially slow as consumers draw down promotion-subsidized stocks. Thus, manufacturers will also often drop coupons to head off a big splash by the competition. Timed to reach consumers in an area just before a competitor launches a product or sponsors a special event such as a concert, coupons effectively knock consumers out of the market by encouraging them to stock up their home pantries.

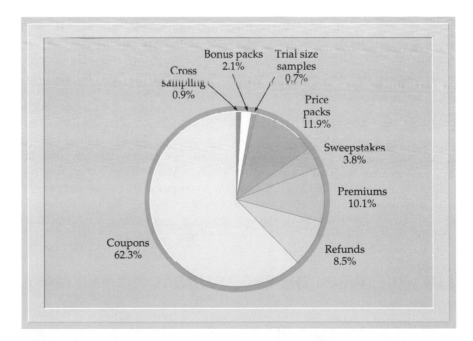

FIGURE 14-2   Consumer Promotions (From Dancer Fitzgerald Sample's "Consumer Promotion Report")

Retailers use price promotions to build traffic. Because they might not be profitable in their own right, but encourage purchases of profitable products, they are known as "loss leaders." Retailers also use price promotions to clear inventories of obsolete products.

New Product Promotions

If a new package good does not establish itself in six months, the lost momentum is hard, if not impossible, to recover. A comprehensive sales promotion plan is consequently a necessity for new product introductions. New products must first be explained to the company's own salespeople. They should be enthusiastic about the product and be convinced that it will be a winner. Second, trade awareness should be built so that when the salespeople arrive, the buyer has some favorable predisposition toward the product.

The presentation to the trade should place its emphasis on the retailer and the consumer's need for the product. The retailer is not about to drop a private label in favor of a branded item. Moreover, the retailer is not interested in simply trading profits with an existing brand. The quantity of buy-in must be decided. An *early-buy allowance* might be used to get a new product into distribution before advertising starts. Such allowances lower a distributor's risk in stocking new brands. Sometimes you have no choice. Mass merchandisers charge package-goods producers *slotting fees* to carry new products in their stores, and these fees may amount to four- or five-figure numbers per item per chain in the United States. Determination of the correct size pack for the appropriate stores and the correct size and type of display are also important. Special promotions for new products can be very expensive. The practical constraints on promotional efforts include the availability of funds and the need to find some reliable measure of sales effects.

If a manufacturer is striving to gain retail distribution, a *stocklift* or *buyback* of merchandise already in the store may be necessary. As retailers consolidate into fewer but larger chains, suppliers are working harder to get into stores and get rivals out—taking an initial hit in the hope that the buyback will pay off in the long run. Retailers say new suppliers bombard them with offers to clear out rival products, and they add that retailers don't make any money on the deals because products are usually sold off at wholesale. Still, for retailers, a stocklift can help them avoid selling remaining inventory at a discount, potentially at a loss, while letting them quickly add a product that they think may sell better. Driving the covert tactic is the emergence of product hit men, contracted to discreetly dispose of competitors' products. In many cases, the firms that do the job are barter companies or liquidators that normally help route overstocked or flawed goods to close-out stores. Their logistical expertise in disposing of merchandise cheaply has become a sophisticated, powerful tool for stocklifting. The process of stocklifting is described in Marketing in Action box 14-4.

As already noted, sampling is a good way to get consumer trial. An example of its use, along with a contest, is given in Marketing in Action box 14-5. Couponing can also play a role. Coupon users need an average increase of 40 percent in coupon face value to try products they don't normally buy. For example, if a user redeems a 50-cent coupon for a favorite product, he or she will require at least a 70-cent coupon to try a new or not normally used product.

CONFLICTS BETWEEN THE PROMOTIONAL MIX AND MARKETING MIX

While the promotional mix is supposed to support the marketing mix, some major concerns have arisen that, improperly used, the promotional mix might undermine the marketing mix. This is especially true in the case of price promotions with respect to list price and advertising.

MARKETING IN ACTION *14-4*

Stocklifting a Competitor's Merchandise

At the Athens, Georgia, giant Lowe's Home Improvement Warehouse store in aisle 23 near the lawn mowers, hundreds of garden gloves recently vanished. The missing merchandise was manufactured by Wells Lamont, the nation's largest garden-glove company. And almost overnight, the empty shelves were restocked last January with gloves made by its archrival, Midwest Quality Gloves Inc. The same scene played out in 100 other Lowe's stores: Wells Lamont gloves were replaced by Midwest gloves in floral, pigskin, cowhide and other designs.

Behind the inventory switch was Midwest. It had struck a deal with Lowe's to buy 225,000 pairs of Wells Lamont gloves and clear them all out so it could fill shelf after shelf with its own product.

Lowe's, the No. 2 home-center chain after Home Depot Inc., has about 450 blue-and-white stores. For years, Lowe's had primarily sold gloves made by Wells Lamont. But last year, it decided to try out another supplier in about 100 stores in the South. Lowe's typically has two ways to get rid of inventory. The new supplier, Midwest, could have paid Lowe's a "markdown allowance" to sell off the Wells Lamont gloves gradually, at discounted prices. But with the crucial gardening season approaching, Lowe's opted for a stocklift, to clear the shelves in one sweep. "It just gives a better presentation to the customer than mixing two different vendors." Midwest declined to discuss the specific stocklift. But in general, Midwest works hard to meet retailers' requests, including hanging the gloves on metal rods attached with clips, called "clip strips," for better shelf display. "We try to make it as easy as possible for the retailer to take our product in." Midwest added that such efforts have helped the company expand aggressively into new retail chains and increase sales an average of 35% a year.

Wells Lamont, the stocklift victim, had no immediate recourse. "Of course we mind it, but that's not illegal. We sold the product to the customer," said the retailer. "It's their inventory, not ours." So, last winter, the Wells Lamont gloves were pulled off the shelves, packed up, and whisked away to a storage room. Meanwhile, Midwest arranged to sell all the gloves to a liquidator, International Purchase Systems. The Wells Lamont gloves arrived in the warehouse and, for weeks, sat in a dark cor-

(continues)

Courtesy Midwest Gloves

MARKETING IN ACTION *14-4*   (continued)

ner. Some were stuffed into a hodgepodge of boxes that once held refrigerators and washing machines. Others still sealed in Wells Lamont boxes, bore a sign that said "Buyback" in magic marker. With rap music blaring from a radio that hung from a pillar, workers sorted out the gloves, discarding the shopworn ones and separating them into about a hundred new cardboard boxes according to size and style—Cotton Hob-Nob, Vinyl-Coated K-Wrist, Work No Sweat and Yard & Garden with extra-long protective cuffs. Ten people working eight-hour shifts took about six weeks to sort out and count the gloves before they were resold. Time was running out. "The season is now. Spring and Fall are when people do gardening." Two weeks later, with the gardening season in full bloom, some of the Wells Lamont gloves surfaced in downtown Manhattan's National Wholesale Liquidators store, amid a jumble of photo albums, vacuum cleaners, cordless telephones and $3.97 salad spinners. In the basement of the close-out store's home-improvement department, an open box marked "Lowe's" sits next to coiled garden hoses. It is filled with Wells Lamont's purple Yard & Garden gloves. The "regular" price tag of $2.99 is crossed out. The gloves are on sale for $1.49.

International Purchase Systems believes that Midwest paid about $700,000 for the 225,000 pairs of gloves—about the wholesale price. In turn, it bought the gloves for about $280,000; the difference, about $400,000, may indicate just how eager Midwest was to get its gloves into Lowe's stores. Then, International Purchase Systems sold the gloves to an array of close-out stores, including National Wholesale Liquidators Inc. and Building 19 Inc. It took in about $70,000, before its own operating expenses. That may seem slim, but it expects to be rewarded in the long run. It has also expanded business by tapping the revenge impulse: After purchasing stocklifted products, it puts in "courtesy calls" to the victims, encouraging them to "return the favor" by working with International Purchase Systems.

— *Buybacks are a necessary evil in gaining market share. You get the market share immediately, but at a price.*

Source: Yumiko Ono, "Where Are the Gloves? They Were Stocklifted by a Rival Producer," *The Wall Street Journal*, May 15, 1998, pp. A1, A8.

Advertising Versus Price Promotion

In boosting list prices and making deep promotional price cuts, consumer goods companies have let their focus be diverted from long-run profits to short-term sales volume and market share. In the process they shifted more and more moneys from consistent theme advertising to consumer and trade promotions. Research from the Promotion Marketing Association of America (not an unbiased source) shows that senior executives believe promotion is more effective than advertising. The executives also said that consumer promotion does build brand equity, and trade promotion can build brand equity. Others believe that price promotions devalue brand image. Managers at Unilever have characterized the process as "promotion, commotion, demotion."

On the other hand, consistent theme advertising strengthens a brand's image for the long haul. The resultant brand equity offers some protection from competitive forays. Reductions in advertising expenditures in order to fund price promotions may weaken consumers' perceptions of a brand. We should note that price promotion costs are variable with volume and permit small regional brands to compete against the heavily advertised national brands.

Research has shown that FSI (free standing insert) coupons generate more penetration when distributed in weeks in which effective advertising is aired than when distributed in off-air weeks. This interaction is of an economically useful magnitude. The interaction is only present when advertising is effective in its own right.[4] Consistent theme advertising and sales promotion can work together in a synergistic manner if executed in the context of an integrated marketing communications (marcom) plan.

MARKETING IN ACTION *14-5*

Targeting Gatekeepers and End-Users

About five years ago, Ledesma, Argentina's largest sugar company, developed a process to make paper out of sugar cane husks. It acquired two writing paper brands—Gloria and Exito—and poised to go to market with an ecological positioning. But there was a problem. The sugar cane paper lacked resilience and tore if one tried to erase on it. Public perception said the paper was substandard. Ledesma scientists and manufacturing executives eventually perfected a viable product, but that meant little if consumer skepticism could not be counteracted.

The key market for Exito Ecologic and Gloria Ecologic writing tablets was school children. The marketing problem obviously called for a sampling solution—but how to get writing paper into the hands of kids at school? Ledesma found two ways. On five successive Sundays, spread ads ran in newspaper magazine sections reaching two million Argentineans a week. A sheet of Ecologic lined notebook paper was inserted in the middle of the spread. Copy told of the unique environmental benefits of the product and invited kids six to 18 to draw pictures of endangered species on the paper and enter them in a contest. Winners in four age groups, chosen by a judging team of internationally known philatelists, would have their drawings immortalized on an actual set of Argentine government stamps. [The government postal service, which had consumer perception problems of its own readily agreed to hitch on to a program with concern for ecology, endangered species, and education.]

The second sampling program was aimed at the primary influencers: teachers. Ledesma distributed paper and contest forms to public and private schools and encouraged teachers to make entering the promotion a class project. On the first day of school in Argentina, most teachers give students a list of the materials they will need to buy, and most times they suggest the name of a [Ledesma] competitor's notebook. "We knew that if we could get them to try our paper, they would see it was as good as the competitor's. And teachers like environment-friendly products."

Ledesma received more than 90,000 drawings from school children. Sales of Exito and Gloria brands grew a combined 11 percent, gaining Ledesma a three-point share gain. And throughout Argentina—as well as around the globe—Ledesma's lined paper could be detected behind the endearing animal drawings on the stamps. That's exposure that cannot be bought.

The four winners and their families also got a trip to the south of Argentina for a whale-spotting expedition—a fitting conclusion to a whale of a promotion.

— *Large rewards come from unearthing the proverbial Big Idea and daring to execute it.*

Source: Amie Smith and Al Urbanski, "Have a More Active Role," *Promo*, December 1998, p. 28.

Courtesy Ledesma, s.a.a.i.

List Price Versus Price Promotion

Many manufacturers believe that a high-list, high-deal policy is more profitable than offering a single price to all consumers. This is because it permits them to price-discriminate among customer segments. This is one aspect of *demand pricing*. Consider the case of a brand targeted at two segments: regular customers and deal-prone, price-sensitive customers. Suppose that you face the (linear) demand curves for each segment shown in Table 14-2 and your product has a unit variable cost of $0.80. If you never did any promotion, what price should you charge? The maximum contribution occurs at a list price of $1.60. Suppose, however, you want to price-discriminate among the segments; what prices should you charge within the ranges given? The best prices would be a $2.00 list price for regular customers and a $1.40 promotion price for deal-prone customers. Demand pricing yields higher profits. You do not want to leave money on the table!

The demand pricing approach is not without problems. Care must be taken in executing it. Two negative things can happen: leakage and slippage. *Leakage* occurs when consumers not targeted for a price promotion manage to take advantage of it. *Slippage* occurs when those who should receive a promotion do not.

Trade deals pose further complications. Distributors may not pass through the benefits of a deal to the consumer. Attractive trade deals may also lead distributors to forward buy or divert goods. *Forward buying* involves purchasing more inventory now than is needed to run a concurrent consumer promotion. The extra merchandise can then be sold at regular prices after the deal period. Enough merchandise may be bought to last until the next deal. *Diversion* involves buying goods in regions where manufacturers are offering unusually deep discounts and moving the goods to regions where the deals being offered are not so attractive. Deep-discount stores and warehouse clubs are especially adept at gaining advantage by these practices. To counteract the advantage of these low-cost retailers, competing chains have demanded that manufacturers sell everything to them at the lowest promotion price offered anywhere the chain operates. This uniform pricing policy limits a manufacturer's ability to engage in regional pricing.

Forward buying and diversion impact a manufacturer's ability to produce in an efficient manner and raise inventory costs throughout the distribution system. Forward buying plays havoc with a firm's manufacturing cycle, creating frantic overtime followed by unproductive lulls. Moreover, deep-discount stores that find these practices attractive are not long-term customers inasmuch as they carry only a few items in any product category and have no commitment to carry any brand on a regular basis.

TABLE 14-2 Segment Demand Curves

Price	List-price Segment		Promotion-price Segment		Total Market (Both Segments)	
	Units	Contribution	Units	Contribution	Units	Contribution
$2.00	70.0	$84.00	00.0	$00.00	70.0	$ 84.00
1.90	72.5	79.75	15.0	16.50	87.5	96.25
1.80	75.0	75.00	30.0	30.00	105.0	105.00
1.70	77.5	69.75	45.0	40.50	122.5	110.25
1.60	80.0	64.00	60.0	48.00	140.0	112.00
1.50	82.5	57.75	75.0	52.50	157.5	110.25
1.40	85.0	51.00	90.0	54.00	175.0	105.00

Source: Paul W. Farris and John A. Quelch, "The Defense of Price Promotions," *Sloan Management Review.* Vol. 29, No. 1 (Fall 1987), p. 67.

To try to regain the initiative some manufacturers have begun to emphasize *everyday low prices* (EDLP) or *value pricing*. Procter & Gamble has tried to implement an EDLP on most of its brands. Some retailers have opposed the plan because they were concerned that they would lose promotional flexibility as well as profits. They believed that P&G's plan favored retailers, such as Wal-Mart Stores, which were already following an "everyday low prices" approach. Competitors moved in, offered substantial deals, and stole share from P&G in the short run. The move to a more rational everyday list price system seems inevitable. The question is whether enough advertising and promotional support will be maintained to keep consumers interested in the product category.

PUBLIC RELATIONS

Today more and more customers are taking the time to phone or write companies when they encounter a problem with a purchase. Sophisticated marketers realize that prompt responses to these complaints can help correct problems and retain customers. Managers know it is a lot less expensive to maintain current customers than to find new ones.

Firms are expanding their customer relations departments because these investments pay off. Most complainers are satisfied with a personal letter and some coupons. Failure to respond to questions, however, can lead to bad word-of-mouth publicity. Inquiries are also a valuable source of information. This approach is detailed in Marketing in Action box 14-6.

MARKETING IN ACTION *14-6*

Maintaining Customer Contacts

APPLYING ... to Consumer Food Products Marketing

Two consumers who objected to the bland flavor of a new potato chip alerted Borden to a manufacturing error in one batch. People who inquire about products can be identified and used later in direct mail campaigns. For example, when Campbell decided to roll out a new line of low sodium soups, its customer relations division assembled a list of every customer who inquired about the salt content of its other soups. These customers were then sent a brochure on the new soups as well as some coupons.

APPLYING ... to Consumer Clothing Marketing

The type of response that customers like to receive can be illustrated by two examples. When a buyer wrote to Liz Claiborne to complain about buttonholes unraveling on a dress, the company replied immediately with a letter of apology. The company included instructions to have the dress repaired by any tailor, along with reassurances that reimbursement would be forthcoming. A letter sent to Health Valley Foods complaining about the lack of raisins in a box of cereal, prompted a two-page reply from the company president. In addition, the company sent a replacement box of cereal, an Oat Bran Jumbo Fruit Bar, a packet of herb seasonings, and a $1 coupon for cookies or bars. Health Valley doesn't advertise and the company is tickled when people take time to let them know about a problem.

— *It is simply good business for you to stay in touch with your customers.*

Source: Kathleen Deveny, "For Marketers: No Peeve Is Too Petty," *The Wall Street Journal*, November 14, 1990, p. B1.

By permission of Campbell Soup Company

Public relations is also responsible for consumer education, publicity, special events, and sponsorships. The idea is that getting attention in a crowded marketplace doesn't have to be expensive. Franklin Sports Industries designed a baseball batting glove of Spandex and English leather to fit around a bat. Most important, the gloves sported the Franklin logo in inch-high letters on the back of the hand. Franklin handed them out by the dozen to every major-league ballplayer. Since then, Franklin's name shows up on television every time a camera focuses in on a batter. It has appeared on batters on the cover of *Sports Illustrated*. As a result Franklin sells about $65 million of all types of sporting goods, yet spends less than a million dollars a year on advertising.

Event marketing can be used to lure the customer into the retail outlet to purchase, while at the same time building awareness and impacting imagery. During the 1988 Olympics, Seagram Coolers launched a program called "Send the Families," designed to raise money to send a family member to accompany an athlete, all expenses paid to Seoul, Korea. The program involved point-of-sale displays with appropriate literature explaining how consumers could participate based on purchase and details about Seagram's contributions. The program was supported by an aggressive public relations effort involving the world's largest greeting card, transported across the country on a flatbed truck and signed by dignitaries and consumers at each stop. Tying all the pieces together was an advertising campaign that got the message out about the program and Seagram's support for American athletes.

MARKETING IN ACTION *14-7*

Using Sports Figures in a Prescription Drug Promotion

Astra Pharmaceuticals hopes to score in the fiercely competitive arena of hypertension drugs with its sports-themed launch of Atacand (candesartan). Atacand joins Pfizer's Norvasc (amlodipine) and Procardia (nifedipine), Hoechst Marion Roussel's Cardizem CD (diltiazem), and other hypertension medications aimed at an estimated 50 million U.S. citizens with the disease. Norvasc leads in sales, with five million total prescriptions in the quarter ending September 1998.

Hall of Fame members Ernie Banks of the Chicago Cubs and football player Deacon Jones of the Los Angeles Rams joined Astra and NY-based Ketchum Public Relations at New York's All-Star Cafe recently to kick off Atacand's four-month, 19-city promotional tour. Banks, Jones, and Hall of Fame member Whitey Ford of the New York Yankees will carry the theme, "Have a Heart—Help Yourself and Someone Else," during visits to community centers and local broadcast shows throughout the United States. "This is the real World Series for people we love," Banks, who is a hypertension patient, told an unusual combination of medical and sports reporters attending the launch. Jones and Ford also suffer from hypertension.

Atacand, an angiotension receptor blocker, is a once-a-day pill that, according to clinical trials, causes few side effects. Dr. Alan Gradman, chief of the Division of Cardiovascular Diseases and director of Cardiology Fellowship Training at Western Pennsylvania Hospital, says nearly two-thirds of hypertension patients stop taking blood pressure drugs within a year of diagnosis because of unpleasant side effects such as dizziness, leg swelling, and headaches.

Gradman says using popular African-American sports figures like Banks and Jones to spread the hypertension message is an attempt to reach those who most need to hear about hypertension treatments. "Scientific findings might impress people like me," Gradman says, "but people typically at risk are interested in talking to Deacon Jones." As many as 30 percent of all deaths in hypertensive African-American men may be attributable to the disease, according to Astra's figures, with men in general showing the greatest hypertension risk up until age 55. The risk in women rises between 55 and 74 years old.

— *Celebrities may create the stir you need to call attention to your message.*

Source: Diane West, "Atacand Up at Bat," *Pharmaceutical Executive*, December 1998, p. S16.

MEASURING CAMPAIGN EFFECTIVENESS

APPLYING
... to
Consumer
Packaged
Goods
Marketing

You have to look at the effectiveness of any marketing activity you undertake. For example, Colgate-Palmolive applies a strict profit-and-loss formula in measuring the effectiveness of its ongoing cause-related sponsorship of the Starlight Foundation, which grants wishes to seriously ill children. Colgate's effort involves free standing insert coupons and is easily tracked. Your ability to track the impact of consumer promotions has been greatly enhanced by the availability of scanner data. The scope of information now available is indicated by a sample page from Information Resources, Inc.'s *Marketing Fact Book* shown in Table 14-3. Using supermarket scanner sales data, Colgate compares product sales in the three weeks following a coupon drop with average sales for the six months preceding it. The difference is then multiplied by the brand's net profit margin and the event's cost on a per-unit basis is subtracted to find the true incremental profit.

A common criterion used to evaluate the success of promotional activity is plus sales per dollar of company expenditure. This ratio shows how sales respond to the prizes and trips used as incentives and allows comparisons to be made among different types of promotions. Some firms break historical sales data into trend, seasonal, and irregular components so that the plus sales produced by promotional efforts can be measured. This method, called "bump analysis," adjusts sales for seasonal factors and removes the trend so the remaining irregular component reflects the impact of the promotion. Figure 14-3 shows the impact of a campaign on the sales. Note that the campaign produced losses in volume both before and after the effective dates of the promotion. The reduced volume before the promotion may have been due to the sales force holding back on deliveries to take advantage of campaign benefits. The drop after the promotion may indicate that the campaign had exhausted the available consumer demand. Total plus sales for the "sales campaign" were obtained by adding in sales for the two 10-day periods before and after the promotion. If the before-and-after losses were ignored, the estimate of plus sales in Figure 14-3 would be inflated. Once a reliable figure for plus sales has been estimated, it is divided by the costs of the promotion to get a ratio that can be used to evaluate the results of current and past campaigns.

There is an automated promotion evaluation system called PROMOTER, which incorporates concepts from expert systems and contains a knowledge base to recognize and adjust for data irregularities. The system estimates a *baseline* of what sales would have been if the promotion had not been run. This is possible because from 30 to 90 percent of the time, a consumer product is not on promotion in a particular store. Thus, using sales data from individual stores, sales from these nonpromotional weeks can be compared with those from promotional weeks. The incremental impact of the promotion can be measured. Experience with PROMOTER gave rise to a more sophisticated decision support system, PROMOTIONSCAN. Whereas PROMOTER measures total incremental volume for only one brand, PROMOTIONSCAN does so for all brands, including competitors. PROMOTIONSCAN also relates that incremental volume to retailer merchandising variables such as features, display, and price reductions.

The incremental impact of a trade promotion can be seen in the representative numbers shown in Table 14-4. As noted earlier, most trade promotions are unprofitable. The brand promotes to the trade at a 15 percent discount over a four-week period. Assume that all the stores in the market feature the brand for one week in their weekly newspaper advertising supplement. What's more, half the stores support the brand with three weeks of in-store display and consumer price reductions, whereas the other half only reduce the price but for the full four weeks. (It is unusual to get such excellent trade support.) Nevertheless, the promotion ends up costing 64 cents for each incremental dollar it generates. Unless the product's gross margin is more than 64 percent, the promotion will lose money. This is because the manufacturer has to sell a high number of cases at the discounted price to cover the normal

TABLE 14-3 Scanner Summary Data

Category—Liquid Soap Volume Is Pounds. Annual—Jan to Dec Including Only Brands Purchased by 0.5% or More of All Households	Ctgry Volume Share	Type Volume Share	— Data Reflect Grocery Store Purchases Only —						% Volume with the Specified Deal						Avg % Off on Price Deals
			% of Hshlds Buying	Volume per Purch	Purch per Buyer	Purch Cycle (days)	Share Ctgry Rqmts	Price per Volume	Any Trade Deal	Print Ad Featr	In-Store Disply	Shelf Price Reduct	Store Coupn	Man-ufactr Coupn	
Category—liquid soap	689.1*	100.0	31.9%	0.9	2.4	94	100%	2.29	24%	8%	6%	17%	1%	31%	35%
Type—liquid soap	100.0	100.0	31.9	0.9	2.4	94	100	2.29	24	8	6	17	1	31	35
Benckiser Cons Prods	9.8	9.8	5.4	0.8	1.5	97	42	1.96	8	1	2	7	0	12	26
Clean & Smooth	9.8	9.8	5.4	0.8	1.5	97	42	1.96	8	1	2	7	0	12	26
Colgate Palmolive	20.6	20.6	8.5	1.1	1.6	92	52	2.21	39	18	14	24	3	22	34
Softsoap	18.9	18.9	8.0	1.1	1.5	93	50	2.15	40	19	15	23	4	23	35
Softsoap Shower Gel	1.7	1.7	0.8	0.7	2.0	92	33	2.82	29	3	1	26	2	12	29
Koa Corp of Amer	17.1	17.1	8.2	0.9	1.7	93	48	1.86	17	4	2	13	2	35	40
Jergens	10.9	10.9	5.4	0.9	1.5	99	44	1.63	12	2	2	10	1	27	41
Jergens Antibacterial Plus	6.2	6.2	3.7	0.8	1.5	81	34	2.28	26	8	4	19	4	50	39
Minnetonka	3.6	3.6	3.2	0.6	1.3	100	30	2.13	40	8	2	35	1	23	44
Softsoap Country Designs	2.2	2.2	2.1	0.6	1.3	96	28	2.12	44	10	3	36	1	26	47
Softsoap Pastels	0.8	0.8	0.8	0.6	1.2	108	27	2.19	34	1	0	35	0	21	36
Procter & Gamble	17.7	17.7	9.5	0.8	1.6	96	45	2.19	15	4	5	10	1	34	37
Ivory Liquid	8.5	8.5	3.0	1.1	1.9	107	57	1.92	6	2	0	4	0	21	27
Ivory Liquid Accents	2.0	2.0	2.1	0.5	1.3	94	24	2.03	16	5	1	14	1	43	53
Ivory Liquid Classics	1.2	1.2	1.2	0.5	1.3	88	23	2.17	16	1	1	15	0	35	43
Safeguard	6.0	6.0	4.6	0.7	1.3	76	30	2.62	28	6	13	15	1	50	34
The Dial Corporation	22.6	22.6	9.4	0.9	1.8	102	59	2.57	25	6	3	21	1	42	29
Dial	22.5	22.5	9.3	0.9	1.8	101	59	2.56	25	6	3	21	1	42	29
Unilever	3.8	3.8	3.5	0.5	1.5	102	33	3.80	30	11	5	20	2	66	39
Dove Beauty Wash	3.8	3.8	3.5	0.5	1.5	102	33	3.80	30	11	5	20	2	66	39
Private label	1.5	1.5	0.6	1.1	1.4	99	48	1.42	17	0	0	17	0	1	13
Private label	1.5	1.5	0.6	1.1	1.4	99	48	1.42	17	0	0	17	0	1	13

*Category volume per 1000 households.

Source: The Marketing Fact Book. Chicago: Information Resources, Inc., 1992, p. 241.

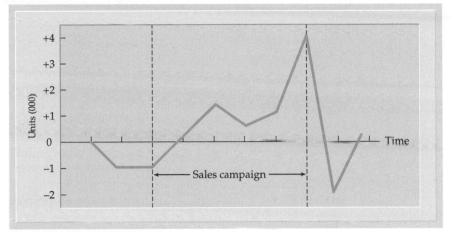

FIGURE 14-3 Measuring the Effects of a Sales Promotion

sales that would have taken place without the promotion. In addition, the manufacturer must also cover the forward buying by the retailer.

A promotion should be judged on the value of new customers attracted to it in addition to the immediate sales volume it generates. New customers may like the brand and, thus, buy it for many years. Therefore, immediate sales may not indicate the real value of a promotion; instead, it would be reflected by the number of new triers and their acceptance of a brand. It is important to distinguish between gaining triers (the job of the promotion) and gaining acceptance (the job of product development).

The value of event marketing is often measured by adding up the number of seconds of TV airtime or column inches of press clipping that feature a company's name or logo, then multiplying that by the equivalent ad cost. Some research companies make a business of doing such research. Some believe that measures such as "media equivalencies" are irrele-

TABLE 14-4   Trade Promotion Economics

	Cases	Gross Dollars
Baseline*		
Sales that would have occurred during a four-week promotion period even without promotion	400	$ 4,000
Incremental sales to consumers†		
Due to a one-week feature	100	$1,000
Due to 50% of stores with three weeks of displays and price reduction	250	$2,500
Due to 50% of stores with four weeks of price reduction only	80	$ 800
	430	$4,300
Ten weeks of forward buying by retailers	1,000	$10,000
Total sales during promotion	1,830	$18,300
Cost of promotion		$2,745
Cost per incremental dollar of sales		$0.64

* Assume weekly base sales of 100 cases and a list price of $10 per case.
† Based on analysis of single-source data and retailer promotion purchases.

Source: Magid M. Abraham and Leonard M. Lodish, "Getting the Most Out of Advertising and Promotion," *Harvard Business Review,* Vol. 68, No. 3 (May–June 1990), pp. 50–60.

vant, and what you should measure are favorable impressions of your brand that remain in people's minds. Thus, researchers recruit event spectators and conduct follow-up telephone interviews several days later to measure sponsor recall and consumers' intent to purchase sponsors' products.

Real-time scanner monitoring and the Internet have some marketers adjusting their promotions while they are ongoing rather than simply doing postmortems of their sales promotions. McDonald's gauges the success of a four-to six-week sales promotion by the reaction in the first five days. RealTime Media does daily promo-tracking for CDNow (Marketing in Action box 14-3). If the day-by-day information indicated that CDNow wasn't getting the traffic it wanted, it would take out additional banner headlines, buy more media support, send out e-mails, and/or seed more offers into the promotion.[5]

Rather than just evaluating each activity in isolation, you should strive to assess the synergistic effects of marketing communications (marcom) because their integration is important. Unfortunately, research methods for showing the effect of integration have not yet been developed.

SUMMARY

The promotion mix allows you to fine-tune your marketing mix. A review of the literature finds these reasons for promotions:

- Enables you to adjust to variations in supply and demand without changing list price.
- Allows you to price-discriminate among consumer segments.
- Rewards consumers.
- Secures distribution for new products.
- Induces consumer trial for new products.
- Encourages different retail formats, for example, shoppers clubs.
- Permits smaller regional brands to compete against nationally advertised brands.
- Adds excitement at point-of-sale to mature products.
- Defends shelf space against existing and anticipated competition.
- Clears inventories of obsolete products.

Thus, the promotion mix gives you flexibility to address very specific marketing situations.

You must approach the consumer with an integrated marketing communications package—sales force, direct marketing, advertising, sales promotion, and public relations all at once. As one observer puts it: "An ideal integrated marketing communications program combines media advertising to build awareness, sales promotion to generate an inquiry or response, database marketing to capture customer or prospect information, and ongoing direct marketing to specifically target customer needs and personalize, perhaps even customize, the communication to achieve measurable results."[6]

NOTES

1. Robert C. Blattberg, and Scott A. Neslin, *Sales Promotion: Concepts, Methods, and Strategies* (Englewood Cliffs, NJ: Prentice-Hall, 1990), p. 3.
2. William M. Bulkeley, "Rebates' Secret Appeal to Manufacturers: Few Consumers Actually Redeem Them," *The Wall Street Journal,* February 10, 1998, pp. B1, B6.
3. Richard Sale, "The Display Police," *Promo,* March 1999, pp. 80–81, 84.
4. Michael von Gonten, "Tracking Advertising Effects," *Admap,* Vol. 33, No. 9 (October 1998), pp. 43–45.
5. Richard Sale, "Evaluation in Evolution," *Promo,* September 1998, pp. 63, 65, 67–68.

6. Neil M. Brown, "Redefine Integrated Marketing Communications," *Marketing News,* March 29, 1993, pp. 4–5.

SUGGESTED READING

van Waterschoot, Walter, and Christophe Van den Bulte. "The 4P Classification of the Marketing Mix Revisited," *Journal of Marketing,* Vol. 56, No. 4 (October 1992), pp. 83–93.

REFERENCES

Abraham, Magid M., and Leonard M. Lodish. "Getting the Most Out of Advertising and Promotion," *Harvard Business Review,* Vol. 68, No. 3 (May–June 1990), pp. 50–60.

Abraham, Magid M., and Leonard M. Lodish "An Implemented System for Improving Promotion Productivity Using Store Scanner Data," *Marketing Science,* Vol. 12, No. 3 (Summer 1993), pp. 248–269.

Blattberg, Robert C., and Scott A. Neslin. *Sales Promotion: Concepts, Methods, and Strategies* (Englewood Cliffs, NJ: Prentice-Hall, 1990).

Buzzell, Robert D., John A. Quelch, and Walter J. Salmon. "The Costly Bargain of Trade Promotion," *Harvard Business Review,* Vol. 68, No. 2 (March–April 1990), pp. 141–149.

Jones, John Philips. "The Double Jeopardy of Sales Promotions," *Harvard Business Review,* Vol. 68, No. 5 (September–October 1990), pp. 145–152.

Schultz, Don E., William A. Robinson, and Lisa A. Petrison. *Sales Promotion Essentials,* 3d ed. (Lincolnwood, IL: NTC Business Books), 1998.

Shapiro, Arthur. "Advertising Versus Trade Promotion: Which Is Which?" *Journal of Advertising Research,* Vol. 20, No. 3 (June/July 1990), pp. RC-13–RC-16.

QUESTIONS

1. Spain's Basque country-based bank, Caja de Burgos, wants clients for its pension plans account. Its pension plans are designed to appeal to self-employed males who already own a minimum of four of the bank's products. The bank has identified its targets—about 10,000 of them. Create a sales promotion to interest these prospects in opening new pension accounts.

2. Warner-Lambert wants to get a trial of its new anti-itch cream Benadryl. Prospects are those most likely to become victims of poison ivy, mosquito bites, and heat rash. Propose a plan for sampling this over-the-counter drug.

3. Visa USA wants customers to use its card more often. Create a sales promotion for the Christmas holiday season.

4. Bass Brewing's market share for Worthington Bitter beer has seen significant growth in the United Kingdom due to increased distribution and product superiority. Create a sales promotion that rewards pub-goers. The target audience is 25- to 40-year-old, blue-collar men who tend to reflect fondly on their laddish days, but now have family responsibilities.

5. With stocklifting, consumers don't know why some products vanish—or turn up—in a store. One critic has pointed out "You've taken away what should drive the market, which is the preferred product." How do you feel about the ethics of stocklifting? How does it fit with having a customer orientation? When might stocklifting violate the law?

6. A relaxation of rules on the marketing of professional services has led to increased interest in the use of promotions to boost sales. For example, an orthopedic surgeon who wanted to specialize in joint replacement came up with a brochure designed to appeal to older people and distributed it by direct mail to retirement communities. This

appeal was so successful that the surgeon had to open two more offices and find a partner. In another case, a dentist who doubled the size of his Yellow Pages ad found that demand for his services doubled as well. How should professionals allocate their marketing budgets across different promotional alternatives to maximize sales?

7. When PepsiCo launched its "Pepsi Stuff" promotion, industry executives feared it might be too challenging for consumers. To win a denim jacket emblazoned with the Pepsi logo, for instance, people had to collect 400 award-points from peel-off strips on Pepsi or Diet Pepsi—the equivalent of 200 two-liter bottles. In fact, the contest wasn't challenging enough. Even before the last phase of media advertising in a six-month campaign was scheduled to run, bottlers reported that redemptions were running about 15 percent of total points available rather than the expected 10 percent—a burden for bottlers who have to pay half the costs of all prizes. How should Pepsi respond to redemptions running 50 percent higher than expected?

8. *Yo quiero Tylenol?* Taco Bell's advertisements featuring a Chihuahua proved surprisingly popular. To capitalize on Chihuahua fever during the holiday season, Taco Bell brought out four toy dogs that spoke lines from the chain's ads when they were squeezed: "Yo quiero Taco Bell"; "Here leezard, leezard" (with the "free-food" picket sign from the Godzilla spot); "Viva Gorditas" (with beret); and "Feliz Navidad, amigo" (with Santa hat). The Chihuahua campaign ran into an unexpected problem. The head of a chapter of the League of United Latin American Citizens, a Hispanic civil rights group, equated Taco Bell's advertising with hate crime. How should Taco Bell respond?

9. Philip Morris Co., with brands such as Marlboro, has about a 50 percent share of the U.S. cigarette market. It supports its consumer "marcom" activities with a sales-incentive program for independent retailers. The program, called Retail Masters, rewards participating retailers with payouts based on sales and display of Philip Morris brands. Under the program, displays of non-Philip Morris brands must be temporary. For agreeing to the display restrictions, the retailer earns "contract money." Moreover, the retailer also earns "Flex Funds" based on the proportion of its sales that are Philip Morris brands. Do Philip Morris's actions unfairly restrict distribution of competing brands?

10. Labor disputes in sports, such as those in Major League Baseball, the National Hockey League, and the National Basketball Association in recent years, can diminish the value of the product and the value of sponsorships of the product by alienating fans. What damage control in such situations might professional sports leagues do? their individual teams? the sponsors?

11. Based on scores of illnesses to consumers who drank Coca-Cola products, Belgium and Luxembourg banned Coca-Cola products in early June 1999. Coca-Cola traced its problems to bad carbon dioxide in its Antwerp plant and to traces of fungicide on wooden pallets used in its Dunkirk, France, canning facility—both owned by Coca-Cola Enterprises. France, and the Netherlands, then banned the sale of any products that came from those plants. Soon health ministers in Switzerland, Italy, and Spain were warning consumers about Coca-Cola products from those plants—even though Coca-Cola did not ship to those countries from the plants in question. How should The Coca-Cola Company and its anchor bottler, Coca-Cola Enterprises, respond to this crisis?

12. McDonald's restaurants and EMI Records Group North America, a unit of the London-based Thorn EMI PLC, teamed up for a purchase-with-purchase promotion. McDonald's customers were given the opportunity to purchase specially-priced 10-track compact disks (CDs) or cassettes of music by four different artists, including Garth Brooks. The $5.99 CDs and $3.99 cassettes were all compiled from previously released music. A coupon was included in the album that could be redeemed at Musicland stores that permitted consumers to purchase other titles by artists included in the promotion at a $2 discount. The promotion was run in over 9,500 McDonald's restaurants. The promotion

was initially scheduled to occur from September 2 to 22, but was extended an additional week and ended September 28. The promotion was accompanied with a $20 million advertising campaign featuring Garth Brooks as a spokesperson. Sales of about 10 million units of special compilation CDs and cassettes took place. EMI is curious about the impact of the promotion on regular sales of its artists. SoundScan data are given in the file garthdat.sav on weekly sales of two older Garth Brooks' albums: *In Pieces,* released the previous summer, and *No Fences,* released 4 summers before. Because each of these albums had been available for at least a year, EMI assumed that any change in sales during the weeks of the promotion could be directly attributable to the McDonald's promotion. Total industry sales serves as a possible control for seasonality.

CHAPTER 15

INTERNATIONAL MARKETING

> Free trade, one of the greatest blessings which a government can confer on a people, is in almost every country unpopular.
>
> LORD MACAULAY

No economies today prosper without international trade. Indeed, some of the strongest (Germany and China) regularly sell more abroad than they import. Even the United States exports 20 percent of its industrial production and sells two out of five acres of its farm produce abroad. Today one-third of U.S. corporate profits is derived from international trade, and this proportion is sure to increase in the future. When you travel, you notice signs for Coke, Pepsi, McDonald's hamburgers, Philips Electronics, Michelin tires, and Caterpillar tractors. These firms have learned how to operate in international markets.

Successful international trade is based on the *law of comparative advantage.* This principle states that countries are better off producing items where they have inherent advantages and buying from others products where they have handicaps. The United States has comparative advantages in the production of agricultural products and airplanes, which it exports, and is at a disadvantage with newsprint and oil, which it imports. Despite the tremendous benefits of trade for the U.S. economy, 58 percent of Americans agreed with the statement that trade is bad because cheap imports hurt wages and jobs.[1] Only people making more than $100,000 a year (56 percent) and college graduates (46 percent) felt that trade creates growth and jobs. Clearly more people need to know how international marketing benefits society.

Another factor supporting international marketing is opportunity. Today the United States represents less than 25 percent of the world market for goods and services. Almost all firms that have achieved national distribution in the United States must become international to continue to grow. For non-U.S. firms the potential outside the home country is even greater. Although the Japanese market is large, the potential market outside Japan is 85 percent of worldwide demand. Our discussion suggests that international markets present tremendous opportunities for growth. This chapter will analyze the special character of international trade and present some aggressive marketing strategies for operating in this arena. An example showing how Nissan made a series of crippling errors in its North American operations is described in Marketing in Action box 15-1.

APPLYING
... to
Consumer
Durable
Goods
Marketing

MARKETING IN ACTION *15-1*

Nissan Drops the Ball in the U.S.

Nissan was one of the first Japanese auto manufacturers to enter the U.S. market in the 1970s with sporty cars like the 240Z. In the early 1990s, they gained ground with the muscular Maxima sedan and in 1995 they sold over 800,000 cars in America. As the third largest seller of foreign cars in the U.S., Nissan was able to construct an assembly plant in Tennessee to build its small Sentra model, the intermediate Altima and small trucks. However, due to a series of blunders, Nissan's U.S. sales declined in 1996, 1997, and 1998 resulting in a loss of $513 million in 1997. Although America contributed 32 percent of Nissan's total sales revenue, the company lost track of the needs of its U.S. customers. Their first mistake was an attempt to make more profit on the imported Maxima by cutting product features and quality. They dropped the sophisticated rear suspension that made the sporty Maxima stick to the road and the American auto press was quick to point out this deficiency. Instead of manufacturing the Maxima in America to compete with Toyota's Camry and Honda's Accord, they chose to build the smaller and inferior Altima in Tennessee to compete in the important intermediate four door sedan market. Nissan was also slow to take advantage of the growing importance of trucks in the U.S. market. In 1998, Nissan's U.S. manufactured truck sales declined an amazing 30 percent at the same time Chrysler increased truck sales 13.8 percent. Indeed, for the first time ever Americans bought more trucks in 1998 than they bought cars and Nissan was unable to participate in this bonanza. Part of the problem was that Nissan did not have a big pickup to compete with Ford and General Motors. They also failed to see the importance of offering the four door option in their small extended cab pickups as was done by their more successful competitors. Also Nissan was advertising its trucks with TV ads featuring a dog who drives its sleeping owner's recliner down a steep slope to a dealer showroom. The ads were a huge hit with everyone except Nissan dealers, who quickly discovered the brand image ads didn't sell cars or trucks. To counter declining sales, Nissan began offering large rebates and low monthly leases that assumed higher end of lease residual values than was the industry norm. As a result, Nissan ended up owning over 100,000 high-priced used cars that they chose to keep rather than accept large losses on their resale. Even Nissan's Infiniti luxury cars were trumped by Toyota's Lexus division.

— *Firms that fail to keep up with consumer preferences in overseas markets can expect their market shares to wilt.*

Source: Robert L. Simison, "Nissan's Crisis Was Made in the U.S.A.," *The Wall Street Journal*, November 24, 1998, pp. B1, B4.

ENVIRONMENT OF INTERNATIONAL MARKETING

International trade provides attractive opportunities for sales increases, but it also carries a number of risks. Part of your job as marketing manager is to know how to balance revenue gains from trade against the possibility of financial losses. Some of the most serious problems include fluctuations in exchange rates, trade barriers, unstable governments, and piracy of trade secrets by outsiders. Perhaps the most difficult issue is what to do about governmental trade restrictions.

Trade Barriers

Economists all agree that trade among countries increases wealth. However, politicians have found that running positive trade surpluses with other countries while maintaining regulations that protect domestic industries from outside competition are popular with the people. Production workers, for example, view international trade as a threat to their jobs. They believe imports close factories rather than provide a source of low-cost merchandise. Thus, while trade clearly helps an economy as a whole, many people see only the negative impact on high-cost local producers.

An example of the politics of trade barriers is shown by Japanese restrictions on the importation of rice, citrus fruits, and beef. Japan runs a huge trade surplus with the United States and could easily afford to buy more American agricultural products. However, Japanese farmers are unusually strong politically and have long been favored with tight import rules. The result is that Japanese consumers pay exorbitant prices for rice, beef, and oranges, although their economy would be better off buying these items from abroad. Politically, it is easier to protect jobs in the short run than it is to maximize wealth.

Tariffs and Quotas   There are basically two types of restrictions that countries use to keep unwanted products out and protect domestically produced goods. The more common one is a tariff, or tax on imports. Tariffs are usually expressed as a percentage of the value of the good and are added on to get the selling price. Tariffs range in size from nuisance taxes of 2 percent to prohibitory values of 50 percent or more designed to stop the importation of certain items. For example, a few years ago, European Common Market slapped stiff tariffs on fresh chickens imported from the United States to protect their own expanding chicken business. The United States responded by slapping a 25 percent tariff on imported trucks, which at that time were primarily small Volkswagen pickup trucks coming from Germany. This high "chicken" tax continues to this day and effectively protects U.S. manufacturers from imported truck competition. The net result is that American manufacturers have been able to raise their prices on trucks to the point where they are much more profitable than automobiles, and margins run to $8,000 per vehicle. Although the 25 percent tariff has helped U.S. firms in the short run, foreign manufacturers have begun to build truck factories in the U.S. to avoid the tariff. Toyota, for example, built a plant in Indiana in 1998 to produce large pickup trucks with V8 engines to compete directly with similar trucks from Ford, General Motors, and DaimlerChrysler. Given the huge profits American firms are making on trucks, the current tariff on imported trucks cannot be justified on economic grounds. American consumers would be better off without the tariff, since they would have more makes of trucks to choose from and would pay much lower prices for pickup trucks.

A second type of import restriction is the quota. This is an absolute limit on the number of certain items that can be imported. Italy, for instance, had an annual quota of only a few thousand Japanese cars for a number of years. Although the low quota helped to protect Italian car manufacturers, there is some question about whether the Italian economy was better off as a result. Germany has no quotas on cars, and the Japanese have a significant share of that market. The Germans, in turn, have the largest share of imported-car sales in Japan. We argue that the absence of German and Japanese auto quotas leads to greater trade and wealth for these two countries.

Another class of trade restriction that can cause problems for export-minded firms is the nontariff barrier. This often takes the form of technical specifications or inspection procedures that make it difficult or impossible to move goods across borders. For example, at one time the French required all videocassette recorders (VCRs) coming into the country to pass a customs inspection at a small interior community. This forced the Koreans and the Japanese to route all shipments through this isolated town. In addition, not enough customs inspectors were assigned to this community to handle the work, so the number of VCRs admitted to France declined sharply.

The United States has disagreed with European Union restrictions on banana imports by American firms. While the United States does not raise bananas in North America, Chiquita Brands International has extensive banana plantations in Latin America and claims to have lost 4,000 jobs and $1 billion in profit to the European banana rules. Europe's banana trade rules tend to favor imports from former colonies and have benefitted Europe's largest banana distributor, Fyffes of Dublin. The United States appealed to the World Trade Organization (WTO) about the discriminatory rules. The WTO ruled in favor of the United States but the European Union's modified rules still favored its former colonies. America countered by slapping 100 percent tariffs on a list of high-priced imported European items. This banana war is foolish and both parties would be better off settling this dispute with fewer restrictions on trade.[2]

Recent Trends Despite the periodic imposition of tariffs, quotas, and nontariff barriers, there has been a gradual loosening of trade restrictions in the world economy in the past 60 years. The General Agreement on Tariffs and Trade (GATT) is one international agreement that has reduced the level of tariffs throughout the world on several occasions. The trend toward free trade is gathering momentum in the European Union (EU). Trade barriers among EU members have been eliminated, and nonmembers are scrambling to gain access to this huge market. However, EU protectionism is slow to die. While the Japanese automobile manufacturers were first kept out with tariffs and quotas, when they built factories in Europe they found they still faced restrictions on the number of cars they could sell. Also EU allows member countries to control pharmaceutical prices to manage their national drug budgets. To sell medicine in France, companies must sign secret agreements that stipulate prices and volume ceilings for each drug sold in the country and may include guarantees on employment levels at French factories and funding for state run research institutes.[3] These agreements stifle competition and make it difficult for outsiders to enter the French pharmaceutical market.

The North American Free Trade Agreement (NAFTA) between Canada, America, and Mexico has increased trade among the three countries and seems to be working fairly well. For example, automobiles and auto parts can move freely among the three countries to benefit all concerned. However, Mexican cattle and pork producers have not been happy with the dramatic increase in shipments of American beef and pork to their local markets. In 1998, the Mexican meat producers had a serious drought and claimed that U.S. producers were dumping beef and pork in Mexico at unfairly low prices.[4] A description of the effect of NAFTA on American producers of brussels sprouts is described in Marketing Strategies box 15-1.

When business firms encounter unfair trade restrictions, they can ask their governments to appeal to GATT to impose sanctions to stop the offending practices. In addition to sanctions such as countervailing tariffs and antidumping fines, governments threaten retaliatory

---

MARKETING STRATEGIES *15-1*

Free Trade in Brussels Sprouts?

Before the North American Free Trade Agreement passed, 93 percent of the U.S. brussels sprouts were grown in foggy, oceanside fields in central California. With the passage of NAFTA, brussels sprouts are now being shipped in from Mexico. About 3,500 acres in California are devoted to producing the smelly mini-cabbages that are hated by children. The problem for U.S. growers is brussels sprouts are labor intensive and must be picked by hand. Where U.S. growers pay their workers $6 per hour, Mexican farmers pay theirs $6 day. This pay differential makes the future for U.S. growers look bleak. NAFTA has some protections against this type of economic damage, but it takes influence that the few U.S. brussels sprouts growers do not have. U.S. brussels sprouts production amounts to only $27 million a year and the average American eats only three a year. To help save their businesses, American growers are trying to persuade the Mexican growers to delay exporting until late January when the U.S. harvest slows. Of course, if the growers could get Americans to eat a few more brussels sprouts the market would let them survive. However, if Mexico continues to ship brussels sprouts in November and December, American growers will have to find something else to grow on their valuable oceanside fields.

— *The law of comparative advantage is quite willing to eat brussels sprouts.*

Source: Martha Mendoza, "Brussels Sprouts NAFTA'd," *The Denver Post*, November 25, 1998, p. 13A.

action. For example, not long ago, the EU said it would no longer accept U.S. beef that had traces of growth hormones. This would have drastically reduced the amount of U.S. beef shipped to Europe. The United States countered by saying it would impose tariffs on an equivalent amount of EU food shipped to the United States. Since neither side wanted trade to decline, there was a strong incentive to compromise on this issue.

Currency Exchange Problems

INTEGRATING
... with
Finance

International marketing is complicated because each country or trading block has its own currency. Thus, when you sell products in Japan, you are likely to be paid in yen. Since the exchange rate between dollars and yen changes hourly, you may receive fewer dollars than you expected. The possibility of serious exchange losses is so high that some small firms avoid international trade altogether. More experienced companies have learned to hedge their financial positions in the futures markets to reduce currency exchange problems.

The impact of realignments among currencies can seriously damage a firm's sales and profits. To help control these problems, 11 European countries have formed a monetary union. The currencies of the 11 EMU nations are no longer quoted separately, but are valued only in terms of their fixed relationship to the new euro. In 2002, national currencies will be phased out and the euro will be the standard currency of Europe. The advantage to business is that they will no longer have to cover the costs of exchanging currencies. Firms outside the EMU will benefit as well since they will no longer have to hedge future exchange risks for 11 different currencies.[5] An example of the impact currency values can have on international marketers is described in Marketing Strategies box 15-2.

An even more serious problem occurs when you want to trade with a country whose currency is not readily convertible. This has been a problem in doing business with the Russians. The ruble has little value outside the country since the Russians have few products that outsiders want to buy. Thus companies that do business in Russia often have to work out complex barter arrangements to extract their profits. PepsiCo, for example, has converted rubles into Russian Stolichnaya vodka for the past 20 years and shipped the vodka to the United States, where it is sold for dollars. Recently, PepsiCo entered a joint venture with three Ukrainian companies to sell $1 billion worth of ships to foreign firms. Some of the proceeds will be reinvested in the shipbuilding venture, and some will be used to buy bottling equipment and to build five Pepsi bottling plants in the Ukraine. The rest will finance the opening of 100 PepsiCo-owned Pizza Hut restaurants in the republic. This example shows the complex financial deals that are needed to get around currency exchange problems and to help Pepsi protect its market share in the Ukraine from inroads by Coca-Cola.

One solution to the exchange problem is for the seller to accept payment only in dollars or other hard currency. However, some countries have limits on the amount of these currencies that are available to pay for imports. Thus, when you trade with countries with foreign exchange restrictions, you have to be imaginative in arranging for payment.

Unstable Governments

When the governments of trading partners change frequently, there is a greater risk of business losses. New governments often modify the rules that determine how business is conducted. The most extreme action is nationalization of the property of foreign firms. Other drastic actions that can cause trouble are restrictions on the transfer of currencies and revisions in tariffs or quotas. When you have to deal with unstable governments, there is a strong incentive to export rather than risk direct investment.

Historical examples of countries where nationalization of industry caused serious problems for foreign firms include Mexico with petroleum, England with transportation, and Italy with cars. In each of these cases, nationalization has led to monopolies for the govern-

APPLYING
. . . to
Business-to-
Business
Marketing

INTEGRATING
. . . with
Finance

MARKETING STRATEGIES *15-2*

Falling Peso Kills U.S. Venture

The U.S.'s biggest distributor of office supplies, Unisource Worldwide Inc., saw an opportunity in Mexico to modernize an industry dominated by small, inefficient family enterprises. Unisource bought up 20 Mexican distributors in 1995 and went to work. They quickly found that the warehouses of the companies they bought often had dirt floors, making it impossible to use forklifts. Also many of the existing accounts were too small to be serviced economically and the field salespeople had to be retrained on how to sell. Unisource stuck with their new venture for three years, but when the Mexican government devalued the peso in 1998 they decided to divest themselves of the Mexican unit and take a $70 million write-down against earnings. Mexico's declining currency hurt because Unisource made its investments in dollars and was earning in pesos. The company was also damaged by falling prices for paper, which accounted for two-thirds of their sales in Mexico.

— *Currency risk can make the difference between success and failure in overseas ventures.*

Source: Joel Millman, "Unisource's Exit From Mexico Is Cautionary Tale for U.S. Firms," *The Wall Street Journal*. October 23, 1998, p. A17.

Courtesy Unisource Worldwide, Inc.

ment firms and losses for foreign competition. Once governments own business firms, they routinely protect them with tariffs and quotas. Thus countries with a history of nationalization are not good environments for international investment. One way you can compete in these countries is to form joint ventures in which capital is raised locally and the outside firm provides technical and marketing expertise. While there are still risks with this arrangement, the chances for massive capital losses are reduced.

Cultural Factors

Successful international marketing demands that you pay close attention to the special needs and customs of your buyers. Overseas buyers often have different concepts of time, space, and etiquette. Thus, before you create a marketing plan for overseas business, you need to find out how these customers regard and use your products. The marketing of automobiles provides a number of examples of the impact of cultural differences.

Selling Cars Internationally   There are many large auto markets in the world where cars travel on the left side of the road (Japan, England, and Australia). This makes it important to have the steering wheel on the right side of the car. For many years American manufacturers ignored this factor and tried, without much success, to sell left-hand drive cars in these countries. American cars also sold poorly in Japan because U.S. automobile firms did not provide the folding side mirrors and the fit and finish demanded by Japanese buyers. On the other hand, when Toyota came to America, they sold only left-hand drive cars, they made their cars bigger, more powerful, and they added the cup holders and extra storage spaces needed by Americans for their long auto trips. Careful attention to cultural differences allowed the Japanese to grab a large piece of the U.S. market while the insensitive American firms have yet to figure out why they failed in the Japanese market.

American firms have also not done well shipping cars to Europe. Part of the problem is that American cars are too big for European roads, parking spaces, and garages. Also many American cars come equipped with automatic transmissions and air conditioning that either are not needed or do not appeal to European buyers. A further problem is that gasoline carries much lower taxes in America than it does in Europe, which means the engines in American cars tend to be larger and consume more fuel than European buyers can afford. In addition, American firms do not offer diesel engines preferred by many European buyers for their high mileage potential. Diesel engines seem underpowered, noisy, and dirty to Americans and are only used in trucks. The only success American firms have had in Europe is to design and build cars locally for the special needs of that market.

Other Social Considerations   Some cultures are more protective of their citizens' privacy than in America and some European countries. Mall interviews to gather consumer data, for example, are totally unacceptable in Muslim countries. In some countries, women are not allowed to drive or to work in certain occupations. In many countries comparative advertising is taboo and sexual innuendo in ads is unacceptable. Other markets severely restrict the content and duration of television advertising. Some further examples showing the impact of cultural differences on marketing plans include the following:

- Japan's Mitsubishi Motors had to rename its Pajero model in Spanish-speaking countries because the term describes the process of masturbation.
- Germans prefer salad dressing in a tube.
- Kellogg's Pop Tart failed in Europe because many homes do not have toasters.
- PepsiCo's Mountain Dew soft drink is difficult to pronounce in Portuguese, and sales have been slow in these markets.
- Two-liter pop bottles failed in Spain because refrigerators were too small.
- Toyota Motors was forced to drop the number from its MR2 car in France because the combination sounds like a French swear-word.

Although these examples suggest that you should adapt products and brand names to fit local cultural norms, it is possible to go too far. Some imported products are successful *because* they are different, and drastic changes can destroy their appeal. For example, when Disney was designing a theme park for Japan, its local partners insisted that nothing be changed from what was available at Disney World in Florida. They cautioned that customers did not want an Americanized Japanese park; they wanted the "real" Disney creation. This means that you must study the needs of each country to determine what portions of the product and marketing program need to be changed and what should be left alone.

WHICH MARKETS TO ENTER

Selecting international markets for expansion resembles the process of segmentation. First, you want to be sure that there are enough people in the new market to make the project worthwhile. Also, it is important that your product or service have distinct competitive advantages. Finally, you need to consider the higher risks that accompany global marketing because of cultural differences and the possibility of government restrictions. For example, many international firms consider South Korea to be a difficult market to enter because of excessive government red tape and the problems in bringing additional capital into the country. However, disposable income there is rising rapidly, and South Korea is now the second largest consumer market in Asia after Japan. Also, the population is well educated, and the number of two-income families is rising. This makes convenience foods and higher-quality products that are popular in the West more attractive among South Koreans. Ralston Purina saw milk consumption rising—the consumption of breakfast cereal closely tracks milk consumption throughout the world—and jumped in. It built a $10 million plant to make Chex cereal, and sales are growing rapidly. Purina's success in South Korea was helped by the absence of strong local cereal manufacturers.

APPLYING
... *to*
Consumer
Packaged
Goods
Marketing

Another way to control risk is to enter markets that are nearby and that share a common cultural heritage. American businesspeople have followed this advice; Canada is our largest trading partner and an important area for investment. Not only do we share a language with English-speaking Canada, but most Canadians live near the border. This makes it easier to deliver merchandise and facilitates cross-border promotion by radio and television.

The ultimate test of international market viability involves a financial analysis to determine the potential return on investment. As a first step, you need a good measure of potential demand. Then you must estimate the costs of making your goods and services available in another country. If you are exporting, you must predict transportation costs, tariffs, and dealer margins. If you are locating production facilities in the new market, the costs of labor, raw materials, and taxes have to be considered. Sometimes the availability of raw materials is a serious problem in less developed economies. McDonald's, for example, learned a great deal about local conditions while developing its first fast-food restaurants in Russia. This market appears to be a tremendous opportunity for McDonald's. The population is large, and there is need for high-quality, quick-service restaurants. However, the limited supply of food in the grocery stores that ensures success of the restaurants also means that it is difficult to get the needed raw materials for its french fries and burgers. Currency exchange problems limit the amount of food that can be imported, and McDonald's has had to work with local suppliers to bring them up to the required quality standards. This takes time, and it will be years before McDonald's has a significant market share in Russia.

APPLYING
... *to*
Restaurant
Marketing

The last step in your evaluation of export marketing is to calculate the profitability for each prospective country. These profits should be compared and adjusted for different levels of risk. Remember that a high profit is less attractive if there is a strong chance for property expropriation and restricted financial transfers. Obviously, the presence of a stable and friendly host government makes international marketing much more attractive.

MARKET ENTRY STRATEGIES

Once you have selected an international market for development, you have to decide on the best way to proceed. A variety of entry strategies can be employed to present your products to global customers. The main choices are exporting, licensing, joint ventures, and investing in your own facilities (Figure 15-1). These alternatives vary in commitment, risk, and profit potential. Note that these approaches are not mutually exclusive. Different entry strategies can be used at the same time in separate markets. Also, you may want to use more than one strategy to enter a single foreign country. A line of products might be licensed for local production and another line manufactured in a joint venture (country B, Figure 15-1). Each of these approaches will be discussed in the following pages.

The emphasis here is on expanding the market for a product from your home country to international markets. You could, of course, acquire brand names that already exist in global markets. To expand as a world marketer of fish products, H.J. Heinz (Star-Kist Seafood) established a beachhead in Europe with the acquisition of the Marie Elisabeth trademark from a Portuguese sardine packer. Also, Thomson, the French electronics giant, invaded the United States by snapping up the GE/RCA television brands.

Exporting

The most common way to enter international markets is through export (Figure 15-1). Extra production from the home market is simply shipped overseas using established distribution channels. This approach only requires transportation and payment of duties, so there is little financial risk. A slightly more expensive approach is to make modest adjustments in your product to adapt it to the special needs of overseas customers. These changes may include modification in the size of the product or package, a new name, local language instructions, and special colors.

Several levels of organizational arrangements can be employed to assist exporting activities. Often, the first step is to hire a special agent or trading company from your own country to help you contact international customers. These people are paid on commission and handle all the paperwork involved in overseas selling. The second step is to set up an export department in your own organization. This department is staffed with an export sales manager and clerks to handle the necessary documents. A third level of commitment involves hiring for-

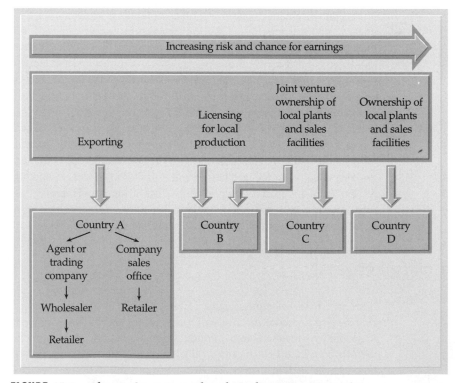

FIGURE 15-1   Alternative International Market Entry Strategies

eign-based dealers or agents. In exchange for exclusive rights to sell your products, these people provide invaluable access to local buyers. For example, in 1998 Honda announced plans to double the number of locally owned car dealers in eastern and southern Europe by the year 2000. Honda wanted to expand its dealer network ahead of the introduction of the common European currency, the euro.[6] The highest level of export investment involves setting up your own international-based sales branch. Although this requires higher fixed costs for salespeople, facilities, and inventory, it gives you more control over the global marketing effort. Your choice of export arrangements depends on the size of the opportunity and the amount of money you have to risk on this venture. A summary of key considerations in developing an international dimension to your business is given in Table 15-1.

> **APPLYING**
> *. . . to*
> *Consumer*
> *Durable*
> *Goods*
> *Marketing*

An example of how to make money exporting bicycles is provided by Cannondale, a U.S. manufacturer of high-priced racing and mountain bikes. Cannondale sells more than 30 percent of its $77 million bike volume in Europe and other countries. Its initial distribution channel in Japan was through Mitsubishi, a large trading company. Mitsubishi insisted that Cannondale add another layer of traditional bicycle wholesalers to sell to retailers (see Figure 15-1, country A). This raised costs, and since the wholesalers handled several manufacturers, they provided less attention to any one brand. Cannondale did not like the service it was receiving, so it terminated Mitsubishi and set up its own sales office in a small town outside Osaka. Next, it hired two Japanese-speaking American professional bicyclists who lived in Japan to promote its bikes. The two raced Cannondale bikes every weekend, gaining a lot of free publicity in the bicycle press. On weekdays they make sales calls on bike dealers. Working directly with the dealers has revealed that Japanese prefer smaller bikes in flashier colors—feedback the company never got from Mitsubishi. In the first year of the new program, Cannondale tripled the number of dealers carrying its bikes and sales quadrupled to $2 million. Despite the startup costs of opening its own sales office, Cannondale Japan earned $60,000 in profits in its first year of operation.[7] These results show that exporting can be profitable.

TABLE 15-1 Marketing Do's and Don'ts for New Exporters

- **Do develop a marketing plan before you begin.** You must have clearly defined goals and objectives and know how to reach them. Don't take this crucial first step without competent advice.
- **Do secure top management commitment for the long haul.** It takes time and money to establish yourself in any new market, particularly one with which you are unfamiliar.
- **Do select overseas representatives with care.** Evaluate personally the people who will handle your account, their facilities and resources, and how they work.
- **Do establish a base for orderly growth.** Concentrate on one or two overseas markets and build them up before expanding worldwide.
- **Modify products to comply with rules and the local culture.** Local regulations and preferences cannot be ignored. Make necessary product modifications at the factory.
- **Do print sales, service and warranty data in the local language.** Be sure to *use an experienced translator.* Don't cut corners here—the results can be disastrous.
- **Do consider using an export management company.** If you don't want or can't afford an export department right now, consider appointing an export management company.
- **Don't neglect export business when domestic sales rise.** Letting exports slide when domestic sales boom discourages your overseas agents, turns off your customers, damaging your reputation abroad, and leaves you without recourse when domestic sales fall.
- **Don't treat export business like a stepchild.** If you regularly boost domestic sales through advertising, discount offers, sales incentive campaigns, and preferential credit and warranty protection, apply these same incentives to overseas markets.
- **Don't assume that the same marketing technique works everywhere.** Cultural preferences and taboos must be respected. Your overseas representative should be able to advise on effective local marketing.

Source: U.S. Department of Commerce

Licensing

Once you get some experience with export marketing, you may want to license organizations in other countries to produce goods and services to expand market coverage. With this approach, a licensor signs contracts with licensees for the use of a manufacturing process, trademarks, or trade secrets for a fixed royalty percentage. These royalties typically run 2 to 4 percent of sales but sometimes amount to 10 percent or more. The licensor gains exposure in new markets without having to risk local investments. Because very little investment is required, the profits on licensing agreements can be extremely lucrative.

Licensees gain production or management knowledge of well-known products without having to spend money on R&D. In addition, licensees benefit from advertising and promotion expenditures by the parent organization designed to build worldwide demand. Coca-Cola and Pepsi both used licensing to expand their business internationally. With the reunification of East and West Germany, Coke moved quickly to license beverage organizations in eastern Germany to bottle and distribute Coca-Cola. Coke advanced $140 million to help its licensees upgrade bottling machinery and vending machines. As a result of such aggressive moves, international sales now account for 80 percent of the company's soft drink profits. Coke and Pepsi maintain control over their international licensees by supplying them with the concentrated syrup that provides the flavor for the soft drinks.

Although licensing can be very profitable and can allow you to expand rapidly, it does carry some serious risks. You have very little control over a licensee's production and marketing efforts. For example, an American company signed a licensing agreement with an Asian firm to produce trademarked fasteners for its Australian customers. After teaching the licensee how to make quality fasteners, the U.S. company was surprised when the licensee began to ship its own private brand of fasteners into the Australian market. The American firm felt betrayed by these actions so they terminated the licensing agreement and bought a plant in China to serve the local market and Australia. Another example of the perils of licensing is described in Marketing in Action box 15-2.

In addition to reducing control over marketing activities, licensing exposes you to potential losses of trade secrets and production technology. To make licensing work, you have to show outsiders how production processes work. This means that you may be training competitors to enter your market when the licensing agreement ends. For example, Quicksilver Enterprises was unable to sell its ultralight airplanes in Brazil because of steep import duties, so the U.S. firm licensed a local firm to build and sell its planes in Brazil. However, six months after Quicksilver's engineers taught the concern how to build, fly, and fix the planes, the royalties stopped. The Brazilian company claimed that it had changed the design, and Quicksilver was out $100,000 in royalties and lost all sales in Brazil for several years.

Another problem is that royalties are paid on the basis of sales reported by your licensee, which means that it is to the licensee's advantage to understate volume to reduce the size of royalty payments. Obtaining an accurate audit of sales figures may be difficult in some countries, and signing up trustworthy business partners is critical to the success of a licensing program.

Joint Ventures

The objective of joint ventures is to find local partners to share the risks and profits of international market expansion. This can be done by buying an interest in an existing local business or by starting up a new venture with a resident business. Teaming up with a local partner cuts the size of your investment and allows you to gain valuable assistance in regard to customers, labor availability, raw material services, and distribution channels. The outside partner often provides the technical and production expertise, and the inside partner provides marketing connections.

MARKETING IN ACTION *15-2*

The Perils of Licensing

A number of international firms have ended long-standing partnerships with Japanese companies. These associations provided outside firms with easy entry for their products, but they often led to problems. Borden ventured into Japan in 1971 with a licensing agreement with Meiji Milk, Japan's biggest dairy company. Initially the agreement worked well, as Borden got access to Meiji's vast distribution network and local production assured prompt delivery of fresh products. Together, Borden and Meiji created a large market for premium ice cream. Their Lady Borden brand secured 60 percent of an eventual $125 million market. However, liberalization of milk product import rules allowed the entry of Häagen-Dazs and Breyer's Grand Ice Cream from the United States. Lady Borden's market share slipped from 60 to 50 percent and Meiji was slow to respond to the competitive challenge.

Borden tried to renegotiate its agreement with Meiji to gain more control over the marketing of Lady Borden. Unfortunately, a change in management at Meiji delayed the implementation of new arrangements. Borden decided to break its ties with Meiji and set up their own sales subsidiary. Meiji agreed to continue to promote Lady Borden for 14 months until its licenses expired. Since Meiji had learned a great deal from Borden about ice cream manufacture, they decided to protect their position in the market by introducing two new premium brands of their own in the interim until the licensing agreement with Borden expired. One brand, Aya, stressed Meiji's Japanese roots. A second brand, called Breuges, is similar in price and content to Lady Borden. Borden did not believe it was fair for Meiji to introduce new brands while it was committed to promote Lady Borden and threatened to sue to stop their distribution. In addition, the loss of local production capacity meant that Borden had to import ice cream all the way from Australia and New Zealand. What appeared to be an attractive deal for Borden turned out to be a public relations and financial disaster.

— *Licensing works well for entering markets quickly but often creates problems in the long run.*

Source: Yumiko Ono, "Borden's Messy Split with Firm in Japan Points Up Perils of Partnerships There," *The Wall Street Journal*, January 28, 1991, p. B1.

Joint ventures are also attractive when the outside firm does not have the financial reserves to start a wholly owned operation or wishes to limit the financial risk of market expansion. Sometimes joint ventures are the price host governments exact when they allow access to their markets. Politicians often view joint ventures as a way to generate jobs, train workers, and reward local business interests.

The main problem with joint ventures is disagreement on how to manage the business. Outside firms often prefer to be majority stockholders in joint ventures so that they can control the operation to minimize the chance of losses. After all, outside partners usually provide the technology and production support for the project and have the most to lose if the project goes bad. Local partners may be more concerned with extracting current profits rather than with long-term success. The control issue is complicated further by rules in some countries that local people must own 50 percent or more of the stock of joint ventures. This has been the case in China until recently. Six Japanese firms negotiated a joint venture for a $4 billion petrochemical plant with two Chinese firms. The plant is located in Liaoning, China, has a refining capacity of 2 million metric tons, and produces 450,000 metric tons of ethylene a year. Ethylene is in short supply in China, and the project looks promising to the Japanese. To protect themselves, the Japanese firms have negotiated a 51 percent stake in the project.

Ownership of Facilities

You can obtain the most control over international marketing activities by constructing your own factories in host countries. Local manufacturing provides significant savings on transportation costs, and resident labor is often cheaper than home market workers. Also, host governments may provide lucrative financial incentives to attract outside manufacturers.

INTEGRATING
. . . with Finance, Production Management

Ownership also gives you a better image with customers because you are creating jobs for residents. In addition, ownership of facilities allows you to learn more about local demand so that you can tailor your products, advertising, and distribution plans to host country needs. Sometimes the operation of factories in other countries is the only way to get around tariff barriers and alleviate political pressures against imported goods.

The main problem with local manufacturing is that you expose yourself to a higher risk of serious financial loss. Overseas facilities may be damaged by war, nationalized by governments, or hamstrung by inflation or local currency exchange problems. In addition, host governments may have stiff requirements on severance pay that make it expensive to close down overseas operations.

APPLYING
. . . to Consumer Durable Goods Marketing

Some of the factors influencing decisions on ownership of facilities are demonstrated by DaimlerChrysler's decision to build Dakota pickup trucks in Brazil. Until the year 2000, Brazil had a 49 percent tariff on imported vehicles. This very high tariff placed an effective limit on the number of vehicles that could be imported into Brazil and forced manufacturers to build local plants if they expected to share in the large Brazilian auto market. Chrysler was late getting to Brazil, a country where 13 auto companies announced plans to invest $19 billion in new factories by the year 2000. The DaimlerChrysler plant cost a modest $315 million and was designed to limit their financial risk in this emerging market. Chrysler arranged for Dana Corporation of Toledo, Ohio, to assemble a rolling chassis consisting of a frame, axles, brakes, and wheels at a nearby plant. The Dakota truck chassis are then rolled into the Chrysler plant where engines, transmissions, and body parts are added to complete the vehicles. Dana's locally produced chassis accounts for 33 percent of the value of the vehicle. Because Dana assembles the rolling chassis in Brazil, Chrysler can count the entire value of the unit as local, allowing Chrysler big discounts on import duties on body panels, engines, transmissions, equipment, and thousands of other cars it brings into Brazil from the United States. If Chrysler made the chassis at its own plant, it could credit only the parts it actually made in Brazil as local. The rolling chassis plan allowed Chrysler to hire fewer people, made its factory smaller, reduced its upfront investment, and shortened the start-up time.[8] Since Chrysler opened its Dakota truck plant, Brazil and Argentina have agreed that the Mercosur trading block will have a common import tariff of 35 percent and eliminate tariffs on trade of cars and parts between member countries. This means that Chrysler will have free access to sell Dakota pickup trucks in Brazil, Argentina, Paraguay, and Uruguay, a market of 200 million consumers.[9]

GLOBAL VERSUS LOCALIZED MARKETING

An ongoing controversy is whether firms should pursue a global or localized strategy in their international marketing activities. Global marketing emphasizes selling the same product with the same ads all over the world. This approach implies that the world is becoming homogenized and everyone wants the same things. One reason global marketing is so effective today is that global communications networks are opening access to more markets. CNN now reaches 78 million households in 100 countries, and MTV has an audience of 310 million in 78 countries. Localized marketing, on the other hand, implies that customers' needs are different in each country, and that you should adjust your product and your ads to meet local market conditions.

Both sides in this controversy have their advocates and a rationale. Global marketing can save money and increase profits. Colgate-Palmolive, for example, introduced its tartar-control toothpaste in more than 40 countries using only two ads. For every country that used the same ad, the firm saved $1 to $2 million in production costs alone. Colgate has saved millions more by standardizing the look and packaging of certain brands and reducing the number of factories that make them. Although global marketing has worked well for some companies and product categories, there seem to be an equal number of examples where it has failed. Marketing in Action box 15-3 describes such a situation in the German PC market.

MARKETING IN ACTION *15-3*

Compaq Dumps Global and Goes Local

APPLYING
. . . to Consumer Durable Goods Marketing

INTEGRATING
. . . with Production/ Operations Management

Compaq is a large and successful company with 8 percent of the world consumer market for personal computers. The company's chief executive is German and it was natural for Compaq to set up its European headquarters in the biggest country, Germany. However, despite the large numbers of technology savvy consumers with money to spend, Compaq was only able to get 1.2 percent of the large German market. Sixty percent of the German consumer PC market is owned by an army of 30,000 mom-and-pop computer assemblers. Although Germany is not known for bargains, personal computers are dirt cheap. The average price of a midrange PC is $1,272 in the U.S.; it is only $1,059 in Germany. Two-thirds of German PC buyers are willing to buy inexpensive no-name brands without features considered essential for U.S. computers. Normally, Compaq uses a global approach and designs computers to sell all over the world without considering differences in local manufacturing costs or market conditions. In Germany, Compaq pinpoints an appropriate German cost and design and tells local developers to design a PC to fit. To meet their price objectives, Compaq has dispensed with expensive custom software and Compaq keyboards and Compaq mouses. This allowed its local manufacturer to swap any component that it could find cheaper elsewhere. The resulting Compaq PCs for the German market do not have the usual internal modem and speakers. They are also taller and thinner to make them easier to ship and move around the factory. As a result of Compaq's decision to go local, its German market share jumped to seventh from 10th with 3.5 percent of the market.

— *Local PC manufacturing can cut costs and raise market share.*

Source: Matthew Rose, "Compaq Finds German Market Tough to Crack," *The Wall Street Journal*, November 20, 1998, pp. B1, B8.

Courtesy Compaq Computer

Problems with Global Marketing

Procter & Gamble took a sexy soap commercial that worked well in Europe and tried to use it in Japan. The Camay soap ad was based on the premise that women want to be attractive to men. In the ad a Japanese woman is seated in a bathtub when her husband walks into the bathroom. The woman starts telling him about her new beauty soap, but the husband, stroking her shoulder, hints that suds aren't on his mind. Japanese saw this ad as rude and intrusive, and it was withdrawn. P&G concedes that it would not have made the mistake if a Japanese woman had been running the campaign there. When a woman was put in charge, a successful ad showing a beautiful European woman, alone, in a European-style bath was created for the Japanese market.

Insufficient Research Often the failure of global marketing programs is due to insufficient research on the intended target countries. Blockbuster, the number-one video rental store in the United States, looked to attractive overseas markets and found that Germany is the fourth largest video rental market in the world. Also, preliminary research revealed that the name Blockbuster had good brand recognition among young and middle-aged Germans. In 1995, Blockbuster opened 7 stores in Munich and 10 in Berlin. Although Blockbuster paid attention to the German market, the stores languished. Subsequent research showed the Germans preferred to watch movies in theaters. Also Blockbuster placed the stores in downtown areas, whereas all competitors were in residential areas. Perhaps Blockbuster's most serious error was that initial research failed to reveal that one-third of all video rentals in Germany are for pornographic films. Even though Blockbuster did not rent pornographic films, all video stores had a negative image in Germany and children were encouraged to stay away from them. After two years, Blockbuster closed all of its stores in Germany. Blockbuster conducted extensive market research on the Japanese market and its 38 stores there have been more successful.[10] Blockbuster was allowed to keep its Japanese stores open every day from 10 A.M. until midnight, whereas store hours in Germany were restricted and Blockbuster had to close on Sundays and holidays. These examples suggest that it is essential to conduct careful research before entering overseas markets.

Overstandardization Sometimes global marketing programs are too rigid about product specifications and the use of standard promotional activities. Ford, for example, has tried on several occasions to develop "world" cars that could be sold in Europe and North America. The company failed in the 1980s to develop a "world" Escort and again in the 1990s with its Mondeo-Contour-Mystique family of midsize cars aimed at both continents. Anyone who has driven a car in Europe realizes how difficult it is to make a car small enough to negotiate the narrow streets of Europe yet big enough to compete on the wide avenues of America. Ford's Contour/Mystique twins did not sell well in the States because they cost almost as much as larger Toyota Camrys and Honda Accords, and their backseat area was very small. Ford has developed another world car about the size of an Escort that they think will do well in Europe and the United States. The Ford executive in charge of global small car development avoided regional jealousies by installing a Briton as chief program engineer, a German as chief technical officer, an Irish woman as project manager, and an Australian as chief designer. To make the car roomier for the U.S. market, the designer made the new Focus model three inches taller so occupants sit up straighter, allowing more legroom and making it easier to enter and exit the car. They also tightened the steering, improved the ride, the crash protection, and occupant comfort. Ford contracted the manufacture of 15 major subassemblies for the Focus to outside suppliers so they could cut the cost of making the new model by $1,000. Ford expects to sell one million of the Focus cars a year worldwide.[11]

Another standardization problem occurred when Heinz tried to expand its 9 Lives cat food and Morris the Cat logo into Moscow. They found Russians thought Morris the Cat

APPLYING
. . . to Consumer Services Marketing

APPLYING
. . . to Consumer Durable Goods Marketing

should be fatter-looking, which they deemed healthier. Also Russian cat lovers prefer to feed their cats beef-flavored food instead of the tuna favored by Americans.[12] These cases show that excessive standardization of global marketing programs can create problems.

Think Global but Act Local

The examples we have discussed suggest that global marketing often works and can save money. Perhaps the best approach is to think global but act local. This means that you should have global objectives but should not ignore local market conditions. While Colgate toothpaste is available worldwide, for example, the company also makes a spicy toothpaste especially for the Mideastern market and sells a baby soap named Cadum only in France. Similarly, PepsiCo allows offices in other countries to edit and dub its global ads and to plan their own promotional activities. The extent of decentralization of marketing planning is shown by surveys indicating that host country marketing managers make up to 86 percent of advertising decisions, 74 percent of pricing decisions, and 61 percent of channel decisions. However, product design decisions are usually reserved for the parent organization. Global marketing is alive, but the trend seems to be to adjust plans to meet the special needs of particular customers in other countries.

Strategies for Localized Marketing

A set of strategies for adapting to local conditions is shown in Figure 15-2. Strategy 1 is a global marketing approach that sells the same product in all countries with the same promotional appeals. This strategy has the advantage of low costs and seems to work best for business products such as airlines, computers, and machine tools. Strategy 2 sells the same product in different markets but changes the message for each set of customers. An example is the motor scooter that is sold as primary transportation in less developed countries and as a recreational vehicle in the United States. Strategy 3 focuses on adapting the product to meet local conditions but uses the same advertising message in all countries. Detergents and gasoline are routinely adjusted to meet water and weather conditions in each market area and are sold with standard promotional campaigns.

Strategy 4 in Figure 15-2 adapts both products and communications for each market entered. When Nestlé tried to break into the British instant coffee market, it found that coffee preferences were more American than European. This forced Nestlé to prepare a lighter blend of instant coffee for the British market. Because coffee is not as popular as tea in England, Nestlé had to use more aggressive advertising to attract the attention of potential customers. Strategy 5 is to invent something to meet the special needs of a local market. This is likely to be an expensive and risky approach to global marketing. For example, because of the lack of electricity in many underdeveloped countries, a South African firm invented a hand-powered radio. Users turn a crank that activates a spring powered generator inside the radio. Each time the spring is tightened it powers the radio for an hour of listening. This radio can be sold anywhere in the world where consumers lack access to electricity or expensive batteries for portable radios. Although the strategies shown in Figure 15-2 do not cover all possible market situations, they do provide a useful set of approaches for many localized marketing problems.

SUMMARY

Every day the world becomes smaller because of improvements in transportation and communications. One result is that international marketing is becoming more important to the success of business organizations. Part of your job as marketing manager is to under-

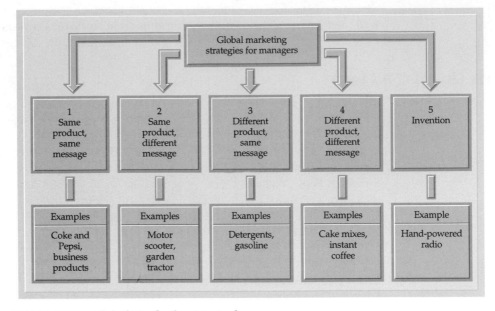

FIGURE 15-2   Global Marketing Strategies

stand the environment of international business and to select the best markets for overseas expansion. This involves calculating the expected rate of return on investment for each country and balancing it against the risk of loss. Next, you must decide on the most appropriate method for entering international markets. In some situations, exporting is the best approach; in others, you may want to use licensing, joint ventures, or direct investment.

A common problem with international marketing is deciding whether to adapt your products and advertising to the special needs of individual countries. Some organizations have been successful with a global approach where the same products and promotions are used throughout the world. Others have had more luck tailoring their products and advertising to the preferences of each market.

NOTES

1. Jackie Calmes, "Despite Buoyant Economic Times, Americans Don't Buy Free Trade," *The Wall Street Journal*, December 10, 1998, p. A10.
2. Robert S. Greenberger, "No Quick Solution Is Seen with EU in Banana Dispute," *The Wall Street Journal*, December 3, 1998, p. A14; James Cox, "The United States vs. The European Union: Two Sides of the Banana Split," *USA Today*, March 3, 1999, p. 3B.
3. Stephen D. Moore, "Hopes Dwindle that EU Will Dismantle Draconian Price Controls on Medicines," *The Wall Street Journal*, December 7, 1998, p. A26.
4. Joel Millman, "Mexican Meat Producers Take on U.S.," *The Wall Street Journal*, November 5, 1998, p. A17.
5. "Review & Outlook: Lessons from Europe," *The Wall Street Journal*, December 7, 1998, p. A30.
6. "Honda to Expand in Europe," *The Wall Street Journal*, November 6, 1998, p. A17.
7. Andrew Tanzer, "Just Get Out and Sell," *Forbes*, September 26, 1992, pp. 68–69.
8. Gregory L. White, "Chrysler Makes Manufacturing Inroads at Plant in Brazil," *The Wall Street Journal*, August 13, 1998, p. B4.
9. Peter Fritsch, "Argentina, Brazil Agree on Car Tariffs," *The Wall Street Journal*, December 11, 1998, p. A10.
10. Khanh T. L. Tran, "Blockbuster Does Boffo In Japan, A Positive Sign for U.S. Retailers," *The Wall Street Journal*, August 19, 1998, p. A14.

11. Robert L. Simison, "Ford Hopes Its New Focus Will Be a Global Bestseller," *The Wall Street Journal*, September 15, 1998, p. B10.
12. Erika Rasmusson, "Global Warning," *Sales & Marketing Management*, November 1998, p. 17.

SUGGESTED READING

Chryssochoidis, George M., and Veronica Wong. "Rolling Out New Products Across Country Markets: An Empirical Study of Causes of Delays," *Journal of Product Innovation Management,* Vol. 15 (1998), pp. 16–41.

Maruca, Regina F. "The Right Way to Go Global," *Harvard Business Review* (March–April 1994), pp. 134–145.

REFERENCES

Cateora, Philip R., and John L. Graham. *International Marketing,* 10th ed. (Homewood, IL: Irwin, 1998).

Czinkota, Michael R., and Ilkna A. Ronkainen. *International Marketing,* 5th ed. (Chicago: Dryden, 1998),

Jain, Subhash C. *International Marketing Management,* 5th ed. (Cincinnati, Ohio: South Western, 1995).

QUESTIONS

1. Dell Computer announced plans in 1998 to invest $125 million over five years to build a plant in the Brazil state of Rio Grande do Sul. International companies with local production plants dominate Latin America's personal computer market. Dell ranked ninth in 1998 with 1.2 percent of the Latin America market. Rio Grande do Sul offered Dell generous tax and financial incentives plus 140 acres of land to build its plant. Why does Dell want to make computers in Brazil rather than export them from Texas?

2. In 1998, overall imported car sales in Japan declined 26 percent while the sales of the Rover Mini rose 17 percent. The squat, boxy Mini has barely changed since the first one was produced in England in 1959. Half the Minis made in the United Kingdom are shipped to Japan despite the Mini's selling price being twice that of equivalent Japanese produced cars. The Mini is popular because it is cute, agile, different, and it looks like the car driven by the hapless Mr. Bean, a popular television character in Japan. Rover's success with the Mini in Japan is also due to their careful attention to special campaigns and fervent fans who have built up an industry that includes Mini shops, Mini races, Mini clubs, and a magazine called *Mini Freak.* Is the Mini triumph in Japan an example of global marketing or is it due to localized marketing?

3. The EU has imposed antidumping duties on 15 Japanese makers of computer printers for selling at prices below those charged in their domestic market. The growing European printer market is estimated to be $1.75 billion a year, and Japan's share has grown from 49 percent to 73 percent in three years. Is the EU really concerned with the evils of dumping, or does it have some other agenda? Are European buyers better off paying the higher prices that the new duties will require? How are the Japanese likely to respond to the new duties?

4. When the Japanese economy was in a recession in 1998, Anheuser-Busch had success selling a cheap, potent low-malt brew by emphasizing its "extra strong" alcohol content. Japanese regulations allow the sale of beverages with a dry weight content of only 25 percent of expensive malt, whereas beer must have 66.7 percent malt. Although the U.S. Bureau of Alcohol, Tobacco and Firearms prohibits brewers from using messages that hype strength on labels or ads, Japan does not have these restrictions. Is it ethical to use alcohol content to sell low malt beverages in Japan when it is illegal to use these tactics in the United States and the higher alcohol content could be detrimental to the health of Japanese consumers?

5. The Chinese have agreed to lower barriers to U.S. exports ranging from cigarettes to refrigerators. The agreement averted a trade war in which the United States threatened to impose 100 percent tariffs on $3.9 billion worth of Chinese imports. Products covered by the agreement include chemicals, computers, integrated circuits, medical equipment, autos and auto parts, telecommunications equipment, fruits, grain, and edible oil products. Why was it to the advantage of China to lower its barriers to American imports?

6. When 3M enters international markets, it typically begins by exporting products from the United States and selling them through company-owned overseas subsidiaries. As volume increases, 3M ships semifinished goods, such as huge rolls of tape, and uses local workers to cut and package the material. The next step is to move into local manufacturing. Why does 3M use this approach instead of licensing or joint ventures?

7. Canada and the United States have the world's largest bilateral trading relationship, valued at $173.4 billion. All tariff barriers between the two countries have been eliminated. Canada has a population of only 26 million compared to 271 million in the United States. Some people have speculated that certain small Canadian businesses will suffer because of the trade agreement. As a marketing person, explain how the new pact will actually help some small Canadian companies.

8. DaimlerChrysler is a manufacturer and a world leader in commercial trucks. Rather than export trucks from Germany, the company has 42 factories spread across five continents. Why has a global strategy of shipping parts among its plants helped it succeed?

MARKETING PLANNING

> A good plan, violently executed today, is better than a perfect plan tomorrow.
>
> GENERAL GEORGE S. PATTON

One of your most important jobs as marketing manager is the preparation of marketing plans. Organizations that plan for the future are more likely to survive. Marketing plans are normally developed on an annual basis and often include actions that take place over several years. A marketing plan is a formal statement that explains where each product or service is today, where you want it to be at the end of the planning horizon, and how you intend to get there. Once marketing plans have been prepared, they are used to guide field marketing activities for the planning period. You must influence others—some of whom you have no formal authority over—to carry out your plans. As the planning period unfolds, you must monitor marketing performance and compare results with the goals set in the marketing plan. Not everything will go as planned; you must *act and adapt*. The objective of this chapter is to show you how to prepare and implement a marketing plan.

BRAND MANAGER AS PLANNER

The most common place for marketing planning to begin is in the offices of brand or product managers. Figure 16-1 provides an example of how product managers fit into the organizational life of a large business. The actual organizational structure used by an individual firm may, of course, be different. Note that brand/product managers are generalists who operate alongside the line field sales organization. Product managers usually report to either a category manager or a group marketing manager. Group managers have responsibility for products in more than one product category. Category marketing managers focus on items in one category, which allows for better coordination of strategic and marketing efforts.

Brand and product managers operate as independent entrepreneurs, with responsibility for generating revenues and profits on the goods and services under their supervision. They create the marketing plans that attract customers, and they function as the key decision makers in the day-to-day management of groups of products. The assignment of planning to product managers is essentially a bottom-up procedure. Plans prepared by product managers go up the organization before they are sent back down to be executed by the sales organization (Figure 16-1).

Brand managers also coordinate pricing, promotion, distribution, and research activities on a daily basis. Some of the duties assigned to product managers are listed in Table 16-1. A

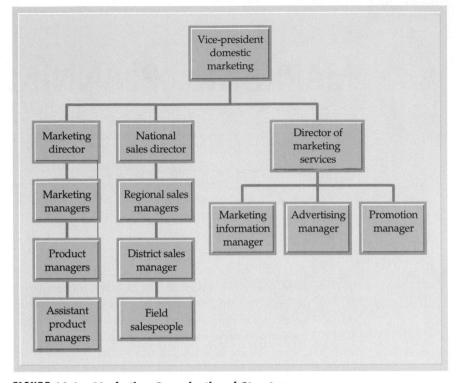

FIGURE 16-1   Marketing Organizational Structure

new assistant brand manager typically starts out developing coupon and promotion programs, examining costs, and getting involved with production and advertising. Brand managers must be brand stewards and assume responsibility for the environmental impact of their products, processes, and packages. The job of a product manager encompasses almost all elements of the marketing mix and is one of the most challenging occupations in the business world.

A key problem at both the product management level and the category level is keeping the same people in place so that they become experts. There is often too much churning, with the average tenure in a position only 18 months. As a result, continuity becomes lost.

TABLE 16-1   Primary Activities of Product Managers

Prepare marketing plans for the following year, including merchandising, advertising, and selling
activities to reach sales and profit goals.
Recommend prices, discounts, and allowances.
Forecast sales and set sales quotas with the sales manager.
Analyze sales results, share of market, competitive activity, and brand profits and adjust plans where
necessary.
Request market research when necessary.
Initiate product improvements in anticipation of, or in reaction to, shifts in customers' requirements,
advances in technology, or actions by competitors.
Continually appraise product performance, quality, and package design.
Recommend products to be eliminated.

THE MARKETING AUDIT

A good place to start marketing planning is with a marketing audit. Audits are periodic reviews of the entire marketing efforts of the firm. They are designed to point out the strengths and weaknesses of marketing plans, objectives, organization, personnel, and operating procedures employed by the organization. The idea is to appraise the overall condition of the marketing program so that the firm can capitalize on its strengths and improve areas that are weak.

Areas to Be Audited

The marketing audit is not concerned with measuring past performance; instead, it looks to the future to see how well the firm's resources are being used to exploit market opportunities. The auditor first looks at marketing objectives to make sure that they are sufficiently broad so that the firm is not trapped with an obsolete product line. For example, an abrasives company would be advised to state its objective as improved sales of metal polishing and removal services rather than just as improved sales of grinding wheels. This approach allows the company to offer a variety of ways to solve customers' problems without restricting itself to the sale of a single product.

The audit should also include an appraisal of the structure of the marketing organization. Does the chief marketing officer have enough power to control all relevant marketing functions? Are the channels of communication open among sales, advertising, promotion, and product development executives? Do the managers of each marketing function have the skills, training, and experience needed to perform their jobs successfully? Should new-product development be handled by a committee, venture teams, or a separate department?

In addition, marketing audits must evaluate the procedures that are used by the firm to implement marketing programs. This means that the auditor must consider how well the product line meets the needs of the perceived market segment. In addition, the auditor reviews the coverage of the sales territories and checks the speed of delivery provided by the warehouse and the transportation network. Auditors should also speak with dealers and customers to find out how they view the marketing operations of the firm. One thing auditors look for in judging operating efficiency is balance across elements of the marketing program. It would be foolish, for example, to spend lavishly on trade promotion unless salespeople are available to make follow up calls. In another case, an auditor found a large proportion of a pharmaceutical manufacturer's ad budget devoted to billboards, which is an unusual way to promote prescription drugs. The selection of billboards as an advertising medium had been made years before and had become such a sacred cow that no one in the company questioned its efficiency. Fortunately, the auditor convinced the company to drop billboard advertising in one area, and sales remained constant. Thus, in this case, a single operational change saved the manufacturer many times the cost of the marketing audit.

Implementing the Audit

A good marketing audit will turn up a number of suggestions for improving the plans and operation of marketing departments. It is the job of marketing managers to take these ideas and incorporate them into the plans being developed for specific brands and product lines. The most effective marketing audits are conducted by someone outside the marketing organization. This avoids the problems of having an audit conducted by a manager who is a weak link in the marketing department. The best audits provide a lighted pathway to the development of moneymaking marketing plans.

BUILDING THE MARKETING PLAN

Marketing plans are a comprehensive statement of what you expect from each brand or service in the future. They evolve from the firm's mission statement which defines the businesses the company wishes to pursue and the customers to be targeted. Plans are prepared on an annual basis, and include both historical data and recommendations on how to improve performance. The plan combines a set of marketing strategies with a timetable for action so that specific financial goals can be achieved. An annual plan usually includes such sections as an executive summary, current company situation, business environment, target markets, objectives, strategy, action programs, anticipated results, and contingency plans (Table 16-2).

Executive Summary

An executive summary is a one- or two-page review of the main facts and recommendations that often appears at the front of a marketing plan. The idea is to highlight the most important parts of the program for top management. This allows executives to gain a quick overview of the plan without wading through the whole report and the supporting exhibits. Managers who need more detail than is provided in the executive summary can go directly to the sections of the marketing plan that include the required information. Executive summaries are designed to make marketing plans more usable, and they are one of the last elements of the plan to be prepared.

Company Situation

The company's situation sets the stage for the rest of the report by telling the reader where the company stands. The situation analysis reviews historical data accumulated for each product. This section includes information on sales, earnings, market shares, shareholder equity, cash flow, and other variables for the past several years. Often this information is presented in chart form to make it easier for executives to grasp trends and relationships.

In addition to providing basic financial data, the company situation should describe current marketing mix variables, such as product quality standards and communication themes, to help show the way to tomorrow. You must know your strengths and weaknesses. You cannot plan for the future unless you know what is going on in the present. Marketing in Action box 16–1 describes how a weak company situation led to a buyout by a more successful firm.

TABLE 16-2   Sample Marketing Plan Headings

1. *Executive Summary:* Short review of the facts and recommendations (optional).
2. *Company Situation:* Current sales, net income, market share, strengths, weaknesses.
3. *Environment:* Competitive plans, opportunities, threats, laws, regulations.
4. *Target Markets:* Who your customers are, where they are, how they buy, and how much they will buy.
5. *Objectives:* Where the firm is going in terms of sales, market share, distribution, stockholder equity, technology, quality, and how objectives will be measured.
6. *Strategy:* Market development, cost reduction, differentiation, penetration, diversification.
7. *Action Programs:* Six-month activity plan, tactics, media plan, individual assignments, timetables, and completion dates.
8. *Anticipated Results:* Projected profit and loss statement and cash budget by month and quarter, break-even analysis.
9. *Contingency Plans:* What to do if sales, profit, and other goals are not met.
10. *Appendices:* Supporting exhibits and tables.

MARKETING IN ACTION 16-1

First Brands Sells Out

First Brands Corp. of Danbury, Connecticut, is primarily known for its Glad plastic wraps and trash bags which account for nearly half its sales. They also sell STP motor oil and several brands of cat litter. Plastic bags and motor oil are mature markets with many competitors that use price cuts and promotional discounts to gain market share. First Brands reported disappointing profits in August of 1998 due to heavy promotional costs for a new line of Gladware plastic containers. Also, First Brands depended on weakening overseas markets for 22 percent of its revenues. First Brands' situation was bleak with aging brands and few prospects for growth. The company's stock declined from $28 in 1997 to a low of $20 in September of 1998. When Clorox Co. made an offer for the firm, an agreement was quickly reached for stock valued at $39 per share. Clorox projected $90 million in annual cost savings as a result of the merger. These savings were expected in advertising terms and costs where both firms have products such as cat litter, charcoal and fire logs. Sometimes when firms are in a weak competitive position, it pays to sell to a more diversified company. Certainly in this case the stockholders of First Brands and their executives were quite happy to receive $39 a share for stock that had been selling for $20 a few weeks earlier.

— *Sometimes a review of a company situation is grim and it pays to sell out.*

Source: George Anders, "Clorox, Still Growing, to Buy First Brands," *The Wall Street Journal*, October 20, 1998, p. A3.

APPLYING
... to Consumer Packaged Goods Marketing

INTEGRATING
... with Strategic Planning

Environment

This section describes the external environmental factors that influence business planning. These include shifting customer demands, technological change, competition, governmental regulations, and availability of labor and materials. New customer wants and needs and advances in technology open opportunities for new markets and products. Competition is a constant threat to business success, and you need to know who the major domestic and foreign rivals are. You also need data on competitive strategies, pricing, cost structure, and distribution channels. Governmental regulations and court decisions also set limits on what marketing managers can do in particular situations. Thus you must be aware of what is allowable in the areas of the environment, employee rights, and competitive practices in pricing and advertising. Sometimes marketing plans are constrained by the availability of skilled labor and raw materials or uncooperative labor unions. You must keep up with these changes so you can plan accordingly. An example of how changing customer needs altered the planning process at Mohawk Industries is described in Marketing in Action box 16-2.

Target Markets

The target market section of a marketing plan provides a detailed explanation of who your intended customers are. The plan should define your market in terms of demographics (age, income, education), geographics (location), and lifestyle. Be sure to include a discussion of the size of each intended market segment. In addition to size, you need to know how fast the target groups are growing and what product or service features customers are looking for. Knowing who your customers are, how much they buy, and when they buy makes it easier to design marketing plans to meet their needs.

Information on target markets can often be gathered over the Internet. For example, the U.S. Patent and Trademark Office now offers simple and free searches of its trademark database through its World Wide Web site. In May of 1998, Microsoft Corp. filed applications

MARKETING IN ACTION *16-2*

Planning to Meet Customer Needs

Historically, architects and builders ordered carpet 45 days in advance allowing mills plenty of time to plan production and ship carpet to commercial customers. However, today with lean inventories, carpet manufacturers are receiving more surprise orders with shorter delivery requirements. In 1996, Mohawk Industries was only able to fill 80 percent of its order queries in the time requested. Since margins in the commercial carpet business are very high, no one wanted to turn away even a single customer. Mohawk needed a better way to predict orders so it could do a better job of planning its production schedules. A DuPont scientist who had been studying production scheduling problems came up with a remarkable solution. Instead of predicting sales for 30 days into the future, why not create a new plan every day, a kind of rolling forecast based on up-to-the-minute customer orders. He wrote a computer program that captured every order and predicted the size and timing of future orders. DuPont offered the program to their nylon customers and now Mohawk runs the program each night to decide which of their 4,000 products should be produced the next day. Now only 35 percent of work in process has actually been ordered, compared to 85 percent in the past. The new planning system allows Mohawk to fill 95 percent of customer's orders on time. This has led to significant revenue and profit gains for the company.

— *Careful planning can lead to increases in sales and profits.*

Source: Thomas Petzinger, Jr., "In This Carpet Mill, The Best Laid Plans Are Rolled Out Daily," *The Wall Street Journal*, October 30, 1998, p. B1.

Courtesy Mohawk Industries, Inc.

for trademarks for Microsoft Taxsaver and Microsoft Taxbreak. These names are to be used with computer software for tax planning and the preparation and filing of tax returns. Knowing that Microsoft is thinking of entering the tax preparation market would be valuable to Quicken, whose Turbo Tax currently dominates this segment, and to others who might want to target this market.[1]

Objectives

The objectives section of the marketing plan describes where you intend the product or business unit to go in the future. These objectives must be in agreement with the overall objectives of the firm, but they do not have to be the same for each line of trade. Thus, the objective for a question mark product might be to build market share, whereas with a cash cow you might prefer to lose market share rather than waste money trying to save a lost cause.

Company objectives, for example, might call for 20 percent sales growth, a 15 percent pretax profit margin, a 1 percent increase in market share, and a 20 percent growth in stockholder equity. Products in attractive markets would be expected to match or exceed these goals, and businesses in more competitive or mature environments would have lower expectations. The idea is to push each business to do as well as it can in the light of differences in potential.

Your marketing plan must specify how the data needed to measure the achievement of objectives will be collected and analyzed. Market share data, for example, can come from store audits, scanner data, A.C. Nielsen figures, trade associations, or from customer surveys. There are also many different ways to measure growth in stockholder equity.

Strategy

The strategy section of the marketing plan provides a statement showing how the business will achieve its objectives. The statement indicates the areas the firm will emphasize in its drive for victory. Effective strategies tell management what paths to follow for key marketing mix variables. For example, you can build a sustainable competitive advantage through brand identification, product differentiation, niche marketing, or low costs. Brand strength and product differentiation can be improved through the use of new advertising themes, increased ad expenditures, reallocation of ad dollars across media vehicles, and special promotional events.

Businesses that need to improve profitability could pursue a strategy of raising prices. This strategy, in turn, could mean selective price increases for high-demand items or across-the-board increases on all products. Cost-cutting strategies can involve a variety of areas both within the marketing department and in other parts of the firm. The most common approach is to redesign products to make them easier and cheaper to manufacture. Another effective technique is to expand the use of Web selling to lower distribution costs. One popular cost-cutting strategy is to drop low-profit items and to restrict the number of product variations offered to customers. Other cost-saving strategies might include staff cuts, reductions in corporate image-building advertising, and temporary cuts in sales training activities. An example of the use of diversification to enhance revenue growth is shown in Marketing Strategies box 16-1.

Action Programs

The next step in the planning process is to translate broad strategy statements into specific actions and tactics. This can be helped along by setting up timetables to show the starting and completion dates for each activity. In addition, it is useful to assign responsibility to one individual to ensure that each project is completed on schedule. For example, a program to identify products for elimination might be given to a group product manager. These managers oversee the work of several product managers, and they have the experience needed to pick items for divestment. The group product managers could also farm out some of the elimination decisions to subordinates who monitor the day-to-day activities of each brand.

MARKETING STRATEGIES *16-1*

Growth from Diversification

Playtex Products Inc. was launched in 1986 as a leveraged buyout from its owner Beatrice Cos. Playtex sold its bra and underwear lines to Sara Lee Corp. in 1991, leaving it with 54 percent of its business derived from the sale of tampons. In 1996, Playtex found itself mired in price and promotion wars with Tambrands, now owned by Procter & Gamble. Heavy promotion by Tambrands for its market leading Tampax tampons forced Playtex to respond with its own two-for-one offers. The resulting battle left a glut of tampons in retail warehouses and consumers' medicine cabinets. This competitive struggle convinced Playtex that it needed to reduce its dependence on tampon sales. Playtex has since bought up Binky Pacifiers, Carewell Industries, a toothbrush maker, and the Personal Care Group which owns brands including Wet Ones, Mr. Bubble, Chubs baby wipes, and Binaca breath spray. Another recent acquisition is Diaper Genie that wraps soiled diapers in plastic. As a result of these purchases, Playtex has doubled its revenue from infant care to 34 percent of sales and feminine care products now amount to only 34 percent of revenue. Playtex's strategy of diversification has given it a 42 percent share of the rapidly growing infant care market to balance its slow growth position in the tampon business.

— *Diversification can lead to revenue growth for narrowly focused firms.*

Source: Tara Parker-Pope, "Playtex to Add Diaper Genie to Buying Spree," *The Wall Street Journal*, January 14, 1999, pp. B1, B3.

**Courtesy Playtex
Products, Inc.**

The steps taken by America Online to protect its number-one position in Internet access provides a good look at a real action program. AOL currently offers slow dial-up service over phone lines that may become obsolete with the very quick broadband service coming from cable companies. To counter this threat, AOL purchased NetChannel, a firm that offers the Internet over TV sets. They also have appointed a manager of broadband marketing and are exploring relationships with Time Warner and other cable providers to reach cable modem customers. Perhaps AOL's most critical action program is lobbying legislators and the Federal Communications Commission in Washington to force cable companies to give them access to broadband cables being installed to give consumers faster Internet access.[2]

Anticipated Results

Once the specific tactics have been selected, managers are in a position to forecast the results of the new marketing plan. These are usually presented in the form of break-even charts, projected profit and loss statements, and cash flow budgets. Anticipated unit sales and total revenues are shown for each model and time period. When price changes are expected to occur during the planning horizon, they are factored into the revenue calculations and are shown in the profit and loss statement as net realized price. Costs are broken into fixed and variable categories for planning and control purposes. Production and physical distribution costs are subtracted from revenues to give estimates of gross margins in dollars and percentages. Next, gross margins per unit are divided into fixed costs to give break-even volumes at different prices. Then budgets are set for the sales force, advertising, sales promotion, market research, product development, and administrative expense categories. The difference between these expenses and the gross margin available is the profit for the planning period.

After the projected marketing budget has been approved by top management, it is used to monitor results. Actual sales and expenses recorded in each period are compared with the projected figures on a monthly and a year-to-date basis. Significant differences between the planned and actual results provide signals for remedial action.

Contingency Plans

Contingency strategies are needed because real-world events such as fires, drought, war, inflation, floods, and price cutting often interfere with even the best market plans. This section asks a series of "what if" questions about possible events in the marketplace and then answers them. For example, what if the market grows faster than forecast levels? A trigger point for action might occur when new orders are 30 percent above the long-range forecast. At this point, the firm could run into capacity limitations, although excess capacity might be available elsewhere in the industry. Possible responses in this situation might be to go to a three-shift production schedule operating seven days a week, advance the timing of capacity additions, be selective in accepting orders, and provide leadership in raising prices. Other contingency plans would be formulated to combat price cutting by competitors and failures to meet sales goals.

Some examples of contingency planning are provided by the interactions between Mexico's largest brewer, Modelo, and America's giant Anheuser-Busch Cos. With the expected passage of NAFTA, Modelo sold a majority stake to Anheuser to protect it from an expected influx of American beers. This did not happen, however, and Modelo saw its share of the Mexican market expand to 55 percent and its flagship Corona brand become the number-one imported beer in America. Corona's success caused Modelo's stockholders to ask Anheuser for more money for the shares they were selling. Anheuser refused, so Modelo renewed a distribution contract with its American distributor for a 10-year period before Anheuser could gain complete control of the company. Anheuser had expected to sell Corona through its own distribution network in the United States and was forced to make contingency plans. To satisfy its U.S. distributor's need for an imported beer, Anheuser began to market three Corona clones—Azteca (made in Mexico), Tequiza (made in the United States), and Rio Cristal (brewed in Brazil) to compete with a beer it already owns.[3]

The main advantage of contingency plans is that they force management to think about a broader range of problems than might occur when strategies are designed only to meet immediate company objectives. Also, contingency plans that have been made ahead of time can be implemented quickly if the need arises. As a former chairperson of General Motors has said, "I don't like people running into my office saying, 'Jeez, this just happened. So what do we do next?' I want to have a plan for just about everything."

Appendixes

This section contains supporting documents and exhibits. Make sure that they are numbered correctly and appear in a logical order. Remember that well-designed charts with three-dimensional shading and color are easier to read and understand. Attractive graphics are also useful if you are called on to give an oral presentation of your marketing plan.

Marketing Plan Example

A sample marketing plan for a product acquired by Cook Inc. is shown in the Appendix. Cook Inc. is a successful medical products manufacturer in Bloomington, Indiana. The company had an opportunity to produce a new machine designed to help remove material from blocked arteries. The new product was an endarterectomy oscillator that fit in well with Cook's current product lines of diagnostic catheters. Our sample marketing plan suggests that the prospects for success with the endarterectomy oscillator looked good. However, the oscillator sold poorly and the item was one of very few product failures at Cook Inc. In this case the product proved to be dependable, it filled a need, was priced appropriately, and distributed effectively. The product failed because surgeons were slow to switch to new approaches to clear blocked arteries. Looking back, Cook should have done more with trial placements and education in hospitals to acquaint surgeons with the product and teach them how to use it. This example shows that marketing innovative surgical machines is much more complicated than introducing new types of catheters.

TESTING THE MARKETING PLAN

To help reduce risk, many marketing managers test their marketing plans using computer simulations. This approach saves time and money compared with field test markets or regional market evaluations. The use of simulations also provides secrecy and prevents your competitors from auditing your tests, stealing your ideas, or sabotaging your plan with special advertising gimmicks.

How Do Simulations Work?

Simulation is the use of a model to replicate the operation of a real system over time. Marketing simulations, for example, feed price, promotion, advertising, and distribution values into a model to estimate the sales volumes or market shares the products might have at the end of a time period. The main advantage of marketing plan simulations is that they allow you to bring together and study the interaction of several marketing variables at the same time. In addition, you can test various combinations of marketing factors without having to spend money to take the risks associated with making changes in the real world.

An example of how simulation is used by managers might be described as follows:

INTERVIEWER: Do you make regular simulation runs for assessing the marketing mix for a new product?

ANALYST: Oh, yes.

INTERVIEWER: Do you implement the results?

ANALYST: Oh, no!

INTERVIEWER: Well, that seems odd. If you don't implement the results, perhaps you should stop making the runs.

ANALYST: No, no. We wouldn't want to do that!

INTERVIEWER: Why not?

ANALYST: Well, what happens is something like this: I make several computer runs and take them to the brand manager. He is responsible for this whole multimillion-dollar project. The brand manager looks at the runs, thinks about them for a while, and then sends me back to make a few more, with conditions changed in various ways. I do this and bring them back in. He looks at them and probably sends me back to make more runs. And so forth.

INTERVIEWER: How long does this keep up?

ANALYST: I would say it continues until finally the brand manager screws up enough courage to make a decision.

Simulation thus encourages manager-model interaction to improve understanding of the business environment and to help make better plans. When you do not agree with the simulation results, the input data can be reexamined and tests run to see how sensitive the results are to changes in parameters. This process of interacting with a model allows you to learn more about your problems without giving up control to the computer.

Simulation Examples

Simulations have been used to test marketing plans in many firms. It is common, for example, to run alternative advertising schedules through simulation models to find which media give the best customer exposure. One new product model is used to evaluate the impact of alternative package sizes, coupon schedules, and promotions on the sales of newly introduced items. This program has proved to be so valuable that it is often run more than 400 times in a single month.

Simulation can help you build better marketing plans by employing models that replicate the operation of real-world systems. Simulation is not a cure-all; it is merely one of several tools available to simplify complex marketing problems. The main problem with marketing simulations is because many variables are involved, it is often difficult to find optimum solutions. One approach is to make a series of simplifying assumptions, but this can lend an aura of unreality to the recommendations. A better approach is to restrict the number of marketing variables in each simulation project. For example, Figure 16–2 shows the results of a simulation designed to find the optimal product mix and prices for an individual firm. This simulation involved a search across 20 product alternatives and preferences of 60 consumers divided into eight market segments. The lines at the bottom of the figure represent combined utility curves for the eight segments. Note that the utility curves rise to ideal points and then decline across product alternatives. In this case, a profit-maximizing solution was found in less than a minute, using appropriate heuristics and a desktop computer. Complex simulations that take hours to run on a mainframe computer are not much help to marketing decision makers.

The solution recommended in Figure 16-2 suggests marketing the three products shown by the dark price bars. Profit maximization raised prices so that segments 1 to 3 were shut out of the market. Segment 4 chose product 4, and segments 5 to 7 chose product 10. Seg-

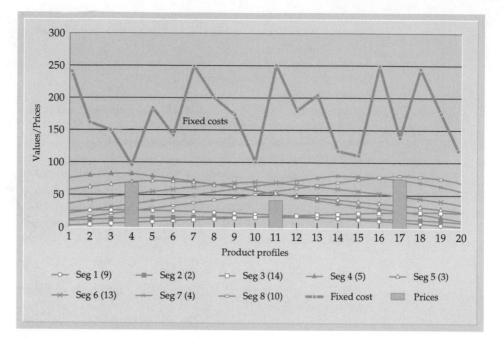

FIGURE 16-2   Using Simulations to Optimize Product Mix and prices for Eight Market Segments (From Gregory Dobson and Shlomo Kalish, "Heuristics for Pricing and Positioning a Product Line Using Conjoint and Cost Data," *Management Science* **[February 1993], p. 170)**

ment 8 selected product 17. The beauty of this simulation approach is that it allows marketing managers to quickly evaluate a variety of price and product mix alternatives. Common applications of simulation in marketing have been to (1) help develop alternative marketing strategies, (2) provide inexpensive test markets to evaluate strategies, and (3) help control the implementation of marketing programs.

IMPLEMENTATION AND CONTROL

The success of marketing plans frequently depends on the level of execution that is achieved by the salespeople, dealers, and advertising agencies that implement programs in the real world. Even the most brilliant plan will fail if it is not implemented correctly. Effective implementation converts marketing plans into individual assignments and makes sure that they are executed on time. Business firms must have a system of control that quickly points out execution errors and helps managers take corrective action. An important first step is to decide what factors best explain the success or failure of an individual marketing plan. Depending on business conditions, a firm might emphasize market share, dollar volume, unit sales, dollar profit, or stockholder equity. Marketing control is basically a set of procedures that allows managers to compare the results of marketing plans with predetermined standards so that corrective action can be taken to ensure that objectives are met. Effective control requires a system that gathers data on market conditions and places them in the hands of executives who can make adjustments in plans and operating procedures.

A flow diagram that highlights the basic elements of the marketing control process is presented in Figure 16-3. The first few steps involve planning and are usually performed on an annual basis. Objectives are adopted; price, promotion, advertising, and distribution strategies are selected; and performance standards are set for sales quotas, selling expenses,

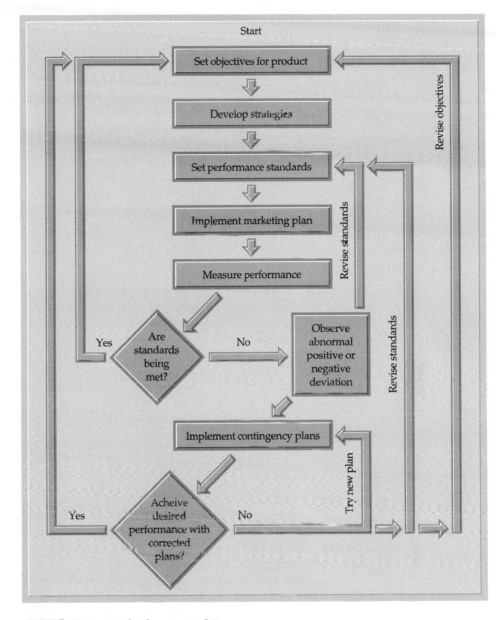

FIGURE 16-3   Marketing Control Process

and other control variables. Next, the marketing program is implemented over a span of time, and periodic measurements are taken to record the reactions of customers and competitors. The basic aim of the control process is to see whether the predetermined performance standards are being met. If they are, the successful results are fed back to the starting point and used to set the objectives for the next planning period (Figure 16-3).

When significant deviations from performance standards are observed, the manager has the choice of changing the standards or implementing contingency plans to attempt to correct the problem (Figure 16-3). For example, suppose that a new product, expected to attain a 3 percent market share after six months, actually captured 10 percent of the market. This suggests that the original estimate was low, and the manager should probably raise the annual forecast to 8 percent or more so that the production, advertising, and distribution efforts can be adjusted to reflect realized demand.

In the more typical situation in which sales fail to reach desired levels, managers can try a variety of short-run strategies to get the product back on target. These may take the form of cents-off coupons, new advertising themes or media, deals for retailers, changes in ad schedules, increased advertising, contests for salespeople, or simple changes in packaging or product specifications. If these tonics fail to do the job, the manager may have to revise the standards or objectives for the next planning period (Figure 16-3). In addition, managers can initiate special market research studies to determine why products do not reach long-run sales goals. These efforts may result in entirely new products, major changes in existing items, new channels, realignments in selling efforts, or a decision to drop the offending products entirely. An illustration showing how a new marketing plan helped save a company is described in Marketing in Action box 16-3.

Setting Standards

Performance standards are planned achievement levels for selected marketing variables that the firm expects to attain at stated intervals throughout the year. Managers do not have time to watch all dimensions of the marketing plan; they must select the most important performance factors to be monitored on a regular basis. In addition to traditional dollar sales, profit, and market share goals, most firms set standards for selling and advertising expenses. These are often expressed as a percentage of sales to simplify comparisons with past performance and the experience of other firms in the industry. For example, a company could measure the efficiency of its sales organization by setting a standard of 10 percent of revenue to cover branch office overhead, salaries of salespeople and sales managers, travel, commissions, bonuses, and customer entertainment. Other marketing factors that can be used for control purposes are shown in Table 16-3.

Measuring Performance

Marketing information systems provide the basic data used by control systems to compare planned performance with real-world results. A control system should permit assignment of responsibility for differences between planned and actual performance. Managers rely on a variety of special reports to point out deviations between standards and actual operations so that corrective action can be taken.

An example showing how a marketing control system operates is provided by the U.S. food company H.J. Heinz. The product was a frequently purchased item found in supermarkets. It was sold in several different sizes, and one size or another was promoted to the trade every four to six weeks. The impact of promotion on market share appeared to vary by container size and across sales districts. To study these effects, Heinz built some response functions for 27 market areas.

Newspaper features were the primary promotional tool used to draw customers' attention to the product. Heinz kept track of the number of features run, the share of the market of the retail chain, the size of the feature ad, and the percentage discount offered by the feature in relation to the average level of discounting to which the customers had become accustomed. These revealed that there was little evidence of any relationship among promotional spending and either the number of newspaper features or market share. The number of newspaper features for competitive products, as well as those for the product, did influence Heinz's market share.

Additional calculations suggested that most promotions were, on average, unprofitable. Accordingly, the number of promotions in most districts was decreased, and those promotions that were conducted were adjusted to include package sizes that seemed to be most

MARKETING IN ACTION *16-3*

Rescuing Quaker Oats

After Quaker Oats lost $1.4 billion on the sale of its Snapple beverage division, they hired a new CEO from Kraft Foods. Instead of selling off the company in pieces as Wall Street expected, the CEO instituted a new marketing plan. First he sold off two food-service divisions and combined Quaker's foods and beverage businesses into one organization, eliminating a layer of management. He also consolidated the sales forces and they now sell Gatorade and snack foods. To push its strongest brand, Gatorade, the company introduced new flavors such as Midnight Thunder, innovative packaging in the form of wide mouthed bottles, and a successful line of flavors under the Frost Label, a lighter-tasting drink. To sustain Gatorade growth, Quaker is focusing on getting the sports beverage into more places where people sweat. This involves expanding distribution for active thirst occasions with vending machines at golf courses, tennis centers, schools, and hospitals in warm weather states. The CEO is also shifting dollars from retail discounts to Gatorade advertising. Since the new CEO initiated his marketing plan, Quaker Oats' unit volume and profits have increased sharply. Also Quaker stock has jumped from $47 when the new manager arrived to $61. When the CEO took over, he was given options to buy 1.3 million shares at $47. The success of his marketing plan has provided him with a paper gain on his Quaker options of $1.8 million.

— *Good execution of a marketing plan can rescue a company in trouble.*

Source: Rekha Balu, "Like Oatmeal, Morrison Proves Good for Quaker," *The Wall Street Journal*, October 27, 1998, pp.B1, B6.

Courtesy Quaker Oats

TABLE 16-3   Performance Measures Used for Control Purposes

Customers	Awareness levels
	Inquiries
	Complaints
	Number of returns
	Warranty expense
Product	Rate of trial
	Repeat purchase rate
	Cannibalization rate
	Price relative to those of competitors
	Coupon redemption rate
Distribution	Average order and delivery time
	Percentage of stores carrying the product
	Months of inventory in dealers' hands
	Distribution costs per unit
Sales and advertising	Advertising cost per unit sold
	Turnover rate of sales force
	Sales calls per day
	Number of new accounts opened
	Sales per order
	Number of accounts lost

effectively promoted within a given district. During the first year in which these actions were taken, the total number of promotions was reduced by 40 percent, yet market share increased by more than three share points.

A marketing control system was designed to monitor Heinz's promotional activities. Each month the newly available data are entered into the system, and the current effectiveness of the promotions is evaluated. The purpose of the marketing control system is to detect changes in the effectiveness of any particular type of promotion. Heinz was concerned that rapidly rising prices in the general economy might make the consumer less loyal and more price conscious. As a result of the system, Heinz found that occasionally promotions for a particular size that had been successful in the past became ineffectual. Moreover, some promotions that had always been ineffective in a district became successful. The marketing control system thus accomplished its purpose in revealing changes in customers' habits.

SUMMARY

This chapter has shown why marketing plans are needed to help guide field marketing activities. In addition, we have explained who prepares marketing plans and how they are organized. The development of effective marketing programs depends on timely data.

The success of marketing planning in the real world frequently depends on how well the various elements of the marketing mix work together. Enlightened managers are now able to pretest the interactions of marketing variables by running examples through special business simulations. These simulations allow the manager to test combinations of marketing factors without spending the money or taking the risks associated with making changes in an actual competitive environment.

Computers can also be used to help monitor the implementation of marketing programs. The basic control process is a check for differences between desired performance standards and actual results. When negative deviations occur, simulation can be employed to determine what has gone wrong with the marketing plans and help develop new strategies.

In addition to monitoring current operations, you must prepare yourself for the future. This means that marketing programs should be audited periodically to make sure that the firm has the right products, personnel, and channels of distribution to fill customers' needs and meet the challenges offered by competitors.

NOTES

1. Nick Wingfield, "Free Search of Trademark Database Can Provide Clues to Companies' Plans," *The Wall Street Journal*, October 20, 1998, p. B8.
2. Thomas E. Weber, "Inside the Race to Grab High-Speed Connections: Cable Providers Could Become Rivals of AOL," *The Wall Street Journal*, October 22, 1998, pp.B1, B8.
3. Jonathan Friedland and Rekha Balu, "Head to Head: For Mighty Anheuser, No Rival Is Too Small—Even One It Owns," *The Wall Street Journal*, October 22, 1998, pp. A1, A10.

SUGGESTED READING

Albers, Sönke. "A Framework for Analysis of Sources of Profit Contribution Variance Between Actual and Plan," *International Journal of Research in Marketing,* Vol.15, No.2 (May 1998), pp. 109–122.
Cohen, William A. *The Marketing Plan* (New York: John Wiley, 1997).

REFERENCES

Gumpert, David E. *How to Really Create a Successful Marketing Plan* (Boston: Inc Publishing, 1996).
Hiebing, Roman G., and Scott W. Cooper. *The Successful Marketing Plan: A Disciplined and Comprehensive Approach* (Lincolnwood, IL: NTC Publishing 1997).
Larkin, Geraldine A. *12 Simple Steps to a Winning Marketing Plan* (Burr Ridge, IL: Probus Publishing Co., 1992).

QUESTIONS

1. In the third quarter of 1998, worldwide shipments of PCs increased 15 percent from the third quarter of the previous year. However, total worldwide revenue for PCs did not increase due to sinking prices. From 1996 to 1998 the average selling price for a PC dropped from $2,000 to $1,100. Meanwhile the five biggest PC marketers (Compaq, IBM, Dell, Hewlett-Packard, and Gateway) increased their share of the total world market from 37 percent to 40.6 percent. How should smaller PC producers adjust their marketing plans in response to these changes?

2. American power companies have been slow to buy new electrical generation equipment because of concerns about overcapacity and the uncertainties of deregulation. However, a shortage of power in the Midwest during a 1998 heat wave caused power companies to scramble to order new gas-powered turbines. Now the order books for turbine manufacturers are full and prices have increased. Should turbine builders, such as GE and ABB, adjust their marketing plans to reduce expenditures on marketing activities?

3. Ames Department Stores has purchased Hills Stores for $127 million to create a firm with sales over $4 billion a year from 456 stores. The combined firm will be the fourth largest U.S. discount store behind Wal-Mart, Kmart, and Target. By targeting lower-income and elderly customers, Ames has found a niche that sets it apart from Wal-Mart. The deal will also provide Ames with increased purchasing power and should mean lower prices for customers. Does Ames's plan to grow by merging two firms that have

recently filed for bankruptcy protection insure success in the future? What other adjustments to Ames's marketing plan do you recommend?

4. General Motors has signed a multibillion dollar 10-year deal to buy substantial amounts of aluminum from Alcan Aluminum Lt. The order suggests that GM plans to design much more aluminum into its vehicles, displacing steel. Why is GM substituting high-cost aluminum for steel and how will this change affect their plans to sell cars and trucks?

5. The nation's largest automobile insurance company has been granted a charter to operate a federal savings bank. State Farm plans to teach its 16,000 insurance agents to market products such as savings accounts, certificates of deposit, money market accounts, and mortgage and car loans to the company's insurance customers. They eventually plan to offer checking accounts. Why has State Farm taken this radical step to broaden their product offerings? What marketing synergies will occur as a result of this planned expansion?

6. Mercedes-Benz of Germany recently purchased America's third largest auto manufacturer, Chrysler. Why did Daimler, a producer of high-priced cares and trucks, want Chrysler that sells such low-priced cars as the Neon? How will the marketing plans of Chrysler be changed now that it is owned by Daimler?

7. Private labels now account for 21 percent of sales in the largest 15 U.S. grocery stores, up from 17 percent in 1992. During this period, a new private label company, American Italian Pasta Co., has grabbed 25 percent of the pasta market from national brands. What adjustments should the national brand firms make to their marketing plans to counter this growing threat to their food business?

8. Granola bars were introduced as a snack for health-conscious consumers. They were made from rolled oats, sugar, and dried fruit or nuts. Unfortunately, many consumers thought they tasted like cardboard, and sales were disappointing. Granola bar makers then added chocolate and peanut butter to their offerings and sales soared. The distinction between granola bars and candy bars has narrowed (Table 16-4). Consumers associate "granola" with "healthy." Granola bar makers reinforce this consumer perception by emphasizing "wholesome" and "goodness" in their advertising. Is the conduct of the granola makers ethical?

TABLE 16-4   Granola Bars Versus Candy Bars

		How Those Calories Break Down			
	Calories (per oz.)	*Fat*	*Added Sugar*	*Complex Carbohydrates*	*Protein*
Quaker Dips Granola Bars	158	40%	23%	29%	6%
Hershey's New Train Granola Bars	143	42	23	28	7
Nature Valley Chewy Granola Bars	138	38	21	35	7
Snickers	137	43	38	11	8
Milky Way	128	33	49	14	4

Source: Center for Science in the Public Interest.

SAMPLE MARKETING PLAN FOR COOK INC. ENDARTERECTOMY OSCILLATOR*

COMPANY SITUATION

Cook Inc. is a rapidly growing medical supply manufacturer. The company is currently profitable selling cardiovascular catheters, ureteral catheters, heart pacemakers, x-ray radiopaque dye, and stents. Cook sells its products throughout the world and markets catheters in the United States with a staff of 20 company salespeople. Their strongest market position is in their core cardiovascular catheter product lines. Cook's greatest strength is its highly trained staff of catheter designers and assembly workers. Recently the company has been given the opportunity to produce and market an endarterectomy oscillator developed by Dr. Everett Lerwick, a leading vascular surgeon. Endarterectomy oscillators move dissecting loops and debrading catheters back and forth inside arteries to help remove material that restricts the flow of blood. Oscillators are less invasive than other surgical procedures and can reduce the cost of treating partial arterial blockages.

ENVIRONMENT

Heart and vascular disease is a leading cause of death in America. New products that make it easier to treat these diseases and reduce death rates have been well received by physicians and governmental regulatory agencies. At the present time, there are no competing endarterectomy oscillators on the market. In addition, Dr. Lerwick's oscillator has a strong patent position that will prevent competitors from copying the present design. The Lerwick oscillator can be manufactured from standard components with the current staff and facilities of Cook Inc. We do not anticipate any threats from competitors, governmental regulators or existing laws that will prevent our product and sale of endarterectomy oscillators.

TARGET MARKETS

The current market potential for endarterectomy oscillators appears to be good. At the present time, artery blockages have to be treated with complex bypass surgery. The endarterectomy oscillator would replace the need for surgery and encourage collateral blood flow in surrounding tissue. If each hospital qualified to do this type of procedure bought only one oscillator and 20 percent of the cardiovascular surgeons purchased as well, total market potential would be 3500 units. This estimate is conservative because many of the hospitals have more than one operating room where cardiovascular surgery is performed. Thus, many hospitals would need more than one unit. If 30 percent of the hospitals bought two units, then total demand would be 4400 units.

A reasonable assumption in this case with respect to the expected life cycle of the oscillator would be about 10 years. This means that 10 percent penetration of the market each year would generate sales of 440 units and if each oscillator produced annual sales of $1,000 for dissecting loops and debriding catheters, sales revenue would be over $1 million per year. These are substantial revenues that could be added to Cook's sales receipts. Given the strong patent position on the oscillator, the target market potential is attractive.

OBJECTIVES

Cook has a reputation for selling high quality technologically advanced health care products. New items are expected to follow in this tradition to build sales and profits. The company favors product expansion that uses the existing manufacturing expertise, distribution channels and sales techniques. As a relatively small player in the medical equipment market, Cook does not require a number one or number two market share position to consider themselves successful.

STRATEGY

Each firm must have its own strategic vision. Cook looks to improve its market position through diversification and differentiation. Strategies for each element of the marketing mix for the endarterectomy oscillator are as follows.

---

* This marketing plan was prepared by Douglas J. Dalrymple from data supplied by Cook Inc. Some figures in the plan as well as some time sequences have been disguised. An executive summary has not been included to save space.

Product Design

The endarterectomy oscillator has been carefully developed and tested by Dr. Everett Lerwick, a leading vascular surgeon. The product was used in 90 successful operations over a period of five years. In addition, the long-run survival rate of patients has been encouraging. Lerwick's oscillator has proven to be durable, and Cook could expect continued sales of replacement loops and debriding catheters to go along with each machine.

In terms of design, the endarterectomy oscillator is fairly simple. The device has an electric motor whose circular motion is converted to oscillations in a 120° arc up to 8000 times per minute. The oscillations are transmitted through a handpiece with special loops that clear the material from the patient's arteries. Speed of oscillation is controlled by a foot pedal. This mechanical device has proven to be reliable, and there are few areas for product failure. All indications suggest that the endarterectomy oscillator is an excellent product that is ready to go to market.

Promotion

Extensive promotion will be needed to help acquaint surgeons with the new oscillator. Several rounds of direct mail are appropriate at a cost of $5000 each. In addition, six journal ads would help prepare the doctors for calls by the Cook sales force. Displays at four trade shows would seem to be a minimum to demonstrate to doctors how the new machine operates. These shows seem expensive ($2800), but they will require Cook to rent extra space and pay Dr. Lerwick's expenses. Trade shows are cost effective because large numbers of surgeons can be contacted in one location.

Distribution Channels

The use of the present distribution channels for the oscillator presents a number of problems for Cook. First, the product sells for a much higher price than the curent line of catheters that are purchased for $5 or $10 and then thrown away. The oscillator will require time-consuming personal sales calls to allow for demonstrations and closing. Moreover, the current salespeople are paid a salary and can sell large volumes of catheters much more easily than they can sell the new oscillator. In addition, the purchase of equipment is likely to be handled separately from supplies, and Cook will have to call on different people than those interested in catheters.

Sales force interest in the oscillator could be improved by offering a 10 percent sales commission,

but this would reduce the profit potential. Another solution would be to assign one of the current salespeople or hire someone to be an oscillator specialist. This would raise fixed costs but probably could be justified by the strong market potential. Another possibility would be to manufacture the oscillator and then get an outside firm to sell it along with other products. If independent reps could be recruited to sell the oscillator for 10 to 15 percent of sales, then Cook would be advised to consider this channel of distribution. The problem for Cook is that independent reps are not interested in new products until it is clear that they have caught on in the marketplace. Reps do not want items that take a lot of time to build market acceptance. In addition, if development work has to be done, the reps will demand a margin of 30 to 40 percent of sales. If Cook has to pay 40 percent to the reps and 10 percent to Lerwick, then there will be very little profit unless a high price is charged.

Pricing

Pricing is a key decision because price will help determine the ultimate profitability of the product. Because the product is patented and hospitals are not expected to be sensitive to the price of this item, a skimming price is indicated. In this case, hospitals could easily charge off the cost of the oscillator to surgical patients over the course of a year. A skimming price of three to five times the cost would suggest selling prices between $1350 and $2250. Although these prices seem high, they are within the realm of possibility.

Because both fixed and variable cost elements are present, a multiple breakeven analysis is appropriate with selling prices of $1350, $1800, and $2250. Three different scenarios for sales force effort can also be considered. They are: (1) give salespeople no added incentive; (2) give salespeople an additional 10 percent commission; and (3) add an oscillator specialist. The resulting set of breakeven calculations is shown in the table in the Anticipated Results section.

With a selling price of $1350, the breakeven is less than one sales per week even when sales force effort is encouraged with a 10 percent commission. Adding a specialized salesperson increases the breakeven to about two sales per week at the same selling price. By increasing fixed costs, the addition of a salesperson increases the risk.

Strategic Choices

Introduction of the oscillator has a number of advantages for Cook. First, the market potential is strong, and the product is patented to keep competition at bay.

Second, the oscillator fits in well as a product line extension for the current line of catheters. Indeed, both the oscillator and Cook catheters can be used in the same surgical procedures. Furthermore, the product will be easy to manufacture with existing tools and labor. In addition, the oscillator can be sold with the same distribution channels used for the catheters. At prices over $1000, Cook makes good margins and the breakeven point is low. The key issue, however, is risk. Cook has spent nothing to develop the oscillator. In addition, production of the oscillators does not require new tooling, new equipment, new plant, or new technology, and promotional costs are modest. Thus, the risk to Cook if it takes on the product and it fails is very low. On the other hand, if the oscillator succeeds, profits will be good because Cook has so little money tied up in the project. The benefits of introducing the oscillator outweigh the risks: add the oscillator to the product line.

ACTION PROGRAM

Set an introductory price of $1350.
Sell extra dissecting loops at $65 each and charge $90 for the debriding catheter.
Sell the oscillator with the existing field sales force.
Promote the oscillator with direct mail and trade shows.
Avoid journal ads and special sales commissions.

ANTICIPATED RESULTS

A multiple breakeven analysis (Exhibit 1) shows that at a price of $1350, Cook only needs to sell 41 units to cover their costs.

Since this is only about one percent of the projected market of 3500 hospitals and cardiovascular surgeons, the oscillator should generate a handsome profit. Also shifting the $9600 ad money shown in the breakeven

EXHIBIT 1   Multiple Breakeven Analysis

Give Salespeople No Added Incentive			
Price	$ 1350	$ 1800	$ 2250
Royalty (10%)	135	180	225
Net revenue	1215	1620	2025
Variable production cost	450	450	450
Margin/unit	$ 765	$ 1170	$ 1575
Promotion	$ 30,800[a]	$ 30,800	$ 30,800
Breakeven volume	41	27	20
Sweeten with 10% Commission			
Price	$ 1350	$ 1800	$ 2250
Royalty (10%)	135	180	225
Net revenue	1215	1620	2025
Variable production cost	450	450	450
Commission (10%)	135	180	225
Total variable costs	585	630	675
Margin/unit	$ 630	$ 990	$ 1350
Promotion	$ 30,800	$ 30,800	$ 30,800
Breakeven volume	49	32	23
Add a Salesperson			
Price	$ 1350	$ 1800	$ 2250
Royalty (10%)	135	180	225
Net revenue	1215	1620	2025
Variable production cost	450	450	450
Margin/unit	$ 765	$ 1170	$ 1575
Promotion	30,800	30,800	30,800
Salesperson	50,000	50,000	50,000
Total fixed costs	$ 80,800	$ 80,800	$ 80,800
Breakeven volume	106	69	52

[a] 6 ads (@$1,600) $ 9,600
     4 conventions (@ $2,800)   11,200
     5,000 direct mail brochures (@$2.00) 10,000
                                           $30,800

analysis to conventions and direct mail will make it easier to reach the breakeven volume of 41 units. Cook did not spend any money to design the oscillator, and it is anticipated that the breakeven volume will be reached during the first year of production.

CONTINGENCY PLAN

If the oscillator is selling at a rate of less than one per week at the end of the first year, discontinue selling it.

INDEX